ROUTLEDGE LIBRARY EDITIONS: SOCIAL THEORY

Volume 34

INTRODUCTION TO THE SOCIAL SCIENCES

INTRODUCTION TO THE SOCIAL SCIENCES
With Special Reference to their Methods

MAURICE DUVERGER

Translated by
MALCOLM ANDERSON

LONDON AND NEW YORK

First published in 1964

This edition first published in 2015
by Routledge
2 Park Square, Milton Park, Abingdon, Oxfordshire OX14 4RN

and by Routledge
711 Third Avenue, New York, NY 10017

First issued in paperback 2016

Routledge is an imprint of the Taylor & Francis Group, an informa business

© 1964 George Allen & Unwin Ltd

All rights reserved. No part of this book may be reprinted or reproduced or utilised in any form or by any electronic, mechanical, or other means, now known or hereafter invented, including photocopying and recording, or in any information storage or retrieval system, without permission in writing from the publishers.

Trademark notice: Product or corporate names may be trademarks or registered trademarks, and are used only for identification and explanation without intent to infringe.

British Library Cataloguing in Publication Data
A catalogue record for this book is available from the British Library

ISBN: 978-0-415-72731-0 (Set)
ISBN 13: 978-1-138-99264-1 (pbk)
ISBN 13: 978-1-138-78744-5 (hbk)

Publisher's Note
The publisher has gone to great lengths to ensure the quality of this reprint but points out that some imperfections in the original copies may be apparent.

Disclaimer
The publisher has made every effort to trace copyright holders and would welcome correspondence from those they have been unable to trace.

Introduction to the Social Sciences

WITH SPECIAL REFERENCE TO THEIR METHODS

by

MAURICE DUVERGER

TRANSLATED BY

MALCOLM ANDERSON
M.A., D.Phil.

London
GEORGE ALLEN & UNWIN LTD
Ruskin House Museum Street

FIRST PUBLISHED IN ENGLISH 1964

This book is copyright under the Berne Convention. Apart from any fair dealing for the purposes of private study, research, criticism or review, as permitted under the Copyright Act, 1956, no portion may be reproduced by any process without written permission. Enquiries should be made to the publisher.

This translation © George Allen & Unwin Ltd, 1964

Translated from the French
METHODES DES SCIENCES SOCIALES
first published 1961

French original © 1959 and 1961 Presses Universitaires de France

PRINTED IN GREAT BRITAIN
in 10 point Times Roman
BY SIMSON SHAND LTD
LONDON, HERTFORD AND HARLOW

CONTENTS

INTRODUCTION: THE SOCIAL SCIENCES

SECTION I. *The idea of social science* — page 11
1. The historical development of the social sciences — 12
   A. The primitive confusion between science and philosophy — 12
   B. The eighteenth and nineteenth centuries: the foundation of an autonomous social science — 15
   C. The twentieth century expansion of social science — 20
2. Characteristics of social phenomena — 24
   A. The collective character: 'sociologism' and 'psychologism' — 24
   B. The objective character: the problem of collective images — 28
   C. The general character and relativity — 31
   D. The positive character: the problem of values — 33

SECTION II. *The various social sciences* — 38
1. The specialized social sciences — 38
   A. Social morphology — 39
   B. Specialist sociologies — 43
2. The global social sciences — 54
   A. The sociology of elementary and intermediary groups — 55
   B. The sociology of aggregations — 59
   C. General sociology — 63

Plan of the Book — 69
General Bibliography — 71

PART ONE: THE TECHNIQUES OF OBSERVATION

CHAPTER ONE: DOCUMENTARY OBSERVATION — 75

SECTION I. *Categories of documents* — 75
1. Written documents — 75
   A. Public archives and official documents — 76
   B. The press — 77
   C. Private archives — 80
   D. Indirect documentation — 82
2. Statistics — 84
   A. Gathering statistics — 85
   B. The value of statistics — 87

INTRODUCTION TO THE SOCIAL SCIENCES

3. Other documents	89
A. Technical documentation	89
B. Iconographic and photographic documentation	91
C. Phonetic documentation	93

SECTION II. *Methods of analysing documents* — 96

1. Classical methods	96
A. The main characteristics of the classical methods	96
B. The various classical methods	98
2. Quantitative methods	102
A. Quantitative semantics	103
B. Content analysis	105

SECTION III. *Technique of content analysis* — 109

1. Units of analysis	109
A. Grammatical units of analysis	109
B. Non-grammatical units of analysis	112
2. The analytical framework	114
A. The categories	114
B. Formulating the categories	120

CHAPTER TWO: DIRECT EXTENSIVE OBSERVATION — 125

SECTION I. *Sampling* — 125

1. Drawing the sample	125
A. The quota method	125
B. Probability methods	128
2. The representativity of the sample	133
A. Measuring representativeness	133
B. Correction of polls	140

SECTION II. *Questionnaire methods* — 143

1. Preparation of questionnaires	144
A. The categories of questions	144
B. Designing the questionnaire	148
C. Formulating the questions	151
D. Corrective tests	157
2. The administration of the questionnaire	159
A. Written replies	159
B. Oral questionnaires	162

SECTION III. *The results of investigations* — 167

1. Processing the results	167
A. Technical operations	167
B. The value of the results	169

Contents

2. Publication of the results	172
A. Practical effects	172
B. Rules for publication	174

CHAPTER THREE: DIRECT INTENSIVE OBSERVATION — 178

SECTION I. *Interviews* — 178

1. General examination of the interview — 178
   - A. Forms of interview — 179
   - B. Interview technique — 181
2. Special interview techniques — 183
   - A. Repeated interviews — 183
   - B. Depth interviews — 185

SECTION II. *Tests and the measurement of attitudes* — 189

1. Test method — 189
   - A. Survey of test methods — 189
   - B. Use of tests in the social sciences — 193
2. Measurement of opinions and attitudes — 196
   - A. Methods of measuring opinions — 196
   - B. Attitude scales — 199

SECTION III. *Participant observation* — 209

1. Participant observers — 209
   - A. Observation by individuals and small teams — 210
   - B. Team observation — 212
2. The observer participants — 216
   - A. Introspection in social science — 216
   - B. Observation of one's own group — 219

PART TWO: SYSTEMATIC ANALYSIS

CHAPTER ONE: ELEMENTS OF SYSTEMATIC ANALYSIS — 225

SECTION I. *Conceptual frameworks for research* — 225

1. Levels of scientific research — 226
   - A. Distinction of levels of research — 226
   - B. Scope of sociological explanation — 228
2. Classifications or typologies — 232
   - A. The different kinds of typologies — 232
   - B. Problem of natural typology — 235
3. Theories and hypotheses — 238
   - A. General theories — 239
   - B. Partial theories and models — 242
   - C. Working hypotheses — 245

Introduction to the Social Sciences

SECTION II. *Experiment*	248
1. Laboratory experiments	249
A. Artificial groups	249
B. The sociodrama	251
2. Experiments in the field	254
A. Passive experiments	255
B. Active experiments	257
SECTION III. *The comparative method*	261
1. Comparing analagous phenomena	261
A. General techniques of comparison	262
B. The two categories of comparison	265
2. Different views of the same phenomena	267
A. General description of the method	268
B. Main uses of the method	269
CHAPTER TWO: MATHEMATICAL AND GRAPH TECHNIQUES	277
SECTION I. *Mathematical techniques*	278
1. Expressing phenomena mathematically	278
A. Quantification in social science	278
B. Synthetic representation of quantities	282
2. Mathematical analysis	286
A. Analysis of associations and correlations	287
B. Factorial analysis	293
C. Operational research	299
SECTION II. *Graphs*	301
1. Mathematical graphs	302
A. Various types of graphs	302
B. Representation of frequency series	311
2. Non-mathematical graphs	316
A. Geographical diagrams	317
B. Charts	325
Index	334

INTRODUCTION

THE SOCIAL SCIENCES

In the world today the social sciences have even more important application than nuclear physics. The techniques of propaganda in totalitarian states, advertising in 'capitalist' countries, public relations, revolutionary war and 'psychological action' have transformed human life even more than nuclear fission.

However, the relative position of theory and practice differ between the social and the physical sciences. In the physical sciences progress in theory precedes practical application; the reverse is the case in the social sciences where practice seems more advanced than theory. There is a striking contrast between the effectiveness of the applied social sciences and the anarchic state of their theory: sociologists are not even agreed on elementary definitions and basic concepts. Each sociologist talks his own language and this makes communication between sociologists difficult. This is doubtless explained by the backwardness of the social sciences compared with the physical sciences—there was a time when practice was in advance of theory even in the physical sciences.

In spite of the importance of their contemporary application, social sciences appear in some respects to be underdeveloped sciences. This is probably a temporary situation but it exists and seems likely to last for some time: it must therefore be taken into account. Whilst it makes absolutely necessary an attempt at a definition of the social sciences before examining their techniques and methods of research, it also makes this attempt very difficult. To avoid increasing the confusion a new definition, new concepts, new classifications must not be added to those already in existence. Our aim must be to look for features common to them all.

Section I. The idea of social science

At first sight, the notion of social science seems easy to define: the social sciences study men living in society, Aristotle's 'political animal', and they are thus concerned with the analysis of human groups, collectivities and communities. But even the notion of a human group is not easy to define. If we suggest, for example, 'a simple agglomeration of individuals' it can be objected that a cinema queue is not a real collectivity—although it could become one. Also, the statements that the social sciences are the 'study of man in society' and that they analyse 'human groups' are not synonymous: the stress is placed on the members of the group in the first and on the community in the second.

To avoid becoming involved in the serious and persistent controversies about the object and nature of the social sciences, a partial definition will be constructed by tackling the problem in a genetic manner. Firstly, the historical development of the social sciences will be traced so that discussions of their object and nature can be put in a context. Secondly, as the definition of the social sciences, 'the sciences of social phenomena', is the most neutral and the most generally accepted, a definition of the general character of social phenomena will be attempted. This brings us to discussions about the definition of 'social phenomena' but these will now be more concrete.

1. THE HISTORICAL DEVELOPMENT OF THE SOCIAL SCIENCES

I am attempting only a schematic and superficial outline, the sole purpose of which is to help understanding of actual difficulties of definition of social phenomena. In this context it is essential to appreciate two things: (1) the primitive confusion, which persisted for centuries, of the objective scientific with the moral and metaphysical; (2) the recent tendency towards splintering into many specialized disciplines, replacing social science by the social sciences. With these as guiding considerations we can delineate three great periods—which are not clearly separated and it is not therefore possible to date the periods exactly.

A. The primitive confusion between social science and social philosophy

Originally the rules of social organization such as they ought to be, rather than of social organization as it exists, were sought. In other words social philosophy rather than social science was practised. This attitude persisted for centuries and has not entirely disappeared. Until the eighteenth century, the authors in whose work a scientific rather than a philosophical attitude predominated were very few in number. After the eighteenth century the number increased considerably; in the nineteenth century the scientific attitude began to predominate.

The Social Sciences

(a) THE GENERAL CHARACTERISTICS OF THE PERIOD

To embark on the study of the principles of an ideal organization, it is necessary in the first place to study the working of existing social organizations: social philosophers were thus drawn towards social science.

1. *The predominance of the philosophical and moral point of view.* In its original form, social science was embedded in a mass of normative considerations of a moral or philosophical nature, rather like a metal mixed with other substances in an ore. The proportion of scientific observation relative to normative considerations varied depending on the author. In every case the normative point of view predominated: it guided the activities of the researcher and it was at the very origin of his research. The first scientific theories were the reflection of moral and metaphysical doctrines and of *a priori* positions.

2. *Importance of collected observations.* The contribution of this early period to the development of the social sciences is important. Many writers were acute and energetic observers. The metaphysical and normative context hindered neither careful analysis of the real world nor the development of the comparative method: in this respect Aristotle remains a model. Two intellectual temperaments are nearly always present: one inclined to reflect on information already available, the other to seek new information. In the period we are considering, the philosophical tendency favoured the former but it did not altogether extinguish the latter. The abundant harvest of observations left by the writers of this period is often more valuable than their general theories which have sometimes created obstacles to the development of the social sciences by interposing an artificial screen between the observer and reality.

(b) THE MAIN STAGES

We will limit ourselves here to pointing out some essential landmarks, emphasizing on the one hand the link with metaphysical doctrine, on the other the quasi-permanent opposition between the temperaments of the philosopher and the observer.

1. *In antiquity*, it is represented in the classic opposition of Plato and Aristotle. This must not be exaggerated. It is true that Plato is essentially a philosopher and that his main analytical tool is abstract reasoning. It is also true that Aristotle had a remarkable talent for observation, and that his philosophical reflexion is based on very wide and varied empirical research: for example, he wrote a series of

monographs on the Constitutions of 158 foreign and Greek city-states, of which only one survives (*The Constitution of the Athenians*). Despite this, the intellectual starting point of Aristotle is philosophical and his metaphysics remains the basis of his conception of society. Moreover, one finds in Plato an 'attempt at a scientific treatment of economic and social facts' (L. Robin): he is well aware of the importance of geographical, demographical and economic conditions in social life. One can even discover the embryo of the theory of the class struggle, when he writes: 'A city is always composed of at least two parts which are at war with one another: the rich and the poor.'[1]

2. *In the Middle Ages* social philosophy mirrored Christian religion and morality. Scholastic methods accentuated the primacy of deductive reasoning over empirical observation. The great synthesis of Saint Thomas Aquinas has the range of Plato: but the scientific element in social research tends to be less. However, the basic principles of Christianity, notably the dogmas of the Fall and the Redemption, tend towards a historical conception of society, the first traces of which are discernable in Saint Augustin's *City of God. Treatise on the first invention of money* (1370) by Nicholas Oresme was the first example of an experimental work, and it also marks the birth of a particular social science: political economy.

3. *The Renaissance and Reformation* disrupted the old intellectual framework, and the great voyages of discovery made new societies known to Western European men; these developments favoured experimental tendencies. Machiavelli's *Prince* (1532) and *The Republic* (1577) of Jean Bodin are more realist than philosophical. In the same period, 'statistics', a descriptive science of the state, the forerunner of political science, made its appearance in Italy (see particularly the treatise of Sansovino, *De governo dei regime e republiche antiche e moderne*, 1567). In 1615, Antoine de Montchrétien published the first *Treatise of Political Economy* (which was a manual rather than a scientific work). In addition to these, the first accounts of exotic travels brought new observations about society and curiosity was turned towards the concrete.

However, the general approach remained more philosophical than scientific. But the context of social philosophy evolved: Christianity ceased to be its unique foundation. The second half of the sixteenth and the seventeenth century saw the beginning of the theory of 'natural right' and a juridical social philosophy in the writings of

[1] *The Republic*, IV, p. 422.

The Social Sciences

Gentilis, Althusius, Grotius and Pufendorf. On these foundations Locke developed the doctrine of political liberalism (*Treatise on Civil Government*, 1689). In contrast, Hobbes's *Leviathan* (1651), in which empirical observation has greatest weight, argues in favour of political authoritarianism.

B. The eighteenth and nineteenth centuries: foundation of an autonomous social science

Before the eighteenth century works in which the scientific attitude predominated over the philosophical are rare: Machiavelli, Bodin, Nicholas Oresme, Montchrétien were forerunners. In the eighteenth century these works became more frequent and the idea of a rigorous separation between science and philosophy appeared. Also, the idea appeared that social phenomena have a regular character, and are therefore subject to natural laws more or less analagous to those which govern the physical universe: the conception of social laws marks a decisive step forward as the purpose of science is to look for laws which can be tested by experiment.

The contribution of the eighteenth century is therefore very important. But the philosophical approach still predominated. The idea of a social law, the notion of an autonomous social science had not been generally accepted. In the nineteenth century they were progressively considered as normal. Also the eighteenth-century authors had neither clearly delimited the field of social science nor precisely defined its purpose. The contribution of Auguste Comte is important in this respect. The contribution of Karl Marx is equally important in establishing the objective and relative character of social phenomena, essential to the constitution of sociology as a science.

(*a*) THE CONTRIBUTION OF THE EIGHTEENTH CENTURY

In the eighteenth century, the tendency to study social facts from the philosophical standpoint, to seek what human societies ought to be rather than examine what they are, remained predominant. It inspired one of the greatest works of the period, *Contrat social* (1762) by Rousseau, which expressly stated: 'I seek right and reason and do not argue about facts.' It remained the basis of the works of the 'philosophers', Voltaire, Mably, d'Holbach, Diderot and the Encyclopaedists. It remains an underlying element even in the writings of Montesquieu.

1. *Development of works based on observation*. *L'Esprit des lois* (1784) can, however, be considered as the first treatise of political sociology; the notion of social laws and the very clear statement: 'I describe here

what is and not what ought to be,' manifests a definite desire to observe scientifically. Apart from *L'Esprit des lois*, the objective social sciences developed in three directions: (1) in political economy, which the French physiocratic school, then the English school of Adam Smith, developed into an autonomous science; (2) in mathematical statistics which were used as a basis of the first demographic work (Graunt, 1662; Halley, 1692; Deparcieux, 1746; Moheau, 1778); (3) in the comparative study of peoples, based on the accounts of travellers and explorers: examples of this are Jean Demeunier, *L'Esprit des usages et coutumes des différents peuples* (1778), and P. Lafitau, *Moeurs des sauvages amériquains comparées aux moeurs des premiers temps* (1724). Thus, the first characteristic of the eighteenth century is the multiplication of works with a really scientific character in which the philosophical element is small or completely absent.

2. *Elaboration of the idea of social laws*. The second, and the most important, characteristic is the elaboration of the idea that social facts are subject to laws: 'physical laws of society' as Dupont des Nemours said (1768). Before him Montesquieu had defined them as 'necessary relations derived from the nature of things' (1748).

The concept of social laws became progressively dissociated from the notion of a providential order: it is symptomatic that one of the founders of statistics, the German Süssmilch, interpreted demographic regularities as the effect of divine will; and that Mercier de la Rivière quotes in the epilogue to *Ordre naturel et essential des sociétés politiques* (1767) a phrase of Malebranche on the sovereignty of the Eternal Order. But the task of searching for the foundations of social science, whether in Divine Providence or in 'the nature of things', belongs to metaphysics: science is limited to stating the existence of 'regularities' and 'necessary relations'. It should be emphasized that this concept of social science has been, from the beginning, drawn in three different directions: statistical laws, derived from the calculation of probabilities (invented by Bernoulli who formulated in 1713 the famous 'law of large numbers'); historical laws regarding the development of mankind (Condorcet, *Tableau historique des progrès de l'esprit humain*, 1794); laws analagous to those of the physical universe. This latter always seems to have had pride of place: its predominance was confirmed in the nineteenth century.

(*b*) THE CONTRIBUTION OF AUGUSTE COMTE (1798–1853)

Auguste Comte is considered to be the founder of sociology; but his contribution to the development of the idea of social science is less important than has been believed.

The Social Sciences

1. *The invention of the term 'sociology'*. Today the term 'sociology' and 'social sciences' are almost equivalent, with the qualifications made below (see p. 43). The term sociology was invented by Auguste Comte. In the eighteenth century the term 'new science' was used, first by J. B. Vico in his important work *Principes d'une science nouvelle* (1725, 1730, 1744), then by some Physiocrats, particularly Dupont de Nemours (1768), and finally by the disciples of Saint-Simon. The Encyclopaedists employed the expression 'science of man' which was adopted by the *Ideologues* (Destutt de Tracy, etc.), by physiologists and doctors (Cabanis, Bichat, Burdin), and then by Henri de Saint-Simon in his *Mémoire sur la science de l'homme* (1813). But Saint-Simon finally preferred the term 'social physics' (already used by Hobbes) which was at first favoured by Auguste Comte.

It was only in volume IV of his *Cours de philosophie positive* (1839), in the forty-seventh lesson, that he gave the new science the name of 'sociology': he did this to avoid confusion with the 'vicious attempts at appropriation' made by the Belgian mathematician, Quetelet, who applied the term social physics to the statistical study of moral phenomena (*L'homme et le développement de ses facultés*, or *Essai de physique sociale*, 1835).

2. *Definition of the object of the social sciences*. The essential contribution of Comte is the first precise definition of the object of social science.

For Comte, 'organic physics' is the science of the individual and 'social physics' is the science of the human species which constitutes an 'immense and eternal social unity'. This social physics, or sociology, has two parts: social statistics, which is the anatomical study of society, 'a positive study, both experimental and rational, of mutual action and reaction which all the various parts of the social system continually bring to bear on one another'; and social dynamics which is to statistics what physiology is to anatomy. Statistics is the study of order, Dynamics the study of progress (in the sense of development, not of becoming more perfect, i.e. implying value judgment). The famous 'law of the three stages' summarizes social Dynamics: mankind passed successively through the theological stage, the metaphysical stage and the positivist stage.

3. *The positive character of the social sciences*. The main contribution of Auguste Comte is usually considered to be the assertion of the positive character of the social sciences and their definitive separation from morals and metaphysics. This is not quite true: this separation was established in the eighteenth-century discussion of 'social laws'.

Auguste Comte was, however, the first to systematize and give a complete analysis of the principle.

In saying this it should not be forgotten that the father of sociology did not succeed in freeing himself from his own philosophical beliefs. Consciously he wanted to limit the scope of social science to a study of what is: unconsciously he could not prevent his sentiments, his aspirations and his desires concerning what ought to be from interfering in his scientific analyses. Thus the old confusion between science and philosophy reappeared in another form. Many sociologists, perhaps all, have followed in the footsteps of Auguste Comte: many works, positive in appearance, really reflect the metaphysical beliefs (religious, philosophical or political) of their authors. Comte believed that it was possible to resolve this contradiction by developing a positive religion and morality based on his sociology: this illusion (sometimes called 'sociologism') was later shared by some of the disciples of Durkheim.

(c) THE CONTRIBUTION OF KARL MARX (1818–1883)

The contribution of Auguste Comte was accepted immediately: Emile Durkheim and the sociologists of the late nineteenth and early twentieth centuries were influenced by him. In contrast, the contribution of Karl Marx was neglected in scientific circles for a long time because of its political context. The political influence of Marx was obvious in the second half of the nineteenth century; his direct scientific influence hardly developed until the middle of the twentieth, although a certain diffuse Marxist influence was perceptible well before this.

1. *The objectivity of the social sciences.* Auguste Comte thought that 'the whole social mechanism rests on opinions': he thus gave sociology a subjective character. The first main contribution of Marx was to place social science on purely objective bases by asserting that juridicial relations, political forms and the whole anatomy of society rested on the economic infrastructure and on the relations of the forces of production. It is possible to argue about the pride of place given to economic phenomena: it is possible that this is neither general nor absolute. But it must not be forgotten that Marx never argued that the action of the economic 'base' on the superstructure was in one direction only—on the contrary, he argued that the superstructure reacted on the base and the relations between the two were reciprocal. This materialist conception, according to Durkheim,[1] had the merit of introducing the 'idea that social life must be explained not by reference to the ideas of those who participate in it but in

[1] *Revue philosophique*, December 1897.

terms of profound causes of which the participants are unaware'. Although he was very hostile to Marxism, Durkheim saw in this a necessary condition for sociology to become a science.

This problem, which raises many difficulties, will be discussed later on: the ideas of those who participate in social life have an important influence on it: they are themselves, to a certain extent, objective phenomena. But we restrict ourselves here to insisting on the importance of the Marxist contribution to the objectivity of the social sciences.

2. *The evolutionary character of social phenomena.* Auguste Comte, Condorcet and many others had thought of the idea of evolution: its first traces can be discerned in Saint Augustin. But the evolution of human society was imagined as a development of the same fundamental organism in the context of which man's nature appeared stable; no one thought this nature could change its essential structure, but only improve or blossom in some way.

Rather like Heraclitus, Marx thought that human nature is the product of history and like history itself develops by a dialectical, not a linear, process. Social cadres, legal systems, art, morals, religion, psychology, manners and behaviour, ideas, philosophy, etc., are linked to a socio-economic infrastructure which is always changing both because of its own internal development and because of the reactions of the superstructure on it. Thus all the elements of social reality are relative both in relation to one another and in relation to history.

3. *The first general theory of the social sciences.* Marxism was the first complete system, the first cosmogony explaining all social phenomena. Before it they were only political syntheses: for example, Montesquieu on political régimes, Adam Smith on economics and so on. One can also argue that as no other cosmogony has succeeded in replacing Marxism, no other system developed since has been as complete, and no other has had an audience beyond a small group of specialists (see below p. 239).

The influence of Marxist cosmogony is therefore considerable. In some respects it serves as a basic framework, a reference system, even for those who criticize it and emphasize its inadequacy and errors. This influence is, however, probably more fruitful for non-Marxists than for Marxists. The comprehensiveness of the doctrine has encouraged Marxists to use deductive reason rather than experimental research, thus developing a new scholasticism within a dogmatic framework: the disciples of one of the greatest among the founding fathers of social science have thus, paradoxically, returned to the primitive confusion between science and philosophy.

C. The twentieth century expansion of social science

Nowadays no one talks of social science, in the singular, but of the social sciences. Sociology is more and more considered as a science of synthesis and, under the title general sociology, covers the various specialist sociologies. Auguste Comte and the French sociologists at the end of the nineteenth century were very much opposed to this and, like Karl Marx, they reaffirmed the unity of social science. But they have not been followed.

(*a*) THE STRIVING FOR THE UNITY OF SOCIAL SCIENCE

The development of particular social sciences is not a twentieth-century occurrence. It antedates the separation of the social sciences from philosophy.

1. *The first specialist social sciences in the eighteenth century.* Some specialist disciplines were founded on the basis of experimental method when social science was still dominated by metaphysical and moral considerations.

This was the case with political economy: the *Treatise on the invention of money* by Nicolas Oresme has already been mentioned as one of the first works based on empirical observation. In the eighteenth century, the Physiocrats, then Adam Smith, established political economy as an autonomous science, clearly separated from philosophy. Demography is an analagous case: in the eighteenth century mathematicians developed statistical methods and applied them to the study of population, notably to mortality (Graunt, 1662; Halley, 1692). The word 'demography' was invented as late as 1855 by Achille Guillard but the discipline already had its object and methods at the end of the eighteenth century. The sociology of history (or the philosophy of history)—the search for the laws of development of events —had a remarkable forerunner in the person of Ibn Khaldoun (1332–1406), the Arab philosopher; in the eighteenth century, J. B. Vico formulated the law of the perpetual return of the three ages—the divine age, the heroic age and the human age. Less developed than the political economy and demography, the sociology of history nevertheless tended to form a separate discipline.

2. *The reaction of the founders of sociology in the nineteenth century.* The founders of sociology in the nineteenth century reacted vigor-

ously against this tendency towards the division of the social sciences. Auguste Comte asserted that 'social phenomena are fundamentally connected with one another' and that study of a particular category of phenomena is sterile. He criticized political economy for this. The disciple of Saint-Simon, Bazard, had made a similar criticism of the separate development of political economy which he attributed to Adam Smith; he exonerated the Physiocrats who linked their system to a global conception of society.

The unity of social science was asserted even more strongly by Marx. Marxist sociology is based on the assumption of the strict interdependence of all social phenomena: none could be validly analysed in isolation. The fundamental character attributed to the economic phenomena (constituting the 'base' whilst other social facts made up the superstructure) seems to permit the development of political economy in isolation. But the superstructure reacts on the base in such a way that economic facts are subject to the influences of other elements of social reality—political economy therefore cannot be isolated from sociology. History is social reality in dialectical movement, its perpetual becoming. Social reality does not exist outside history: the complete interpretation of history in sociology is a fundamental principle of Marxism.

(b) THE CONTEMPORARY MULTIPLICATION OF SPECIALIST DISCIPLINES
The exhortations of the founders of sociology have not been effective. Social science has splintered into more and more specialist disciplines: ethnography, social psychology, anthropology, economics, demography, ecology, linguistics, sociology of law, political science, etc. An attempt will be made later to define each of these (see p. 38).

1. *The necessity of specialization.* The complexity of social facts and the diversity of techniques used for observing them makes specialization inevitable. No sociologist today can take in the whole of social reality unless by doing it at second hand, relying on the results of specialist researches. Of necessity the different branches of social science must be separated. Even in Marxist countries where there is great concern for unity, there are economists, historians, demographers and so on—in other words specialists in a sector of social research. But the economist, the historian, the demographer, etc., should not lose sight of the general connections between social phenomena: as they go deeper into their own specialization they should preserve an awareness of the relations between it and other parts of social life. This is not without practical difficulties because a specialist in one branch of the social sciences is an amateur in others.

2. *The absence of a general theory of the social sciences.* In the USSR and the socialist countries the unity of the social sciences is guaranteed by the specialists' acceptance of the Marxist cosmogony, by their belief in the same basic philosophy. If an acceptance and a belief of this kind does not exist it is much more difficult to maintain the unity of social science. In Western countries there is no generally accepted cosmogony; in the absence of a global theory, social scientists are reduced to constructing partial theories within the framework of each discipline. The connection between all social phenomena is thus lost sight of.

3. *Departmentalization in the universities.* The university departments and the diversity of the formative training of specialists in the social sciences has further aggravated the tendency towards division. People come to the social sciences by many routes (but nearly always specialized ones within the organizational structures of Universities, Faculties, Research Institutes, etc.) such as statistics, philosophy, ethnography, psychology, psychiatry, medicine, etc. In France, for example, no sociologist has at present a real sociological training. Sociology is always a superimposition on another basic training. Everyone therefore tends to study the social sector for which he is best equipped intellectually and professionally and to consider the others, which he knows less well, in terms of his specialization. Departments of sociology have, of course, existed for a long time in certain, particularly American, Universities but most of the time they have been in conflict with adjacent departments such as political science and psychology with the result that they developed only one aspect of the social sciences and do not provide an antidote to specialization.

4. *The recent reactions against the splitting up of the social sciences.* The coherence of social phenomena and the profound unity of the social sciences have never been seriously doubted and there has, therefore, been a search to remedy the proliferation of the specialist disciplines. One method could be that recommended by Auguste Comte—the training of 'specialists in generalities'. General Sociology, in attempting to synthesize the results of social sciences, works in this direction. This raises great difficulties which will be discussed later. The second method would be to construct a generally acceptable doctrine, a cosmogony which would provide for Western scientists the same kind of framework and basic philosophy as the Marxists have. At the moment, many people call for this but no one has yet been able to provide one.

THE SOCIAL SCIENCES

The third method consists of specialists in each of the disciplines collaborating in common research projects. 'Interdisciplinary' researches and regular contacts between workers in different fields are becoming more and more fashionable. The growing unity of research techniques is an influence in the same direction. It is striking that most of the Anglo-Saxon manuals are on the methodology of the social sciences (this book follows their example), and not on any particular one of them, because the different sciences are progressively using the same analytical procedures. In some respects it seems that the phase of the fragmentation of the social sciences is passing and a phase of relative reunification is commencing. But the difficulties and limits of such an enterprise, however necessary it is, should not be obscured.

(*Translator's Note:* Works in English are published in London, works in French in Paris unless otherwise stated. The bibliographies have been abridged and reference should be made to the French edition for more extensive bibliographies, especially for works in French.)
A. CULLIVIER, *Manuel de sociologie*, 3rd ed., 1958, pp. 1–96, gives a good summary and bibliography of the history of the social sciences. It has been much drawn on in the preparation of this chapter. J. TOUCHARD (*et al.*), *Histoire des idées politiques*, 2 vol., 1959, should be consulted. For a more elaborate analysis see F. ZNANIECKI, *Cultural Sciences: their origin and development*, Urbana (Ill.), 1952; F. N. HOUSE, *The Development of Sociology*, New York, 1936; E. BOGARDUS, *The Development of Social Thought*, 3rd ed., Los Angeles, 1955; H. E. BARNES and H. BECKER, *Social thought from Love to Science*, 2 vol., 2nd ed., New York, 1952; H. E. BARNES, *An Introduction to the History of Sociology*, Chicago, 1947, and *Historical Sociology*, New York, 1948; A. W. SMALL, *Origins of Sociology*, Chicago, 1924.

On the Greeks: L. ROBIN, *Platon et la science sociale*, 1942; E. BARKER, *The Political Thought of Plato and Aristotle*, 1906; *The Politics of Aristotle*, 1946; M. PRELOT, *La Politique d'Aristotle*, 1950; W. W. JAEGER, *Aristotle, fundaments of his development*, 2nd ed., 1950.

On the Middle Ages: H. ARQUILLIÈRE, *L'Augustinisme politique*, 1931; J. FIGGIS, *The Political Aspects of Augustin's City of God*, 1921; E. BRIDREY, *La Théorie de la monnaie au XIVe siecle: N. Oresme*, 1909.

On the sixteenth and seventeenth centuries: P. MESNARD, *L'Essor de la philosophie politique au XVIe siecle*, 1936; J. W. ALLEN, *A History of Political Thought in the Sixteenth Century*, 1928; H. SÉE, *Histoire des idées politiques en France au XVIIe siecle*, 1920; G. MOUNIN, *Machiavel*, 1958; C. BENOIST, *Le Machiavélisme*, 3 vol., 1907–36; A. RENAUDET, *Machiavel: étude d'histoire des doctrines politiques*, 2nd ed., 1955; R. CHAUVIRE, *Jean Bodin, auteur de la République*, 1914; J. MOREAU-REIBEL, *Jean Bodin et le droit public comparé*, 1933; L. STRAUSS, *Hobbes's Political Philosophy*, 1936; H. NEZARD (*et al.*), *Les Fondateurs du droit international*, 1904.

On the eighteenth century: G. ATKINSON, *Les Relations de voyage au XVIIIe siècle et l'évolution des idées*, 1925; P. HAZARD, *La Crise de la conscience européenne*, 5 vol., 1935; R. HUBERT, *Les Sciences sociales dans l'Encyclopédie*, 1923.

On Montesquieu: J. DEDIEU, *Montesquieu, l'homme et l'oeuvre*, 1943; the collective work published for the bicentenary of *Esprit des lois: La Pensée politique et constitutionnelle de Montesquieu*, 1952; J. STAROBINSKI, *Montesquieu par lui-même*, 1956.

On A. Comte: J. LACROIX, *La Sociologie d'Auguste Comte*, 1956; L. LÉVY-BRUHL, *La Philosophie d'Auguste Comte*, 1900.

On Marxism: H. LEFÉBVRE, *Pour Connaître la pensée de Karl Marx*, 2nd ed., 1956, and *Le Marxisme*, 1952; P. BIGO, *Marxisme et humanisme*, 1954; J. MARCHAL, *Deux essais sur Marxisme*, 1955; M. RUBEL, *Karl Marx: essai de biographie intellectuelle*, 1957; F. ENGELS, *Anti-Dühring* (various editions).

2. CHARACTERISTICS OF SOCIAL PHENOMENA

The most neutral definition, with the fewest theoretical difficulties, of the social sciences is that their object is the study of social phenomena But this is almost a tautology—it depends on the definition of social phenomena. This definition has provoked many controversies since August Comte attempted to define clearly the aim and scope of sociology. The questions raised have not yet been resolved but there seems now to be some areas of agreement. It is generally admitted that social phenomena are: (1) collective, (2) objective, (3) general and (4) positive. But there is not general agreement on the definition of these terms.

A. The collective character: 'sociologism' and 'psychologism'.

The social sciences are concerned with the study of human groups or collectivities: a social fact is firstly a collective fact, that is to say a fact common to several individuals. But every collectivity is a series of relations between individuals: collective actions are conceived and performed by men. From this arose, even at the very beginning of sociology, an opposition between two tendencies—one stressing the collective character, considering groups as objective realities apart from the individuals which compose them; the other insisting on the fact that it is the individuals alone who think and act, thus reducing the concept of the collectivity to the 'interindividual.'

(a) SOCIOLOGISTIC TENDENCIES

In the 'individual-group' relationship the second term is stressed. The group constitutes a fundamental reality whilst the individual is in some way only a 'derived' reality.

1. *Organicism* is historically the first, and the most absolute form, of this tendency. Human societies are regarded as biological organisms. These latter are composed of groups of cells: similarly men are regarded as cells in the social organism. The important feature in societies, as in living things is not the cells which compose it but the organism itself.

Herbert Spencer (1820–1903) who invented the theory did not present it in its absolute form. He sought only to show that the laws of biological evolution are also applicable to human societies (increase in numbers, growing integration, movement from homogeneity to heterogeneity, etc.). His disciples pushed the analogy further: The Russian, Lilienfield, studied 'human society as a real organism' and the Belgian, De Greef, called it a 'hyper-organism'. However organicism was progressively abandoned. The fact that individuals are endowed with consciousness is a fundamental difference between them and cells of a biological organism. The design on the cover of the first edition of Hobbes's Leviathen—a monster formed by the juxtaposition of thousands of men—is only a design: organicism is only a metaphor.

2. *The 'ontology of the community'*. The second communitarist strand, sometimes called the 'ontology of the community', is derived from Hobbes and even more from Hegel's theory of the State. A human group is a spiritual not an organic reality, but it is nonetheless a fundamental reality—the individual only exists by it, in it, through it. As the German philosopher, Otto Spann said: 'Before entering the community man is pure potentiality; it is only in the spiritual community that he develops his individuality and his moral essence.' Some schools of thought in Germany have been associated with this position. One example is the 'psychology of peoples' school founded in 1859 by M. Lazarus and H. Steinhal who discerned in the people (volk) a collective spiritual reality—the individual consciousness is only a product of a 'collective soul.' Another example is Oswald Spengler who was more of a philosopher than sociologist, and more of a political theorist than a philosopher. Just before the advent of national socialism, and throughout the nazi period a host of pseudo-thinkers vulgarized ideas of this kind.

(*b*) THE PSYCHOLOGIST TENDENCIES

At the opposite extreme, some sociologists considered that groups and communities have no reality in themselves and are only modes of relations between individuals.

1. *Classical political economy*, founded by Adam Smith and the Manchester School, established the first kind of psychologism. They conceived all economic activity as relations created between individuals. These are not considered in concrete terms but as abstractions, schematized in the famous *homo oeconomicus*. Classical economic science thus consisted more of reasoning on the basis of the psychology of *homo oeconomicus* than of the experimental observation of facts.

2. *Inter-psychology and social psychology*. The first sociologist to adhere to the psychologist point of view was Gabriel de Tarde (1843–1904) who, reacting against organicism, asserted that sociology ought to be an 'intermental' psychology which he termed 'interpsychology'. Tarde did not have much influence in France (where Durkheim was preferred) but he had considerable influence in the English speaking countries, especially the United States, and he can be considered the father of contemporary social psychology. The Englishman, Macdougall (1871–1938), the American, F. H. Giddings (1855–1931), and above all the 'relationist' Chicago school limited the group, in the same way as Tarde, to reciprocal relations between individuals. But the English and American authors differed from Tarde in the methods which they used to study the psychology of the relations between individuals. Tarde's method was essentially introspective whilst the anglo-saxon psychologists examined the actions of individuals by the so-called 'behavioural' method.

(*c*) THE ATTEMPTS AT RECONCILIATION

Two great attempts at reconciliation, the Marxist and the Durkheimian, must be mentioned. The problem has today lost most of its urgency and most sociologists guard against the excesses both of communitarism and psychologism without having really succeeded in defining the collective character of social facts.

1. *Marxism*. Some consider Marxism as a communitarist doctrine which submerges the individual in the collectivity. In asserting that man is the product of history, that there is no constant 'human nature', that ideas, sentiments, artifacts, are the reflections of socio-economic conditions and of the factors of production, Marxism obviously gives the collectivity primacy over the individual. Moreover, the theory of classes makes fundamental realities of these groups. But, from another point of view Marxism insists on the essential importance of man 'the most precious form of capital'. Man is the product of history, but history is also the product of

man—man makes his own history. Each individual is determined by socio-economic conditions: but by being conscious of this, the individual can make history.

Even the idea that impulses to social change originate in techniques of production and the factors of production in the end gives pre-eminence to man, the inventor, the worker, the technician, in the collective evolution. In Marxism the role of man is not comparable to a cell in a biological organism nor an element in a communitarist entity. In fact Marxism makes the first attempt at compromise between the communitarist and psychologist tendencies with greater concessions to the former than to the latter.

2. *Emile Durkheim (1858–1917) and the 'collective consciousness'.* Marx's attempt at reconciliation was not a conscious one: he cared little about the organicist or psychologist theses of the sociologists, which, moreover, mainly postdate his own work. In contrast Durkheim's famous theory of 'the collective consciousness' is a conscious attempt to reconcile the opposing points of view of Spencer and Tarde. Durkheim wrote in *The Rules of Sociological Method*, 'Undoubtedly, nothing collective can be produced if individual consciousnesses do not exist, but this necessary condition is not in itself sufficient. It still remains necessary that these individual consciousnesses are associated, combined—and combined in a certain way; social life is the result of this combination.' 'The group thinks, feels and acts in a quite different manner than its members would if they were isolated individuals: therefore if one starts with the individuals one can understand nothing that happens in the group.'

Durkheim's conception of the collection consciousness always remained very fluid: examined from a certain angle it looks like a kind of 'social soul' and this degenerates into communitarism; from another angle, it is only the product of the co-operation between individual consciousnesses and this brings us back to psychologism. Durkheim tried to keep to the middle way, as the following passage illustrates: 'In relation to us as individuals, society is at the same time transcendent and immanent in us, and we feel it as such. It extends beyond us and at the same time is a thing internal to us since it can only live by us and through us. Or rather, in a certain sense it is ourselves.'

3. *The present situation.* The definition just quoted expresses very well the fundamental ambiguity of the collective character of social phenomena. Discussion about Durkheim's theses was once very

lively but today it has become quieter, not because of the victory of one side or the other, but through weariness. In fact, the attempt to define the frontier between the individual and the collective has been renounced because it has been realized that neither has a separate existence: every collective fact is a fact of consciousness which can only be reflected in individuals and as no individual has lived alone since his birth the individual psychology is marked by the collective context.

Phenomenology and existentialist philosophy have facilitated this evolution by fostering the understanding that individual consciousness does not think in isolation, that the consciousness of the self is not separable from the consciousness of the other or from the consciousness of ourselves: 'What I am is not the consciousness of an isolated being. I experience myself in communication' (K. Jaspers); 'I exist socially in the same way as I exist physically' (M. Dufrenne). There is a difference of point of view rather than of subject between social science and psychology of the individual (and even, in some respects, of biology). Social science examines human phenomena from a collective standpoint, psychology from the individual—but they are the same phenomena. The collective character is an angled version of rather than an intrinsic element in phenomena.

B. The objective character: the problem of collective images

Rather similar controversies have arisen concerning the objective character of social facts and these have often been mixed up with the argument just mentioned. Durkheim, in *Rules of Sociological Method*, proposed the treatment of social facts as 'things'. This does not raise difficulties for some of those which are materially objective; but for most, considering them as 'things' raises a variety of objections because they are 'collective images' and, as such, phenomena of consciousness.

(a) THE TWO CATEGORIES OF SOCIAL PHENOMENA

In one sense all social facts are phenomena of consciousness, of images, like all physical, biological and other phenomena: 'The world is my imagining of it.' But certain social facts are only images and have no existence outside consciousness. Others, in contrast have existences external to consciousness and are also something else as well as images. These can be called 'materially objective' facts.

1. *Materially objective facts.* For some social science disciplines these are the main objects of observation. In demography, for example,

the problem of objectivity hardly arises because the size of a population, the age, the sex, the morphological characteristics are as objective as the phenomena studied by the physician or the biologist (see, however, p. 41). This is equally true for the economist examining the level of wages and prices, the distribution of raw materials, the structure of industry, working conditions, etc.; and for the historian with events, battles, treaties, decisions by a head of state; for the political scientist with governmental structure, the organization of elections, the structure of parties or pressure groups, systems of financing public expenditure; for the criminologist with the distribution of juvenile delinquency, the progress of certain types of crime, methods of punishment, etc. Thus a great number of phenomena studied by social sciences have a materially objective character.

2. *Collective images.* However, a more careful consideration of the preceding examples shows that they confuse two distinct categories of facts. Some are complete, in that the observer finds in them all the elements of his observation as in population statistics, the level of prices and salaries, electoral and penal statistics. Others reveal only one aspect of reality; the other aspect has the character of an image, of a phenomenon of consciousness, the objectivity of which is more open to question. For example, in the study of a political party, the official statutes, the real structure, the ways in which the leaders are chosen, the number of members and militants, the methods of support, electoral programmes, the content of its press and the speeches of its parliamentarians and so on are materially objective elements. But the images of the party which its members, its opponents and the indifferent have and the motives for joining or, opposing it are collective images which are not objective or, at least, are objective in a different way.

There are therefore three categories of fields of study in the social sciences: the first comprises materially objective facts only: the second, both materially objective facts and facts about collective images; the third, facts about collective images only (such as the study of public opinion, political and religious beliefs, etc.). In practice, excluding demography and economics, the social sciences deal more with collective images than with materially objective facts.

(*b*) THE OBJECTIVE STUDY OF COLLECTIVE IMAGES

How can the danger of subjectivity be escaped in the study of collective images when their only manifestation is in individual consciousness? Durkheim developed his theory of the collective consciousness partly to remove this difficulty. Today the solution is looked for elsewhere. A certain degree of objectivity is attained by treating collective images partly as 'things'.

1. *W. Dilthey's theories on the 'internal understanding' of social facts.* The subjectiveness of collective images resides in their being internal to each individual consciousness. If an internal study is attempted then a subjective method is being used, like the introspective technique of the psychology of the individual. This is the method proposed for sociology by certain German thinkers following Wilhelm Dilthey (1833–1911) who made a radical distinction between the natural sciences and the *sciences d'esprit*, counting the social sciences amongst the latter. 'Social facts,' wrote Dilthey 'are comprehensible to us, so to speak, from the inside.' Methods totally different from those of the physical science would have to be used to analyse them, methods based on a kind of direct intuition, of a more or less affective communion: 'We will explain nature; but we will *understand* the life of the soul.' Dilthey's ideas have had a very important influence on German sociology and philosophy. A certain tradition continues to accept them partially. But, in practice, they are ignored by the majority of contemporary sociologists.

2. *The objective procedures of analysis of collective images.* The study of the individual psychology has transcended the subjectivity of internal analysis of individual consciousness, through the study of the physiological and biological bases of psychological phenomena and through the study of the external behaviour of individuals. By these means it has been able to establish itself as a science. The 'behavioural' method in particular is becoming more and more widely used. The social sciences have followed this example in that they now utilize many behavioural procedures which have an objective character. They also use other techniques which are peculiar to them. These are based on the fact that collective images manifest themselves not only in individual behaviour but also in collective attitudes and behaviour. Public opinion, for example, can be studied in the press, in 'rumours', in parliamentary debates, radio and television, the cinema and so on. These are means of collective expression which are themselves materially objective facts.

However, the social sciences have not entirely abandoned the analysis of individual consciousness nor has psychology (the techniques of psycho-analysis have, on the contrary, revived it). In the social sciences the study of personal documents and, even more, personal interviews play an important role. Both are more or less based on introspection and thus they have a subjective character.

This character is limited when the inquiry is a general one. Analysing the opinions of a single person in an interview is completely subjective, but the collation of the interviews of a large number of people in order to find common elements in them is a partial return to objectivity (these common elements reflect the collective character of images).

Another problem is the subjective impressions of the observer. There is a tendency to mix with pure observation, the intuition and the 'internal comprehension' of Dilthey. This is not an absolutely insoluble problem. There are various mathematical procedures which can control, for example, the objectivity of interviews in public opinion polls and of analysts in content analysis studies and so on (see pp. 122, 158). In spite of these controls, subjectivity cannot be entirely suppressed.

C. The general character and relativity

'What is everything which is not eternal?': 'We will never again possess the spirit of this evening.' These two lines of bad verse taken together express very well the tension within the social sciences. On the one hand 'there is only science of the general': on the other, every social fact is a human fact of a place and of a time, expressing a particular moment of history. The general character of social facts might be opposed by what one could call the 'historical objection'. It is not a decisive objection because it is not really opposed to the general character. However, it expresses a truth which cannot be ignored: the general character of social facts is relative.

(a) THE OBJECTION OF HISTORICITY

This has been refuted by the distinction between the 'evential' and the 'institutional'. But the 'evential' itself can be made the subject of general studies.

1. *The distinction between the 'evential' and the 'institutional'.* This was formulated in 1894 by the historian Paul Lacombe. It had a great success and today a whole school of French historians write institutional history. One of them, Fernand Braudel, distinguishes three 'stages' of history: 'The top layer is evential history concerned with short periods; this is a micro-history. At mid-range, there is conjunctural history which has a larger and slower rhythm. This has been mainly concerned with the study of material life, of economic cycles and intercycles.... Beyond this "recitative of the conjuncture" there is structural history or the history of long periods: it is at the limit of movement and immobility and by its long-standing values

it appears as a fixed point in relation to other histories which, finally, gravitate around it.' Thus 'history is not only the different, the unique, the unexpected—the things which will not occur again'. In the last two stages the distinction between generality and historicity does not exist: across the conjunctural cycles and the long persisting structures, the facts of social history are sufficiently general to be the object of sociological analysis.

2. *The general character and the 'events'*. It must be stressed that events can be collated and compared in a manner which introduces generalization. Even physical and biological facts have a certain unique quality. The conditions of 'temperature or of pressure' are never the same. Strictly speaking, no one oak tree resembles another and no one dog another. Generalization originates not in the nature of things but in an attitude of mind, from an intellectual process which we call abstraction. Undoubtedly uniqueness is more apparent and individuality more developed in social phenomena than in biological and physical facts but it is a matter of degree rather than of kind.

Also the uniqueness of events can be questioned. The economist Francois Simiand, in a controversy with Paul Lacombe, said: 'There is no relationship in which one cannot distinguish an individual as well as a social, a contingent as well as a recurrent element.' Paul Lacombe, in a rejoinder, said that in the battles of Pavius and Rocroy there was 'a system of armaments, tactics, habits and customs of war which can be found in many of the other battles of the period'. Every historical event is a combination of elements which one finds in other events; it is the combination which is unique rather than the elements which compose it. But even the various combinations which have occurred can themselves conform to types which have a general character.

(*b*) RELATIVITY OF THE GENERAL CHARACTER

The objection of historicity cannot be completely rejected. Contemporary sociologists are generally agreed in recognizing that social phenomena are historical facts and that this is an essential part of their nature. But this does not appear to them to conflict with their general character, which is simply considered as relative.

1. *The notion of 'historical context'*. Generalizations and regularities are valid only in a given historical context and they cannot be transposed directly from one context to another. The notion of 'historical context' is difficult to define. 'Cultures' and 'civilizations', 'periods'

and 'eras' express it well enough but in a rather vague way. The proposition of some historians such as Fernand Braudel to distinguish short-term contexts, conjunctural cycles and long-term contexts has already been mentioned. The duration of historical contexts varies greatly and it is possible that it tends to diminish. Georges Gurvitch talks of the 'plurality of social periods' and essayists have dwelt on the 'acceleration of history'; in the contemporary world change is more rapid and therefore 'periods' are shorter. Whether this is the case or not, it is not very difficult to discern in history a certain number of eras or civilizations limited in both time and physical location which have had clearly defined characteristics. For example, Western society in the Middle Ages, Europe in the eighteenth century, contemporary Western industrial societies form relatively homogeneous units (see p. 65).

2. *Relativity related to 'historical contexts'*. The generality and regularity of social phenomena applies only to each of these 'historical contexts'. Sociological laws, structures, types and classifications have no absolute character and are general only in a partial sense. They express the reality only within the limits of a historical context. All analyses in the social sciences are relative to a certain moment in a historical period and to a certain geographical area. The possibility of a general sociology applicable to all eras and all countries is not rejected in *a priori* grounds but it would probably have a relative character. Rather than a schema of unchangeable types expressing a human or a social 'nature' identical for all times and places, it would be a system of translation, a kind of general key for deciphering, to pass from the phenomena of one period to those of another—rather like the general theory of relativity for the physical universe (see p. 66).

D. The positive character: the problem of values
In Auguste Comte's language 'positive' is contrasted with religious and metaphysical: after passing successively through the theological and the metaphysical stages mankind arrives at a third stage, the positive stage. In current usage the word has almost the same meaning: science is positive because it is the study of what is, not of what ought to be. The distinction between positive and non-positive is that between is and ought. The notion of a positive phenomenon contrasts with a 'value'.

(*a*) THE NOTION OF VALUE
The notion of value implies an attitude within the categories of good

and evil, just and unjust, beautiful and ugly, good and bad, agreeable and disagreeable, useful and harmful. Some social phenomena are 'neutral' in value: for example, most people are indifferent to the seasonal migration of Nomads in the Middle Atlas, of the decline of tribal civilization in Africa and so on. But phenomena which are neutral for some are the object of value judgments by others: for instance, many Frenchmen attach no importance to the privileges of the *bouilleurs de cru* whilst many others are violently for or against them. In practice, there are few social phenomena which are really neutral for all the members of the group under consideration: most phenomena have value judgments applied to them but the degree and the form of these varies considerably.

1. *Value hierarchies.* Among the categories of values already mentioned certain hierarchies can be discerned—some categories have greater 'value' than others. For example, many civilizations consider that good and evil, justice and injustice are superior values to useful and harmful, agreeable and disagreeable. This hierarchy varies, however, between social groups and between individuals in the same group. The place of the beautiful/ugly range in the scale of value is particularly interesting in this respect. Moralists who place most highly 'good/evil' condemn materialists for placing 'useful/harmful' and hedonists for placing 'agreeable/disagreeable' at the top of the hierarchy. Drawing up the value scales for different social groups and different 'periods' or 'civilizations' is one of the important fields of study in the social sciences.

2. *The non-positive nature of value judgments.* To 'evaluate' a fact is to make an appreciation or judgment of it in terms of the categories already mentioned (just/unjust, good/evil, etc.). The main point about this judgment is that the criterion on which it is based is not positive but a certain idea of what ought to be. This is not clear for certain kinds of value, for example, the useful and the harmful, the agreeable and the disagreeable. There are objective criteria possible for these and in this sense they are not value categories. No objective criteria exist for the other categories. These are the basic value categories: just/unjust, good/evil. The criteria of justice and injustice, of good and evil in any given society can be described, but these criteria vary from society to society and from period to period and nothing permits us to say which are the true criteria. Only an *a priori* judgment based on beliefs, on a commitment of heart and mind, can define what 'ought to be'.

(b) THE DISTINCTION BETWEEN NORMATIVE AND POSITIVE SCIENCES

This distinction is widely accepted amongst lawyers and moral philosophers who consider their subjects as normative sciences.

1. The normative sciences: ethics and law. There are two main normative sciences, ethics and law. Both study the rules (the 'norms') which ought to be observed in social life. They are thus distinguished from the other social sciences which analyse social life in practice. The distinction between ethics and law lies in the origin and sanction of the rules with which they are concerned: legal rules are established and sanctioned by public authority, moral rules are immanent in the human conscience, and are sanctioned by guilt feeling (religion is also important in defining and sanctioning them).

The concept of 'normative sciences' is explained by the prestige of the world 'science' in intellectual and university circles. It is symptomatic that the Faculty of Letters in France has taken the title (in 1957) of 'Faculty of Letters and the Humane Sciences'. Similarly lawyers more and more frequently call their discipline 'legal science' but they have to stress that the object of legal studies is very different from the other social sciences—hence the title 'normative sciences'.

2. The contradiction in the notion of a 'normative science'. If one studies moral and legal rules as social phenomena like other social phenomena, without being concerned about their intrinsic value, attempting only to discover their operation, effectiveness, evolution and so on, then this is positive social science—the sociology of morals and the sociology of law. Inquiries into whether they are good or evil, just or unjust, is the job of a philosopher or moralist or metaphysician and not of a scientist. Law, ethics, philosophy, metaphysics are eminently respectable disciplines—but they are not scientific disciplines. There are no normative sciences, only positive sciences.

(c) THE POSITIVE STUDY OF VALUES

It is impossible for the social sciences to ignore values. Firstly, because value judgments are involved in nearly all social phenomena. Secondly, because values usually give social phenomena their essential meaning: the meaning which a social group attributes to phenomena or institutions is a fundamental element in them. From this point of view Durkheim's definition is false—social facts are not 'things'.

1. The principle of treating values as facts. It is possible to study values positively and to consider them as facts. In a given social group, a certain conception of justice and injustice, of beauty and ugliness exists. These conceptions are positive facts inasmuch as they express the beliefs of the group and provided the observer does not adopt a position concerning them. In any country at a particular moment there usually exists a certain 'consensus' regarding the form and origin of the power, structure and investiture of the government. In a positive sense the government is legitimate in so far as it corresponds to this 'consensus'. It is thus possible to analyse legitimacy in a scientific manner. For a democrat only a popularly-elected government is legitimate, but this legitimacy is based on a value judgment or a personal belief and not on sociological analysis.

2. *The practical difficulty to the personal bias of sociologists.* There are difficulties in the path of adopting a positive attitude because sociologists are men who cannot easily separate their activities as scholars from other concerns involving value judgments. Certain value judgments permeate their scholarship. I myself have written 'if political science did not have as its aim making men freer, happier, more complete masters of their destinies, it would not be worth a moment's effort'. It is remarkable that the sociologists, such as Auguste Comte and Durkheim, who have most strongly asserted the positive character of their research have often confused their own scientific analyses with value judgments. The attitude of others, such as Karl Marx and certain contemporary Americans who more or less openly run together scientific propositions with personal value judgments, cannot be justified. The most honest attitude is to strive for the maximum separation between scientific analysis and normative positions and also to make explicit what these latter are so that others can take into account the 'coefficient of personal bias' which affects all sociologists.

General: E. DURKHEIM, *The Rules of Sociological Method*, Glencoe, 1950, and *Sociology and Philosophy*, 1953; G. GURVITCH, *La Vocation actuelle de la sociologie*, 2nd ed., 1957.

On the collective character: H. SPENCER, *Principles of Sociology*, 3 vols., 1876–96; R. WORMS, *Organicisme et société*, 1896; O. SPANN, *Gesellschaftslehre*, 3rd ed., Leipzig, 1931; O. SPENGLER, *Der Staat*, 1933; E. DURKHEIM, *Suicide*, Glencoe, 1951; *Elementary forms of religious life*, 1926; *The Division of labour in society*, Glencoe, 1947; G. GURVITCH, 'Le problème de la conscience collective dans Durkheim' in *Essais de sociologie*, p. 115; M. DUFRENNE, *Phénoménologie et sociologie*, 1947.

On the objective character: E. DURKHEIM, *Sociology and Philosophy*, 1953; R. BENEDICT, *Patterns of Culture*, Boston, 1934; J. M. BLACKBURN, *Psychology and the Social Patterns*, 1945; W. I. THOMAS, *The Behaviour*

The Social Sciences

Pattern and the Situations, 1927; H. A. HODGES, *Wilhelm Dilthey, an Introduction*, New York, 1944; R. ARON, *Essai sur la théorie de l'histoire dans l'Allemagne contemporaine*, 1938.

On the general character: F. BRAUDEL, 'Histoire et sociologie' in G. GURVITCH, *Traite dé sociologie*, Vol. I, pp. 82–97; M. BLOCH, *The Craft of the Historian*, Manchester, 1954; L. FEBURE, *Combats pour l'histoire*, 1953.

RECENT REACTIONS AGAINST POSITIVISM. The positive character of the social sciences has always been denied by some writers who denounce it as 'sociological scientism': F. VON HAYEK, *Scientisme et sciences sociales*, 1953. There is a certain anti-positivist trend in American political science: see D. WALDO in *Political Science in the U.S.A.*, UNESCO, 1956, who emphasizes what BERNARD CRICK calls 'The Strange quest for an American Conservatism', *Review of Politics*, July 1955. Some American political scientists consciously look towards conservative ideals: for example, E. VOEGELIN, *The New Science of Politics: an Introduction*, Chicago, 1952; J. H. HALLOWELL, *The Moral Foundation of Democracy*, Chicago, 1954. Bertrand de Jouvenal represents a similar tendency in France.

Various criticisms of positivism are made. The very great importance of values in politics is emphasized—the positivists have never denied this but they have wished to treat values like other 'facts'. It is alleged that many ostensibly positive studies are based on implicit value judgments. It has been argued, on the one hand, that in refusing to adopt a position on values leads in practice to conformity to the values of the group, and, on the other hand, that placing good and evil on the same level for the purpose of analysis is immoral and leads to the denial of the existence of values. None of these criticisms calls positivism seriously into question. To consider values as facts and as relative is a methodological attitude and does not deny the validity of personal value judgments. Moreover, positivism is an essential condition of science.

On values in the social sciences, see G. MYRDAL, *Value in Social Theory*, 1958; E. DURKHEIM, *Sociology and Philosophy*, 1953; F. ADLER, 'The Value concept in Sociology', *American Journal of Sociology*, 1956, p. 272; A. M. ROSE, 'Sociology and the study of values', *The British Journal of Sociology*, 1956, No. 1; B. M. ANDERSON, *Social Values*, Boston, 1911; C. BOUGLÉ, *Leçons de sociologie sur l'évolution des valeurs*, 1911.

SOCIAL CONSTRAINT. This concept, considered by Durkheim to be fundamental, has not been dealt with. It is very vague and covers many different things such as the prestige of leaders, the pressure exerted by fashion and tradition, so it is hardly possible to establish a single consistent notion. On the other hand, it cannot be completely emptied of content. On social constraint, see E. DURKHEIM, *Rules of Sociological Method*, Glencoe, 1950; the investigations of G. L. DUPRAT on the various forms of social constraint published in the *Revue internationale de sociologie*, 1927–30; J. S. ROUCEK (*et al.*), *Social Control*, 2nd ed., Princeton, 1956; T. T. SEGERSTEDT, *Social Control as a Sociological Concept*, Upsala 1948; *American Sociological Society:* Papers and Proceedings, Vol. XII, 'Social Control', Chicago, 1930.

Introduction to the Social Sciences

Section II. The various social sciences

After the breaking down of sociology into specialist disciplines the number of social sciences has increased. Distinctions between the social sciences are made on empirical and not on logical grounds and follow either the original training of the researchers (history, economics, philosophy, law, etc.) or the kind of research techniques used (demographic, linguistic, technological, historical, ethnological, etc.). Every rational classification of the social sciences is artificial. However, it is interesting to attempt a classification in order to show the links and connections between the various disciplines.

Crudely two types of classification can be made: a vertical one, following the various aspects of social life within the same groups (demography, economy, religious sociology, politics, legal sociology, aesthetics, etc.); a horizontal one according to the various categories of social groups—ethnography (the study of the societies which at one time were called 'primitive' or 'savage'), history (the study of the past), the study of small or medium-sized groups within a larger society and so on. In theory these categories are quite clear but are very much less so in practice because inquiries cut across them. For example, rural and urban sociology are concerned at the same time with a particular aspect of social life, human geography, and the study of intermediary groups—towns and rural societies. The categories, however, remain useful for the purposes of clarification. Particular social science disciplines will be classified here as those dealing with a particular aspect of social groups and global social sciences which deal with all the aspects of one or more groups (including general sociology which deals with all aspects of all groups).

On the relations between the various social sciences see the collective work *The Social Sciences: their relation in theory and teaching*, 1936; W. F. OGBURN and A. GOLDENWEISER, *The Social Sciences and their interrelations*, New York, 1927; M. KOMAROVSKY, *Common Frontiers of the Social Sciences*, Glencoe, 1957.

1. THE SPECIALIZED SOCIAL SCIENCES

Specialized social sciences are concerned with particular aspects of the study of structure and function—the geography, demography, economy and other aspects of social groups. A preliminary classification into two categories can be made: firstly, human geography and demography, the examination of the external structure, the morphology of groups; secondly, other specialized social sciences which mainly analyse the internal structure of groups. The term social morphology is generally accepted as a descriptive title for the first category. Social physiology can, although it is not generally, be used for the second category.

The distinction between the two categories is questionable from many points of view. Social morphology is not restricted to demography and human geography and the other social sciences contain a morphological element. There are, for example, economic, political, legal morphologies. If the title 'social morphology' is retained for human geography and demography because it is common usage, 'social physiology' will not be used—we will call the other social sciences 'sociologies'. This is not entirely satisfactory because 'sociology' and 'social science' are often used as synonyms. We will use the term in a stricter sense to signify a specialized social science which examines both facts of structure and facts of function and having both a morphological and a physiological aspect (see p. 43).

A. Social morphology

The term social morphology is used in three different ways. In the widest meaning it is the study of the structure of social groups and in this sense all social sciences have a morphological aspect. The sociologist Maurice Halbwachs uses it in a very restricted sense—only demography falls within his definition—but this definition has not been widely accepted. There is a third definition, narrower than the first and wider than the second, which has gained general acceptance: 'The study of social facts in their material substrata' (A. Cuvillier). This definition is derived from Durkheim: 'Social life rests on a substrata which is fixed in size and form, composed of the individuals which make up society, the utilization of the soil and the nature and configuration of all sorts of elements which affect collective relations.' Thus, in practice, social morphology includes human geography and demography.

(*a*) HUMAN GEOGRAPHY

The terminology of this field is not well established. The German school, following Ratzel, call it 'anthropogeography'. The American school call it 'human ecology' (ecology being the science of the relations between a living organism and its environment). The French school prefer the term 'human geography' and it will be used here.

1. *Influence of geographical factors: determinism or possibilism.* There has been for a long time an awareness of the influence of geography on social life. Plato mentions it and Aristotle discusses it at length. Malebranche thought that the lively imagination of the Gascons came

from a quality in the air. Montesquieu elaborated on the theme of a relationship between political régimes, climate and the fertility of the soil. Taine accorded to the 'milieu' pride of place in intellectual formation. The study of the influence of geography became more systematic with Le Play and the 'school of social science' and it was thought of as having a determining influence. Le Play gives examples which have become famous: the high plateaus of Asia consist of fertile steppes the soil of which occasionally becomes exhausted—this produced a hard raising economy and frequent migrations, making necessary the formation of large patriarchal families with rigid hierarchies and strong traditions; a contrasting situation was found in the isolated Norwegian fjords which engendered individualism and particularism. The disciples of Le Play, however, progressively diluted his determinism.

The anthropogeographical German school was rigidly determinist. Its founder, Frederick Ratzel (1844–1904), the father of sociological geography, wrote that 'the apparent liberty of man seems obliterated by the action of the soil', that 'the whole life of the State has its roots in the soil' and that 'the soil rules the destiny of peoples with blind brutality'. The scientific work of Ratzel is of considerable importance but political considerations, attempts to justify German expansion, are often embedded in it. His analysis of the importance of 'space' in the life of people formed the basis of Hitlerian theories of 'living space'. His book *The Sea as the Origin of the Greatness of Peoples* (1900) voiced the ambitions of some German groups of the period which wanted naval rivalry with England. Between the two wars the followers of Ratzel moved in the direction of 'geopolitics', borrowing this word from the Swedish Rudolf Kjellen (in his book *L'Etat comme forme vitale* (1917)). Sociological geography became a means of political propaganda supported by apparently scientific arguments.

The French school of human geography has replaced the idea of geographical determinism by that of 'possibilism'. Vidal de la Blache explained it in this way: 'At every step nature offers possibilities; between them, man chooses ... Geography provides the backcloth on which man embroiders the design.' Man also change the geographical milieu. Huntington's assertion 'man is only clay in the hands of nature' can be turned on its head—'nature is clay in the hands of man'. Man is assisted not only by technology but by collective ideas and images: 'Thought is one of the great factors in changing the land' (P. Demangeon). It is, of course, true that social structure sometimes reflects geographical conditions. But conversely geographical configurations are often moulded by social structure.

This is true for modern cities, primitive tribes and Kabyle villages; in all of them the plan of settlement reflects the composition of society. Possibilism is less satisfactory than the consideration of reciprocal influences between man and nature.

2. *Main themes of human geography.* Three main themes in current research in human geography can be distinguished. Firstly, there are general inquiries into the relationships between particular geographical features and social structure, or, conversely, between particular social structure and geographical features. Examples of this are P. Deffontaines, *Géographie et religion* (1948), Georges Hardy *Géographie psychologique* (1939), Cavaillès, *La Route française* (1946) and the important work of the American human ecology school concerned mainly with natural ecological zones or 'human areas', the distribution of juvenile delinquency, mental illness, social disorganization, the segregation of social classes and so on; and general theorizing about the relations between geography and society.

Urban sociology is the second theme. This was first developed in the United States under the influence of the human ecology school. It broke away from this influence in America and elsewhere because urban sociology belongs only partly to human geography. The same thing can be said for the third theme—rural sociology. Urban and rural sociology concentrate on a particular kind of community utilizing different disciplines to examine particular aspects of social life. We shall return to these in the discussion of the horizontal classification of the social sciences.

(*b*) DEMOGRAPHY

Achille Guillard invented the word 'demography' in 1855. But the science was developed long before this. At the end of the eighteenth century the influence of demographic factors on social development was brilliantly illustrated in Malthus's famous law (1798).

1. *The evolution of demographic concepts.* Very simply, demography has shifted from mathematical to sociological concepts. As Sauvy said: 'The science of population, demography, is everywhere and nowhere. It has no natural limits only conventional limits: if it is limited to the observation of age, sex and matrimonial state, theoretical demography is only a branch of mathematics (...) and applied demography a branch of applied statistics.' This was its form in its early days. Demography was conceived at the moment when statistics assumed its modern meaning, a mathematical technique, losing its original meaning as a descriptive science of the

State (in Italian *statista* means statesman). The first works of mathematical statistics were demographic studies—the tables of mortality by the astronomer Halley in England (1692) and by Deparcieux in France (1746). The place of statistics and ennumeration in demography obviously remains a large one. Censuses of population remain the essential working documents of demographers.

Mathematics long ago ceased to be the only element in demography. In order to analyse population statistics demographers must take into account other evidence. They have to analyse social situations and collective images with which population movements are closely linked. 'The marriage rate does not follow the process of sexual maturing alone; it is subject to the cultural norms of societies and groups and to economic contingencies which raise or lower the age of marriage. The birth rate is affected by the existence of controls and limitations of many kinds ... the birth and death rates ... are the consequences of the concerted will of social groups and to external circumstances associated with the forms of civilization quite as much as they are biological phenomena.' (A. Girard). To give one example, in 1951 in France infantile mortality varied as much as the ratio of 1 to 5 according to social group. The number of children and birth control varies according to religion, social level, period, etc., independently of biological conditions. Demography therefore tends more and more to use the procedures of sociological analysis side by side with statistical techniques.

2. *Contemporary development of demography*. The importance of demography in the social sciences is growing. There has been a striking increase in the number of demographical studies in recent years and a place has been found for it in university curricula. This seems due to two causes: firstly, the development of means of population control; secondly, the fundamental importance of the influence of demographic phenomena on some contemporary societies.

In the first place, the discovery of contraceptives has opened the way to real family planning. Contraceptive pills will make this even easier. The only limitations of this control are social taboos—particularly religious taboos like those of the Catholics and the Moslems. The progress made in medicine and hygiene in the last half century has increased man's influence over the death rate. In advanced countries the average life span has increased from thirty to seventy (which approaches the average biological age of death). States (even those with economically liberal governments) are

The Social Sciences

progressively tending to control national and international migratory movements to secure the best use of natural resources.

The second factor is the growth of the influence of demographic factors on contemporary social life. The progressive establishment mastery of man over birth and death has resulted in the unequal reduction in the rates of both. There has been an intermediary period when the death rate has been reduced much faster than the birth rate and consequently there have been considerable increases in population. Increase in population is a general phenomenon and it worried demographers long before the contemporary progress in hygiene and medicine. In 1798 Malthus formulated the celebrated law according to which the population grew in geometrical proportion (if this growth is not checked in some way) whilst means of feeding the population grew only in arithmetical proportion. Mankind was thus threatened with famine. However, the real growth in Malthus's time was quite low and his so-called law has never been verified. The actual growth of population in the underdeveloped countries is much greater and famine is an immediate threat. The life of some contemporary societies is in this way partly dominated by demographic phenomena.

B. The specialist sociologies

Some regard the terms 'social science' and 'sociology' as synonyms. Others apply the title 'sociology' to the synthesizing of the results of the specialist disciples. However, this is usually called 'general sociology' (see p. 63). There is a noticeable tendency to give a more restricted meaning to the term 'sociology' than to 'social science'. This usage will be followed here and those social sciences which examine facts of function as well as facts of structure, in contrast with those which are limited to morphology and consequently remain more descriptive, will be called sociologies. Thus amongst specialist sociologies are economic science, political science, sociology of law, religious sociology, moral sociology and sociology of art.

(*a*) ECONOMIC SCIENCE

This is one of the oldest of the social sciences. As had already been mentioned the name political economy was invented by Antoine de Montchrestien in 1615 and Nicolas Oresme published a treatise on money in 1370. Economics today is the first of the social sciences both in the number of specialists in economics and its practical importance. This practical importance is reinforced by certain doctrines (in particular by Marxism, which asserts the primacy of economic phenomena over other social phenomena).

1. *Political economy.* The title economic science today tends to replace the traditional title political economy but they are synonyms. Political economy has been defined as the science which examines the production, the distribution and consumption of goods and services—the 'science of wealth'. Today economic science is considered as based on one fundamental proposition—that of scarcity, i.e. the disproportion between human needs and the goods and services available to satisfy them. It has been defined as 'the science of the administration of scarce resources in human society' (R. Barre). Lionel Robbins makes a similar statement: 'The scarcity of the means of satisfying ends of varying importance is an almost universal factor in human behaviour ... Political economy is the science which studies human behaviour as a relation between ends and scarce means.' Scarcity provokes competition and tension: from this, Francois Perroux derives his definition of political economy as the science 'which analyses and reduces tension between men in their collective efforts to order rationally all the energies of the cosmos in the service of all those purposes which deserve to be described as human'.

Since the beginning two strands have co-existed in economic science. One is the attempt to interpret economic reality with the individual as the starting point. The individual is analysed in order to determine economic motives and to decide upon ends; a scheme of economic activity is built, in a network of relations between individuals. The other starts by considering human groups, societies and 'global quantities' of goods and services. These two types of analysis are called micro-economics and macro-economics (it is interesting to compare this to the distinction between psychological and sociological analysis in the other social sciences. (See pp. 24, 57, 231). The Physiocrats were macro-economists whereas the classical economists (Adam Smith, J.-B. Say, etc.) tended to be micro-economists. All liberal economics leans towards micro-economics. Marx and the socialists re-established macro-economics whilst the marginal theorists fostered the popularity of micro-economics. Keynes furthered the cause of macro-economics. At the moment both in capitalist and socialist countries macro-economics tends to be dominant. Individualism and micro-economics are defended only by a small minority.

A second fundamental characteristic of economic science should be stressed. Before 1914 the great majority of economists worked within the context of a single system. They considered that elements within the capitalist system were general: so-called primitive economies seemed to them backward forms which would of necessity evolve towards capitalism as they were modernized. They considered economic laws had an absolute validity and that the capitalist system was 'natural'. Since 1914 the idea of relativity has penetrated into economic science under the influence of historical analysis and the appearance of non-capitalist systems in the contemporary world (more than half the present population of the world lives under a socialist system). Economic laws are only valid in a particular context. Laws common to several systems, or transposable from one system to another are, however, possible: an analogous situation is found in other social disciplines.

2. *Social economics.* The twin tendencies within economic science towards macro-economics and towards relativism brings it closer to other social disciplines. In this sense it can be said that all political economy is 'social' but it has been the usage for a long time to call the study of human relations which are derived from economic phenomena 'social economics'. Work relations are particularly important amongst these. The 'sociology of work' is establishing itself as an independent discipline. The development of industry in modern societies has raised 'industrial sociology' into the most important branch of the sociology of work. Technology—the science of instruments, tools, machines and technical procedures—has received a new stimulus after being confined for a long time to the role of an auxiliary to ethnography or history (on technology see p. 89).

The sociology of work tends to enlarge its scope to consider the whole of human activity from the point of view of work. This leads firstly to the analysis of the commitments and activities connected with work such as syndicalism and social conflict and this leads on to the examination of social stratification, of the groups and classes which are more or less the direct products of the diversity of jobs and wage scales. This leads to a consideration not only of man at work but man outside his work (the sociology of leisure develops at the same rate as the hours of work diminish). This eventually leads to the analysis of the total development of the activity of work in the human life span and particularly to the problem of professional careers. In extreme cases the sociology of work runs the risk of becoming a general sociology based on the hypothesis that work is the most important factor in explaining social phenomena. The same risk applies to all the specialist branches of the social sciences and it must be remembered that the frontiers between the disciplines are artificial and have no value in themselves.

Introduction to the Social Sciences

(b) POLITICAL SCIENCE

The term political science entered common usage in the second half of the nineteenth century: it is symptomatic that between 1859 and 1872 Paul Janet felt the need to change the title of his magnum opus from 'political philosophy' to 'political science'. Established by Aristotle, Jean Bodin, Machiavelli, and Montesquieu, the first great work of political science, *Democracy in America* by Alexis de Tocqueville, was written in the first half of the nineteenth century. Karl Marx had a decisive influence on the development of the subject. However, until 1945 it was established on a university level only in the United States. Chairs and departments were in America between 1890 and 1914. This was associated with the movement to purify American political life and to replace the adventurers who had built up powerful political machines by honest men. After 1945 European universities accepted the subject with some difficulty.

1. *The two conceptions of political science.* The last born of the social sciences, political science is in the grip of two controversies, one about its aim the other about its methods. There are two conceptions about its aim that are closer in practice than in theory. On the one hand political science is thought of as the science of the State. This definition is closest to normal current usage of the world 'political'. In the public mind the word 'political' and the word 'state' are connected. The definition of the dictionary of the *Académie française* is: 'Politics (noun): knowledge of everything which relates to the art of governing a state and of directing relations between states.' Littré defines politics as 'the science of the government of states'. M. Marcel Prélot adheres closely to this definition. In his lecture course given in the Faculty of Law (Paris) in 1956–57, he developed the theme at length by examining: '(1) Politics as knowledge of individual states; (2) Politics as the science of all states.' Other important authors have belonged to the same school of thought. Georg Jellinek, for example, wrote in 1903: 'The terms *science politique, scienza politica*, political science or politics apply to the science of the State.'

For others political science is the science of power. This conception is of more recent origin but it has become very popular and most specialists in politics today accept this. It is possible to give a large number of quotations from authors of widely differing views. 'Politics means the rise towards participation in power or influence in the distribution of power between states, within states or within the groups which make up the state.' (Max Weber). 'Politics is the study of the authority relations between individuals and groups and the hierarchy of power which establishes itself within all numerous and complex communities.' (Raymond Aron). 'A brief definition of the scope of political science is the study of power. [Its object is] the study of the phenomena arising out of power, in other words with the phenomena of command which appear in a society' (Georges Vedel). 'The object of political science does not raise great difficulties: it is the science of authority, of governors, of power.' (Maurice Duverger).

What then is power?—Basically there is what Léon Duguit calls the distinction between the governed and the governors. In every social group, there is on the one hand those who give the orders and on the other those who obey. The word 'power' describes both the governing group and the function which it fulfils. Political science is the science of governors and leaders: it examines their origin, structure, prerogatives, and the scope and foundations of the obedience given to them. Power should not be confused with a similar phenomenon which, for lack of a better word, we call 'superiority' or 'domination'. Superiority or domination is not at the level of the antagonism between the governed and the governors but at the level of the antagonism between the governed.

The differences between power and superiority or domination are of two kinds. Firstly, superiority is a material fact whilst power is also a phenomenon of belief. Power is recognized as power and its authority is admitted. If it is not embodied in the desired form, if it is not legitimate (in the sociological sense of the word) then there is a revolt against it. There is a reaction against its excesses if it passes the limits considered normal. But the necessity of power and of obedience to power is generally admitted. In contrast a superiority is only submitted to: as it is a phenomenon of competition there is a constant struggle against it and a hope either to destroy it, thus establishing equality, or to re-form it to one's own advantage. Secondly, power has an organized and structured character. It is thought of as the skeleton of society and it belongs to the social framework. The juridical study of power in the state is called 'constitutional law' which expresses very well this character. In contrast, domination results from conflicts and struggles inside the social framework.

2. *Intermediate conceptions.* Some sociologists, whilst admitting that the object of political science is the study of power, do not think that it is concerned with the analysis of power in all its forms and in all human groups. They try to define a 'political power' different from other forms of power. For some, political power is characterized by

the ultimate recourse to physical violence and by organized sanctions. Under a different form this is the same as the position that political science is the science of the State because the State is defined, by Léon Duguit and others, as the consistent utilization of physical force within the framework of organized sanctions. In fact, this definition is very vague. Undoubtedly the State is, crudely, and in general, the human group in which sanctions are most effective and best organized. But other groups have analogous characteristics. Criminal gangs and societies have 'irresistible' and very well organized sanctions. Also, force and sanctions play only a secondary role in well established States in which propaganda and beliefs are much more important: 'gouverner, c'est faire croire'. All power is a mixture of violence and beliefs. There is no way of measuring the degrees of violence and belief.

For others, political power appears only in complex societies. Power in elementary groups does not have a political character: 'In a strict sense a political hierarchy necessarily concerns more than one group at the same time ... all political organization supposes a plurality of groups subject to a common order.' (F. Bourricaud). This is a very popular theory. In practice it corresponds to a generally respected division of labour between political scientists and other social scientists. Until now the first have concerned themselves hardly at all with the analysis of power in small groups. From a scientific point of view there appears to be a clear difference between the problems of authority in small groups and complex societies (see below, p. 57).

However, this is an uncertain distinction. It is difficult to establish the dividing line between simple and complex groups. Firstly, 'inside any group, however small, the process of differentiation creates "cliques" and "coalitions": the unity of a group, whilst this process of differentiation is going on, presents a problem which can be strictly called political'. Another point of view is that it is impossible to define a small group. For example a small industrial firm is a small group: a large firm is a complex group. Size and complexity have the same importance in distinguishing between groups, although one is partly the function of the other. But the lines are impossible to draw in this sphere. Would one say, for example, that the phenomena of authority within the Council of Ministers—a small and simple group—are not the concern of political science?

These controversies about the objects of political science have less importance in practice than in theory. The protagonists of the theory that political science is the science of the State consider that it must also be concerned with the relations between the State and other human groups; thus in practice the object of political science extends beyond the State and impinges to a considerable extent on other human communities. On the other side of the coin, the protagonists of the science of power position consider that the State possesses the best-organized and most efficient form of power; it has the role of a kind of 'ideal type' in relation to other human groups. It is therefore natural that a particularly important place is reserved to it and that power in the State is studied more widely than power in other social groups. There is also a general tendency to study complex rather than small elementary groups.

3. *Controversies about methods.* In practice these controversies are more important than those about aims. They seem, however, to be approaching a resolution.

Like all the social sciences, political science was for a long time confused with morals and philosophy. This produced two results: firstly, a mixture of the analysis of objective facts and the affirmation of normative principles, 'judgments of reality and value judgments' as Durkheim put it; secondly, the predominance of *a priori* reasoning over observation. Like the other social sciences, political science has progressively been emancipated from these primitive aspects. But political science is not as advanced as the others and the moral point of view and implicit or explicit appeals to values are still very common. It is not by chance that contemporary efforts to reintroduce value judgments to social science are mainly restricted to political science (see above, p. 37). But these efforts are very limited in scope; the objective and positive character of political science is no longer seriously questioned. On the other hand the use of the deductive method remains widespread and many works of political science are really political philosophy, wrongly arrogating the name of science.

This is now an old fashioned controversy and the separation of political science from political philosophy is almost accomplished; those who analyse political phenomena in books and in their minds are only a very small minority. The development of methods of observation (which was very considerable in the United States between 1919 and 1939) has created other difficulties. The lack of systemization and conceptual frameworks for research has resulted in the collection of an impressive quantity of information which did not lead to many conclusions. An American author in 1950 thought that American political science (at this time the most advanced) suffered from 'hyperfactualism'. This is a feature common to most of the social sciences in the middle of the twentieth century. But for some time there has been a reaction against it in America and elsewhere.

(c) THE OTHER SPECIALIST SOCIOLOGIES

To complete the picture a few words must be said on the sociology of law, religious sociology, the sociology of morals and the sociology of art. This is not an exhaustive list of the remaining specialist sociologies and it must be insisted on once again that the dividing lines between the specialist sociologies are drawn for pedagogical reasons or by the facilities for specialization. There are, therefore, very flexible and if an aspect of social activity becomes the focus of specialized research it can always be raised to the level of an autonomous discipline.

1. *The sociology of law.* Law and the sociology of law are concerned with the same things: Constitutions, legal codes, laws, decrees, legal texts and institutions in general. But they do not study them in the same way. For the lawyer, texts and institutions express the rules of positive law and the significance and scope of these rules must be established by a rigorous analysis based on fixed rules so that one can establish what the law is. The sociologist studies laws as an expression of a certain social condition, every society being reflected in its juridical system. He seeks to establish how far these rules are applied in practice and how far they represent an ideal which is far removed from reality. The lawyer studies the rules as rules, in their normative aspect: for the sociologist, the rules of law are objective social facts. Law is a 'normative science' (see p. 35): the sociology of law is a positive science.

When this is said it must be pointed out that law and the sociology of law are very much intermixed in practice. For a long time lawyers have not limited themselves to the internal analysis of texts to establish their significance. Pure exegisis has been abandoned and there has been a progressive tendency to establish the meaning and significance of juridical rules by placing them in their social context. In this way the lawyer is compelled to be a sociologist. Conversely, the sociologist cannot ignore juridical analysis if he is to understand the meaning of the texts he is studying. This interpretation of sociology and law varies greatly from one branch of law to another. It is much less developed in *droit privé* where legal definitions have been established for a long time and habits of scholastic reasoning are very firmly established. But in at least one branch of *droit privé* there is a close link with sociology—this is criminal law which cannot today be separated from 'criminology' (penal sociology). It is in constitutional law which strictly juridical analysis remains on the surface and where the political import of the texts is fundamental. In practice it is not now possible to treat constitutional law seriously in isolation from political science.

The sociology of basic legal principles was established at the beginning of the twentieth century, particularly by the disciples of Durkheim in France, who looked for the sociological foundations of law, of obligation and so on. Important results have been achieved in this field particularly concerning the distinction between rules of law, moral rules and social usages. Without neglecting these traditional concerns, the sociology of law has moved on to more concrete inquiries: for example, research into criminality, the evolution of the family and divorce, the kinds of contract used, decentralization and the types of local administration, etc.

2. *Religious sociology.* Religion is a social phenomena of fundamental importance. Some sociologists, particularly the followers of Durkheim, have argued that primitive societies are completely dominated by religious or magical beliefs and that 'laicization' of a part of social life appears only at a late stage of development. Political life, law and morals are only slowly separated from religion. The first studies in religious sociology were therefore concerned with underdeveloped societies or societies in the past. The study of contemporary religions has either been restricted by the respect of the faithful or deformed by the bias of their opponents.

This is of course true to differing degrees with the phenomena studied by the other social sciences; religious phenomena are not the only ones placed in the category called 'sacred', placed in a category of values adhered to on *a priori* grounds which are absolute, revered and unquestioned. In politics, morals, family life, sexual relations and so on, the 'sacred' is always very much present; the idea that facts concerning them can be subject to scientific study and treated just like other phenomena can appear sacrilege in the strict sense of the word. Religion belongs completely to the category of the sacred, whilst some facts about the others are outside it and more and more are regarded as being 'profane'. A religion which loses its sacred character ceases to be a religion. It is therefore natural that the sociological study of religious phenomena has aroused and continues to arouse much opposition.

Opposition is, however, tending to disappear. In modern societies the sociology of religions was originally developed by opponents of religion. Auguste Comte, Durkheim and their disciples sought more or less to establish that religion is a survival of a primitive mentality.

More concrete and less ambitious studies of religious practice are favoured today, and although these studies touch only the external and superficial aspects of the phenomena, the 'behavioural' method has had the advantage of introducing objectivity and precision. In this field the works of Gabriel Le Bras have had a great influence.

3. *The sociology of morals* is closely associated with religious sociology and the sociology of law. Morals are usually based on religious concepts and law is still based on moral principles. The development of an autonomous sociology of morals at the end of the nineteenth and at the beginning of the twentieth century, mainly as a result of Durkheim's influence, is explained by the desire to create a secular system of morals based on scientific concepts without any religious content—morality would thus be based on a 'science of habits'. This attitude has been abandoned and it is generally recognized today that it is impossible to move from 'is' to 'ought' and to base moral obligation on sociological analysis. However, an apparent separation of religion and morality has been occurring in Western societies and the decline in religious belief has been accompanied by the maintenance of the original moral standards.

Nobody any longer denies the interest of the sociology of morals and the possibility of developing a 'science of habits', provided it is limited to the consideration of facts. Freed from its early ambitions, the development of the sociology of morals is now hindered because it has not succeeded in freeing itself from philosophy and theoretical considerations about values. There is a vast field for the sociology of morals in the analysis of the behaviour of social groups and comparing it with accepted principles and 'taboos'. In spite of their methodological inadequacies, the famous works of Professor Kinsey on the sexual behaviour of male and female Americans should be mentioned because they showed how far actual conduct in this respect was removed from the accepted moral principles.

4. *The sociology of art.* The admirable paintings of Lascaux have shown that art goes back to the very beginnings of the human race and is a fundamental social activity. It has always been one of the concerns of sociology. The analysis of artistic activities forms an important part of all ethnological studies. The study of the so-called popular arts has given rise to a separate social science, that of 'folklore': historians attribute great importance to the history of the arts; Marxists stress the close connection between art and socio-economic development, and so on. One cannot say that the sociology of art is

neglected. However, it has not been very much developed as a separate discipline. Perhaps this is because too often it is associated with the philosophy of art (or aesthetics).

On human geography: M. SORRE, *Les Fondements de la géographie humaine*, 4 vols., 1943–52; A. LE LANNOU, *La Géographie humaine*, 1949.

On urban sociology: the bibliography in *Current Sociology*, Nos. 1 and 4, 1955; E. A. BERGEL, *Urban Sociology*, 1955.

On rural sociology: the bibliography by H. MENDRAS in G. GURVITCH, *Traité de sociologie*, p. 312; LOOMIS and BEEGLE, *Rural social systems*, New York, 1950.

On demography: A. SAUVY, *Théorie générale de la population*, 2 vol., 1952–54; *Richesse et population*, 1944; L. CHEVALIER, *Démographie générale*, 1951; M. HALBWACHS, *Population and Society*, Glencoe, 1960.

On economics: R. BARRE, *Economie politique*, 2 vols., 2nd ed., 1960; J. N. KEYNES, *The Scope and Method of Political Economy*, 1891; L. ROBBINS, *An Essay on the Nature and Significance of economic science*, 1932; T. PARSONS and N. J. SMELSER, *Economy and Society*, 1956; O. LANGE, 'The Scope and Method of Economics', *Review of Economic Studies*, 1946, No. 33; Ch. GIDE and Ch. RIST, *Histoire des doctrines économiques*, 7th ed., 1947; E. JAMES, *Histoire de la pensée économique au XXe siècle*, 2 vols., 1955.

On political science: M. DUVERGER, *Méthodes de la science politique*. 1959; UNESCO, *La Science politique contemporaine*, 1950; W. A. ROBSON, *The University Teaching of the Social Sciences: Political Science*, UNESCO, 1955; R. BENDIX and S. M. LIPSET, 'Political Sociology', *Current Sociology* 6, 1957; D. WALDO, *Political Science in the U.S.A.*, UNESCO, 1956.

On the concept of power as the basis of political science: articles by J. LHOMME in *Revue économique*, 1958, p. 859 and 1959, p. 481; B. DE JOUVENEL, *Power*, 1948; C. E. MERRIAM, *Political Power*, 1934; H. D. LASSWELL and A. KAPLAN, *Power and Society*, 1952.

On the biological aspects of power: M. SIRE, *La Vie Sociale des animaux*, 1960; P. CRAWFORD, 'Social psychology of the vertebrates', *Psychological Bulletin*. 1939, p. 407. D. O. HEBB and W. R. THOMSON, 'The Social significance of animal studies', in G. LINDZEY (*et al.*), *Handbook of Social Psychology*, Cambridge, 2nd ed., 1956, Vol. I, p. 552.

On the 'science of the State': M. PRÉLOT, *La Conception française de la science politique*, Roneotyped, Faculty of Law, Paris, 1956–57; A. CARRO MARTINEZ, *Introduction à la ciencia politica*, Madrid, 1957; D. EASTON, *The Political System*, New York, 1953; F. BOURRICAUD, 'Science politique et sociologie', *Revue française de science politique*, 1958, pp. 249 ff.

On the sociology of law: H. LÉVY-BRUHL, *Aspects sociologiques du droit*, 1955; COLLOQUE DE STRASBOURG, *Méthode sociologique et droit*, 1958; COLLOQUE DE TOULOUSE, 'Droit, economie et sociologie', *Archives de la Faculté de Droit de Toulouse*, Vol. VII, 1959; R. VOUIN and J. LÉAUTÉ, *Droit pénal et criminologie*, 1956.

On religious sociology: J. WINCH, *Sociology of Religion*, 1945; J. M.

YINGER, *Religion, Society and the Individual*, New York, 1957; G. LE BRAS, *Études de sociologie religieuse*, 2 vols., 1955–56; *Current Sociology*, 1, 1956; *Archives de sociologie des religions*, 1956.

On the sociology of morals: G. GURVITCH, *Morale théorique et science des moeurs*, 1937; J. C. FLÜGEL, *Man, Moral and Society*. 1955; S. J. HOLMES, *Life and Moral*, New York, 1948; M. GINSBERG, *On the Diversity of Morals*, 1957; A. C. KINSEY, *The Sexual Behaviour of the Male*, Philadelphia, 1948; *The Sexual Behaviour of the Female*, Philadelphia, 1953; D. P. GEDDES (*et al.*), *An Analysis of the Kinsey Reports*, New York, 1954.

On the sociology of art: P. FRANCASTEL, *Peinture et société*, 1954; S. FINKELSTEIN, *Art and Society*, New York, 1947; D. W. GOTSCHALK, *Art and the Social Order*, Chicago, 1951; R. MUKERJEE, *The Social Function of Art*, New York, 1951; R. ESCARPIT, *Sociologie de la littérature*.

2. GLOBAL SOCIAL SCIENCES

I propose to call those social sciences which examine the whole of the activities of one or more social groups 'global' social sciences: for example, ecology, demography, economics, politics, law, morals, religion and aesthetics. Specialization of teaching and research is here not made according to the nature of the activity but is defined by the groups studied; instead of analysing a type of activity in all social groups, all the activities of a type of social group are studied. The latter method seems preferable to the former because the various kinds of social activity are difficult to distinguish and they are very much dependent on one another. Social reality is a 'totality of interdependent parts'. On the other hand, the specialist social sciences allow a more profound analysis of each type of activity. In addition, the distinctions between types of social group present difficulties and they are often questionable.

There are three categories of global social sciences. The first is concerned with social groups artificially isolated within larger groups of which they form a part: examples of this are the sociology of 'small' or 'elementary' groups which is very popular in the United States, the sociology of political parties, pressure groups and 'intermediary' groups in general, the sociology of towns and communities, etc. The second is concerned with complex groups which are more or less autonomous: examples are ethnography which is concerned with underdeveloped societies and what can be called the 'sociology of nations' (in which history has an essential place). The third studies all social groups in all societies: this is a general social science in relation to both the specialist social sciences and the global social sciences and is usually called 'general sociology'.

The Social Sciences

A. The sociology of elementary and intermediary groups

Human societies are usually complex: they are rarely simple groups but are usually collections of groups which cut across one another. An individual belongs to a family, a local community, a Church, a trade union, a firm and to various other associations. Each of these groups has its own characteristics; one can thus establish a typology of elementary and intermediary groups inside a society. The specialization of teaching and research can be drawn up on the basis of this typology and a new definition of the social sciences according to the types of groups with which they are concerned can be established. Starting from this point of view, the sociology of the family, the sociology of small groups and the sociology of intermediary groups can be distinguished.

(a) THE SOCIOLOGY OF THE FAMILY

In all human societies the family seems to form the basic elementary social group but it varies very greatly in form. In current usage the word applies both to the domestic society which includes kinsmen (sociologists sometimes call this the 'extended family') and the conjugal family which is limited to a married couple (sometimes called the 'elementary family'). At one time the two were to some extent fused, the second being dominated by the first. Recent changes have tended progressively to distinguish them and have given primacy to the small unit.

1. *Ethnological studies of the family.* Various kinds of social science cut across one another. The sociology of the family has been developed by ethnologists. In the societies studied by them, family ties play a primordial role. Ethnological studies have thrown light on basic phenomena which have necessitated the revision of preconceived ideas derived from the observation of the modern family.

Thus the notion of kinship which is now based on descent (blood relation) or alliance (marriage ties), in other words on physiological connections, had not this character in so-called primitive societies. Some of them (for example the Melanasians of the Tobriand Islands) are unaware of the role of the father in procreation and the notion of kinship is therefore purely social. But in other primitive societies in which descent through the father is known, the social character of kinship predominates over the physiological aspect. To be kinsmen means participation in a group, in its rites, and share its religious and moral values. This notion was present in Greece and ancient Rome, where, according to Fustel de Coulanges 'It was religion that determined kinship' and this was the source of the primacy of agnatic kinship (through the males) over cognatic kinship (through the females). It is possible that modern legal systems which give primacy to juridical kinship over natural kinship are a survival of these primitive ideas, although this primacy is usually explained on grounds of social utility.

The types of 'primitive' family are very numerous because these families are based on myths and social bonds, of which there are a great number, and not on blood or marriage ties, of which there are a limited number of combinations. Some sociologists attempted to generalize their ethnological findings concerning particular societies but this attempt has now been abandoned. The 'totem clan'—a group which is attached to a common and mythical ancestor, the totem, which is its symbol and emblem—is found in its pure form in some Australian societies and in a hybrid form in others but it appears completely absent in many other societies. It cannot be ascribed the importance which many of the disciples of Durkheim gave it: it is simply not true that humanity has evolved 'from clans to empires'. Similarly the verification of family divisions by the system of 'halves' or 'phratries' is not general. New dimensions have been given to the typology of families by the recent studies of Claude Lévi-Strauss who has endeavoured to translate the various 'elementary structures of kinship' into mathematical symbols.

2. *Studies on the modern family*. The sociology of the modern family was first developed by Frederic Le Play (1806–88) who inaugurated the monographic method and made a number of studies of families, particularly of working class budgets in the middle of the nineteenth century. The school of Le Play later tended to confuse sociological research with social reform and lost its early scientific orientation. The development of the sociology of the family has been generally hindered by moral and religious considerations and by attempts to justify *a priori* conceptions of the family or to do battle against some change considered bad. On the other hand, the moralizing point of view has provoked sociological research especially on the phenomena of the 'disorganization' of the family, resulting from the increase in the divorce rate, the decrease in the number of children and the contraction of the family as the 'extended family' gives way more and more to the 'elementary family'. Eventually the separation of sociology and morality has been achieved in this field as in the others: there is even a tendency today to reject the concept of 'disorganization' which implies a value judgment and replace it with the 'new organization'. The sociology of the family is now being fully developed as a positive social science.

(b) SOCIOLOGY OF SMALL GROUPS

In the last few years the sociology of small groups has been greatly developed in the United States. Important results have been obtained but they cannot be generalized.

1. *Development of the sociology of small groups.* The sociology of the family, or at least the elementary family, can be considered as part of the sociology of small groups. American sociologists have studied many other kinds of small groups, for example student seminars, school classes, groups of friends, air force squadrons, gangs of adolescents or adults, and boards of administration and management. They attempt to define the interpersonal relations inside the group and the conditions and forms of the authority of the leaders. A whole theory of leadership has been elaborated.

Two things can explain the development of small group sociology in the United States. The first is theoretical: the study of small groups is associated with a very widespread tendency in the United States to look at sociology from the point of view of social psychology, in other words to consider social facts as phenomena of relations between individuals (see pp. 25, 68). Small groups are thus thought of as 'elementary' groups and social life as consisting of a complex collection of temporary or permanent liaisons between these basic elements. The second reason is a practical one: some researchers have stated that small groups allowed the construction of real sociological experiments and thus experimental procedures more or less analogous to those of the physical sciences could be introduced into the social sciences (see p. 249).

2. *The limits of small group sociology.* Some American sociologists have generalized the results of observing small groups and have regarded 'leadership' theory as a general theory of power in all groups, large as well as small. This generalization ignores the fundamental distinction between 'macro' and 'micro' which will be discussed later (see p. 231). The authority of the leader of a small group is obviously based on his personal ascendancy over the members of the group who know him intimately and live in day to day contact with him. The political leader has prestige with people who have no direct human contact with him—except the illusory and factitious contact of the radio, television and cinema. The point is valid not only for leadership but for all other interpersonal relations which differ if they are based on a direct, intimate and regular contact rather than on an occasional contact within a large group. The conclusions based on observations of small groups are valid only for small groups.

(c) SOCIOLOGY OF INTERMEDIARY GROUPS

The notion of an 'intermediary group' is very vague. All those groups contained within a complex whole (a nation, a tribe or people) other than the family or the 'small groups' in the American sense are contained in this category. This to some extent corresponds with the idea popularized by corporatist theories of 'intermediary bodies' between the family and the state. In fact, there is no expression 'the sociology of intermediary groups' in current use and it is used here to group various social researches: the sociology of political parties, of pressure groups, of towns, of rural communities, etc.

1. *The sociology of associations.* In each nation there is a multitude of associations of all kinds—industrial and commercial companies, trade unions, political parties, youth movements, ex-servicemen's groups, professional associations, sports clubs, clubs for hobbies, learned societies, literary and artistic academies, Churches, secret societies and so on.

However, the sociology of associations hardly exists as an autonomous discipline except as part of general theory. The famous distinction made by the German sociologist Tönnies (1855–1935) between 'community' and 'society' as the two fundamental types of association should be mentioned here. 'Community' (*gemeinschaft*) is based on blood, sexual relationship, geographical proximity or friendship (it is the 'community of the spirit'): it has a natural, intimate and trusting character. By contrast, 'society' (*gesellschaft*) is based on interest and exchange and has an artificial, mechanical and quasi-commercial character. This classification is not clear: in the mind of the author it applies both to ideal types with a normative character and to concrete types—and the first aspect dominated the second. It was associated with a mystique of 'community' which was regarded as morally superior to 'society' and this mystique was one of the foundations of national socialism. The same mystique is present in a third category which another German sociologist, Schmalenbach, suggested adding to Tönnies's categories: the *bund*, a voluntary association not founded on interest, characterized by tension, exaltation and effervescence (a recently founded religion, a marriage of love, a revolutionary party are examples of *bund*). The typology of Tönnies is interesting as a first basis of classification of associations. But it should not be forgotten that it is proposed as a general typology, applicable not only to associations but to all human groups. Even on a theoretical level these are not really part of a true sociology.

In empirical research the study of associations is split up between the different specialist sociologies. Industrial and commercial companies are analysed by economists; churches and religious associations by specialists in religious sociology; political parties, pressure groups and administrative bodies by political scientists and so on. All kinds of associations present similar structural problems such as those concerning the choice and the authority of the directors, the relations between members of the group, the nature and intensity of their allegiance, the motives for and significance of joining, etc. Political science—as the science of power—does this in everything which touches the problem of authority. It also does it, in a more general way, for all the associations which more or less directly influence the government of the State. As nearly all associations fall within this category, at least in a partial and occasional way, the sociology of parties and pressure groups is tending to lay the foundations of a general sociology of associations.

2. *The sociology of local communities.* As a result of their geographical situation, towns and rural communities constitute intermediary groups within nations. But urban and rural sociology are divided between human geography (according to the vertical classification of the social sciences) and the sociology of intermediary groups (according to the horizontal classification). In the study of towns and human communities it is impossible to determine exactly what belongs to human geography and what is properly speaking sociology The influence of environment and physical conditions, in other words urban and rural ecology, belongs to the former, the study of human relations and community structure to the latter. But the two are closely linked and the geographer who is primarily concerned with the first cannot ignore the second and, conversely, the sociologist who is primarily concerned with the second cannot ignore the first.

B. The sociology of aggregations

There is no satisfactory distinction between 'elementary and intermediary' groups and 'aggregations': most groups are more or less complex aggregations (even the family and some small groups). The human race forms a social web in which all groups are intertwined. However, some aggregations can be isolated. Some are completely isolated like so-called primitive societies which have a simple structure and little contact with the rest of the world. Others are less easy to isolate but are separated from others by clearly defined boundaries: for example, nations in the contemporary world, cities and empires throughout history and the supra-national units which are being formed. They have a more complicated structure.

Some of them make up interdependent entities and have to be studied as such. Indeed, recent evolution has moulded them more and more into a common entity, the human race: the isolation of under-developed societies is rapidly disappearing and the frontiers between nations are becoming less important. But at the present time mankind does not form an integrated society: nations and under-developed societies have a more real social existence than the total human community.

(a) ETHNOLOGY

The terminology is still imprecise in this field. It is generally admitted that ethnography comprises 'the observation and analysis of human groups considered in isolation'. (Claude Lévi-Strauss) whilst ethnology 'makes use of the evidence obtained by ethnography in a comparative fashion'. In English speaking countries there is a tendency to use the term anthropology instead of ethnology.

1. *The object of ethnology.* The groups studied in ethnography, ethnology and anthropology are generally those societies which were once called 'primitive' and are now called 'under-developed' or simply 'different', for example those societies in America, Asia and Africa which have not left traces in history and only in the last few years have existed as nations. Ethnology is sometimes described as 'the history of peoples without a history': this is not true because these societies have a history but no archives and no collections of written documents so their history cannot be analysed by the usual methods of the historian. Sometimes these societies are considered as 'simple' societies and contrasted with complex modern societies. This is a very suspect contrast because although the former are less complex mainly because they cover smaller areas, they are 'simple' societies only in exceptional cases. They usually have a very complex character and cannot be regarded as similar to elementary and intermediary groups. They are aggregations although less complex and certainly smaller than nations and modern industrial societies.

Some ethnologists now tend to extend the scope of their discipline. Claude Lévi-Strauss has written that the groups studied by the ethnographer are 'often chosen amongst those which are most different from our own, for theoretical and practical reasons which have nothing to do with the nature of the research'; this implies that the study of all groups, including highly developed modern ones, comes within the scope of ethnography. He goes on to explain that if one regards the term sociology as covering all the research on complex societies then it has become 'a specialism of ethnography'.

The imperialism of the ethnologists and their desire to extend their discipline to cover all human groups is expressed well in the term anthropology. In practice, ethnographic methods are used to study modern societies; for example a French village and a sports club. But in current usage the terms ethnography, ethnology and anthropology are still used to describe the social science concerned with primitive or different societies.

2. *The significance of ethnology.* The change in the terms used to describe the societies studied by ethnologists illustrates a change in the significance attributed to the discipline. At the end of the nineteenth and the beginning of the twentieth centuries these societies were considered as primitive types of social organization petrified at the beginning of their development. It was thought that through ethnological studies the earliest history of mankind could be pieced together. The famous book *From Clans to Empires*, by G. Davy and A. Moret, illustrates this, now abandoned, attitude. Some societies seem very close to those of pre-history such as those, according to Marcel Maus, of the Fijians and Australians. But most have gone through a long evolution the traces of which are being discovered by ethnologists. The implicit assumption of the primitivist theory is that climatic and natural conditions and isolation caused the petrification of societies at the first stage of the evolutionary process. But the difference of climatic and natural conditions always existed and they probably gave the primitive societies of Europe different features to those of the societies which ethnologists study. These original differences brought about a different evolution.

The attempt to use ethnology as a method of reconstituting the first stage of the evolution of mankind has been abandoned although comparisons are still made between apparently analagous features of the structure of African or Australian societies and Gallic or Germanic tribes. In terming the societies studied by the ethnologist 'different' their original and particular features are stressed. Comparison of their respective institutions is essential to indicate the relativity of each and to highlight common features. No sociologist, in whatever branch of sociology he works, can afford to ignore the work of ethnologists. The comparative method has a fundamental role in the social sciences; ethnographic comparisons constitute one of its bases—they are a type of 'distant comparison' (see p. 266).

(*b*) SOCIOLOGY OF NATIONS AND SUPRANATIONAL AGGREGATIONS

Unlike so-called primitive or under-developed societies, the complex modern societies of the nation and the supranational groupings in process of formation have not been widely studied. Their historical genesis is studied more than their actual structure and operation.

1. *History.* History is not an autonomous social science but an auxiliary of all the social sciences. There is economic history, political history, religious history, history of law, history of art and demographic history. There is history of the family, of political parties, of trade unions and of associations. There is national history, there is general history and the history of civilizations which is the auxiliary of general sociology. We will not dwell on the problem of the 'science of history'. The fundamental distinction between 'institutional' and 'evential' history has already been made (p. 31): the former is a genuine historical sociology whilst the latter provides essential raw material for the social sciences.

One of the basic frameworks of historical analysis is the nation. This framework is however open to criticism. A general history of Europe is being written by a group of historians from the various European countries. UNESCO has a similar project under way for the history of the world. These projects have the double purpose of reducing the national bias of historians and to diminish the importance of national boundaries in historical analysis. They are helping history to become a science by reducing the personal bias of the historian but they can only succeed in the second aim in so far as national groups are themselves becoming less important and where supranational groupings (Europe, the communist bloc, the Western world, etc.) are becoming the basic 'complex aggregations.'

The importance of the nation in history is the reflection of the importance of nations as complex aggregations: the former reinforces the latter. In his famous definition of the nation, Renan rightly emphasized the role of history in the formation of national sentiment. National solidarity, the social and political structure of a country, national temperament are the reflection of the mythical history taught in schools more than of real history. The distinction between real and mythical history is the same as the general distinction between 'things' and collective images in all social phenomena. History is, in effect, the genetic sociology of nations, and as such, is at present the most highly developed branch of the sociology of nations.

2. *The study of contemporary nations and supra-national groupings* is less developed. The focus of political science, 'the science of the state', is the analysis of nation states; it remains central even when political science is considered as the science of power. In practice

political science is concerned mainly with nation states almost exclusively from the point of view of power; in other words, it is concerned with government, administration and political forces. It tends, however, to a certain extent to pass beyond the limits of its own field to embark on global sociology of national societies (which has not had an autonomous development of its own). It synthesizes the evidence presented by human geography, demography, economics, religious sociology and other specialist sociologies.

A sociology of the nation is, however, being established by using ethnological methods in the study of advanced societies. The forerunners of this development are the studies of 'national temperament' and the 'psychology of peoples' although these had no claim to being scientific. There has been some attempt in the past few years to revive the 'psychology of peoples'. Geoffrey Gorer's work on the Americans although open to criticism is of a serious nature. The great difficulty in adapting ethnological techniques is the size of national communities. But the image of a whole nation can be evoked by the study of quite small groups and very good American work (W. L. Warner on the United States and L. Wylie on France) has been done along these lines.

C. General sociology

Few sociologists deny the need for general sociology but many criticize the themes and the results of it. It is very difficult to disengage it from the clutches of philosophy. *A priori* reasoning and deductive method play a large role and at worst it is often (according to Andre Marchal) 'empty of all substance' and degenerates into 'pure verbalism'. It is not easy to rectify this because general sociolgy is not in direct contact with the facts but deals with them at second hand. As generalization and abstraction are its functions there is, in the absence of restraints, a natural tendency to excess.

There are two branches of general sociology. Firstly there is 'relativist' (or historical) general sociology which attempts to define the basic 'civilizations' or 'epochs' inside which sociological laws and typologies have a general validity. Secondly, there is a general systematic sociology which attempts to define the framework for research and the theories and typologies applicable to all eras and civilizations. These are different 'levels' rather than 'branches' of research, systematic sociology being on a higher level of generality than 'relativist' general sociology.

(*a*) HISTORICAL OR RELATIVIST GENERAL SOCIOLOGY

Its main object is the definition of 'civilizations', 'epochs', 'cultures', and so on (the terminology is imprecise) which form entities inside which structures, types, sociological laws relative to them can be defined (see p. 33). At the moment the most highly developed branch is the sociology of knowledge. The sociology of civilizations is in general still very vague and very much involved with the philosophy of history.

1. *The sociology of knowledge.* The American sociologist R. K. Merton has defined this as being 'essentially the correlations between knowledge and other existential factors of society and culture'. The basic idea of the sociology of knowledge is that not only ideologists, myths, moral prescriptions, systems of values (i.e. beliefs without objective foundation) but also scientific knowledge, and objective 'truths' are dependent on society and history. Their appearance or discovery is linked to an historical conjuncture and to a type of 'civilization' and they have, like ideologies and values, a relative character. The sociology of knowledge is a sociology of ideologies, of science, of logic, of modes of reasoning and a sociology of sociologies.

Marx opened the way to a sociology of knowledge by asserting the direct link between ideas and the economic infrastructure; systems of ideas which do not accord with the existing or developing system of social forces are eventually rejected in favour of ideas which express it more exactly. According to Marxist doctrine, the conditioning of knowledge by the social system is not absolutely rigorous. Systems of ideas contrary to the social system can form but they have no influence; these aberrations have no roots and do not penetrate society. Eventually they disappear or remain confined to very small groups separated from the mainstream of the community. Marxism was criticized by Max Weber for being able to explain any development which does not fit in with Marxist doctrine as a 'survival', an 'anachronism' or an 'accident'. Whether this is true or not, the Marxist hypothesis is a very fruitful one. A politician can obviously use it in bad faith to prove that he is always right, but the scientist can use it honestly as a means of arriving at correct explanations of the facts. As has already been said, it is not appropriate to give a privileged place amongst social forces to economic forces; or, rather, the description of this privileged place can be regarded as relative and one which must submit to the sociology of knowledge.

2. *Philosophy of history and sociology of civilizations.* Philosophy of history attempts to formulate general laws of development of human societies. It is the attempt to explain and predict the origin,

The Social Sciences

evolution and decline of the various kinds of 'civilizations' and 'cultures'. Philosophies of history are now judged harshly by sociologists. They tend to regard them as works of the imagination with implicit metaphysical or political postulates rather than as scientific studies. Some, such as Oswald Spengler's *Decline of the West*, certainly warrant this criticism. Even more serious works such as those of Arnold Toynbee are open to it.

But it must be remembered that philosophy of history was an important stage in the development of a valid general sociology. Before philosophy of history appeared philosophy was essentially static in that it attempted to formulate theories valid for all time and all places and was to varying degrees based on a concept of unchanging human nature. The philosophy of history had the great virtue of introducing the idea of evolution into philosophy. Ibn Khaldoun's law of the three generations, Vico's law of the three ages and the eighteenth-century idea of progress now appear simple-minded and false but in their own time they represented great advances. Although it is doubtful whether contemporary theories give satisfactory explanations they provide ideas which could prove useful. For example, Toynbee's concepts of 'challenge' and 'response' as motor elements of civilizations have not the general and fundamental character which he attributes to them but they sometimes provide apartially valid explanations.

It is not now usual to design explanatory panorama of the general development of civilizations and the corresponding stages of civilizations; it is now preferred more modestly to distinguish one from another. This is properly speaking the aim of the sociology of civilizations. It is an important aim because inside the categories defined, classifications, typologies, sociological laws should be valid although they are relative to and remain limited by the boundaries of each civilization (see p. 33). It is a difficult aim and categories proposed can usually be criticized on the grounds of arbitrariness, artificiality and excessive abstraction. The classification of types of civilization proposed by Georges Gurvitch can be used as an example.

Gurvitch distinguishes six historical types: (1) Charismatic theocracies (following the terminology of Max Weber who contrasted authority based on tradition, authority based on reason and authority based on irrational belief, prestige and admiration which he called 'charismatic power'); (2) patriarchal societies; (3) feudal societies; (4) global societies giving birth to capitalism and to so-called 'enlightened' despotism; (6) global liberal-democratic societies with free market economies. In addition, he lists four other types 'which in the contemporary world struggle against one another: 1. Planned society which is fully developed, organized capitalism; 2. Fascist society with a technocratic, bureaucratic base; 3. Society planned according to the principles of pluralist collectivism'. It is interesting to compare these classifications with those of the ethnologists, historians, economists, etc., which they attempt to synthesize.

(b) SYSTEMATIC GENERAL SOCIOLOGY

The sociology of civilizations and the sociology of knowledge are concerned with the systemization of the results of the various social sciences which operate within each 'civilization'. Philosophy of history is at a higher level of generality in attempting to explain the sequence of the various civilizations. Systematic general sociology is at an even higher level of generality in trying to define a common language for all frameworks and to construct theories and typologies applicable to all civilizations. It has a double aim: 1. Establishing a common typology: 2. Formulating general theories or 'cosmogonies'.

1. *General typologies.* All classifications and all typologies of social phenomena are relative to a civilization. Systematic sociology attempts to establish a common typology for all these special typologies. This is not a concrete typology representing a natural classification of phenomena of one or more 'civilizations' but an abstract typology, a kind of common selection for all the particular typologies. This is, for example, the objective of the work of Georges Gurvitch defining 'the stages in depth' of sociological research. Unfortunately there is as yet no agreement on a general typology: each sociologist has his own. This is a great weakness of the social sciences and is a sign of their under-development.

2. *General theories.* The same thing can be said about general theories. At the level of each particular social science and each category of social group there are certain theories which are generally accepted. It is more difficult to find them at the 'civilization' level and they do not exist at the level of a cosmogony applicable to all 'civilizations', all groups and all the specialist social sciences. We will return to the consequences of this later (see p. 241).

Does the relative character of social phenomena exclude the very idea of a general theory as each explanatory system is valid only for a certain type of civilization? The possibility of a general typology can be admitted because of its schematic and formal character—but an explanatory system for all social phenomena cannot have this character. Many general theories still have a static and absolute character which is incompatible with the relativity of social phenomena. However, these are giving way to two other types of general theories. The first is explanations of the sequence of the various civilizations through history. This is the traditional concern of the philosophy of history which can pass from the philosophical to the sociological plan. The second corresponds in the social field to the general theory of relativity in the field of physics: it is concerned with the definition of a general system of transposition enabling the transfer of laws of one social universe (or 'civilization') to those of another. The first has not yet been separated from the philosophy of history; research has scarcely commenced on the second.

On the sociology of the family: R. HILL, *Current Sociology*, 1, 1958; I. GALDSTON, *The Family in Contemporary Society*, New York, 1958; N. W. ACKERMAN, *The Psychodynamics of family life*, New York, 1958; R. D. HESS and G. HANDEL, *Family Worlds*. Chicago, 1958; W. WALLER and R. HILL, *The Family: a dynamic interpretation*, New York, 1951.

On the sociology of small groups: D. CARTWRIGHT and A. ZANDER, *Group Dynamics* Evanston, 1953; P. MORRE, E. F. BORGATA and R. F. BALES, *Small Groups*, New York, 1955; A. W. GOULDNER, *Studies in Leadership*, New York, 1950; J. KLEIN, *The Study of Groups*, 1956.

On the sociology of associations: M. DUVERGER, *Political Parties*, 1955; J. MEYNAUD, *Les Groupes de pression*, 1960; F. TÖNNIES, *Fundamental Concepts of Sociology*, 'Gemeinschaft und Gesellschaft', New York, 1940; *Kölner Zeitschrift für soziologie und sozialpsychologie*, VII, 1955 (special number on Tönnies).

On ethnology: C. LÉVI-STRAUSS, *Anthropologie structurale*, 1958; J. GILLIN, *For a science of social men*, New York, 1954; A. L. KROEBER (*et al.*), *Anthropology Today*, Chicago, 1953; A. R. RADCLIFFE-BROWN, *Structure and function in Primitive Society*, 1952.

On history and nations: E. RENAN, 'Qu'est-ce qu'une nation?' in *Discours et conférences*, 1928; K. W. DEUTSCH, *An Interdisciplinary Bibliography of Nationalism*, Cambridge (Mass.), 1956; W. BUCHANAN and H. CANTRIL, *How Nations see each other*, Urbana, 1953; A. MIROGLIO, *La Psychologie des peuples*, 1958.

On the sociology of knowledge: W. STARK, *The Sociology of Knowledge*, 1958; K. MANNHEIM, *Essays on the Sociology of Knowledge*, 1952; B. BARBER, *Science and the Social Order*, Glencoe, 1952; P. A. SOROKIN, *Social and Cultural Dynamics*, 4 vols., New York, 1937–41.

On the sociology of civilizations: R. E. PARK, *Human Communities*, Glencoe, 1952; K. MANNHEIM, *Essays on the Sociology of Culture*, Oxford, 1956; A. L. KROEBER, *Culture, a critical review of concepts and definitions*, Chicago, 1952.

On the philosophy of history: R. ARON, *Introduction to the Philosophy of History*, 1961; J. TOYNBEE, *A Study of History*, 12 vols., 1934–61; O. SPENGLER, *The Decline of the West*, 2 vols., 1926–28.

On general typologies: G. GURVITCH, *La Vocation actuelle de la sociologie*, 1957, and *Traité de sociologie*, 1958.

On social psychology: O. KLINEBERG, *Social Psychology*, New York, 1954; G. LINDZEY (*et al.*), *Handbook of Social Psychology*, 2nd ed., 2 vols., 1956; J. W. THIBAUT and H. H. KELLEY, *The Social Psychology of Groups*, New York, 1959; A. R. LINDESMITH and A. L. STRAUSS, *Social Psychology*, 2nd ed., New York, 1956.

General works on sociology (the French edition should be consulted for the main works in French, German and Spanish); R. K. MERTON, L. BROOM, L. S. COTTRELL, *Sociology today: problems and prospects*, New York, 1960; J. S. ROUCEK (*et al.*), *Contemporary Sociology*, New York, 1958; J. F. CUBER, *Sociology: a synopsis of principles*, 4th ed, New York, 1959; A. R. RADCLIFFE-BROWN, *A Natural Science of Society*, Glencoe, 1957; R. ROSE and E. VAN DEN HAAG, *The Fabric of Society*, New York, 1957; A. M. ROSE, *Sociology*, New York, 1956; R. MACIVER, *Elements of Social Science*, 9th ed., 1956; G. A. LUNDBERG, C. C. SHRAG and O. N. LARSEN, *Sociology*, New York, 1954; G. GURVITCH and W. E. MOORE, *Sociology in the Twentieth Century*, New York, 1945.

PLAN OF THE BOOK

There are two elements in all scientific work: (1) Research and observation of the facts; (2) Systematic analysis of the evidence. Without the second element observation and research remain merely empirical; without the first, systematic analysis remains philosophical reasoning. Both elements are the subjects of separate parts of this book. But it must be remembered that there are not different or successive stages of research. The facts are not first observed and then analysed. Systemization is present at and essential to the observation stage—in the formulation of hypotheses, the establishment of a typology and so on. The distinction between the two is only made for the sake of clarity and logic.

THE POLITICAL IMPLICATIONS OF THE NEW SOCIAL SCIENCE METHODS.—Most of the new methods have been developed in the United States where they have been used not only as research procedures but also, on a certain level, as means of improving social relations. This later function assumes that the general social structure is good and needs only improvement in detail; American social science can thus appear very conservative. Some have even accused it of being an instrument for maintaining the power of the dominant groups and the subordination of the inferior groups.

1. *The accusation that it is a 'reactionary science'*. The main purpose of 'public relations' is to make employees and workers accept the authority of the employers to reduce internal tensions in the firm and in general to obscure the class struggle. In the United States large firms employ psychiatrists who recruit auxiliaries amongst the work people in order to keep a watch on them and locate the first sign of 'mental derangement' considered the main cause of difficulties in the firm. It is obvious how this can be abused and some have seen in it a 'gigantic attempt by the capitalist class to preserve their power'. (Michel Crozier.)

A whole aspect of modern social science is conservative. 'Statistical democracy', which public opinion polls tend to create, would eventually have everybody accept a superficial 'normality'. The consequences of the very concept of the 'normal' is that opposers are treated as ill or slightly ill people and subversive opinions and the spirit of revolt are treated as neuroses. Also the sociologist Daniel Guérin considers that the exposure of abuses by scientific investigations has a kind of purgative function which helps people to bear the evil with patience. It can be argued that great attention to detail in applying highly developed research techniques is sometimes a diversionary tactic in politics—although this is not always its conscious purpose. The enthusiasm for games theory as a means of explaining political decisions deflects attention from the main problems (which are the interests, the hidden forces, the motives and the significance of the issues behind these decisions). 'Political scientism' might have the same role as that of the theory of the 'State, the director of the common good' in other periods. It is perhaps the most recent and most subtle incarnation of formalism.

2. *Criticism of this accusation.*—This aspect of contemporary social science certainly exists but some have exaggerated it and there is another side to the picture.

The social sciences can also assist human emancipation and they have thus a revolutionary character. This is of more profound significance than their reactionary uses. All techniques used by men to dominate others in modern States, where the masses have reached a level of education and culture at which they cannot be kept in ignorance, consist of camouflaging behind myths or deliberately obscuring facts about oppression and exploitation. The social sciences can assist this through propaganda but if the effects of propaganda are not known it runs the risk of being ineffective. But in so far as its effects are known, and above all the extent to which they are vulgarized, its influence tends to diminish. It has less influence on advanced populations than on primitive populations.

In general the social sciences tend to throw light on things which some would prefer to remain in obscurity, they disperse artificial smokescreens and false appearances. In their very essence they are an attempt at demystification and therefore of human liberation. In the long run the more perfect their techniques become the more they will help towards this end. In the short run an exaggerated enthusiasm for some research procedure may deflect attention from the main and most urgent problems. These deflections are only temporary and they cannot turn the social sciences from their true vocation.

On the conservative or reactionary tendencies of the new methods of the social sciences see Michel Crozier, 'Human engineering', *Les Temps modernes*, 1951, pp. 44-75; see also the preface to the same number; D. Guerin, 'Gunnar Myrdal et le problème noir aux Etats-Unis,' *Contemporains*, 1951, pp. 434–47; see also the bibliography cited on p. 247.

GENERAL BIBLIOGRAPHY

L. Festinger and D. Katz, *Research Methods in the Behavioural Sciences*, New York, 1953.
D. Krech and R. S. Crutchfield, *Theories and Problems of Social Psychology*, New York, 1948.
G. Gurvitch (*et al.*), *Traité de Sociologie*, 2 vols., 1958–60.
H. D. Lasswell, D. Lerner (*et al.*), *The Policy Sciences in the United States*, New York, 1951.
M. Weber, *The Methodology of the Social Sciences*, Glencoe, 1955.
C. Sellitz, M. Jahoda, M. Deutsch and S. W. Cook, *Research Methods in Social Relations*, 4th ed., New York, 1959.
P. Lazarsfeld and M. Rosenberg, *The Language of Social Research*, Glencoe, 1955.
W. J. Goode and P. K. Hatt, *Methods in Social Research*, New York, 1952.
A. M. Rose, *Theory and Methods in Social Research*, 1954.
H. Eulau, S. J. Eldersveld and M. Janowitz, *Political Behaviour: a Reader in Theory and Research*, Glencoe, 1956.

For criticisms of the use of the new techniques of observation for excessively detailed studies:
P. Sorokin, *Fads and Foibles in Modern Sociology*, Chicago, 1956.
C. N. Parkinson, *Parkinson's Law*, 1958 (humorous, but with a serious basis).
C. Wright Mills, *The Sociological Imagination*, 1959.

Bibliographies:
A. W. Spieseke, *Social Studies: Curriculum and Methods*, Washington, 1955.
unesco bibliographies of the social sciences.

PART ONE

THE TECHNIQUES OF OBSERVATION

Like all sciences the social sciences are experimental; they start with the facts. The basic element of their method is to look for the facts and observe them. No one questions this attitude. Those who accuse American sociologists of 'hyperfactualism' are attacking the empirical way in which research and analysis is performed and the absence of systemization and hypotheses but not the principle of observation and research. Moreover, in social science research into the facts has a greater importance than in other sciences because the subject is underdeveloped. Vast unknown territories remain unexplored, and this is why simple documentary studies, simple factual descriptions can be major contributions.

Research and observation of the facts are faced in some social sciences with a particularly difficult obstacle—that of secrecy. Religious, political and sexual phenomena still belong, at least partially, to the sociological category of the 'sacred'. In France it is not polite to interrogate people about their political allegiance or their religious beliefs and still less about their private life. The desire to hide embarrassing information strengthens this convention. The argument about 'State secrets' protects the State less than the private interests which make use of the State. But there are 'State secrets'. The shadows can only be partially illuminated.

Research and observation can follow two kinds of method: (1) The analysis of documents such as written documents, films, photographs, gramophone records, etc., which throw light on social phenomena; (2) the direct observation of social reality by inquiries, interviews, questionnaires, etc. Direct observation can itself be divided into two parts. Either samples are used to analyse large communities and this does not permit very profound analysis; or small communities (and even individuals) are observed and this gains in depth what is lost in scope. The first will be called extensive observation, the second intensive observation. It is sometimes difficult to distinguish between them, especially in borderline cases. Some techniques are common to both although they differ somewhat in their application. For example, interviews by questionnaire used in extensive inquiries are a particular variety of the general technique of the interview, which is widely used in intensive observation. However, the two categories are sufficiently distinct to be studied separately.

CHAPTER ONE

DOCUMENTARY OBSERVATION

Social phenomena leave traces in a great number and variety of documents: archives, censuses, the press, personal documents, instruments and tools, pictures, photographs, films, records, tape recordings, etc. A general outline of these various kinds of documents will be given and then the problems of the techniques of documentary analysis will be examined. Amongst the latter a very detailed study of 'content analysis' is required because of its complexity.

Section I. Categories of documents

The simplest classification is the distinction between written documents (books, journals, archives, etc.), statistical documents (censuses) and others (such as films, photographs, records, tools and instruments, etc.). Another classification, which cuts across the the preceding one, distinguishes between original documents and reproductions. Private archives are documents; photocopies of these archives are reproductions. This distinction is sometimes blurred: the recording of a conversation is a reproduction but it is the only means of conserving in a document something which otherwise would have left no trace. It is perhaps necessary to distinguish between 'spontaneous' and 'artificial' documents.

1. WRITTEN DOCUMENTS

These are numerous and very varied. An exhaustive list of them cannot be given here. The student in the social sciences must work in an imaginative way; unexpected and unusual documents can sometimes provide useful information. As an attempt at classification four categories of written documents will be distinguished: 1. Public archives and official documents; 2. the press; 3. private archives; 4. indirect documentation.

A. Public archives and official documents

There are several categories of official documents: public archives containing the original documents of public administration (reports, instructions, notes, etc.) which can only be consulted by the public under special conditions; censuses and statistics (see p. 84); and the various official publications which are more or less freely available to the public.

(*a*) PUBLIC ARCHIVES

If all official documents were kept in the archives and if the archives were open to the public, the social sciences, and political science in particular, would be greatly advanced. Public documents do not reveal everything but they reveal a great deal. Unfortunately many documents are not kept and those in the archives are often inaccessible.

1. *Central archives.* There is a special administration in France with responsibilities for conserving the archives—the *Archives nationales*. In principle all official documents must be deposited in the *Archives nationales* after a certain time.

Two sorts of difficulties are met with in using the National Archives. In the first place there are important gaps. In spite of the law the ministries do not deposit all their papers: the Ministry of the Interior, in particular, the documents of which have a special importance for political scientists, has retained or destroyed many categories of documents. In 1940, during the German advance on Paris, many documents were destroyed. In the second place, recent holdings cannot be consulted by the public. France has a fifty-year rule; documents of a date later than 1910 cannot be consulted. Most countries have similar rules. As the social scientist often works on contemporary subjects this rule is a great hindrance.

2. *Local archives.* The départemental archives have a centralized organization. The archivists are appointed by the Minister of National Education. In principle the same rules apply for the communication of documents in the départemental archives as in the National Archives.

Municipal archives are the responsibility of the mayor and their conservation is an obligatory charge on the commune. Access to them is easy, particularly in the small communes, but their content is often disappointing. According to the law, consultation of the records of sessions of the municipal council is unrestricted.

(b) PARLIAMENTARY AND ADMINISTRATIVE PUBLICATIONS

The main one is the *Journal officiel* but there are also bulletins of ministries and public services, collections of local administrative orders and so on.

1. *Journaux officiels* and their appendices are documents of great importance in the study of parliament and political parties. They are too often neglected. The reports of the parliamentary debates can be subject to content analysis (see p. 105) to throw light on the political positions of the parties; detailed studies can be made of the divisions. The appendices, called parliamentary documents, contain all the bills proposed and these can be used to analyse the preoccupations of the most powerful sections of public opinion.

2. *Administrative publications* are very varied. Studies of top administrators can be made in the administrative annuals. The collections of administrative orders and the bulletins of the ministries can be used for the study of the public services. The collections of departmental administrative orders and the records of the debates of the General Councils provide documentation on local political life. The *Bibliographie selective des publications officielles françaises* published by *Documentation française* provides a survey of all official publications.

B. The Press

Three different documentary uses of the press can be distinguished: general documentation, documentation on particular social groups or categories and as a source of documentation on the press itself.

(a) GENERAL DOCUMENTATION

Newspapers are the main documentary basis for historical periods for which the archives are not open and even for those periods for which there is access, newspapers are the best source for establishing the general course of events.

1. *Factual documentation.* There are two problems here. Does the press record the facts accurately? Does it report all the facts? It cannot be denied that newspapers distort events but usually by the context and the presentation rather than in the material content of the reporting. The truth can usually be established by comparing newspapers of different views. The study of the different ways in

which newspapers present the same news is in itself interesting. It should be remembered that in the last resort it is not the facts—what really happened—which influences public opinion and consequently the government, but the facts as the public sees them.

Can important events escape the notice of the press? For example, secret agreements between states. Modern means of communication make this unlikely. Events can certainly be obscured for a certain length of time but in one way and another they always become known. A French specialist in international relations (Francois Le Roy) has formulated the theory that at the present time all events leave 'perceptible traces'. This seems to be the case.

2. *Documentation on public opinion.* The press provides basic documentation on public opinion. The press tends to form public opinion as much as reflect it (although people are not always in agreement with what they read in their newspaper). This is even true of commercial newspapers whose first aim is to please; it is true to a very much greater extent of political newspapers.

However, it can be admitted as a general rule that people regularly buy the political newspaper which fits in best with their way of thinking. The geographical and social distribution of political newspapers provides evidence on the various 'spiritual families'. The distribution of the so-called informative press corresponds approximately to the preoccupations of its readers. A more detailed examination of each newspaper, its management, its financial backers and so on, is revealing about the way in which a paper is intended to influence public opinion.

(*b*) DOCUMENTATION ON SOCIAL GROUPS AND CATEGORIES
The specialist press, particularly the professional press, is very important in this respect.

1. *Pressure groups.* As a result of the lack of documentation, the study of pressure groups (fundamental phenomena in Western democracies) remains very neglected. The specialist press can provide a useful starting point. Most professional journals provide a great deal of information on about, for example, the objectives, the results of lobbying parliamentarians and the approaches to the administration of the groups which publish them. In France a profound and systematic study of the professional press would revive the study of politics.

The journals of other pressure groups besides the interest groups such as ex-servicemen's groups, ideological groups, university associations, Churches and so on can also be analysed.

2. *Other kinds of documentation.* The analysis of the journals of political parties is an important means of acquiring information about them. It is often necessary to distinguish between internal news-sheets and newspapers designed for the public at large, and between the official organ of the party controlled by the party leaders and the newspapers which are less directly associated with the party. Sometimes various tendencies within the same party publish separate journals and the comparison of these is interesting.

Certain social categories can be analysed through the newspapers which are aimed at them. For example *L'Aurore* is considered as the newspaper of the petite bourgeoisie, *Le Figaro* the newspaper of the upper middle class: the dominant preoccupations of the groups which read them can be found in their pages. This kind of study is less rigorous than the one about political attitudes because the coincidence between newspapers and social class is less precise. The extent of this coincidence should be examined by means of polls because actual readership does not always correspond to supposed readership. Such polls—or the analysis of records of subscribers—would be very interesting but the management of newspapers would not willingly co-operate.

(*c*) THE PRESS AS A SOURCE OF DOCUMENTATION ABOUT ITSELF

The press is a very important social phenomenon. In democratic States the press can be called the 'fourth estate'. Studying the press of a country is in itself a major contribution to political science and to the other social sciences. There are many ways of doing it. The following list is not exhaustive.

1. *The content of the press.* The content of newspapers, the facts reported, the manner of presentation, the nature and slant of comment, the leading articles and so on can be examined. A catalogue of the sustenance of public opinion can be made. The press is not alone in this—other important sources are radio, cinema and personal contacts.

2. *The distribution of the press.* Establishing the sphere of influence of each newspaper by geographical area, professional and social categories, political tendency and so on is very important. Comparison with the distribution of votes and other political and social phenomena provides useful evidence. Unfortunately the study of the

distribution of the press meets with considerable difficulties.

3. *The control of the press.* Who are the 'press lords'? This question is easily answered in some countries where companies controlling the press are compelled to publish information on the shareholders and the distribution of the shares among them, the composition of the boards of directors and so on. Even here it is possible to use pseudonyms and it is sometimes difficult in those countries where there are no rules or where, as in France, the law is not enforced.

Moreover, it is not sufficient to know who holds the capital to know who controls the newspaper. The working capital often bears no relation to the capital investment and in order to discover the controllers of the newspaper it is necessary to find out where this money comes from. It has been proposed in some countries (of which France is one) to distinguish between the commercial press which seeks only to make profits and does not attempt to influence opinion, and the 'press of commerce'—political journals selling at a loss which is met by financial groups wishing to have means of influence on public opinion and of pressure on the government. In practice there is not always a clear distinction. It must not be forgotten that a large part of the revenue of newspapers comes from advertising and this implies some subordination to large advertisers and advertising firms.

4. *The press as a nucleus of a pressure group.* Newspapers can be the auxiliaries of pressure groups or political parties but newspapers can also be a focus of ideology and action: a pressure group or even a party can be formed around them. The analysis of journals of this kind is important in political science.

C. Private archives
Two types are included under this title: archives of organizations such as political parties, pressure groups, trade unions, association and Churches; and archives of individuals and personal documents. Both are very important as some essential information can be found only in them. Unfortunately access to them is usually even more difficult than to public archives.

(*a*) ARCHIVES OF ORGANIZATIONS
Associations, trade unions, political parties, pressure groups (usually) and Churches keep records of their deliberations, lists of their members, copies of correspondence and so on.

Documentary Observation

1. *The gaps in the archives of organizations.* The importance of the archives of organizations varies. In most cases, in France at least, it is small. When access has been gained to them the most striking impression is usually the gaps in them.

There are numerous causes of this. The period 1940–44 was fatal for the archives of many parties and trade unions; some were dispersed to prevent capture by the enemy and then lost, others were the object of police investigations during the course of which they destroyed. But in most cases the main cause of deficiencies in the archives is lack of organization. Well established and well run archives presuppose a high level of organization and before 1945 this was rare in France.

It is sometimes possible to supplement central archives by research in local archives but these are still more rare and less well kept. But it occasionally happens that local groups have been well organized and their archives have not been dispersed.

2. *The difficulty of access.* Access to the archives depends on the goodwill of the directors of the organizations, and this varies greatly. As a general rule, and especially in France, it is very difficult to obtain access. Political parties, pressure groups and private firms are usually convinced that secrecy is one of the sources of their strength. Consequently they refuse in principle to open their archives or they open them partially, for the least interesting subjects. Access is usually easier on the local level because of the more direct human contact.

This difficulty is overcome when members of an organization, for whom access to the archives is easier, undertake the study of their organization. Their impartiality can be doubted. Collaboration on objective studies between organizations and scientific institutions is not, however, out of the question.

Distrust of sociological investigations is diminishing as these become more numerous. The social sciences are fashionable. Snobbery can help to open both doors and files. The scientific study of an organization also gives it some publicity; it causes it to be taken seriously and extends its public. This consideration also helps to break down traditional distrust.

(*b*) PERSONAL ARCHIVES

Politicians usually keep their personal archives containing correspondence, notes, documents, etc. The title 'politician' includes not only deputies, and ministers, but also organizers of small groups, party militants, journalists, notables and so on. In general, personal documents can be used to analyse psychology, social relationships and behaviour.

1. *The content of personal archives.* This varies greatly. Two broad categories of documents can be distinguished.

Firstly, there are the documents, which are strictly speaking personal, the main content being unpublished correspondence, notes and memoires. Their interest varies according to the man's importance, his personal relationships, his qualities as an observer, etc.

Secondly, these archives contain documents which are not personal. Most politicians keep brochures, pamphlets, internal party news-sheets and other documents which generally can only be found in private collections. This documentation is usually of great importance.

2. *The difficulty of access.* Rather similar difficulties as those of access to the archives of organizations are encountered. A living person usually considers consultation by someone else of his private archives as a compromising divulging of the details of his career. Families often make greater difficulties after a politician's death either because they wish to preserve a certain image of the dear departed or simply through neglect. It is essential that an organization such as the *Fondation nationale des sciences politiques* should be bequeathed as many of these archives as possible. Here also the development of social studies will help to overcome the obstacles which exist at present.

Documents of the second type (non-personal ones) should not in principle be difficult to obtain. Systematic propaganda undertaken by an organization like the *Fondation nationale des sciences politiques* ought to have considerable success. It was also pointed out at the international congress of sociology held at Lille in 1953 that the archives of notaries are important (J.-P. Poisson) and they could be an interesting source.

D. Indirect documentation

Unlike the types just mentioned, many documents are not directly concerned with social matters but can give indications or provide background material about the problems studied. Brief indications only can be given here: the researcher must use his imagination to choose which lines to explore. There are two particularly important categories which can supply indirect documentation: annuals and directories, and literary works.

Documentary Observation

1. *Annuals and directories.* Much can be found in telephone directories: for example under the heading 'association' in the Washington telephone directory there is a good basic list of 'lobbies'. The départemental directories are useful in studying local élites and the professional directories in studying pressure groups. Judiciously used, the *Bottin mondain* can provide useful information on certain social milieu: membership of certain clubs is, for example, revealing.

The careers of higher civil servants, members of ministerial cabinets and so on can be traced in the directories of the ministries and the great public bodies. The influence of certain corps (Inspection des Finances, Conseil d'Etat, Cour des Comptes, Corps des Mines, etc.) can be gauged in this way. The directories of *grandes écoles* (Normale supérieure, Polytechnique, Ponts et Chaussées, etc.) should also be studied. The military directories, the ecclesiastical 'Ordo' and others are important.

2. *Who's Who? and biographical dictionaries.* For several years, following the anglo-saxon example, the who's who fashion has been spreading. Some operate in rather a closed circle: the publisher sends a biographical questionnaire to all the lawyers, doctors, teachers, industrialists, etc., who appear in the specialist directories; he then sends a subscription form for *Who's Who?* and for the pleasure of seeing their names in print the majority of those included buy it. There is, therefore, no selection by the editor—the only selection arises from the failure of some to return the questionnaire. In spite of this, *Who's Who?* of this type contain useful information which supplements the other directories.

More interesting are the true biographical dictionaries of contemporaries which are selections of well-known people with biographical entries established by the editor. For France the best is *Pharos* (2nd ed., 1954, with quarterly supplements). This has been used as a basis of a study (started in 1957) on the ecology of famous men undertaken by the *Institut national des études démographiques* (see p. 160).

(*b*) LITERARY WORKS

Literature mirrors the whole of a society. This remark is valid, to differing degrees, for all forms of artistic expression (the theatre and the cinema are analogous to literature; painting and music are somewhat different).

1. *Social literature.* Some literary works are directly inspired by

social problems. Setting aside memoirs, pamphlets and doctrinal essays, literary works (narrowly defined) such as novels, short stories and plays touch on political economic and social life. Some have an unquestioned documentary value. The importance of *Lucien Leuwen* and *L'Education sentimentale,* not to mention the works of Balzac, for the nineteenth century is an example. Works of contemporary writers are an important source of documentation for certain periods or certain events. For example the novels of Drieu La Rochelle, André Chamson and André Malraux are essential for the understanding of the 1930s; so, too, are many literary works produced between 1940 and 1945 for understanding the Resistance or the concentration camps; some of Aragon's novels provide important evidence on the communist mentality. Minor works, often of poor literary quality, which describe a political or social happening such as a strike, a revolt, the life of a militant, a rise up the social scale, a class conflict or conflict of milieu and so on, are very important. It would be useful to compile a bibliography of this literature.

2. *Pure literature.* Even literature which seems furthest removed from the political and social life of society gives evidence of a certain conception of society. The student of sociology must be profoundly aware of the truth that there is no 'social culture' without 'culture', and that extreme specialization which is perhaps valid in technology is out of place in the social sciences: social life is not a separate field of human activity, cut off from the others; the whole man is reflected and is engaged in it.

Particular importance must be accorded to works which are not strictly speaking literary, but which have a great political and social importance: reading matter for children, especially educational works and textbooks come within this category. Textbooks on civics and history provide basic materials on the political mentality of a people, on the formation of public opinion and on the more or less conscious image a country creates of itself.

2. STATISTICS

Statistics are documents containing the results of census taking. The idea of counting the number of inhabitants in a country and their distribution according to age, sex, profession, etc., is very old. The Chinese took censuses more than 4,000 years ago. The Bible cites several—the one ordered by the Emperor in the year of the birth of Christ for the whole Roman Empire is the most famous. The object of these censuses was military and fiscal—to find out how many men were capable of carrying arms and how many taxpayers there were. The original object undoubtedly explains the distrust which the public still have of censuses; for millenia people have been worried about their consequences.

In modern states censuses and statistics have acquired considerable importance. Their fiscal and military object has become secondary, their first use now being economic. The main purpose today of statistical surveys is to provide as exact knowledge as possible of the elements of production and the distribution of wealth in order to make possible the co-ordination and the direction of the national economy. Planning is only possible on the basis of exact statistics. This produces a distrust of statistics amongst those individuals and classes which are opposed to the intervention of the state in the economy.

A. Gathering statistics

There are two main methods of making statistics—direct and indirect. The first is the oldest and, although still used, tends to give way to more and more to the second.

(a) DIRECT ENUMERATION

This consists of collecting all the relevant facts, trying to miss none. In practice, this has two forms: continuous registration and static enumeration.

1. *Static enumeration.* This is the current form of census taking: all the relevant elements are counted at a particular moment. General population censuses are the best example of this. These took place every five years in France from 1831 until they were interrupted by the Second World War. Between 1936 and 1946 there was no general census. The last census, a work of great precision, was made in 1954. Other statistical studies have been made by INSEE and by the *Institut de Démographie:* examples are the decennial surveys of agriculture from 1862 to 1892, and the surveys of 1929 and the general agricultural census of 1956.

Static enumeration meets with the same difficulties as all census operations: the distrust of those being counted who consequently do not give accurate information; the inefficiency of the census takers, which distorts the results; and failure to understand the questions asked. These difficulties will be analysed later in the section on polls (see p. 125) and the general techniques of interview (see p. 178).

2. *Continuous registration* is the constant keeping up to date of a census. For example, the general population census of 1954 can be kept up to date on births, deaths and the sex and age distribution by using the registration of births and deaths. Income declarations and taxation statistics, changes in employment and unemployment, the electoral roll are other examples of continuous registration. It is a valid method only in so far as it is rigorous: in practice this is the case only for registrations of births and deaths.

(*b*) INDIRECT METHODS

Instead of counting all elements, a representative cross-section can be taken and general conclusions arrived at by extrapolation. Two main methods are used—the indicative method and sampling.

1. *The indicative method.* This proceeds on the basis of easily obtained and measured information which, although external to the object of the inquiry, can be regarded as providing accurate indications about it. The classic example is the estimation of national wealth on the basis of legacies. Since on average people live thirty years after they have inherited their patrimony, it can be assumed that every year a thirtieth of all inherited money changes hands. By multiplying the evaluation of legacies by thirty the gross national wealth can be arrived at. In 1913 legacies totalled 6.6 billion francs: the total wealth of France in private hands could be estimated at 178 billion. This estimate is, however, questionable because of deliberate undervaluing of estates to evade tax—in 1913 the direct valuation of national wealth was 297 billion francs.

Another example is a population census on the basis of the number of households, this number being easier to count than the number of individuals. If previous calculations have accurately established the average number of persons in each household, this average can then be multiplied by the number of households to give the total population.

2. *Sampling.* This is the most popular method at the moment. There are two main techniques. Either the sample is constructed artificially according to a certain image of reality: for example, one could try to construct a sample of communes in France to correspond to the geographic and demographic diversity of all the communes. Or the sample is chosen strictly at random. The differences between 'empirical' and 'probability' methods and general techniques of sampling will be examined later on in the section on opinion polls (see p. 125).

DOCUMENTARY OBSERVATION

B. The value of statistics

The famous quip of Disraeli that statistics are the art of lying with precision has become commonplace. Sections of the public, particularly the most conservative groups, have readily accepted it because of the suspicions already mentioned (fear of the tax collector, fear of the intervention of the State in the economy, etc.). In Disraeli's time when statistics were not very accurate there was an element of truth in it. Today techniques have been perfected and results are more precise. But some errors are inevitable and their nature and extent must be realized.

(a) ERRORS DUE TO STATISTICAL PROCEDURES

These can be classified in two categories: some errors are common to all statistical methods, others are found only in polls.

1. *The errors common to all statistical methods.* These arise from the inadequacies of the investigator and from the techniques themselves. The investigator can make a wrong count either through negligence or laziness.

The personal bias of the investigator can lead, without his knowledge, to a distortion of reality (see p. 165). The efficient training of investigators can undoubtedly reduce the chance of error although it cannot be removed altogether.

The errors which can arise in the process of enumeration must not be disregarded. Counting errors are now reduced to a minimum through the use of mechanical methods. But these are not the only kind of errors: the geographical area and the categories of classification of a survey can be important sources of distortion. The classic example of this is the increase in the birth rate in certain suburban communes following the opening in them of numerous lying-in clinics. It is also necessary to be very careful about counting things twice: the classic case is counting raw materials in stock and in process of being manufactured; another case is the comparison of the expenditure of the State and local authorities (some State expenditure being subsidies of local authority budgets).

2. *Errors in polls.* The error peculiar to polls is that the sample may not be representative. It is obvious that the sample and the total population do not correspond exactly. In random samples the margin of error can be calculated with great accuracy but this is not the case in empirical polls which is a disadvantage of the method. The calculation of the margins of error will be described later in the section on opinion polls (see p. 133).

(b) ERRORS ATTRIBUTABLE TO THE NATURE OF THE THINGS BEING ENUMERATED

These are of two kinds: the difficulty acquiring exact knowledge about the things; and their lack of homogeneity. The second is of particular importance in the social sciences.

1. *Difficulty of acquiring exact knowledge about the things being enumerated.* Some things are physically visible to the investigator, such as the number of rooms in an apartment, the area of a cultivated field and the types of crops grown. Others are invisible and can only be known as a result of a declaration by an individual who has knowledge of them. If these things are neutral—of no consequence to the respondent—the declaration is usually honest and errors are minimal. If, on the other hand, the things are very important to the respondent then there will be dissimulation and the chance of error is great. The obvious example is income tax declarations: except in the case of employees where declarations can be checked with the employer these declarations bear no relation to reality. Economic statistics based on declarations by producers suffer from the same weakness, because of distrust of the State: they are more accurate for industry than for agriculture where this distrust and the taste for dissimulation is deeply rooted.

2. *The non-homogenous character.* A census assumes that the things enumerated are the same as one another. If this homogeneity does not exist then the census is absurd—a worthless precision in a context where precision is out of place.

In the social sciences there is a great danger of using statistics in fields where they are inapplicable. To take a simple example, let us suppose that a census of religion shows that 70 per cent of the population of a country declare that they are Catholics this does not mean that 70 per cent are in fact Catholics or share the same religious beliefs. The term 'Catholic' can mean very different things to different respondents: the homogeneity of the declarations is only a appearance and the statistical assessment of them has limited significance. One can say that all the respondents shared a common attribute—that of having declared they were Catholics. But if this declaration does not have the same meaning for each respondent then the homogeneity is only apparent. Unfortunately many social statistics are based on facts of this kind. We will return to this fundamental problem in the discussion of the application of procedures of mathematical analysis to sociological sciences (see p. 278).

Documentary Observation

3. OTHER DOCUMENTS

All objects made or used by man—for example, clothes, tools, instruments for work or pleasure, works of art or craftsmanship, songs, valued signs and symbols, the ways of using space and methods of changing the appearance of the countryside, the form of houses and gardens and the arrangement of towns—provide basic documentation for the social sciences. Ethnologists, geographers, pre-historians use them a great deal but all branches of the social sciences have an interest in them. They can be arbitrarily classed into three categories: technical documentation (in the widest sense), iconographic, photographic and cinematic, and phonetic documentation.

A. Technical documentation

This title is used broadly to include all the subjects which man uses —edifices and buildings as well as movable objects. The distinction between technical and iconographic documentation (the latter includes drawings, engravings, pictures and sculptures) is not always clear—many utilitarian objects have decorative motifs. This is not important as the distinction is used only for convenience.

(*a*) CATEGORIES OF OBJECTS

Man uses a great diversity of objects. The examples given here are intended to illustrate the wide meaning of the term 'object'.

1. *Classification according to the use of the object.* The following can be distinguished: (1) Instruments and tools used in productive processes; (2) domestic objects such as houses, clothes, furniture, kitchen tools; (3) objects used for games, leisure and pleasure; (4) objects for defence or war such as arms and armour; (5) religious or magical objects such as priestly clothing, images and charms; (6) 'political' objects such as insignia of authority and government, the dress of public servants, flags and emblems.

2. *Classification according to the nature of the object.* The term here is used in a wider sense than is common usage and refers not only to inanimate objects but also to living things such as domesticated animals used in productive processes, for transport and for war. It is also applied to fixed property such as houses, buildings, soil and space used by man, as well as to movable property.

(*b*) THE DIFFERENT WAYS OF STUDYING OBJECTS

Three different types of analysis can broadly be distinguished— material, technological and symbolic.

1. *Material analysis* consists of examining the external aspects of the object. The simple fact that a human group possesses objects made of bronze or iron indicate a more advanced state of civilization than if it had only things made out of carved wood and stone. The techniques of manufacture and construction are also very revealing. Even if we did not know the use and symbolism of Cyclopean masonry, the very size of the stone blocks and the way in which they had been moved indicates a high level of social organization and a construction of this kind must rest on rational collective effort. Pre-historians and historians who study dead civilizations without written records have developed this technique of analysis.

2. *Technological analysis* consists of examining the practical uses of objects. Technology is a branch of social science which is concerned with the tools and instruments men use and the enormous consequences of their use. The replacing of the wooden by the iron plough, the invention of the wheel or a new system of harnessing draft animals radically altered modes of production and disrupted social systems: it is possible to demonstrate that the suppression of slavery was made possible by technical progress. Great scientific discoveries have brought about several technological revolutions since the eighteenth century, which in turn have generated social and political revolutions.

Marxism has illuminated the fundamental character of the techniques of production in the development of economic, social, political, religious and intellectual structures. Even though Marxism may have exaggerated their consequence, it remains very great and technology provides basic documentation for the social sciences.

3. *Symbolic analysis* is concerned with the meaning and value which men attach to objects. Some objects have value only through use; their practical utility alone is taken into consideration. Others have no practical utility and their significance is purely symbolic. But most have both a material utility and a symbolic significance: food has a ritual significance as well as providing nourishment. In so-called 'primitive' civilizations symbolic significance usually has primacy over utility. But even the most highly developed technical civilizations conserve traces of this 'primitive mentality'. Symbolic significance remains very important, and in such matters as clothing, housing, food and cars, prestige and ritual preoccupations often occupy an important place. From the point of view of collective images, purely utilitarian and technological analyses of objects and social behaviour may only touch on the most superficial aspects.

B. Iconographic and photographic documentation
This is visual documentation. The invention of photography has vastly increased its resources.

(*a*) ICONOGRAPHY
This covers all visual documentation other than photographs. It remains important in spite of the contribution of photography.

1. *Iconographic material* includes drawings, paintings, pictures, miniatures and sculptures whether they are separate pieces or elements in a decorative motif. They include works of specialists and the works of amateurs who decorate familiar objects or who while away leisure hours. Popular art such as drawings for children's books and the decorations and images of folklore come within this category.

2. There are various ways of interpreting this material. Crudely, one can distinguish between a realist and a symbolic interpretation. The distinction between figurative and non-figurative in contemporary art is a particular case of a general distinction: pictures can either be attempts at faithful representation of reality or creations, the value and significance of which are more or less symbolic. But the two types are often mixed and it is not always easy to discern whether an image, in appearance realist, does not have a hidden symbolic meaning. Examples of this difficulty can be found in the famous controversies about medieval cathedrals and Egyptian temples. This is of great sociological importance because realist and symbolic interpretations often tend to give very different pictures of the societies studied.

(*b*) PHOTOGRAPHY AND THE CINEMA
These can be used as methods of reproducing documents but they can also provide original documents.

1. *Reproductions.* The invention of photography can be compared with the invention of printing. Before they were invented documentation was a manual operation and documents consequently remained few and not easily accessible. Since their invention it has been possible to reproduce documents by mechanical means and this makes possible practically universal distribution.

The social sciences benefit in two ways from the wide diffusion of photographed documents. Many research workers can see a particular document and consequently there can be many interpretations of it giving rise to fruitful controversies: what escapes some is seen by others and exaggerations are rectified. Also each researcher can have at his disposition, at one time and in one place, or almost one place, a mass of documentation; his appreciation of this documentation is not distorted by failure of memory, and the use of the comparative method, fundamental in social science, is made easier. This refines the intelligence, the intuition and the scientific culture of the researcher in the same way as the reproduction of works of art develops artistic culture.

2. *Direct documentation.* Photographs and films make possible the recording of social phenomena such as ceremonies, festivals, political demonstrations and street riots. Ethnographers use still- and cine-photography a great deal and other social scientists are following their example. They are beginning to use the important documentation gathered by the unconscious auxiliaries of the modern sociologists, the cinema and news photographers. To understand national socialism, for example, archives, books, written documents and various sociological inquiries are not enough: the photographs and films of the congress of Nuremburg, the nazi parades, the speeches of Hitler and the concentration camps are indispensable. All these documents exist, but the official research institutions are not greatly interested in them. It is incredible that at the present time photographic and cinematic libraries parallel to libraries of books do not exist in universities. The creation of these is indispensable to the social sciences.

Photographs and films give a certain vision of social phenomena which would be impossible without them. They can isolate and enlarge a particular detail. They can also give a comprehensive synthetic picture of some phenomena. Aerial photography is at the moment renewing the documentary basis of geography: aerial photographs of towns are fundamental to the study of urban sociology.

The cinema both as an art and as a distraction is a basic social phenomenon of our time. Films can be the object of sociological analysis in the same way as literary, poetic and dramatic works. The cinema seems to play a fundamental role in the creation of contemporary myths. These myths, together with sport and fashion, seem to occupy a larger place in the lives of many men and women than religious beliefs, political ideologies or any other system of values. Analysing them is an essential part of the understanding of contemporary societies.

Lastly, cinema and television news are, like the press and radio, at the same time sources of information, means of propaganda and publicity and revealers of the mentality of a society. The distinctions already made about the press can be applied to them (see p. 77).

DOCUMENTARY OBSERVATION

C. Phonetic documentation

This title refers to recorded sounds. A new source of sociological documentation is being created as a result of technical advances in sound recording. An old source—linguistics—has been greatly extended in recent years. It must be remembered that, like the press, the radio is an important source of documentation.

(*a*) LINGUISTICS

Linguistics is the science of language which, as the principal means of communication between men, is a social phenomenon *par excellence*.

1. *Linguistics and the social sciences.* Linguistics are concerned with the technical aspects of syntax, stylistic techniques and so on which, although not his direct concern, cannot be ignored by the sociologist. The structure of language is an element of the structure of thought and thus lies at the base of the general concepts of society and of the spoken and written communications between its members.

It is also concerned with more directly sociological matters. Comparative linguistic study shows relationships between societies and civilizations: in this field the phonetic analysis of words ('phonics') is a valuable research technique. The study of the history of a language helps to establish what changes have occurred in that society: it is important to fix the date of the entry of a word into common usage, the changes in its meaning, the distortions of meaning and so on. Equally important is the comparison of written and spoken language, the different vocabularies of different social classes and social groups and the various dialects and 'argots'. Political science would gain much by undertaking studies of the political vocabulary of parties and tendencies.

2. *Modern methods of linguistic analysis.* Linguistics employ analytical procedures which are not intrinsically different to those of the social sciences but some have been more highly developed in linguistics. An example is the comparative method: the nature of language allows a precision in the use of this method which is seldom achieved elsewhere. Another example is mathematical analysis. Recent progress in quantitative semantics makes possible the statistical analysis of vocabulary and even stylistic techniques.

According to Claude Lévi-Strauss, the contemporary developments in phonology will be greatly extended in the future: 'Phonology will play, in the social sciences, the same role of renovation as nuclear physics has played in the exact sciences.' His argument is that phonology progresses from the study of conscious linguistic phenomena to their unconscious infrastructure and that its basis is not in separate phenomena but in interlocked structured systems.

The first aspect eliminates almost entirely the more or less conscious subjectivity in sociological analysis. Scientific laws between elements treated really as 'things', as objective as laws relating physical things, could be established. The second aspect links up with the 'structuralist' theories of Lévi-Strauss and also gives them an objective basis. Even allowing for a certain exaggeration in this position, it must be admitted that the results of linguistics are very important for the social sciences.

(*b*) THE RECORDING OF SOUNDS
There are today very simple and convenient methods of recording sounds such as tape recorders.

1. *Recordings* are widely used in the social sciences. Recordings of songs, musical themes and dance music, sometimes accompanied by films, are used by ethnologists and specialists in folklore. In free-ranging interviews a recording of the whole interview rather than the taking of notes by the interviewer is becoming more and more the practice; it makes it easier to analyse replies to questions in all their complexity and in all their shades of meaning. The analysis of music and military, patriotic and popular songs could be very useful in political science. Unrehearsed interviews of politicians and those who play a role in political events are primary historical sources: for example, the press conference given on May 14, 1958, by General Massu is essential to the understanding of the coup of May 13th; the recordings made by reporters on the barricades in Algiers in January 1961 capture the atmosphere of the attempted coup.

2. *The problem of secret recordings.* In the examples cited recordings are made with the knowledge and the consent of those being recorded. But it is possible by using miniature microphones to record people without them being aware of it. The advantages of doing this is considerable because the mannerisms and effects for the observer or the public are absent. Recordings of conversations on current political issues can be an important contribution to the understanding of the real thoughts of citizens. The same thing can be said about conversations on religion, morals and the family.

This procedure, however, raises several objections. There are no great dangers provided that the recordings are made in public places (cafés, restaurants, shops, buses, trains, etc.) and are used by impartial scholars concerned only to further knowledge, and anonymity is strictly preserved. But it is easy to see the use to which it could be put in police states—and all states have a tendency to be police states. From a moral point of view secret recordings are questionable and even, in some respects, inconvenient from a purely scientific point of view. Friendly conversation often has the character of a 'game' or diversion (especially among certain peoples) and has not always the purpose of clarifying the thought of the participants. Distortion is sometimes greater than that springing from a desire to impress an interviewer or the public at large. A text must be considered in its context.

On the general problem of unpublished documentation: R. STAVELEY, *Guide to Unpublished Research Materials*, 1957.

On the official French Archives: J. FAVIER, *Les Archives*, 1959; F. GOGUEL and G. DUPEUX, *Sociologie électorale*, 1951, pp. 38 ff.

On official publications: E. BROWN, *Manual of Government Publications: United States and Foreign*, New York, 1950.

On private archives and documents: L. GOTTSCHALK, C. KLUCKHOHN and R. ANGEL, *The Use of Personal Documents in History, Anthropology and Sociology*, New York, 1945; G. ALLPORT, *The Use of Personal Documents in Psychological Research*, New York, 1942; M. JANOWITZ, 'The Systematic Analysis of Political Biography', *World Politics*, 1954, p. 405; W. I. THOMAS and F. ZNANIECKI, *The Polish Peasant in Europe and America*, 2nd ed., 2 vols., 1927; H. BULMER, *Critiques on Research of the Social Sciences: I. An Appraisal of 'The Polish Peasant'*, New York, 1939; C. R. SHAW, 'Case Study Method', *American Sociological Society: Papers and Proceedings*, Vol. XXI, 1927.

On the press: J. KAYSER, 'La Presse de province sous la IIIe République', *Revue Française de Science Politique*, 1955, pp. 547-71; M. DUVERGER, F. GOGUEL and J. TOUCHARD, *Les Elections du 2 janvier 1956*, 1957, pp. 69-130; the periodical, *Études de Presse*, 1948; and the *Centre de documentation* at the Institut des Sciences Politiques, Paris.

On literature: I. HOWE, *Politics and the Novel*, New York, 1957; R. ESCARPIT, *Sociologie de la littérature*, 1958.

On statistics: A. PIATER, *Statistique et observation économique*, 1960; H. GUITTON, *Statistique et méthodes d'observation économique*, 1959.

On technology and the study of instruments and tools: A. LEROI-GOURHAN, *Milieu et techniques*, 1955; L. MUMFORD, *Technics and Civilization*, 1934; M. GRIAULE, *Méthode de l'ethnographie*, 1957; P. SAINTYVES, *Manual de folklore*, 1936.

On linguistics: N. TROUBETZKOY, *Principes de phonologie*, 1949; R. JACOBSON and M. HALLE, *Fundamentals of Language*, The Hague, 1956; M. COHEN, *Pour une sociologie du langage*, 1956; C. LÉVI-STRAUSS, *Anthropologie structurale*, 1958.

Section II. Methods of analysing documents

Reading a document cannot extract all its meaning. In many cases, to establish the value, the degree of veracity, the exact meaning and significance of a document, a reading according to precise rules must be made. In other cases the quantity of documents is so large that special analytical procedures are necessary.

In general there are two kinds of technique for analysing documents: firstly, the classical methods derived from literary or historical analysis; secondly, the newer methods with quantitative bases. Content analysis, developed in the United States over the last twenty years, is one of these new methods. This distinction can be compared in some respects with the distinction which will be made later between intensive direct observation and extensive direct observation. Classical methods are intensive; they are analyses in depth. Quantitative methods are extensive, attempting to extract the essential features from a mass of documents.

1. CLASSICAL METHODS

We often unconsciously use classical methods of analysing documents. Anyone who reads a newspaper, a political work, an electoral poster, or election results, seeking information objectively and not confirmation of prejudices, is using them. It is worth describing the main characteristics of this method and some of its variants.

A. The main characteristics of classical methods

These methods are mainly derived from literary and historical criticism. They are applied to both internal and external analysis of documents, but more frequently to the former than the latter. The latter, which helps to establish the significance of documents is unfortunately sometimes neglected.

(*a*) INTERNAL ANALYSIS

Restricting ourselves to the main characteristics which illustrate the differences with quantitative methods, we can say that it is a subjective analysis with a rational basis.

1. *The rational basis.* Analysis by classical methods is an intellectual operation. The basic themes of a document are discerned; the links between them and secondary aspects and between the ideas contained in the document are sought.

The rational content of the analysis, of course, varies. There are two types of literary criticism: impressionistic criticism aimed more at an impression of the whole work, and a rational criticism based on a more logical approach. The distinction can be transposed to the analysis sociological of documents although this always leans more towards the second type: but rational analysis can exclude neither artifice nor intuition. Impressionistic criticism also implies a kind of unconscious rational (in the sense we are using the word) analysis. The main difference lies between these two methods and quantitative methods, in that the latter breakdown the text in order to examine words separated from phrases, and phrases separated from the links between them.

An illustration of the rational character is that if the length of the document makes it necessary to divide up the work of analysing it, this would be done as far as possible according to the natural divisions within the document. In this sense it can be said that classical analysis is organic. Quantitative methods, especially content analysis, follow different procedures and usually result in the quasi-mechanical dividing up of the document. A simile might illuminate the difference: classical analysis is like cutting up a chicken, quantitative methods are like slicing a sausage.

2. *The subjective character.* The content of a text is interpreted by the person who examines it. This person must interpret it with maximum impartiality, trying to avoid all distortions arising out of his personal preferences. Considerable 'objectivity' (in the current meaning of the word) can be attained. To the extent that it is purely a matter of collecting information about material facts (dates, statistics, etc.) the analysis can be equally as objective in the scientific meaning of the word—the results do not vary from one researcher to another. But as soon as interpretation is necessary then subjectivity appears; the personal bias of the interpreter becomes an important element. When the interpreter is exceptionally competent this sometimes has advantages but these usually do not compensate for the disadvantages. The most inconvenient aspect is not distortion but the difficulty of using collectively the results of several analyses of documents by classical methods.

From this point of view alone quantitative methods represent an important advance. Although they make the attempt they do not succeed in being 100 per cent objective. But they succeed to a far greater extent than the classical methods. This is why they lend themselves much better to collective works and team research. They are extensive methods; the analysis is less profound but it is much wider in scope.

(b) EXTERNAL ANALYSIS

Great importance is attached in the classical methods to placing a document in its context in order to judge its authenticity. They also attempt to discern its influence. Classical methods thus differ from quantitative methods which examine documents in isolation.

1. *The context of a document.* The word context is here used in a broad sense. It refers not only to the collection of documents of which the document studied forms a part but also the circumstances in which the document came into existence. 'The man, the milieu, the time'—these old principles of literary criticism can be generally applied to classical methods.

They are indeed more important in their general application than in literary criticism. A poem or a novel are, after all, works in themselves and their literary value is independent of the human, social and historical context. By contrast in the social sciences the context is as important as the document itself. It illuminates its significance and allows its authenticity and exact meaning to be established. The role of 'background' information is essential in social science. One can dip into Stendhal, but one cannot study the electoral programmes of 1830 if one is completely ignorant of nineteenth-century history. Once again the role of general culture in the social sciences must be insisted on.

2. *The influence of a document.* Under this heading a distinction must be made between documents which contain only material facts and other kinds of document. It is not essential to know the influence of a statistical document on public opinion in order to be able to analyse it correctly; this influence can be studied separately. But for documents in the second category the analysis of their influence and consequences cannot be separated from an internal analysis.

In any event, it is less the real influence than the supposed influence that matters; less the end achieved than the end aimed at. To appreciate the general significance and the authenticity of document it is essential to know the effect sought by its creator. Letters cannot be analysed without knowing to whom they were addressed, speeches without knowing their public, newspapers by disregarding their readership, etc.

B. The various kinds of classical methods

No method of analysis of documents is strictly confined to the social sciences. Social scientists generally use procedures analogous, although adapted and refined, to historical analysis. One can speak of a sociological method of analysis (see p. 100), but this has a general character and is used outside sociology. For some documents specialist methods, such as juridicial and psychological, are used.

(*a*) THE GENERAL METHOD

This is, as has just been said, essentially derived from historical analysis. Two types of documents should be distinguished: those which give information about facts and those which are, in some way, facts themselves. Examples of the first type are the memoirs of a politician describing the events in which he has been involved and the releases of a press agency. Examples of the second type are an electoral poster, a speech in parliament and the programme of a party: the document itself is the social phenomenon. This distinction (which is important from a methodological point of view) has already been mentioned in discussing studies of the press.

1. *The procedures of historical analysis* are used mainly for documents in the first category. The problems presented are in effect the same as those which historians face in analysing their texts.

The first problem is one of authenticity. To what extent is a document what it is believed to be? Is it a forgery or an apochryphal document? This is a difficult problem in ancient history but less so in recent and contemporary history (which is one of the branches of political science). The authenticity of the great majority of documents is not disputed: if there is a doubt it can be quite as difficult to establish the authenticity of a modern document as an ancient one. Closed archives present special problems which the historian does not face; questions which could be settled by access to the archives remain unanswered because of the fifty-year rule.

The second problem is the veracity of a document: to what extent does a document accurately report the facts? This depends on two factors: the opportunity which the author of a text had of really knowing the facts and the honesty with which he reported them. All the precautions taken by historians should be used by sociologists. It should also be remembered that political passions are often very strong and distort the vision of honest people. Secondary sources are suspect when the documents on which they are based are not known. First-hand testimony must also sometimes be treated with caution. Deliberate lying by the witness is a less likely distorting factor than deficient powers of observation. Comparison of the testimony of different witnesses is necessary, unless there is a witness who can be regarded as particularly reliable.

2. *The procedures of sociological analysis* supplement or take the place of the historians procedures for documents in the second category. In theory, the problem of authenticity is always present, for example, in an electoral poster or a party programme, but in practice it is usually easy to resolve. The 'truth' of an electoral programme is never questioned because it does not state facts but attempts to exert influence in certain directions. In this context the second aspect of historical analysis has no significance. But it is essential to put documents of this kind in the context of the whole process of 'social communication': their origins, significance, the effect which they try to make, the effect which they actually have, and so on, should be examined.

Sociological methods of analysis of this kind of document have been perfected (mainly in the United States). Paul Lazarsfeld, one of the pioneers of the science of information, has summarized the problems involved as: 'Who says what, to whom, with what effect?' This is a good definition as long as the result desired and the result obtained are distinguished.

(*b*) SPECIAL METHODS

Some kinds of documents call for special methods such as juridicial, psychological and mathematical analysis.

1. *Juridical analysis* is applied to international treaties, constitutions, laws, decrees, regulations and other legal texts. It can also be used with certain precautions on pseudo-juridical texts—the statutes of parties, the rules of unions and associations, etc. Only the broad outlines of juridical analysis will be described here.

Firstly, this analysis demands a knowledge of legal vocabulary. Words used in law have a very exact sense and ridiculous mistakes can be made if their meanings are not known. Secondly, juridical analysis rests on a classification of general concepts often called 'juridical categories' (for example, the moral person, the legislative power). Each juridical category has a precise definition and well-defined rules. It is very important to decide the juridical category to which notions belong.

The categories themselves are grouped into what are called 'juridical constructions'. The method used is typical of legal reasoning. Starting from concrete rules applicable in each category, general principles describing the characteristics of a group of categories are formulated. These principles are then used to draw up the rules for other categories (which are not yet defined) by analogy. It was in this way that the theory of the moral personality of societies and associations arose. This kind of reasoning must be linked with the older kinds of reasoning by prescription, by fictions and so on. More can be found out about these things in legal textbooks.

Knowledge of legal techniques, especially of constitutional law and administrative law (but also social law, the law of associations and societies, penal law, etc.) is necessary in the social sciences, particularly in political science. A political scientist does not, as has often been believed, despise the techniques of juridical analysis. They should be used in political science along with other techniques appropriate to the subject being analysed.

2. *Psychological analysis.* Social psychologists make considerable use of psychological analysis of personal documents. G. W. Allport has described the basic procedures used. He regards autobiographies, letters, private diaries, literary and artistic works as personal documents: the same kind of techniques are used to analyse these documents as psychiartists use to diagnose illness. The analysis is centred on the author of the documents and the different aspects of his personality are examined in his work.

It is also possible to use these documents to study the opinions and attitudes of the authors concerning political or social events. This can be done on an extensive scale (for ordinary people) to illustrate certain aspects of public opinion and on a limited and intensive scale to discover the attitudes of political personalities, social élites and the holders of power. The first was used in the United States during the war: analysis of intercepted letters written by German civilians revealed the reactions of the German people to strategic bombings (studies of Dr Herbert Hyman, 1944). In 1930 Stouffer used 238 biographies to discover attitudes to prohibition; a comparison of the evaluations made in this study with the results of a direct analysis of the subjects examined, produced a positive correlation of .96 which confirms the validity of the method.

3. *The analysis of statistical documents.* Quantitative methods of analysing documents will be described later: only the analysis of a special category of documents, statistical documents, will be discussed here.

Mathematical procedures, similar to those used in the study of all other statistics, are followed. Social science statistics do not have peculiar characteristics except sometimes a greater decree of imprecision. In this case, giving the illusion of precision in the results should be avoided. For example, the plotting of points on a graph is most often preferable to the calculation of a correlation coefficient (see

p. 289). There are two categories of statistics in the social sciences. The first are based on opinion polls, the scrutiny of documents and so on, and attempt to give statistical expression to tendencies, attitudes, etc.: they are rather imprecise because of the nature of the facts on which they are based. The second are based on things which can be exactly measured and are as precise as statistics used in the other sciences: examples are, election statistics, the political composition of parliaments, etc.

A brief survey of statistical analysis will be given in the last chapter of the book on the application of mathematical methods to the social sciences. There has been a very lively controversy about this, which is now tending to die down. Mathematical techniques provide the social sciences, like all other sciences, with analytical tools of great precision. But using them in fields where the basic data is imprecise should be avoided (see p. 278).

2. QUANTITATIVE METHODS

In the last quarter of a century methods of quantitative analysis, the purpose of which is to complement and not to replace classical methods, have been developed. They have a great advantage—objectivity. By using these methods an attempt is made to eliminate the subjective element in the interpretation of texts and arrive at an interpretation which is independent of the personality of the interpreter. Documents can thus be examined by a team and calculating machines can be used.

These methods generally have the drawback of breaking up the text and neglecting the internal structure, the arrangement of ideas, the links between them, etc. They tend to substitute for the rational and 'organic' classical methods, a much more superficial mechanical analysis. But one must be cautious about generalizing. Methods of quantitative analysis of texts are still in their infancy: the few attempted studies of texts using IBM machines have already produced important results, attaining a degree of precision unknown in classical methods.

There are two categories of quantitative methods. One is mainly associated with the study of vocabulary, of style and of modes of expression: this can be called 'quantitative semantics'. The other is concerned with the meaning words and this will be called 'content analysis'. The terms are not fixed and usage varies. The two categories merge at many points.

DOCUMENTARY OBSERVATION

A. Quantitative semantics

This method involves the counting of words in a text, classifying them according to the various parts of speech (verbs, nouns, adjectives, etc.), calculating by mathematical means associations of words, analysing the characteristics of the style of an author, revealing interpolations, completing gaps in the text, etc.

The aspects of quantitative semantics, which do not directly concern the social sciences, will not be described here. An outline of the principal directions of research will be given in order to suggest possible transpositions into the social sciences.

(*a*) COMPARISON WITH THE CONVENTIONAL VOCABULARY

Language is a means of communication. Speech presupposes the use of words comprehensible to those who hear them, and therefore commonly used words. Each author uses some of these common words in preference to others: the frequency with which the author uses words is not the same as the frequency of their current usage in the community at large. This difference constitutes the originality of the style of the author and it can be studied by statistical methods.

1. *General principles of analysis.* In principle the method of comparing the frequency with which an author uses words with the general frequency of their use is very simple.

The first step is a methodical census of words in common use showing frequency of use. There are certain basic works of this kind. For example, the Ministry of Education published in 1954 the results of an inquiry which attempted to establish 'basic' spoken French. Before this, there were two working documents for written French: the word list drawn up by V. A. C. Henmon of the University of Wisconsin in 1924 and the one by G. E. Van der Beke in 1929. The first is based on the scrutiny of 400,000 words, the second on 1,200,000. The Van der Beke compilation is based on the systematic analysis of texts drawn from Balzac, Musset, Bergson, Proust, Paul Morand, etc.—a total of 33 novels, 13 plays, 16 histories and critical works, 13 scientific and philosophical works and 14 newspapers and periodicals. Lists of frequency of words and parts of speech can be established by a compilation of this kind.

The style of an author can be defined: the frequency of the words and parts of speech used in a sample of his work should be compared with the frequencies in common usage.

2. *Value of the method.* Some argue that this method involves effort out of all proportion to the results obtained. At the moment this is

true, but the number of times the method has been applied is too limited to draw valid conclusions.

A more serious argument is that the notion of 'current vocabulary' used as the basis for comparison is much too vague. Placing on the same level, Balzac and Paul Morand, Michelet and Bergson, who were a hundred years apart, is an illustration. So too is the mixing of the vocabulary of newspapers, poetry, science, philosophy, etc. There is not one but several vocabularies at any given time: the spoken vocabulary and the written, the vocabulary of novels and of newspapers, etc. A work should be compared with a particular type of vocabulary (and eventually with other types). A vocabulary changes quickly: statistical lists of vocabularies should be made for each period and works should be compared only with the lists of the relevant periods.

Interesting studies can be made of social and political vocabulary. An examination of *Barodet* for a general election can provide elements of a political vocabulary of a period; the political vocabulary of a party can be obtained by examining the election manifestos. Comparison between the two can be interesting. The same work done on different periods would be useful in the study of the evolution of political vocabulary. Analogous studies are possible using the *Journal officiel* (parliamentary debates) by legislature and so on. The recording of conversations can facilitate analysis of the vocabularies of social classes, regions, etc. Numerous research projects could be undertaken using these methods.

(*b*) INTERNAL ANALYSIS OF THE TEXT

In this method nothing external to the text is taken into consideration. The use of computers has opened up interesting possibilities.

1. *General principles of analysis.* The analysis can be identical with that outlined in comparing words used in a text to current vocabulary. For example, a kind of general index of words used by the author with the frequency with which they are used can be made to illuminate the thought of the author. One can go further and examine the context in which each word is used, in other words the concordance between several words: the frequency of each concordance can be established. The length of words and phrases, their rhythm and so on can be measured. It is possible to characterize very accurately the style of a work.

This method has the advantage of using mathematical procedures and computers make it possible to use them on a large scale. Without these machines the task would not be possible. Father Busa, an

Italian Jesuit, who has studied Saint Thomas Aquinas, remarked that: 'I was able to finish the edition of *Summa contra gentillos* in 1951, two years after I started with a simple punch card file. Today with the IBM 705 this would take me a few months. Without either it would have taken me the rest of my life.'

2. *Value of the procedure.* Quantitative methods in depth utilizing electronic equipment to analyse texts can give very significant results. An author's thought can be examined with a previously unattainable precision. The procedure is of particular value in a branch of the social sciences—the history of ideologies.

The subjective reactions of the interpreter can be suppressed. Also the 'memory' of electronic brains can remember all the details of a work in a way that a human brain cannot; the electronic brain keep the details in the correct proportion in relation to the work as a whole. Father Busa can again be quoted: 'To penetrate the thought of an author, the terms he uses and the way in which he uses them should be very closely examined. Interpretation is translation and therefore something of a betrayal. It should be preceded by a scrupulous philological inquiry, above all into the vocabulary generally used, so that the falsification might be the least possible. The electronic brain has made it possible to do this with unexpected (until a few years ago unsuspected) efficiency.'

The method has been used to establish the missing passages in the famous Dead Sea Scrolls. An electronic brain 'suggested' the missing passages on the basis of the rules of periodicity and of associations of words in the whole manuscript. This procedure was checked on temporarily blacked out passages: the machine re-established up to five consecutive words without a mistake. The same procedures used on the synoptic gospels have established the precedence of Saint Mark's gospel.

B. Content analysis

Content analysis is a special simplified form of quantitative semantics. The results obtained are more superficial than those mentioned above but the method is much quicker and easier to use.

Content analysis is concerned less with the style of the text than the ideas contained in it. The distinction is rather artificial because words express the ideas; as we have just seen the use of electronic brains in quantitative semantics makes analysis of ideas more rigorous by introducing greater precision into philological study. But content analysis is characterized by the fact that the entities analysed are not usually words but meanings (synonyms or words with similar meanings are grouped in the same category) and often include themes or whole phrases.

(*a*) DIFFERENT FORMS OF CONTENT ANALYSIS

The diversity of the technical procedures of content analysis will be examined later. A few elementary distinctions will be made here to illustrate the nature of the method.

1. *The distinction according to the material analysed.* Content analysis is applied mainly to written texts and it can be applied to all categories of documents: books, newspapers, periodicals, parliamentary speeches, sermons, posters, slogans, propaganda pamphlets, etc.

The method is not limited to written texts. Many analyses have been made on broadcasts, speeches, interviews, films, newsreels, cartoons, television programmes, comic strips, children's papers, illustrated magazines, etc. An attempt has been made to extend the method to the analysis of music, various forms of art, gesticulations and mimes, etc.: but there are difficulties in these fields.

Generally speaking, content analysis is a method of studying 'communications'. It was developed in the United States as a branch of social psychology known as 'communications research'. The science of communications, an important branch of the social sciences, covers all communications whether public or private and includes propaganda and advertising.

The method cannot be applied to all documents. The distinction already made between documents which report facts and those which are facts is relevant here: historical criticism is more appropriate to the former, sociological analysis to the latter. Content analysis is usually applicable to the latter and not to the former. Some criticisms made of the method misunderstand this essential fact.

2. *The distinction according to the depth of the analysis.* It is interesting to distinguish real content analysis from a simplified and superficial form which can be called a 'quantitative index'. Content analysis is only a deepening and systematization of this procedure.

If one wished to give a brief description of the evolution of the *Revue du droit public et de la science politique* from its origin in 1894 until the present day an index could be drawn up for ten-year periods, grouping into categories every article published. The categories could be articles, reviews, chronicles, legal notes, etc., and sub-categories could, for example, divide the articles into political science, constitutional law, administrative law, international law, economics, etc. The number of the size (or both) of the articles could be recorded.

One would thus obtain a series of quantitative lists of the content of the review which would provide useful information about its tendencies over the years. Analyses of this kind have been made of book publishing, radio programmes and so on. D. Waldo used a similar procedure in his trend report on political science in the United States to show the changes in the focus of interest in the books and articles in political science. These are not genuine content analyses: content analyses are more searching and precise.

(*b*) BASIC CHARACTERISTICS OF CONTENT ANALYSIS

It can be said that content analysis is half-way between quantitative semantics and the quantitative indexes. Not all the words, associations of words, concordances, are counted, as in quantitative semantics, but it is not as superficial and limited as quantitative indexes.

1. *Comprehensive analysis and analysis of samples.* It is important to know whether all the available documents or a sample of them are being analysed. In practice this depends on the quantity of the documents. If an enormous mass of documents is being used to establish general tendencies over a period of years (e.g. the evolution of a journal, the radio, etc.), sampling is necessary to save time. The different methods of sampling will be examined later during the discussion of opinion polls (see p. 125). The techniques used in content analysis differ somewhat in detail from those used in opinion polls. But the general principle that only 'probability' methods are really valid holds good.

However, in content analysis, random samples are often rejected in favour of samples constructed more or less according to the quota system in opinion polls. This procedure is easier and eliminates certain distorting factors. For example, in studies of the press samples chosen by a principle of rotation are often used: in an analysis of the American local weekly press, the first week of February, the second in May, the third in August and the fourth in November were taken. In an analysis of magazine stories the first, third and fifth story of each issue was taken. In another study of the press, successive days of successive weeks were taken. In practice the sample depends on the nature of the material and the purpose of the analysis. Tests must be carried out before the final choice of sampling method is made.

2. *The preliminary choice of categories.* The basic idea of content analysis is to place the parts of a text (words, phrases, paragraphs, etc., depending on the units chosen) in a number of predetermined categories. Content analysis is from one point of view, the ranging of

all these parts in a series of pigeon holes, and describing the text by the number of elements in each pigeon hole.

The analogy with the quantitative index method is obvious. In that method elements are also placed in previously defined categories but they are elementary categories and do not raise problems of definition. Establishing categories in content analysis raises difficult questions. It can be argued that the analysis is worth only as much as the definition of the categories. An *a priori* systematization, a group of co-ordinated hypotheses, is the basis on which definitions are made.

In quantitative semantics there is no prior definition of categories. Counting the words and associations of words is done directly without an intervening 'screen' of categories of classification. Results in quantitative semantics are purer, more diversified and also less prone to error: the categories of content analysis risk being artificial. But the processes of quantitative semantics take much longer and are more complex: it cannot be done without computers. Content analysis is much simpler and does not require complex equipment.

3. *Classifying and processing the results*. Once the categories are established, classification can begin. This is not a purely mechanical operation. The categories are defined in a more or less abstract manner; it is often difficult to place a word in one category rather than another. There is some similarity with the problems of 'coding' the results of opinion polls which will be examined later (see p. 167). Tests are necessary to confirm the validity and accuracy of the categories. It is essential that the classifying is objective and not dependent on the preferences of the classifier. The claim to objectivity is one of the essential features of the method. Without objectivity, it is not possible to organize team research.

When the classification is completed the text is in a series of 'piles' of words, phrases, paragraphs, etc., which can be accurately measured. The text is translated into a set of statistics which can be analysed by the usual mathematical procedures: percentages, averages and medians can be calculated for the purpose of comparison, and on these bases correlations, factorial analyses and so on are made. Mathematical procedures are rigorous in themselves, but the rigorousness of the results depends on the value of content analysis—in other words the value of the categories and the precision of the classification.

On historical analysis: M. BLOCH, *The Historian's Craft*, Manchester, 1954; L. E. HALKIN, *Initiation à la culture historique*, 1956.

On psychological analysis of personal documents: G. W. ALLPORT, *The Use of personal documents in psychological science*, New York, 1942.

Documentary Observation

On juridical analysis: J. Carbonnier, *Droit civil*, 1960; L. Duguit, *Traité du droit constitutionnel*, 3rd ed., 1927; R. Bonnard, *Précis de droit administratif*, 4th ed., 1943.

On quantitative semantics: G. Herdan, *Language as Chance and Choice*, Groningen, 1956; G. U. Yule, *The Statistical Study of Literary Vocabulary*, Cambridge, 1944; P. Guiraud, *Bibliographie de la Statistique linguistique*, Groningen, 1954; Ministère de L'Education Nationale, *Le Français élémentaire*, 1954; W. A. C. Henmon, *A French Word Book*, Wisconsin, 1924; G. E. Van der Beke, *French Word Book*, New York, 1929.

Section III. Technique of content analysis

The general features, without going into too many technical details, will be described here. The main outlines of the method (which has been in use for some time in the United States) are settling down. Adaptations are, however, necessary for each particular piece of research.

1. UNITS OF ANALYSIS

Content analysis consists, as has been said already, of classifying the elements of a text (or, more generally, of a 'communication') according to predetermined categories. Various elements can be selected—words, phrases, paragraphs, whole documents, etc., and they can be divided into two groups, grammatical elements and others. Only one category at a time can be used but it is valuable to do several analyses, based on different categories, of the same text and to correlate the results. In practice this is seldom done because of the time factor and the difficulty of the operation.

A. Grammatical units of analysis

It is of interest to isolate these because they are closer to the units of quantative semantics than other units and a comparison will illustrate their differences. Grammatical units of analysis are mainly words, phrases or paragraphs.

(a) ANALYSIS OF WORDS

Lasswell called this the analysis of 'symbols', Leites and Pool, the analysis of 'terms'. But the terminology used does not matter. The essential feature is that the basis of analysis is single words. Two types of analysis must be distinguished: one considers all the words, the other only a selection which are considered as symbols or key words.

1. *The analysis of symbols or key words* consists of establishing a list of symbols or key words expressing attitudes or tendencies and counting the number of times they appear in a text. Similar words can be grouped around a symbolic word. The unit of analysis is the meaning of a word rather than a word as a grammatical entity.

In 1936 Martin studied nationalist symbols in children's literature. In 1937 Macdiarmid analysed key words in presidential messages. Lasswell and his disciples developed the study of symbols in the press, political speeches, electoral programmes, propaganda, etc. Comparative studies of the world press have been based on a count of symbolic words (liberty, fascism, democracy, communism, etc.) in editorials. In France studies were made of key words in electoral speeches of the campaign for the elections of January 1956.

2. *The general analysis of the words* in a text comes much closer to quantitative semantics; the essential difference lies in the pre-determined categories.

It is less often used in the social sciences but there are possibilities for development. The speeches of politicians have sometimes been analysed by distinguishing between active and passive words—those which personally involve the speaker and those which concern other 'actors' (people, parliament, government, parties); those which are angled towards the past or present and those towards the future, etc. An example is the analysis made in 1955 of the speeches of Mendès-France whilst he was Prime Minister.

General analysis of words is naturally used most often in literary studies as a method of examining style. A considerable amount of work has been done in this field in Britain and the United States, particularly on the vocabulary of poetry. It is often difficult to distinguish here between genuine quantitative analysis and content analysis; the dividing line is blurred.

An important development in content analysis, which is of indirect interest to the social sciences, is the making (particularly in the United States) of studies of 'readability', especially of the press. The object is to establish the degree of difficulty of reading a text. The rules of a readable style, based on the length of words, their common usage, the number of words with prefixes and suffixes, the presence of words with personal references can be formulated. This kind of study is usually based both on analysis of words and of phrases.

(*b*) ANALYSIS OF PHRASES AND PARAGRAPHS

Here the unit of analysis is a group of words which are grammatically linked together: either the phrase (a group of words between two full stops) or the paragraph (a group of words between two indentations). These concrete definitions are not, however, sufficient. This kind of content analysis introduces the more complex notion of the 'theme'.

1. *Two conceptions of the phrase and the paragraph as units of analysis.* Firstly, the grammatical definition just given has variants: one can, for example, take as the unit of analysis the group of words between two full stops or between a full-stop and a comma, or between two commas: the main thing is to fix a standard at the beginning. The choice of standard depends on the nature of the text being examined.

But the usual practice is to define the phrase or the paragraph, not on grammar, but on the meaning of a group of words. This is similar to the use of key words or symbols in the analysis of words. The 'theme' is the most frequently used unit of analysis but the least well defined. The theme is an assertion, an affirmation, or a proposition concerning a particular subject. The theme can be associated with either the phrase or the paragraph. If it is repeated several times in the same paragraph a single theme it is only counted once; but if a paragraph contains two or three different themes each of them is counted. The same thing applies if the phrase is chosen as the unit of analysis.

The difficulty is that themes can be mixed together in the same phrase. To give an example: 'Tito's intelligence has preserved the neutrality of Yugoslavia between the power blocs.' This contains at least two assertions: Tito is intelligent; he has preserved the neutrality of Yugoslavia. Both must be counted in an analysis by theme. But one can also restrict oneself to the principal theme of the phrase or the paragraph. It depends on the basic conventions: it is essential that they are very specific to avoid confusion.

2. *Uses of these analyses.* Most content analyses done in the social sciences, particularly the analyses of propaganda, of the effect of communications on opinion and so on, are based on one or the other of these units. A few examples can be given.

The most important and the most famous is the analysis by Lasswell of Axis propaganda during the war. He examined the propaganda content of Axis broadcasts and the content of newspapers published in the United States by the German American Bund. He was able to show the very close parallel between nazi propaganda and the themes contained in the newspapers. This was used as evidence in the legal action involving the Bund. It should be stressed that this does not furnish proof (but only a presumption) of collusion between the Bund and the Nazis. This use of content analysis could easily become dangerous.

The studies of Berelson and de Grazia of the reactions of Berlin radio and the BBC to Churchill's wartime speeches can also be cited. In another order of ideas, Hamilton's analysis of optimistic and pessimistic tendencies in protestant sermons in the United States is interesting. The study in depth by R. K. Merton of the propaganda campaign run by Kate Smith in support of war bonds should also be cited.

B. Non-grammatical units of analysis
The most often used non-grammatical units of analysis are either whole documents or particular sections of them.

(*a*) WHOLE DOCUMENTS
Analysis of whole documents is almost the same as the quantitative index method. The units of analysis are articles in newspapers or periodicals, letters in collections of correspondence, books in bibliographical studies, etc. Each unit is categorized by one of its elements, according to the purpose of the analysis. This method produces a summary overall view of a subject and is often used in the social sciences.

1. *Use in political science.* The technique is widely used in studies of the press, in the analysis of news, editorials, etc. Similar analyses are made of broadcasts, in the comparative study of programmes, in comparisons of different categories of news, etc. (see the important work of Lazarsfeld, *Radio Research*, 1941, 1942–43).

Interesting studies have been made on political slogans. Jacobson and Lasswell have analysed the slogans of May 1st in the Soviet Union. This can be compared with the work done on advertising slogans by R. B. Schumann in 1937; these slogans are outside the field of political science but comparison of political and advertising slogans is illuminating.

Many other fields in political science can be explored using this method. A comparative study of propaganda posters, covering several countries, ought to be done. The analysis of correspondence received by parliamentarians can show what image the electors have of their representatives: some work of this kind has been done in the United States and it is to be hoped that it will be done elsewhere. The study of newspaper editorials over a long period of time can illustrate the evolution of the political parties. These are just a few of the many examples which could be given and a little imagination could open up many useful lines of research. The analytical

DOCUMENTARY OBSERVATION

method is quick and simple and the work required is not disproportionate to the results.

2. *Use in other social sciences.* A few examples to show the variety of possible analyses will be given here. Numerous bibliographical analyses have been done in the United States. Some of them were pioneering works in content analysis (at least one was done as early as 1923). Berelson and Salter made an important study of magazine stories, analysing them according to the roles played by minority and majority social groups. Changes of attitudes and interests in magazine stories have been examined by Hart.

Similar work has been done on films. The American and the German character expressed in popular theatre has been studied (Macgranaham and Wayne, 1948). Radio drama has been analysed by Lazarsfeld and Stanton. Various studies have been made on public opinion expressed in cartoons and caricatures (notably Albig, 1939). P. Sorokin has transposed the method into the field of painting; J. H. Mueller and K. Hevner have applied it to music, etc.

(b) SECTIONS OF DOCUMENTS

The text or document analysed is divided into a number of equal parts and these constitute the units of analysis. This type of content analyses is furthest removed from classical methods, the least rational, the most mechanical and the one which is most similar to the slicing of a sausage.

1. *The kinds of unit used.* These depend mainly on the nature of the document analysed.

In analysing a book the basic unit is generally the page (or the half or quarter page, etc.). In studies of the press the column is usually chosen. In both cases the line is also often used. If the analysis covers several books or newspapers variations in the unit of measurement have to be carefully guarded against. A page of small letters is not the same as a page of large letters, nor is a page in a four-page newspaper and in the Sunday edition of the *New York Times*. The same observation applies to the column, the line, etc.

In studies of broadcasts the unit of analysis is generally the minute of broadcast time; in studies of films a length of film.

2. *Uses of these units.* They are used very often and it is important to understand how they are used. A text of document is not first cut into equal slices and the sections placed in analytical categories according to the theme treated in them. The procedure is exactly the

reverse: first the themes are distinguished and then the amount of space they fill is measured. This provides a basis for a general census of themes contained in the text.

A large number of studies of the press have used this technique. The column provides the basis of one of the oldest content analyses—Willey's on 'socialization' tendencies in American local newspapers (1926). The quarter of a page was used by B. J. Novack in a study of scientific textbooks in the United States and of scientific articles in the *New York Times*. The line was used in an interesting study by Carpenter on the treatment of Negroes in American history textbooks published between 1826 and 1939. The minute was the unit used by Albig in his study of broadcasts of the period 1925 to 1935. Dale used feet of film in his studies on the cinema.

(*c*) CHARACTERS

Some content analyses have been focused on persons or character traits and these have been used as units of analysis. This is rather a difficult operation and studies of this kind are less numerous than of the kind just discussed.

One of those of particular interest to social scientists is the study of Berelson on the character traits mentioned as desirable to obtain the nomination for the vice-presidency at the conventions of the American parties (see below, p. 119). In the study by Berelson and Salter, already cited, on majority and minority groups in American magazine stories, characters as well as stories themselves are used as units of analysis. These units can also be used in the study of national stereotypes, in the analysis of biographies, plays, films, radio series, etc. Interesting studies have been done on biographies in popular magazines in the United States.

2. THE ANALYTICAL FRAMEWORK

In his classic textbook Berelson writes: 'Content analysis succeeds or fails by its categories.' This is very true. Content analysis is the reverse of an empirical method; it supposes a detailed and previously established system of categories. The actual work of examining the text is almost secondary to the formulation of the categories. In the last resort the interest of the analysis depends on the analytical framework.

A. The categories

The variety of categories is almost infinite and it is nearly always possible to invent new ones for each analysis. Some authors such as

DOCUMENTARY OBSERVATION

Lasswell and White have sometimes seemed to think that general and abstract categories are possible. They have not worked out this idea and it seems impossible to do so, at least on an empirical level; it assumes a general systemization of the social sciences which does not at present exist.

It is even difficult to classify types of categories. Berelson suggested a distinction between categories of 'What is said' and 'How it is said' but in practice there is no clear distinction. Many categories used in content analysis have been formulated by Lasswell whose language is rather obscure and they are sometimes difficult to use. We will attempt here to divide the categories used into two main types; this in itself is open to criticism.

(*a*) CATEGORIES OF MATERIAL

The content of the text analysed is classified in several categories and these can be grouped into two main types—topics and proposals.

1. *Topics.* A great number of content analyses are based on classifications of the topics treated in the documents. This is, for example, the case in quantitative indexes and also in more intensive studies.

Short content analyses of broadcasts usually distinguish between variety, news, classical music, light music, jazz, plays, educational broadcasts, etc. In studies of the press, politics, miscellaneous news, sport, fashion and so on are distinguished. In an analysis of private conversations made in the United States in 1924, five subjects were distinguished—work, clothes, sport, the weather and health. Studies of publications distinguish between fiction and non-fiction, etc.

Lasswell proposed a group of five general categories for the analysis of political phenomena: people (politicians, etc.); groups and communities (Americans, communists, Jews, parties, etc.); organizations (Congress, Supreme Court, etc.); politics (war, peace, reforms, etc.); ideologies (democracy, dictatorship, etc.). This comprehensive framework can serve as a basis for many classifications but the correct formulation of sub-categories applied to the documents remains very important.

2. *Proposals about methods of techniques.* This is really a type of categories based on subjects. Possible kinds of action are taken as the basis for an analytical framework. For example, the following categories of proposals were used in a political analysis done by Berelson and Waples in 1941: 1. Analysis of the facts; 2. propaganda; 3. negotiation; 4. organization; 5. use of economic means; 6. violence; 7. show of force.

(b) FORM

There can be categories not only of the content of documents but also of form; The following are the main kinds of categories in this field used in American analyses.

1. *Form strictly defined.* Lasswell suggested a distinction between statements of fact, of preference and of identification. According to Lasswell 'The communists are going to conquer the world' is a statement of fact; 'The communists are right (or wrong) to conquer the world' is a statement of preference; 'I am a communist' is a statement of identification. These can be interesting distinctions and they have numerous variations.

In a study by Wyant and Herzog (1941) of letters received by American Congressmen the following categories were used—threats, compliments, criticism, offers of help. Berelson has also used in some analysis references to the future, the past and the present (these categories were used on the speeches of Mendès-France).

Stewart in his studies of the American press used the distinction, familiar to all journalists, between news and comment. In the category of news four kinds of 'facts' were distinguished: facts presented as definite; facts presented as possible (uncertain); facts, the certainty of which was based on a value judgment; facts, the uncertainty of which was based on a value judgment. The category of comment was divided into: personal comments of the author or some other direct source; comment by a reported statement with an identified source; comment by a reported statement with an unidentified source; comment by a direct quotation of an identified source; comment by a direct quotation of an unidentified source.

2. *Intensity.* This concerns the supposed effect a communication has on the public to which it is addressed. It is important to make an attempt to calculate the extent to which a text affects the public although this is very difficult.

Sometimes 'emotive' terms have been defined and their frequency measured. In other analyses there has been an attempt to measure the intensity of actions described in the text. For example, Jacobs in a study of propaganda made in 1941 attempted to define a 'scale of atrocities' in propaganda directed against the enemy: atrocities on men being graver than those on inanimate objects; face to face atrocities being graver than those perpetrated impersonally, etc. The scale was constructed on the basis of the opinions of a group of judges by a method somewhat analagous to those used for the Thurstone scales (see below, p. 201).

Documentary Observation

3. *Devices.* Berelson used the term 'device' to describe the analysis of a text according to the rhetorical devices used often to camouflage propaganda messages. Categories of this type are difficult to define and use.

Palmer in 1934 used a distinction between types of argument (arguments from authority, arguments by division, etc.) in analysing of speeches. Runion in 1936 examined the types of rhetorical figures of speech (metaphors, personification, etc.). In the literary field, Miles in 1942 studied the frequency of the pathetic fallacy in English poetry for a period of a century.

(c) EVALUATIVE CATEGORIES

Units of analysis can be classified according to evaluations of them by the author of the document; in other words, according to the values to which he refers or according to the authorities behind which he shelters or according to the standpoint which he adopts towards them.

1. *Standpoints.* Berelson termed this category 'direction' Allport and Foeden 'orientation', Harris and Lewis 'character'. In this field the simplest distinctions are between approval and disapproval, pessimism and optimism, affirmation and negation, etc.

These categories, can, of course, be refined. Kaplan and Golsen in 1943 suggested a distinction between different levels: a strongly positive attitude, a positive attitude, a balanced attitude (partly positive and partly negative), a neutral attitude (neither positive nor negative), a negative attitude and a strongly negative attitude. Identical scale are found in opinion polls. Assigning the units of analysis to these categories presents difficulties.

The combination of various standpoints can give depth to the analysis. The study by Lazarsfeld and Berelson on the presidential elections of 1944 is an interesting example. The newspapers, magazines, broadcasts, etc., were analysed firstly, according to whether they supported the Republican or the Democratic position; secondly, according to whether within each party they defended the candidate of the party or attacked the candidate of the opposing party (whether Democratic Party literature praised Roosevelt or vilified Wilkie).

2. *Values.* Under this heading are grouped the categories called 'standards' by the Lasswell school and 'values' or 'ends' by Berelson —good and bad, just and unjust, beautiful and ugly, happy and unhappy, strong and weak, useful and harmful, healthy and unhealthy and so on.

The values to which documents refer can be divided into a number of categories. For example, Lasswell suggested a distinction between wealth (income, money, material goods), and deference or respect (power, repute, fame). Other categories can be added to this list and those mentioned can be formulated more clearly. In their analysis of American magazine stories, Berelson and Salter distinguished the categories of values of the heart, and of the mind. The former are romantic love, the state of marriage, idealism, affection, patriotism, adventure, justice and independence, the latter were the solution of concrete problems, personal success, money and material goods, economic and social security, power and domination. The distinctions can be criticized in detail (and are revealing in themselves) but the principle is valid.

White has attempted to establish a general and standardized classification of categories of values. He formulated a schema of twenty-one values which can be used in different ways (e.g. social, egotistical, physiological, practical, etc.). These comprehensive frameworks for content analysis must be treated with great caution. I repeat once again that analytical categories must be defined according to the documents analysed.

Categories of values can be widely used in political science. All political activity is based on a system of values. Propaganda makes frequent appeals to values. Classifying the types of values used and comparing the values to which parties and other political groups appeal by analysing electoral manifestos, speeches in parliament, editorials, etc., can make interesting content analyses. General tendencies can be discerned. On the basis of an analysis made in the United States in 1947, Kris and Leites formulated a hypothesis of the decline in the use of moral values in political speeches of the previous ten years. They showed in the same study that themes concerning 'our force and our power' were frequently used in war propaganda during victorious periods and themes concerning the immorality of the enemy during periods of defeat.

3. *Authorities.* This title refers to the people, groups, principles, etc., in whose name declarations are made. For example, in an American study of German broadcasts during the war, the frequency with which American sources were cited with approval was calculated. An analysis of the propaganda about the *Altmark* affair (German ship with 314 English prisoners aboard captured in Norwegian territorial waters by a British destroyer in 1940) distinguished the following authorities: universal disapprobation, factual evidence, authority of neutrals, historical precedents, etc.

DOCUMENTARY OBSERVATION

(*d*) CATEGORIES OF PERSONS AND ACTORS

There are two main groups of categories: first, those which concern personal status, character traits, etc.; second, those distinguishing the various 'actors' (individuals, groups, entities, etc.), to which the documents refer.

1. *Personal status and character traits.* In studies of personalities of the theatre, novels, stories, broadcasts, films, etc., the analytical framework is naturally based on personal traits: sex, age, social position, education, standard of life, religion, place of residence, nationality, race, etc. These categories are easy to use when the units of analysis are 'characters' (see above, p. 114). Others can be added—physical traits, tastes, preferences, etc. An analysis according to psychological traits can be equally interesting.

Studies of this kind can be made in political science, for example, in comprehensive analyses of the establishments of parties, of élites, local notables, parliamentary and administrative personnel. Berelson made an interesting study in 1944 of the personal characteristics most frequently invoked by the candidates for the nomination of vice-presidency during their speeches to the Democratic Party Convention. These are the frequency of traits invoked (in twelve speeches):

Loyalty to the party and work done for it	11 times
Liberalism	9 "
Military service and veteran status	7 "
Support for Roosevelt's programme	6 "
Youth and vigour	5 "
Modest origins	1 "

2. *The Actors.* This title covers the persons, groups or entities which are presented in the documents analysed as occupying a central position and as being the initiators of action.

Studies made in 1947 by Berelson and de Grazia on the relative frequency of the themes 'German forces' or 'Italian forces' or 'Axis forces' (in North Africa) in German broadcasts during the war showed a certain correlation with subsequent offensive military action: predictions could have been made on the basis of such analyses. Another correlation found was that the Führer was mentioned during periods of victory but not during periods of defeat. In the analysis of the broadcasts of Mendès-France the distinction between 'myself, the government, parliament, the nation' was used but proved difficult to apply.

Waples and Berelson suggested in 1941 a kind of general classification for the possible actors in political activity. They distinguished between countries, groups of countries and regions within countries; political, economic, religious and national racial groups; and individuals and non-personal actors—journals and opinion polls. This is an interesting idea but it suffers from empiricism. The authors attempted to fill a gap in the systemization of political science—the absence of a serious typology of groups and political 'actors'.

(e) CATEGORIES OF ORIGIN AND DESTINATION
Analytical categories can be based on the origin of documents and their intended destination.

1. *Origin.* Some studies of the press have used categories based on the origin of news. For example, Taeuber (1932) in his analysis of the American local press distinguished between local, county, State, national and foreign origins. He was able to show how large the proportion of local news was over a long period of time.

Ferster's study of the origin of news concerning the war, published in American newspapers between 1914 and 1917 showed that very little came from German sources and most came from allied sources. This finding is of obvious interest.

2. *Destination.* Berelson called this category the 'target'. It is those to whom a communication or a propaganda message is addressed. For example, one passage of a speech can be addressed to the workers, another to the lower middle class and so on. Interesting analyses along these lines can possibly be made of political speeches, election posters, etc. Few analyses have been completed and those which have are not very illuminating: Waples and Berelson (1941) tried to do this for a presidential election campaign in America but did not achieve worthwhile results. This was probably due to the absence of strong class feeling in the United States and the desire not to take class distinctions into account. This hypothesis should be tested.

B. Formulating the categories
The picture just outlined of the various types of categories used in content analysis is only useful in providing examples. It is intended to suggest ideas to researchers faced with a new subject. Analytical frameworks must be adapted to each particular inquiry. The mechanism of adaptation must now be described—the way in which analytical categories are formulated and the *a priori* means of verifying them.

Documentary Observation

(a) FORMULATION

Systemization cannot be separated from research: it cannot be placed 'above' or 'below', 'before' or 'after'. It is intimately linked to the process of research. This theme will be developed in the second part of the book.

1. *General categories.* General categories exist in the sense that there are categories which can be applied to many particular cases, sometimes after some adjustment. Examples of this are categories of socio-economic levels, of sex, of age, etc.

These general categories are at the moment not very well worked out. The failure of the attempts of Lasswell and White have already been mentioned. Content analysis suffers from the gaps in systemization in the social sciences, the absence of typology valid for most of its branches and the absence of a 'cosmogony'. The attempts of Lasswell and White—like those of Berelson and Waples concerning the 'actors' in political activity—have the fault of being too empirical. Special categories defined for particular analyses suffer from a similar fault—but they are better suited to the material under consideration. This empiricism is unfortunate but inevitable.

2. *Particular categories.* The formulation of these is accomplished in three stages.

First of all it is necessary to define working hypotheses. The formulation of hypotheses will be discussed later. It need only be said here that they are not based solely on an examination of documents. Naturally a brief examination of some documents can suggest ideas and help the analyser to see relationships and contribute to the formulation of hypotheses. But this is not sufficient. A much wider study of the problems to which the documents refer (and their background) must be made. Comparison, reflection and considerable intuitive effort are necessary. A partial and limited systemization in the field of the proposed study must be attempted.

When the working hypotheses have been defined they must be translated into analytical categories. To give an example, the first hypothesis of Berelson and Salter about the treatment of different ethnic groups was: 'The great majority of sympathetic dominant characters belong to the ethnic majority group; unsympathetic or secondary characters usually belong to minority groups.' This hypothesis provided the basis of three analytical categories: (1) Identification by ethnic group of the characters of the story; (2) the roles in the story; (3) the degrees of approval of the characters.

The third stage is the precise formulation of the analytical categories. Precise and very detailed rules must be made so that each of the collaborators in the inquiry understands the same thing by them and so that the assigning of units of analysis to the categories is uniform. These rules are established in several stages. Using a preliminary formulation, a sample of documents is analysed and the rules are modified, and some categories perhaps suppressed, in the light of this. Several preliminary trials produce a satisfactory standard of precision.

(b) VERIFYING THE CATEGORIES

Two things must be verified—validity and reliability. The distinction between them is a general one and will be found again in the verification of questionnaires of opinion, of tests and so on.

1. *Accuracy of the reliability.* Content analysis tries to be objective. In order to be objective the interpretation of analytical categories must vary neither according to the analyser nor the time of analysis.

The techniques for verifying reliability are very simple. Firstly, the documents are given to different research workers at the same time and the correlation between the results obtained by each is calculated. Secondly, the same documents are given to the same research workers at different times and again the correlation between them is calculated. The first test is more precise than the second where memory can distort the result. The first is also more important in practice; if reliability among several research workers is good, reliability over time is usually satisfactory.

In practice many content analyses are made with insufficient testing and this deprives them of all precise meaning. Admittedly the objection is less strong if the categories are formulated and the inquiry carried out by one man; in this case the results cannot be distorted by inaccurate classification, although they will be affected by subjective considerations. No serious analysis can dispense with reliability tests.

2. *Validity of the categories.* An instrument of measurement is accurate if it always measures the same things in the same way whoever uses it. It is valid if it measures correctly. Validity does not necessarily follow from reliability. Supposing we have a metre measure which is in fact 90 centimetres long. The measurements obtained by using it would be identical whoever used it and whenever it was used —but they would be wrong. The instrument would be reliable but not valid.

The problem of validity does not exist unless there is a scale of measurement which exists independently of the instrument used. In many cases in the social sciences it does not. The categories used in content analysis define themselves. The measurements obtained are valid only in relation to this definition and there is no independent scale of measurement.

This is so every time special categories conceived for the analysis of particular documents are used—and, as has been said, this is very frequent. It is therefore necessary when presenting the results of an analysis to give the definitions of the categories used. But if general categories are used the problem of validity is present. If, for the purpose of analysis, categories such as 'communism, democracy, fascism' are used, there are general concepts concerning these notions and the definitions used for the analysis should correspond to these concepts. But, in practice, direct verification is almost impossible and consequently the definitions used should be stated.

Some have suggested a validation procedure by qualified persons using classical analytical methods. For example, Baldwin, having made a content analysis of a series of letters to determine the personality traits of a writer, compared the results with an impressionistic interpretation by trained psychologists. This procedure is rather vague and uncertain.

On content analysis: B. BERELSON, *Content Analysis in Communication Research*, New York, 1952; H. D. LASSWELL, N. LEITES (*et al.*), *Language of Politics*, New York, 1949; W. SCHUTZ, *Theory and Methodology of Content Analysis*, 1950.

On 'readability': R. FLESCH, *Marks of a Readable Style*, New York, 1943; *How to Test Readability*, New York, 1951.

Analysis of books: E. W. HUME, *Statistical bibliography in relation to the growth of modern civilization*, New York, 1923; S. W. KAPPEL, 'Book Clubs and the evaluation of books', *Public Opinion Quarterly*, 1948, pp. 243 ff.; M. E. CARPENTER, *The Treatment of the Negro in American History School Text Books* (1826–1939), 1941; A. WALWORTH, *School Histories at War*, Chicago, 1940; J. KOMIDAR, *American History textbooks for different educational levels*, Chicago, 1948.

Analysis of newspapers and magazines: J. L. WOODWARD, *Foreign News in American Morning Newspapers*, Columbia, 1930; W. C. ROGERS, *The Presentation of Foreign News*, Chicago, 1941; F. HARRIS, *The Presentation of Crime in Newspapers*, 1932; R. W. LOGAN, *Attitude of the Southern White Press Towards Negro Suffrage, 1932–1940*. 1940; Report of the Royal Commission on the Press, 1949; E. LERNER, 'Rumours in Paris Newspapers', *Public Opinion Quarterly*, 1946, p. 382; I. DE SOLA POOL, *The 'Prestige' Papers: a Survey of their Editorials*, Stanford, 1951; B. BERELSON and P. SALTER, 'Majority and minority Americans: an Analysis of Magazine Fiction', *Public Opinion Quarterly*, 1946, pp. 168 ff.

Analysis of broadcasts: A. L. GEORGES, *Propaganda Analysis: a Study of Inferences made from Nazi propaganda in World War II*, Evanston, 1959; P. LAZARSFELD and F. N. STANTON, *Radio Research 1941, Radio Research 1942–1943*, New York, 1942, 1944; *Communications Research*, New York, 1949; R. K. MERTON, *Mass Persuasion: the Social Psychology of the War Bond Drive*, New York, 1946; E. KRIS and H. SPEIER, *German Radio Propaganda*, 1944.

Analysis of speeches: J. MACDIARMID, 'Presidential Inaugural Addresses', *Public Opinion Quarterly*, 1937, p. 72; R. K. WHITE, 'A Quantitative Analysis of Hitler's Speeches', *Psychological Bulletin*, 1942, p. 486, and 'Hitler, Roosevelt and the Nature of War Propaganda', *Journal of Abnormal and Social Psychology*, 1949, p. 157; A. MACLUNG LEE and E. B. LEE, *The Fine Art of Propaganda: a study of Father Coughlin's Speeches*, New York, 1939.

Analysis of propaganda material: S. YACOBSON and H. D. LASSWELL, 'May Day Slogans in Soviet Russia, 1918–1943' in H. D. LASSWELL and N. LEITES, *Language of Politics*, p. 233 ff.; H. D. LASSWELL and D. BLUMENSTOCK, *World Revolutionary Propaganda*, New York, 1939; R. B. SHUMAN, 'Identification Elements of Advertising Slogans', *Southwestern Social Science Quarterly*, 1937, p. 342; H. A. BONE, *Swear Politics: an Analysis of 1940 Campaign Literature*, 1941; I. DE SOLA POOL, *The Symbols of electoral programs in France*, Chicago, 1939.

Analysis of cinema, television and theatre: E. DALE, *The Content of Motion Pictures*, New York, 1937; M. WOLFENSTEIN and N. C. LEITES, *Movies: a psychological study*, Glencoe, 1950; D. SMYTHE and D. HORTON, 'Analysis of Television Programmes in New York City', *News-letter of the National Association of Educational Broadcasters*, January-February 1951; D. V. MACGRANAHAM and I. WAYNE, 'German and American Tracts Reflected in Popular Drama', *Human Relations*, 1948, p. 429.

Analysis of personal documents: R. WYANT and H. HERZOG, 'Voting via the Senate Mailbag', *Public Opinion Quarterly*, 1941, pp. 359 and 590; R. S. CAVAN, P. M. HAUSER and S. A. STOUFFER, 'Note on the statistical treatment of life history material', *Social Forces*, 1930, p. 200.

Analysis of painting, design, music, etc.: J. K. LIVELY, 'Propaganda Techniques of Civil War Cartoonists', *Public Opinion Quarterly*, 1942, pp. 99 ff.; W. ALBIG, 'The Graphic Arts and Public Opinion' in the collective volume *Public Opinion*, New York, 1939; J. H. MUELLER and K. HEVNER, *Trends in Musical Taste*, Indiana, 1942; J. H. MUELLER, 'Methods of Measurement of aesthetic folkway', *American Journal of Sociology*, 1945, p. 276; P. SOROKIN, *Social and Cultural Dynamics*, New York, 1937.

CHAPTER II

DIRECT EXTENSIVE OBSERVATION

The most popular form of direct extensive observation is by polls: a small sample of a large community is examined and the conclusions drawn from it are generalized. This is valid only if the sample is really representative.

This technique has three essential phases: the drawing up of a list of people to be questioned (the sample), the questioning of this sample (the inquiry) and the utilization of the results of the inquiry.

Section I. Sampling

To discover the opinion of 45 million French people (or more exactly 25 million adults) 1,500 to 2,000 individuals are questioned (this is the average for public opinion polls in France). The sample presents two main problems: (1) How the people in the sample are chosen; (2) how the representativeness of the sample is measured.

1. DRAWING THE SAMPLE

The sample can be decided according to two main procedures. One is rigorous but difficult to apply—the random sample. The other is less precise but easier and cheaper—the 'quota' method. There has been a sharp controversy on this issue between institutions (such as statistical and demographic institutes) which use random samples and opinion pollsters who mainly use the quota method. But the debate is dying down because the increasing use of polls has lead both groups to use both, depending on the circumstances.

A. The quota method

The method of choosing the people in a quota has two stages. First a sort of miniature model of the total group to be examined is constructed. Then the number of people in each category (quota) is decided. The first operation is not restricted to the quota method. It is occasionally used in some kinds of random sample; the second is not.

(a) CONSTRUCTION OF THE MODEL

This is a matter of establishing various social categories which are relevant to the inquiry. The proportion in each category should be as close as possible to the proportions in the whole population.

1. *The categories.* The main categories used relate to the person, the family, profession, habitat, region and so on.

(a) Personal or family categories. — Categories according to sex or age can be established. For example, the French Institute of Public Opinion (IFOP) generally distinguishes between four age groups: 20–34, 35–49, 50–64 and over 64. Family categories can then be made: single, married, widow, divorced, married with one, two or more children.

(b) Socio-professional categories. — These are based on official population statistics. The IFOP usually uses the following categories: farmers, workers, employees and civil servants; managers and employers in commerce and industry; liberal professions; retired and rentiers; women without a profession. Some of these categories are not entirely satisfactory: for instance, the confusion of employers and managers of industry and commerce is a great handicap in political analyses.

(c) Categories of habitat. — Distinctions are made between rural areas (according to the French definition, communes with administrative centres of less than 2,000 inhabitants), small towns (2,000–20,000 according to IFOP), medium-sized towns (20,000–40,000), large towns (40,000–100,000) and very large towns (over 100,000). These are examples, and other categories are possible. Other kinds of categories of habitat are types of dwelling place (house or apartment) and the degrees of comfort found there, etc.

(d) Regional categories. — The bases here used are the economic regions established by the National Institute of Statistics and Economic Studies which can be grouped according to the purpose of the inquiry.

2. *Combinations of categories.* The construction of a model of the population supposes that several categories are combined. For example, if the total population comprises 51 per cent women, 49 per cent men: 25 per cent farmers and 45 per cent workers, employees and civil servants: 20 per cent rural dwellers, 35 per cent inhabitants of small and medium-sized towns, 25 per cent inhabitants of large towns, etc. In the 2,000 people questioned exactly the same proportions should be found. Difficulties of adjustment make it necessary to limit the number of categories.

The categories used in the construction of the model (the plan of the inquiry) and those used in presenting the results ought not to be confused. One can present the results of answers in categories which were not used in constructing the model. If, for example, socio-professional categories had not been built into the model, representatives of various socio-professional groups would in practice be contained in any sample of 2,000 people and in the results the replies made by members of groups could be compared. But the proportion would not necessarily correspond to the proportions in the population as a whole and there is therefore a possibility of error and distortion (an analogous phenomenon is found in random samples).

(*b*) QUOTAS AND THE CHOICE OF SUBJECTS TO INTERROGATE

When the plan of the inquiry has been formulated, interviewers are given a list of people to question.

1. *Mechanics of quotas.* In the list attributed to each interviewer, the characteristics (e.g. 51 women, 49 men, 25 of less than 35 years of age and so on) of the people he must question are specified. This is a small plan which fits into the general plan of inquiry.

The quotas are numbers and not names as in random samples. This is the main difference between the two methods: in random samples names are selected at random whilst in the quota system the interviewer himself chooses the people to question.

2. *Criticism of the quota method.* Simplicity and speed are the main advantages of the method. If the persons to be questioned are identified by name it takes the interviewer some time to get in touch with each of them. It is often necessary for him to visit their place of residence more than once to find them at home. Random selection can also result in people living very far apart being chosen and this increases the difficulties. Quotas allow the polls to be conducted much more quickly and at less cost.

But they have serious faults and some people do not regard them as scientific. The interviewer naturally chooses people who are easiest to contact and this can lead to distortion because the opinions of these people are not necessarily the same as those who are difficult to contact. The interviewer also tends to choose people who are like himself (in race, colour, character, social status, etc.), and it has been argued that the quota method leads to the exclusion of those at the top and the bottom of the social scale.

Attempts have been made to educate interviewers so that they become aware of their own natural inclinations and realize the necessity of eliminating them in their choice of subjects. But this is not enough; interviewers should not only be given rules about whom they should not select but also positive techniques of choice. The only existing ones are the techniques of random choice. The quota system is always less rigorous than the random sample. Most important the eventual margin of error in the former cannot be measured.

B. Probability methods

In some polls the sample is selected at random; the people to be questioned are selected by lot. The representativeness of the sample is based on the law of large numbers and calculation of probabilities —these can be calculated precisely (see p. 135). One should not be misled by the expression 'random sample': the word 'random' has a precise meaning which differs from normal usage. The sample is random if each unit of population has the same chance of being selected as any other, as in a lottery each number has the same chance of being drawn. It is very difficult to establish a rigorous system of random selection.

(*a*) METHODS OF DRAWING A RANDOM SAMPLE

If every Frenchman and Frenchwoman had an identity number it would be easy to make a random sample. This is not the case so a selection on the basis of assigning numbers to people is only possible in a few special instances. In most cases indirect procedures must be applied such as areola and cluster sampling.

1. *Selection from directories.* If there is some kind of directory of the section of the population to be examined, extracting a random sample is easy. If the names in the directory are numbered (which is the ideal situation) then a list of random numbers can be used to select the sample. If the names are not numbered then a selection of names at regular intervals can be taken. Various techniques can be used. The simplest is to take one name in every ten (or twenty, or a hundred, etc.). Other techniques are quicker—if the directory is composed of equal pages, taking the first name on every page (or every n pages), taking one name in every n centimetres of cards (as long as all are the same thickness), etc.

2. *Areola samples (or area samples).* If there is no directory then the problem is more difficult. The most usual technique employs large scale maps or aerial photographs divided into squares to form area units as nearly equal as possible. These units are numbered and a

Direct Extensive Observation

random sample is selected; all the dwellers in these areas are questioned. Streets are often used to divide towns into area units and the same principle of random sample of units is applied.

If this method is to be accurate the areas have to be as nearly equal as possible. This makes necessary the definition of zones inside which unit areas are drawn. Sometimes several divisions into squares are superimposed according to the techniques of stratified polls which will be described later.

3. *Cluster samples*. The term covers several different but allied procedures, the main common idea being that elements of a sample are not chosen individually but in groups or 'clusters'. Areola samples are examples of cluster samples; the area units chosen form clusters of people. The techniques overcome the difficulty of having no directory for the relevant section of the population.

A situation which frequently occurs is that a directory of 'clusters' of elements in the population exists but not one that records the name of each individual. If, for example, an inquiry is being made into French school children, there is no directory of these school children but there is a directory of the 38,000 communes of France. A random sample of communes can be selected and all the schoolchildren living in the sample can be questioned. The sample of communes is a cluster sample. Cluster samples have been used to simplify and facilitate inquiries. In an inquiry into housing, for example, samples of groups of three or four adjacent housing units and not individual units can be used.

4. *Multi-stage samples*. In multi-stage samples clusters are selected and within each cluster a further selection of the people to interrogate is made; this is a two-stage sample. There can be three, four or n stages.

An example is the technique used in the United States for inquiries in the countryside. A random sample of counties is selected, then there is a further random sample of smaller administrative units and finally the squaring technique of the areola sample is used and a random sample of these is selected. Finally a census of the inhabitants of these units is made and one person in three or four is questioned. The sample is constructed in four stages and different procedures used in each stage.

5. *Multi-phase samples*. This is a different technique to the multi-stage sample. The general idea is to conduct an inquiry in several phases on varying fractions of the population. In the first place there

is a large sample on the basis of which a rapid inquiry is made and the results of this are used to restrict the size of the second sample used for an inquiry in depth. Some examples illustrate the usefulness of the technique.

If one wishes to investigate people aged over 65, as no directory of old people exists, a directory of dwelling places can be used. The first phase would be to take a random sample of a large number of dwelling places (50,000, for example) and conduct a rapid survey to discover those having people of over 65 in them. A list of these is made and a random sample of one or two thousand people is selected for the final inquiry (this constitutes the second phase).

The technique was used in the United States in a detailed inquiry into household expenditure and consumption (1937). This kind of investigation can only be made on a small sample because each household must fill in an account book for a period of several days, the interviewer must visit the household often, etc. If a small and random sample had been taken from a directory there would have been a sufficient number of average income households but too few very high and very low income households. A two-phase procedure was therefore adopted: 1. A large sample was selected and a rapid survey made to find out the level of household resources; 2. The actual inquiry took in all the households at the extremes (very high or very low incomes) and a random sample of households with average incomes.

(b) STRATIFIED SAMPLING

In the example just quoted the notion of 'strata' and stratified sampling appears and these are worth examining. They imply the division of a population into *a priori* categories (called strata) by a procedure which has already been examined in the discussion of models in non-random samples. Stratification introduces a systematic element into random samples. However, 'quota' samples and systematic stratified samples should not be confused: in the first the choice of the individuals to be questioned is left to the interviewer, in the second the selection is random.

1. *Definition of the strata.* The general idea is that each category or 'stratum' must be as homogeneous as possible and taken together the strata should be heterogeneous. Various methods are used to achieve these ends.

Statistical criteria can be used. For example, the 38,000 communes of France can be classified according to their population. INSEE has formulated strata of communes of less than 10,000 inhabitants, of 10,000 to 50,000, etc.; of communes with less than 2,000 inhabitants in the administrative centre (rural communes), and over 2,000 (urban communes); of rural communes where more than 80 per cent are dependent on agriculture, etc. Paris has been divided into 5,000 small areas and some statistical information about their inhabitants has been collected: number of people to each room, the number of dwelling places with a bathroom, etc. This information is put on punched cards and strata can quickly be identified: e.g. the areas where there are fewer than 20 per cent of dwelling places with a bathroom, 20 per cent to 50 per cent with, etc.

These statistical strata require a previously composed and detailed statistical survey. The dividing lines between the strata, the threshold between one strata and the next, must be carefully chosen. This is also true when geographical criteria are used. 'Natural'—agricultural and other—regions can form strata. The main difficulty lies in definition. An appeal is usually made to the authority of experts in the geographical and the socio-professional fields.

2. *Choice of strata.* Stratification must be adapted to each individual inquiry. A series of strata used in studying political opinions is irrelevant in investigations of the height and weight of schoolchildren or of the distribution of the active population. It is desirable to make a serious study of the strata which could be used in an inquiry to discover the most appropriate; but research of this kind is usually long and costly and therefore often dispensed with.

A good general rule is to define the categories by using as many different independent criteria as possible and using as many categories as possible relating to each criterion. Every investigation has several purposes and the questionnaire contains numerous questions. A stratification based too narrowly on one criterion can result in many useless questions.

The number of strata is limited in relation to the size of the sample because, according to the law of large numbers, the number of units in each stratum has to reach a certain level in order to be representative (this problem will be discussed later). If the number of strata is increased, the sample should be enlarged: this costs time and money.

3. *Combination of strata in multi-stage sampling:* Stratification is often combined with multi-stage sampling and this makes complex stratification possible. Only one example of this technique will be quoted.

Basing the first stage on administrative units, a random sample of communes, cantons or arrondissements is selected. These basic units are classified into strata, for example by geographical region, size of population, urban or rural character. These criteria can be combined by stratifying the population within each region according to other categories. A random sample can then be taken inside these categories.

These basic units selected at random can then be stratified themselves into age, profession, property and other groups, forming 'substrata' and the individuals to be questioned are selected at random from within these substrata.

(c) MASTER SAMPLES

This does not differ from procedures already described, but it has special applications to some other procedures.

1. *Notion of a master sample.* It has been assumed up to this point that a sample is made at the same time as and specifically for the purpose of an inquiry: this is generally the case. But besides these 'made to measure' samples, it is possible to construct 'ready made' samples which can be used many times. To pursue the metaphor further the technique resembles 'industrial measure' rather than 'ready-made'.

The sample made is much larger than those used in conventional investigations. It is selected at random by techniques already described. As time is not limited, accurate and refined methods can be used. This large sample is the master sample or the *a priori* sample.

When an inquiry is undertaken the sample is drawn from the master sample. This is a very easy and quick process because all the units in the master sample are filed. The stratification which seems appropriate to the inquiry can be used with great ease because the units in the master sample have their characteristics recorded on a punched card. Using a master sample takes the form of sampling in two stages at two different times.

The master sample is, as far as possible, kept up to date by following as closely as possible population changes. The difficulties faced by many samples (the age of the directories and card indexes on which they are based) is thus avoided.

2. *Examples of master samples.* Two examples will be given to illustrate the saving of time and money and also the difficulty of establishing a master sample and keeping it up to date.

The American Bureau of the Census constructed a master sample based on aerial photographs and maps of towns on which area units were drawn. The rural master sample contained 67,000 area units

Direct Extensive Observation

covering $\frac{1}{18}$ of the agricultural territory of the United States: it contained three separate samples, each representative of the whole ($\frac{1}{54}$ land, $\frac{1}{54}$ cultivation units, $\frac{1}{54}$ rural population, etc.) The urban master sample was based on small areas which could be used to determine the number of households, commercial establishments, dwelling places, etc.

The French National Institute of Statistics and Economic Studies has established a master sample for public opinion polls based on electors only. It has two stages: communes and electors. The sample of communes is slightly larger than is necessary for an investigation. The sample of electors selected within the sample of communes is ten times larger than necessary and is made on the basis of the electoral register (every nth line or, in the case of the small communes, the whole register). It is kept up to date by using the annually revisions of the electoral register. The inevitable delay in making an investigation is, as a consequence, much reduced.

2. THE REPRESENTATIVENESS OF THE SAMPLE

Opinions polls rest on the assumption that a small sample, on which the polls are based, is representative of the population as a whole. The representativeness of the sample is thus a central problem: if the sample is not representative the replies of those questioned lose all meaning.

The problem has two aspects—measurement of representativeness and attempting to rectify distortions in the sample.

A. Measuring representativeness

This is only possible in probability methods of sampling and cannot be done in quota sampling. Samples rely essentially on the law of large numbers and on mathematical calculation of probabilities.

(a) THEORY OF MEASURING REPRESENTATIVENESS

No sample is exactly representative: one cannot say that n persons must be selected in population p for a sample to be representative. But it is possible to calculate, for each size of sample, the probability of not going beyond a certain margin of error.

1. *Margin of error and probability.* Probability is mathematically defined as the ratio between the number of cases favourable to the occurrence of an event to the number of possible occurrences, when all can be considered equally possible.

For example, if the ninety pieces in a Lotto game are put in a bag

Number of balls	Sequence of draws (B=white ball, N=black ball)				Probability of the results	Proportion in percentages of white balls in the whole draw	Probability of having this proportion
1	B				1/2	100	1/2
	N				,,	0	1/2
	1st draw	2nd draw					
2	B	B			1/4	100	1/4
	N	B			,,	50	1/2
	B	N			,,	50	
	N	N			,,	0	1/4
	1st draw	2nd draw	3rd draw				
3	B	B	B		1/8	100	1/8
	B	B	N		,,	66	
	N	B	B		,,	66	3/8
	B	N	B		,,	66	
	N	B	N		,,	33	
	B	N	N		,,	33	3/8
	N	N	B		,,	33	
	N	N	N		,,	0	1/8
	1st draw	2nd draw	3rd draw	4th draw			
4	B	B	B	B	1/16	100	1/16
	B	B	B	N	,,	75	
	B	B	N	B	,,	75	1/4
	B	N	B	B	,,	75	
	N	B	B	B	,,	75	
	B	B	N	N	,,	50	
	N	B	B	N	,,	50	
	N	B	N	B	,,	50	3/8
	B	N	B	N	,,	50	
	B	N	N	B	,,	50	
	N	N	B	B	,,	50	
	B	N	N	N	,,	25	
	N	B	N	N	,,	25	1/4
	N	N	B	N	,,	25	
	N	N	N	B	,,	25	
	N	N	N	N	,,	0	1/16

Fig. 1.—Sequences for 4 draws

what is the probability of drawing from it a number which ends in three? There are nine favourable cases (3, 13, 23, 33, 43, 53, 63, 73, 83)[1] and ninety possible cases (which are all equally possible if the pieces are well mixed); the probability can be expressed:

$$P = \frac{9}{90} = \frac{1}{10}$$

To take another example, if a bag containing a large number (n) balls, half of which were white the other half black, each time a ball is drawn out the chances are that it will be white are half. If the proportion of white balls to black is not known, how many draws have to be made to have a precise indication of the size of the proportion? This is exactly the problem of the representativeness of the sample. Figure 1 is a table of possible results of four draws. It can be seen that the probability of a 50 per cent. error is 1 in 8, with eight draws the probability is not more than 9:128 (about 1 in 14), with sixteen draws it is not more than 697:32,768 (or about 1:47). With sixteen draws the probability of having more than a 25 per cent error is not more than 1: 4.7. The probability of passing a certain margin of error diminishes the greater the number of draws.

It is unnecessary to increase indefinitely the number of tests because the probability of passing a certain margin of error diminishes very quickly up to a certain point and after this threshold has been passed it diminishes much less quickly.

2. *Meaning of representativeness of a sample.* It can never be asserted that the proportions in a particular sample do not exceed by 10 per cent the real proportions in the population. One can only say the chances of a 10 per cent error are so many in a hundred. The probability of not passing it can be great—99.9 per cent or even greater—but it remains a probability, it can never be an 100 per cent certainty. There will always be a possibility of a greater error, that is to say, of a random sample very different to the population being examined. The same principle operates in a lottery—the more numerous the participants, the less chance each of them has of winning first prize, but in spite of this there is always a winner.

(b) PRACTICAL METHODS OF MEASURING THE REPRESENTATIVENESS OF A SAMPLE

The calculations necessary to measure the representativeness of a

---

[1] This is for an 'exhaustive' draw (each unit drawn is not replaced—if it is then this is called a 'non-exhaustive' draw). All the following examples are based on exhaustive draws.

sample are long and complicated. But tables or graphs can be constructed which make possible the checking by a simple operation the representativeness of the results of an inquiry. A few of the most frequently used will be described here.

1. *Direct measurement of the representativeness of a sample.* The graph of S. S. Wilks is the most practical method. It has a great advantage over methods of direct calculation which only give the size a sample must have (or the number of tests to be made) in order not to exceed a certain margin of error.

In Wilks's graph the proportions found by a poll are recorded on

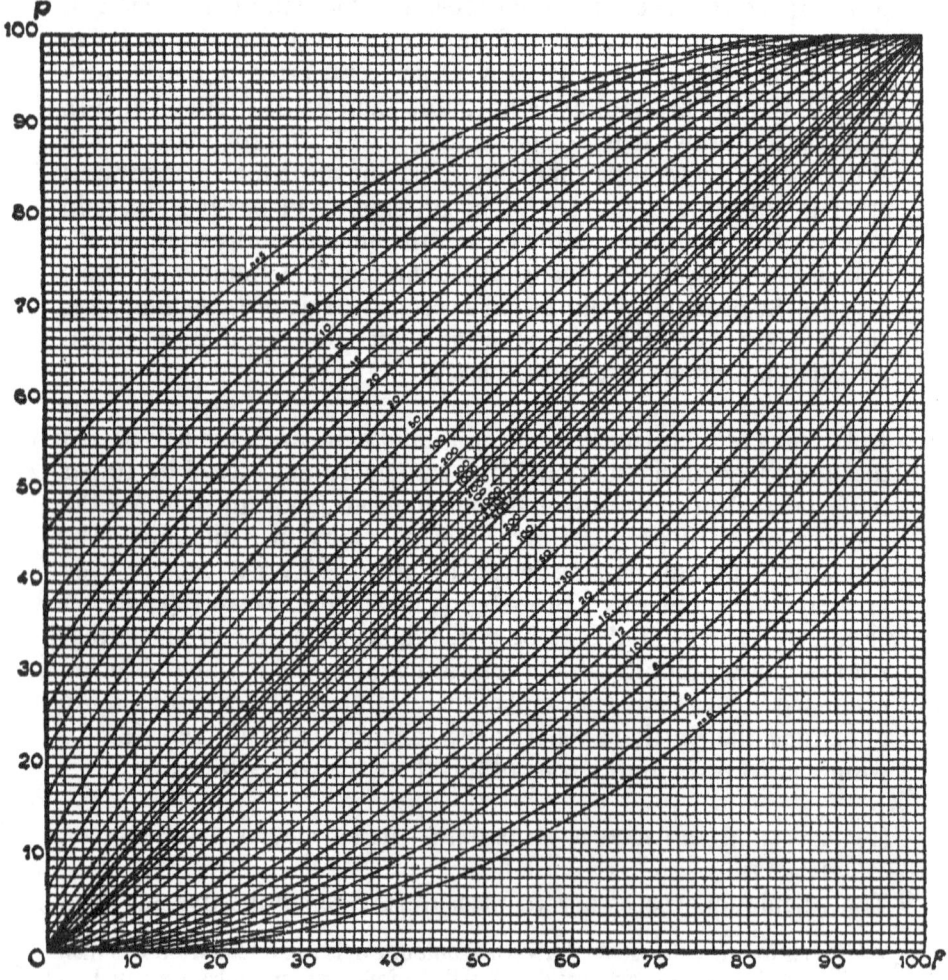

Fig. 2.—Wilks's graph for 95% probability

the horizontal axis, the true proportions on the vertical axis; the curves indicate the number of people questioned. The intersections of the horizontal and the vertical on the curve representing a given size of sample show the limits of the true proportion. Each graph is made for a certain degree of probability. In a graph with a 99 per cent probability there is only one chance in a hundred that the true proportions shown by the graph will be exceeded; in a 95 per cent graph only five chances in a hundred (see figs. 2 and 3).

2. *Tests of significance.* Methods of ensuring the representativity of the sample are often insufficient to determine what conclusions are

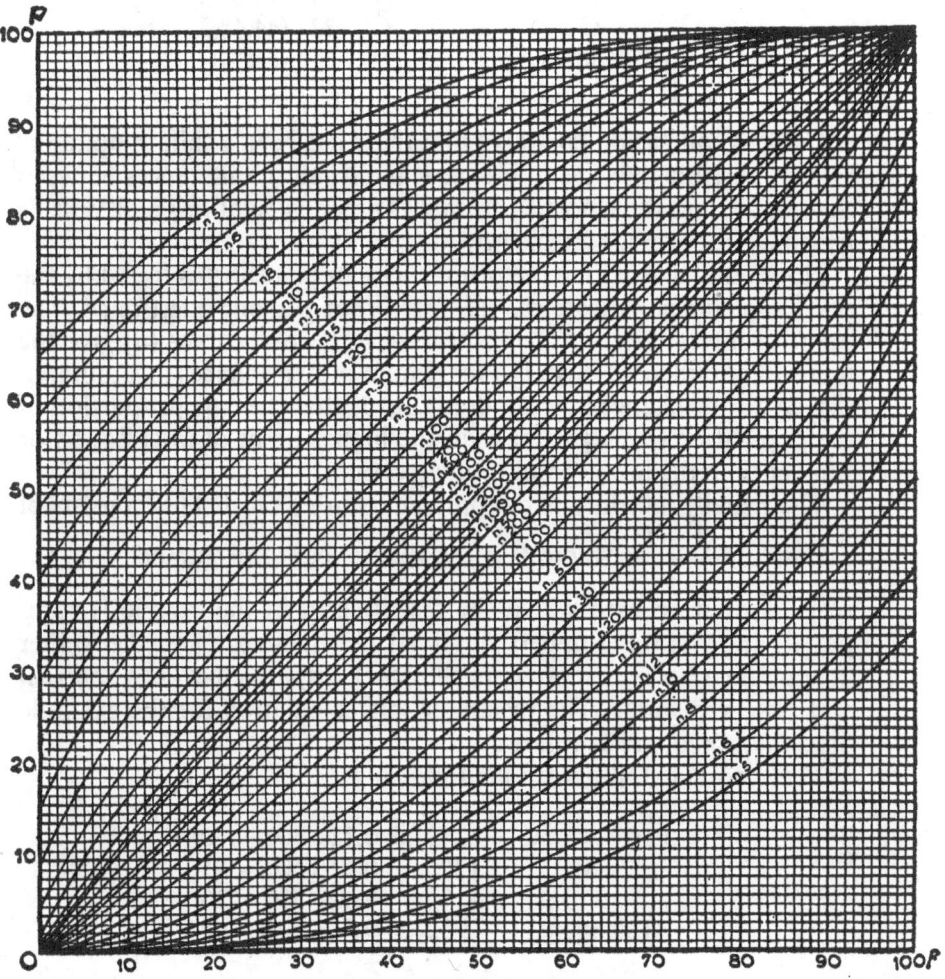

Fig. 3.—Wilks's graph for 99% probability

INTRODUCTION TO THE SOCIAL SCIENCES

legitimate and what are not. To take a specific example, in the elections of January 2, 1956, the results in one constituency were as follows:

Party A	32% of electorate
,, B	17% ,,
,, C	42% ,,
Abstentions	9% ,,

According to a poll made on 500 electors in the constituency in 1958 the following replies were obtained:

Party A	143 (28.6%)
,, B	93 (18.6%)
,, C	222 (44.4%)
Abstentions	42 (8.4%)

Can the conclusion be drawn that there has been a shift in opinion? Or is it possible that the difference is the result of differences between the sample and the whole electorate? Direct calculations and Wilks's graph do not provide an answer.

Horizontal axis (f) are the proportions in percentages found by the poll. The curves indicate the number (n) of persons questioned. The point of intersection of the vertical with the two curves (n) give the limits of confidence: there is a maximum of five chances in a hundred (fig. 2) or one chance in a hundred (fig. 3) that the true proportion of the population (p) is greater than the higher point of intersection or smaller than the lower point of intersection.

The usual procedure is to apply Pearson's χ^2 test. This consists of calculating $\frac{(F-f^2)}{F}$ where F is the theoretical total number (i.e. the real distribution with which the distribution in the sample is compared) and f is the numbers observed. All these are added together giving the χ^2 which represents the total disparity between the real and observed totals. The results of this calculation for the example already quoted, are as follows:

The theoretical totals are the following:

Party A	32% i.e. 0.32 × 500 = 160
,, B	17% ,, 0.17 × 500 = 85
,, C	42% ,, 0.42 × 500 = 210
Abstentions	9% ,, 0.9 × 500 = 45
	500

DIRECT EXTENSIVE OBSERVATION

From these the following table can be made:

	F	f	$F-f$	$(F-f)^2$	$\frac{(F-f)^2}{F}$
Party A	160	143	+17	289	1.80
" B	85	93	− 8	64	0.75
" C	210	222	−12	144	0.69
Abstentions	45	42	+ 3	9	0.20
χ^2					3.44

It can be shown that the value of χ^2 tends to diminish as the number of classifications and the number of 'degrees of freedom' diminish (degrees of freedom are the number of classifications less 1). The number of degrees of freedom are the number of independent variables since the size of any one classification can be established if the size of the others is known—hence $n-1$.

The value χ^2 for a given number of degrees of freedom increases in proportion as the observed distribution deviates from the theoretical distribution and to the extent that probability P of the sample being drawn from a total corresponding to this distribution diminishes. Fisher calculated the values χ^2 for different levels of probability (see fig. 4). In the preceding example where $\chi^2 = 3.44$ it is found that χ^2 is slightly below the threshold of probability of 30 per cent (χ^2 corresponding to this threshold is 3.665). This is to say that there are a

Degrees of liberty	P=95	P=99	Degrees of liberty	P=95	P=99
1	12.71	63.66	16	2.12	2.92
2	4.30	9.93	17	2.11	2.90
3	3.18	5.84	18	2.10	2.88
4	2.78	4.60	19	2.09	2.86
5	2.57	4.03	20	2.086	2.845
6	2.45	3.71	21	2.080	2.831
7	2.37	3.50	22	2.074	2.819
8	2.31	3.36	23	2.069	2.807
9	2.26	3.25	24	2.064	2.797
10	2.23	3.17	25	2.060	2.787
11	2.20	3.11	26	2.056	2.779
12	2.18	3.06	27	2.052	2.771
13	2.16	3.01	28	2.048	2.763
14	2.15	2.98	29	2.045	2.756
15	2.13	2.95	30	2.042	2.750

Fig. 4.—Fisher's table giving the values of Pearson's χ^2

P=the different probabilities (the number of chances in 100 that the sample is drawn from a total identical to the one used as a reference).

little more than thirty chances in a hundred that the sample analysed would be drawn from an identical total identical to that of the elections of 1956: and, thus, that political opinions had not changed between 1956 and 1958. This hypothesis is plausible, but neither certain nor almost certain. The disparity between the theoretical and the observed distribution is only considered significant if the probability is less than 5 per cent.

B. Corrections of the poll

Some elements of the sample and the population observed can be compared. For example, the socio-professional composition, the composition by age group, sex, domicile, etc., of a country are known. If the proportions in the population at large and those of the sample do not correspond the composition of the sample, and even the results of the poll, can be corrected.

(*a*) CORRECTION OF THE SAMPLE

This is done before the inquiry is made and the problem is to prevent the correction damaging the random character of the sample. Various techniques have been suggested.

1. *Balanced samples.* This technique was perfected by Yates in 1949. To give an example, if a stratum of farming households comprises 65 per cent of the population and the random sample produces only 60 per cent the sampling process is continued until the correct proportion of agricultural households is obtained. This must be done at random otherwise the sample will lose its random character and the replacing of names is done in the following manner.

A 101st name is selected and it replaces the 1st; if the former is an agricultural household and the latter is not, the proportion comes nearer to being correct; if it is the reverse then the proportion becomes more dissimilar; if they belong to the same category then the proportion is unchanged. The selection of names continues until the correct proportion is established. According to the law of large numbers the longer the random selection of names proceeds the greater become the chances of getting the true proportion.

2. *Controlled samples.* This method, invented by Bowley in 1926, attempts to make the sample accurate, not according to the units of the sample (for example households), but according to certain elements in the units of the sample.

DIRECT EXTENSIVE OBSERVATION

This can be done if the units of the sample are composed of a cluster (in the sense already given to this word) of other elements. If, for example, we suppose that the proportion of individuals (heads of families and others) whose profession is farming is 42 per cent and there are only 36 per cent in the sample, proceeding in the same way as Yates more households are selected at random in order to produce the right proportion of individual farmers (one of the elements of the cluster).

The same procedure can be followed for the size of units. If we suppose that the area covered by woods and forests makes up 20 per cent of the total area of a département and a sample of farms with an average area of 20 per cent woods and forests is required, Yates method could be used; if one wanted a sample where the average area of woods and forests was 20 per cent per acre, the sample could be controlled by Bowley's method.

3. *Compensated samples.* Controlled samples are based on a system of compensation between units of the sample; 'compensated' samples are those where compensation is made between strata. The principle of this system only will be described because its application is very complex.

Instead of selecting a random sample within each stratum, a random sample is made covering several strata. Coincidence between the proportions, not of a single stratum, but of several of the strata and the population at large is sought. Compensation between the strata operates in this way. A plan of different combinations of interdependent samples is drawn up and a random selection of these is made.

(*b*) CORRECTION OF THE RESULTS OF POLLS

When a poll has been made it is possible to correct the results by applying weighted coefficients to certain units of the sample or by extrapolating results. In either case, the known characteristics of the whole population are the bases of the correcting process.

1. *Removing the distortions in the sample.* The results are corrected before they are assessed; only some of the elements of the sample are subject to correction.

The most frequent case is the elimination of distortion in the samples resulting from refusals to reply, absences, etc. If these are identical for all the categories in the sample representivity will not be affected. In practice refusals or absences vary greatly according to category (they are usually higher for old people, women, etc.).

INTRODUCTION TO THE SOCIAL SCIENCES

If, for example, the following results were obtained:

	Sample made			Sample questioned		
	Men	Women	Total	Men	Women	Total
65–69 years	16	20	36	6	14	20
70+ years	25	34	59	29	32	61
Total	41	54	95	35	46	81

The following weighting coefficients would have to be applied:

Men 65–69	2.67
„ 70 and over	0.86
Women 65–69	1.43
„ 70 and over	1.06

This procedure can be criticized because the refusal to reply might correspond to particular characteristics which are ignored by applying weighted coefficients. A possible element of error is introduced.

2. *Extrapolation of the results.* This is the use of documents external to the poll to correct the results where direct comparison between the composition of the sample and the composition of the whole population is not possible.

(a) Rectification by quotient.—This is the simplest and most frequently used technique. The following example provides a good illustration. In 1946 a sample of one commune in ten in Meurthe-et-Moselle gave an area of 17,714 hectares of cultivated land. The agricultural census of 1929 recorded 18,914 hectares of cultivated land. The sample, therefore, showed a decrease of 6.34 per cent. If the sample of 1946 is generalized to the whole department the area of culitvated land was 177,140 ha.

But in 1929 the area of cultivated land in the sample of communes selected was not 10 per cent of the total cultivated land of the département; this was 177,840 hectares—theoretically 17,784 for the sample of ten whilst in fact, it was 18,914. The difference apparent in 1929 was taken into consideration in 1946 and the agricultural administration finally calculated the area of cultivated land in the département as 166,564 (a reduction of 6.34 per cent on the 1929 total—the reduction shown in the sample of ten communes).

(b) Correction by *a posteriori* stratification.—If we imagine that an investigation has shown in a given sample that the proportion of individuals having a special premium because they earn exceptionally low wages is the following:

Steel industry	3 %
Food industries	10.6%
Textile, clothing, wood and furniture	15.5%
TOTAL	7.6%

This shows that the influence of a group of activities on the phenomena studied is basic because the sample had not been stratified according to groups of activities. A kind of *a posteriori* stratification is made by comparing the total number of wage-earners and the number of wage-earners obtaining the premium with the number of establishments existing in a group of activities in the region (and not by the number of establishments contained in the sample).

This procedure can be generally used to correct the sample. Socio-professional or political categories can, for example, be adjusted. If the number of workers in a sample is 20 per cent whilst in the total population they form 25 per cent the replies of the workers can be weighted and similar weightings can be applied to the other categories.

The two procedures which have been described—the quotient and the *a posteriori*—can thus be combined.

On sampling: F. YATES, *Sampling Methods*, 1953; F. F. STEPHAN and P. J. MACARTHY, *Sampling Opinion: an Analysis of Survey Procedure*, New York, 1958; W. G. COCHRAN, *Sampling Techniques*, New York, 1953; *Bulletin des sciences sociales*, UNESCO, 1953, No. 3; R. GOODMAN and L. KISH, 'The Use of Controls beyond simple stratification in the probability selection of a sample', *Journal of the American Statistical Association*, 1950, pp. 350–72; F. CHARTIER, *Les Sondages à plusieurs degrés*, 1955.

On probability methods and quotas: M. H. HANSEN and W. N. HURWITZ, 'The Problem of non-response in sample surveys', *Journal of the American Statistical Association*, 1946, pp. 517 ff.; D. MANNHEIMER and H. HYMAN, 'Interviewer Performance in Area Sampling', *Public Opinion Quarterly*, 1949, pp. 82 ff.; W. E. DEMING, 'On Errors in Surveys', *American Sociological Review*, 1944, p. 359, and *Some Theory of Sampling*, New York, 1950.

Section II. Questionnaire methods

The main type of polls procedure is the interview by questionnaire. It is a particular variety of the general technique of interview which will be examined later (p. 178). It is sometimes associated with other procedures, for example, the tests or projective methods usually found in intensive observation (discussed in the following chapter); in comparison to the questionnaire they have a secondary role and usually serve the purpose of broadening the inquiry and furnishing information which complements the questionnaire.

1. PREPARATION OF QUESTIONNAIRES

This is a complex and delicate operation. The nature, form and order of the questions is of great importance to the results of the inquiry.

A. Categories of questions

The fundamental distinction rests on the degree of freedom in the reply: the main distinction is between 'open' and 'closed' questions (although intermediary categories exist). Another important distinction is based on the nature of the reply sought.

(*a*) CLASSIFICATION ACCORDING TO THE DEGREE OF FREEDOM IN REPLYING

All questions are open in the sense that a person is not obliged to reply or can reply saying that he has no opinion on the matter. But if the respondent accepts to reply, his liberty can vary and the precision of the reply can vary at the same time.

1. *Open and closed questions.* A closed question is one to which 'yes', 'no' or 'no opinion' are the only possible replies or where the alternatives are of the same nature. An open or 'free' question is one in which the respondent can answer as he likes and he is not limited to a single alternative. An example of an open question is: 'What do you think of the policy of the French Socialist Party towards the Communists?'; an example of a closed question is: 'Are you in agreement with the French Socialist Party's policy towards the Communists?'

Open and closed questions have exactly the opposite advantages and disadvantages. The first allows a much less superficial inquiry and a better understanding of the motives and meaning of the attitudes and opinions of respondents can be obtained. Closed questions have the great advantage of being easy to handle; interpretation of the results does not present problems and 'codification' (see p. 167) is automatic. Open questions leave much room for subjectivity both in the transcribing and interpretation of the replies. The subjects are often baffled by open questions and the investigator has to help them (suggestions are particularly dangerous here).

Direct Extensive Observation

In practice a good questionnaire should include both categories of questions for all the main problems investigated. The results obtained from one category can be completed and corrected by the results of the other. Great care should be taken to see that the open and closed questions about the same problem do not contaminate one another.

2. *Questions with a series of alternative replies.* The following question is an example of a question with a series of alternative replies: 'What do you think characterizes a man of the Left?' 'Anticlericalism. The desire to defend individual liberties. Anticapitalism. Interest in the problems of the proletariat. Opposition to racism. Anticolonialism. Desire for international co-operation. Pacificism.' These are sometimes called 'cafeteria questions' because answering them is to some extent analogous to the procedure used by customers of self-service restaurants.

The series of alternative replies offered to the subject can be either open or closed. It is open if, at the end of the list of specific suggestions, the subject is given the opportunity of giving another reply. It is closed if the subject is limited to the alternatives offered. An open series of alternative replies is the most popular procedure because it is more convenient than simple open questions and it reduces the number of non-replies. The subject is usually also allowed to choose several of the alternatives offered (indicating what he regards as most important) and not just one of them.

This procedure has a number of advantages. It allows almost as much exploration in depth as the open question and has much greater depth than closed questions. Codification and interpretation is almost as easy as with closed questions, limiting to the minimum the risks of personal bias. The subject is helped to reply by the provision of points of reference which assist him to clarify his thinking. But this has a serious drawback; the points of reference tend to suggest replies. The subject often chooses replies which he had not really thought of before seeing the questionnaire; the attitude of the investigators can aggravate this. Proper training of investigators can diminish without entirely avoiding it.

3. *Evaluative questions.* These are a particular variety of the closed series of alternatives. Instead of a quantitative series requiring replies different in nature, the subject is offered a quantitative series and the replies are classified into degrees. Questions of this type introduce an element of measurement or quantification in the attitude or opinions of the subject.

A first and very crude type was the closed question where the alternatives were yes or no, but this has been replaced by a more subtle series of alternatives. For example: 'What is your opinion of the policy of the Socialists *vis-à-vis* the communists? 1. Completely approving. 2. Qualified approval. 3. Neutral (neither approving nor disapproving). 4. Qualified disapproval. 5. Complete disapproval.' Taken with the 'no-opinions' and the no replies, the subjects have the choice of seven alternative positions of which five are of different intensity.

The evaluative question can take an even more refined form by asking the subject to place himself on some kind of scale. The most popular form in France is the graduated line (see p. 197). It must be remembered that the evaluation thus made by the subject is only an indication because it is essentially subjective and has no value as a measurement. Two subjects with the same opinion may place themselves at different places on the scale because they form a different impression of the significance of the degrees on the scale. Attitudes and opinions cannot be measured by using this procedure. Various other techniques have been perfected for objectively measuring opinions and attitudes (p. 199).

(*b*) CLASSIFICATION ACCORDING TO THE NATURE OF THE REPLIES
A person can be asked to give information on a fact or an action; or give his opinions; or give an apparently innocuous reply which is in fact of great significance.

1. *Questions of fact or about actions.* In censuses questions of fact are very numerous. The subjects are asked, for example, the area of the land which they farm, the number of rooms in their dwellings and the size of their income. In opinion polls there are a certain number of indispenable questions of fact—age, sex, profession, habitat, resources, etc.—in order to classify the replies. Replies to questions of fact are easy: the subject is questioned on something tangible and easily understood. In principle, there is a high level of honesty of the replies and there are not many refusals to reply. The exceptions are in those cases where the subject fears that his reply will damage his interests. For example, in France the distrust of the tax collector creates difficulty in assessing replies to questions about standard of living, size of resources, the number of rooms in an apartment and so on.

Questions about actions can be taken together with questions of fact: a subject can be asked if and in what way he has done something. For example, he can be asked if, and for what party, he voted in the last elections. Here, too, the reply can be accurate because the question is about something concrete. The only inaccuracy can arise as a result of a considerable lapse of time. The question 'What party did you vote for in 1958?' would obtain more accurate replies than the same question for the November 1945 elections. If the question is about an act which deeply involves the subject there is a greater chance of distrust, an increase in number of non-replies and of the possibility of dishonesty.

2. *Questions about intention and opinion.* It is necessary to make a sharp distinction between questions about acts and questions about intentions. It is more difficult to answer a question about an action in a hypothetical situation because it is more difficult to imagine a hypothetical action than to remember a real action. The context and the circumstances surrounding an action have a great effect on it. The reply to a question about intention must be interpreted as an opinion on the action and not necessarily as a prediction of how the subject will act. The question 'For which political party would you vote if there were elections today?' is very useful to discover opinons of the subject at the moment of the inquiry. But if in fact there were elections, many external pressures—an electoral campaign amongst them, might influence the subject into voting for another party to the one which he indicated. The comparison between the results of the election and replies to an investigation conducted later do not always indicate a change in climate of opinion because two things of a different nature are being compared.

Questions about intentions are therefore more like questions about opinions. 'Which political party do you most prefer?' is a question of opinion. The question of opinion asks the subject what he thinks and not what he does or what he knows. It is more difficult to reply to questions of opinion and the replies are less precise because opinions are less easy to define and express. The risk of insincerity and non-reply is generally greater. Everything depends on the nature of the opinions. Those of great personal importance are the most difficult to discover. This problem varies between countries and civilizations. Political opinions are regarded as very personal in France which makes political science investigations difficult; in Anglo-Saxon countries this is not the case.

Questions about opinions are the basic element in opinion polls. But it should be remembered that they are not the only kind of sample survey. The distinction already made between closed and open questions and the series of alternative replies or evaluations mainly applied to questions about opinions.

3. *Test questions.* In test questions the interest lies in the hidden significance of the reply: the reply is regarded as an indication of a fact or opinion which the subject would not wish to reveal directly.

For example, to avoid a direct question about size of income the subject can be asked whether he has a car, maid, telephone, radio, television and so on. In an investigation of the bourgeois family in France in 1950–51 there was an attempt to find out whether the young girls were chaste by collating and analysing the replies of two or three questions (which appeared innocuous); a direct question would have risked a high proportion of non-responses. In investigations of the Right or the Left several test questions define the position of the subject objectively and distinguish it from his subjective identification. In many opinion polls there are test questions to establish the general degree of sincerity of the subject.

Test questions are very valuable but they have dangers because of the difficulty in interpretating the replies. Subjective and intuitive interpretations should be avoided. Numerous verifying tests are the only way of validating test questions. We will return to this problem later on (see p. 189).

B. Designing the questionnaire

A questionnaire is not a series of questions in any order. It is, on the contrary, a group of questions the order of which is very carefully studied. The order, the number of questions about the same subject, their grouping in 'batteries' present difficult and important problems.

(a) THE ORDER OF QUESTIONS

Questions should not contaminate one another nor offend the subject, making him adopt a defensive attitude towards the inquiry.

1. *Contamination of questions.* This is one of the main dangers to avoid in designing a questionnaire. There have been many instances of contamination completely falsifying results.

A poll made in the United States in 1939 (after the declaration of war) contained two questions: 'I.—Do you think that the United States should permit American citizens to engage in the German army? II.—Do you think that the United States should permit American citizens to join the British army?' The results were very different according to which order the questions were asked:

		Order I–II	*Order II–I*
Question I	Yes	22%	31%
	No	74%	61%
	No opinion	4%	8%

Question II	Yes	40%	45%
	No	54%	46%
	No opinion	6%	9%

In France at the end of 1944 the writers Paul Chack and Henri Béraud were condemned to death for collaboration; Georges Albertini, *directeur du cabinet* of the minister Marcel Déat (who had 'collaborated' more directly), was condemned to five years' hard labour. At the beginning of 1945 an opinion poll was conducted to find out whether the public approved of these sentences or whether it found them too heavy or too light. When the Albertini question was asked before the Chack-Beraud question 53 per cent thought the sentences too light; asked in reverse order the proportion was 59 per cent.

Neither order is more 'true' than the other. The two series of responses are equally valid facts but the questions contaminate one another. If uncontaminated answers are desired the questions must be dispersed in the questionnaire to separate the questions which might be contagious. Contamination, however, is in itself very interesting; to study it systematically the sample must be divided into groups in which questions are asked in different orders.

2. *The funnel technique.* To avoid contamination it has been suggested that the questionnaire should be arranged like a 'funnel', in other words to start with the most general questions and finish with the most specialized to avoid suggesting answers to the subjects. The same arrangement can be used in ordering the series of alternative replies to a single question. For example, in a poll made at Cornell University in 1947 on the opinion of the American public about the attitude of the government towards the UN the main questions were grouped in the following order: '1. What is your opinion about the general activities of an organization like UNO? 2. Are you satisfied with the work done up to now by UNO? 3. Do you think that the United States has made too many or too few concessions or pursued too selfish a policy in UNO? ... (etc.).'

This technique assumes that the opinions of the people questioned have a logical structure and that particular positions fit in with general opinions. This is not always the case and the funnel arrangement therefore tends towards the contamination of the replies of the particular questions by the replies made to the more general questions; the subject is concerned to rationalize his attitude which may not have been rational before. It can also result in the subject being involved in dilemmas which falsify his previous replies. Thus in most cases the techniques of dispersion is preferable but this depends on the nature of the questions.

3. *The problem of the non-co-operation of the subject*. One of the main difficulties in a questionnaire are the delicate questions which make the subject wary. They can increase the number of non-response and contaminate ensuing questions. Several techniques are used to avoid this.

Questions are often placed at the beginning of questionnaires which are not of direct relevance to the investigation with the purpose of 'relaxing' the subject and to gain his confidence. Investigators must always try to create a relaxed atmosphere. When certain very delicate questions must be asked they are generally put at the end of the questionnaire; by this time the subject is in a trusting frame of mind and there is more chance of obtaining a reply; if, even so, the subject takes offence the preceding answers will not be distorted. If there are several delicate questions, they are dispersed throughout the questionnaire amongst questions which tend to make them appear innocuous. Trials are made before the final version of the questionnaire is drawn up in order to achieve this.

(*b*) NUMBER OF QUESTIONS

There are two problems under this heading; the total number of questions contained in the questionnaire and the number of questions about the same subject (which involves the technique known as 'batteries of questions').

1. *Total number of questions*. This must not be too great to avoid tiring the subject, resulting in the last questions being answered less well—a serious nuisance when these are the most important. Opinion polls are generally composed of about thirty questions, some of which are sub-divided into sub-questions.

Much longer questionnaires of over a hundred or even several hundred questions are, however, used in special cases. A high number is, for example, essential in certain factorial analyses (see below p. 293). But fatigue on the part of the subject limits the validity of the replies and consequently the results of the analysis. This difficulty can be circumvented by giving the questionnaire to people of above average intelligence who are more accustomed to analyse themselves and who can therefore manage a long questionnaire more easily. But these people represent only a special category of the population.

The total number of questions obviously depends on the nature of the questionnaire: if the questions are easy then there can be a considerable number; if they are difficult the number should be restricted. Questions on the same subject seem easier to answer than questions about a number of different subjects.

2. *The number of questions relating to each subject.* As the total number of questions is limited it would appear logical to restrict the number of questions about any problem to one so that a greater number of problems can be included in a single questionnaire. But, as one has just seen, in addition to the diversity of questions affecting their total number, there are other reasons for asking several questions on the same subject: confusion in the mind of the subject and errors are limited; answers can be compared and cross-checked; and the analysis can be given depth. Consequently, two or three or even more questions are usually focused on the same subject and they are usually grouped together in order to facilitate answering. Sometimes they are dispersed in order to measure the degree of contamination and the degree of coherence of opinions; it is interesting to ask the same question in different forms in different places in the same questionnaire.

Sometimes a very great number of questions are asked about a single problem and this is known as a 'battery' of questions. A whole questionnaire can consist of a single battery. Batteries are a means of giving depth to an analysis, throwing light on various aspects and motivations of a single attitude or opinion. They contribute towards 'relaxing' the subject on delicate problems by submerging the most serious questions amongst others which have an anodine appearance. They can also be used as measuring instruments when the questions in the battery have to some extent been standardized by the construction of attitude scales—this will be examined later (see p. 199). An interesting example of the use of batteries is the investigation made in America at the beginning of the Second World War on the 'interventionist' and 'non-interventionist' attitudes and their constituent parts.

C. Formulating the questions

The form of the questions has a great influence on the replies. Some of the basic rules of formulating questions do not call for any explanation: the text of the questions should be as simple as possible; the language used should be familiar and easily comprehensible to all the subjects of the inquiry; the questions should be formulated with the least intelligent subject in mind.

Whether or not the text of the questions should be personalized presents a problem. Should the subjects be addressed in a personal way: 'in your opinion, should one...' or 'Do you think that...' The answer is usually yes. Experience has shown that personalized questionnaires obtain a greater number of responses and their results are generally more accurate. But a psychologist has shown that the personalization of questions slightly diminishes the validity of the responses.

Other, more specialized problems warrant further analysis because of their important influence on results. An investigation conducted in the United States (March to September 1941) under the direction of Hadley Cantril on aid to Britain, the entry of the United States into the war and the dispatch of American forces to Europe, it proved possible to vary the percentage of some of the replies between 8 per cent and 78 per cent. This illustrates the fundamental importance of the way in which questions are formulated. Possible types of deformation will be examined.

(a) THE CONSERVATIVE DEFORMATION

A series of studies have shown that opinion tends naturally to lean in a conservative direction. We will call this the 'Panurgic complex'; it has many manifestations extending far beyond opinion polls. As far as polls are concerned we will examine two aspects of the complex: the attraction of saying 'yes' and the fear of change.

1. *The attraction of replying 'yes'.* The same opinion can be expressed by 'yes' or 'no' according to the way in which a question is worded. For example, those favourable to a new constitution in France in the years 1945–46 could have replied 'yes' if they had been asked 'Should the Constitution be changed?' or 'no' to the question 'Should the Constitution of 1875 be kept?' Experience has shown that the same opinion expressed positively will have a higher percentage of agreement than when expressed negatively. Governments know this very well and usually formulate the text of referenda so that the reply 'yes' corresponds to the solution they desire. In opinion polls the phenomena is well established and generalized (it does not seem to vary much from country to country).

In France the same question about the invitation of Roosevelt to General de Gaulle after Yalta was asked in two different forms: 'A. Do you think that General de Gaulle should have accepted the invitation of President Roosevelt to meet him in Algiers?—(B) Do you think that General de Gaulle was right to refuse President Roosevelt's invitation to a meeting in Algiers?' Approval was expressed by 'no' in A and by 'yes' in B. These were the results:

	A	B
Approval	58% (no)	63% (yes)
Disapproval	27% (yes)	15% (no)
No opinion	15%	22%

The parliamentary debates on validating the elections of Paul Reynaud and Edouard Daladier in 1945 gave another illustration of the same thing. The two forms were '(A) Should the election of M. Paul Reynaud (or M. Daladier) have been validated?—(B) Would have you preferred the election of M. Paul Reynaud (or M. Daladier) to be invalidated?' These were the replies:

	A	B
Paul Reynaud		
Approval	36% (yes)	33% (no)
Disapproval	36% (no)	40% (yes)
No opinion	28%	27%
Edouard Daladier		
Approval	35% (yes)	34% (no)
Disapproval	37% (no)	40% (yes)
No opinion	28%	26%

2. *The fear of change.* Tests made in the United States tend to show that respect for existing institutions, particularly laws, tend to influence responses: supporters of certain measures are less numerous and their opponents more numerous if the framing of the questions makes it appear that these measures necessitate changes in existing legislation. It is difficult to say whether this conformism is general or restricted to the United States. *A priori* one tends to think that the phenomenon does not exist in France where the (verbal) desire for legislative reform is great: but the various tests done tend towards the opposite conclusion.

Two examples of legal conformism in the United States can be given. In September 1939 the same question on aid to France and Britain was asked in two different forms: '(A) Do you think that Congress should modify the law of neutrality so that France and Britain could buy war materials?—(B) Do you think that France and Britain ought to be able to buy war materials in our country?' These were the answers:

	A	B
Yes	53%	61%
No	33%	31%
No opinion	14%	8%

In November 1939 a similar test was made concerning Roosevelt's third term. The two forms of the same question were '(A) Are you in favour of a strict interpretation of the Constitution in order to prevent the President of the United States seeking a third term of office?—(B) Do you favour a constitutional amendment to prevent the President seeking a third term of office?' These were the replies:

	A	B
Yes	36%	26%
No	50%	65%
No opinion	14%	9%

(b) THE FEAR OF WORDS AND THE INFLUENCE OF STEREOTYPES

The supporters of a measure become less numerous if a stereotyped word appears in the question against which there is a natural bias (war for example). This is a particular variety of the tendency towards conformism.

In September 1939 the question of military aid to Canada from the United States if the former was invaded by an European enemy was asked in the two following ways: '(A) If Canada was invaded now by a European enemy do you think that the United States should use its army and navy to help her?—(B) If Canada was invaded now by a European power do you think that the United States should go to war to defend her?' These were the replies:

	A	B
Yes	71%	64%
No	23%	29%
No opinion	6%	7%

In April 1938 a similar question about military preparedness by the United States gave similar results. Form A was: 'Should military training form part of the studies of those who take part in CCC camps?' Form B was: 'Do you think that part of the duties of those who take part in CCC camps is to be trained for war?'

	A	B
Yes	70%	50%
No	23%	35%
No opinion	7%	6%

The most typical—and the most extraordinary—example of this fear of words is the question asked in the last week of October 1941 in the United States. In the form 'Should the United States enter the war now?' 24 per cent of the subjects asked replied 'yes'.

DIRECT EXTENSIVE OBSERVATION

In the form 'Should the United States declare war on Germany now?' only 17 per cent made the same reply. An official declaration of war on Germany seemed more dangerous and more irrevocable. Such results justify (unfortunately) rulers who seek to avoid formulas which frighten and hide realities under reassuring words.

(c) INFLUENCE OF PERSONALITIES

Reference to a person in the wording of a question has an inevitable influence on replies in either an approving or disapproving direction. Prestige can be either positive or negative.

1. *Positive prestige.* Reference to a personality can increase the number of supporters or diminish the number of opponents of an opinion. This was illustrated by including the name Roosevelt in surveys made in the United States in 1941.

A question about aid to Britain was asked in the two following forms: '(A) In so far as it concerns you personally, do you think President Roosevelt has gone too far or not far enough in his policy of aiding Britain?—(B) In so far as it concerns you personally, do you think that the United States has gone too far or not far enough in its policy of aiding Britain?' The answers showed a 'polarization' around Roosevelt, approving his action:

	A	B
Too far	20%	15%
Far enough	57%	46%
Not far enough	17%	32%
No opinion	6%	7%

Another question asked in September 1941 gave even more interesting results. Form A was: 'It has been said recently that to keep the Germans away from North and South America we should prevent them capturing the islands off the West coast of Africa. Do you think that we should prevent the Germans reaching these islands?' Form B commenced: 'President Roosevelt has said recently . . .' and the remainder was the same. The result was as follows:

	A	B
Yes	50%	56%
No	21%	24%
No opinion	29%	20%

It should be noted that it was the decrease in the 'no opinion' categories which made the second result different—the number of opposers increased as well as the number of supporters. It thus seems that people who do not have a definite position on a problem will adopt a position according to their sympathy or antipathy towards a person.

2. *Negative prestige.* The growth of opposition in the preceding example is an illustration of negative prestige. Several very clear examples of this can be quoted.

In September 1940 a question about isolationism was posed in the United States in the two following forms:

'(A) Lindbergh says that if the Germans win the war the United States should try to have amicable commercial and diplomatic relations with Germany. Are you in agreement with this opinion or not?—(B) It is said that if the Germans ... (the rest unchanged)'. These were the replies:

	A	B
Agreement	46%	57%
Disagreement	41%	25%
No opinion	13%	18%

Thus numerous isolationists who basically agreed with Lindbergh adopted a contrary position when their views were expressed by Lindbergh. This is doubtless explained by allied propaganda violently denouncing Lindbergh's pro-German stand. Facts of this kind tend to show that campaigns directed against the reputation of political figures are profitable in that those who share his ideas no longer care to draw attention to the fact.

(*d*) INFLUENCE OF SYMPATHY OR ANTIPATHY
Numerous tests have shown that the answers to questions can be influenced by introducing into the question emotive words which provoke sympathy or antipathy in the subjects.

A typical example is that in an American survey of March 1940. The question was asked in the two following forms: '(A) Do you think that the United States should do more than it is doing to help Britain and France?—(B) Do you think that the United States should do more than it is doing at the moment to help Britain and France in their struggle against Hitler?' The replies were as follows:

	A	B
Should not do more	22%	13%
Should do more	66%	75%
No opinion	12%	12%

The part played by antipathy towards Hitler is obvious.

DIRECT EXTENSIVE OBSERVATION

Another example can be given to show the tendency to say 'yes' being suppressed and even reversed by replacing 'allow' by 'forbid', coupled with the word democracy: the natural sympathy with liberty (associated with the word 'allow') and natural antipathy towards limitations of it (expressed by the word 'forbid') influences replies. The different forms were as follows: '(A) Do you think that the United States should allow public speeches against democracy?—(B) Do you think that the United States should forbid public speeches against democracy?' The replies were:

	A	B
Allow	21% (yes)	39% (no)
Forbid	62% (no)	46% (yes)
No opinion	17%	15%

A question asked in France in 1946 during the period of authoritarian rationing policy showed that the word 'government' caused hostility and influenced the replies. The two forms were: '(A) Do you think that the provisions situation would be better or worse if the government decided today to allow the free sale of all food commodities?—(B) Do you think that the provisions situation would be better or worse if there were free sale of all food commodities?' The replies were:

	A	B
Better	62%	60%
The same	17%	13%
Worse	13%	16%
No opinion	8%	11%

D. Corrective tests

Various procedures are used to eliminate distortions resulting from bad formulation of questions. It is important to distinguish between the two qualities of a good questionnaire—reliability which is easy to control and validity, which is not.

(a) TESTS OF RELIABILITY

A questionnaire is reliable if when it is applied to the same subjects at different times by the same investigators it gives the same results (assuming that the subjects have not changed their views). Beside reliability relating to the subjects (which is of the first importance) there is also reliability of investigators in questionnaires with indirect responses (see p. 162)—a questionnaire is reliable if it is presented to the same subjects at different times by different investigators and the same results are obtained (reliability in relation to the subjects having previously been tested).

1. *Reliability in relation to the subjects.* The verifying test consists of the same investigators asking the same subjects the same questions at different times. This is currently used in many procedures of observation of social reality and is not confined to opinion polls. Moreover, for the latter difficulties are encountered. If the questionnaire is used after short intervals of time the subjects remember the questions and their second replies can be influenced by this. If there is a long interval between applications of the questionnaire the subjects may have changed their opinions. About two months is thought to be a suitable interval.

The procedure is more often used to verify the reliability of tests rather than opinion questionnaire because the same difficulties are not encountered. Reliability can be accurately measured by calculating the correlation between the two sets of replies which gives a coefficient of reliability.

2. *Reliability of investigators.* In this case the test takes the form of different investigators asking the same questions of the same subjects at different times. It is useful to combine this test with the preceding one, applying one to a section of the subjects, the other to the remainder. By comparing the two, inaccuracies relating to investigators and to the subjects can be isolated.

(*b*) TESTS OF VALIDITY

A questionnaire is valid if the results reflect social reality. A questionnaire can be reliable but not valid if the questions are interpreted wrongly but coherently and consistently by the subjects. An analogy already used in the discussion of content analysis, can be made by imagining the measurement of the height of conscripts with an inaccurate measure (the centimetres marked being in fact 0.9 cms.); repetition of the measurement would always give the same result but it would always be false: the measuring instrument would be reliable but not valid.

1. *Preliminary tests.* The first procedure of verifying the validity is a preliminary test. The questionnaire is given to a small sample of subjects by very experienced investigators who note the reactions to the questions and who hold conversations with the subjects in order to find out about their behaviour in other ways. They can thus determine the tendentious and the valid forms of the questions.

Direct Extensive Observation

This is an empirical test. There is no true criterion to measure precisely the tendentious and the non-tendentious questions. In practice, however, this empirical test gives quite satisfactory results.

2. *Sub-divided inquiries.* An apparently more rigorous procedure is the preparation of several questionnaires in different forms. These are applied separately to different sections of the sample. The average of the results is then taken.

In fact this method is open to much criticism. It is not at all certain that the average of the several errors represents the truth. Also the small size of each sub-division of the sample produces supplementary distorting effects.

2. ADMINISTRATION OF THE QUESTIONNAIRE

After the questionnaire has been constructed the investigation commences. It can have two main forms. The subject either makes written replies or answers questions verbally put to him by an investigator.

A. Written replies

Questionnaires requiring written replies have two main disadvantages Firstly, the subject can read all the answers before starting to answer them and his replies may be influenced by one another. Secondly, if the subject does not understand a question there can be no supplementary explanation; the proportion of non-responses, therefore, tends to be higher than in oral questionnaires.

There are two main categories of questionnaires requiring written replies: postal questionnaires and those which require group replies.

(a) POSTAL QUESTIONNAIRES

The questionnaires are sent and returned by post. Modification of this procedure—the questionnaire being delivered personally by an investigator who would explain the significance and purpose of the inquiry—produces a higher proportion of replies. If the questionnaire is also collected by the investigator this produces even better results but it becomes almost as expensive as oral questionnaires and the main advantage of postal questionnaires (cheapness) disappears.

1. *Disadvantages of the procedure.* As well as the two main disadvantages already mentioned there are others which are peculiar to it. It demands a personal effort on the part of the subject to return the questionnaire. Experience shows that many do not do it.

Various ways have been tried to circumvent this difficulty: stamped addressed envelopes for the reply have been sent later with requests for return of the questionnaire; the telephone has been used —this is possible only for brief questionnaires concerned with facts rather than opinions. Questionnaires are also sent to other people in the same categories as the non-respondents but general difficulties concerning the sample are raised by non-response which will be again encountered later on. It cannot be known whether the non-respondents constitute a heterogeneous group in the relevant social categories and whether replacing them by others can introduce a distorting element into the sample.

Another difficulty is the different conditions under which subjects complete the questionnaires. Some do this straight away, others delay and think about the questions or talk them over with their families or friends. The distortions are not important for questions of fact or for basic and clear-cut opinions but with more difficult questions considerable distortion can result.

2. *Use of the procedure.* It is only used in a limited number of cases—primarily for inquiries concerning facts rather than opinions. For example, experience has shown that investigations of business concerns can easily be conducted by post because firms have highly organized administrative services which cuts down the number of non-responses. In the United States surveys of business leaders are often made by telephone.

Another type of postal poll has been tried in France for investigations of social élites, concerning people in certain categories with particular levels of education, culture and so on. Individuals in these categories write more easily, are more used to analysing things and understand the significance of the inquiry more easily than the average man; the number of non-responses is consequently less. A first and not very satisfactory attempt was made at this kind of survey in France in 1955 under the direction of Daniel Lerner concerning reactions to the European idea. A much larger and better organized investigation of the 'ecology of famous men' is being made under the direction of the National Institute of Demographic Studies. The questionnaires are composed essentially of questions of fact about family, education, various activities and so on.

(*b*) QUESTIONNAIRES WHICH REQUIRE GROUP REPLIES

These have fewer disadvantages than postal questionnaires but they can only be used for limited categories of subjects.

DIRECT EXTENSIVE OBSERVATION

1. *The technique.* It is necessary that all the subjects can be collected together in one place. The questionnaire is distributed, the subjects asked to answer the questions immediately and the completed questionnaires then collected. Or, alternatively, people can be approached at the entrance and exit to a library, a course of lectures, a meeting, an entertainment, a factory, a workshop and so on. Another procedure is that subjects are gathered in one place, the investigator explains the significance of the inquiry, distributes sheets on which there are numbers and not questions, reads out the questions and asks that answers be written down straight away.

The advantages of this procedure are obvious. Firstly, all the replies are made in identical conditions. Secondly, contamination of questions is reduced and even disappears completely if there are no questions on the answer sheets. Thirdly, the number of non-responses is greatly reduced especially with the second procedure where the subjects have been specially collected for the purpose. The great danger is 'copying': a subject who is not sure how to reply to a question may look over his neighbour's shoulder and make the same reply. The risk of this can easily be reduced.

2. *Use of these questionnaires.* The only drawback of this procedure is that its use is limited to situations in which it is possible to gather the subjects together in one place. This is possible only in a few cases such as investigations in universities: students are ideal 'material' for investigation because it is easy to hand out questionnaires during a course, at the entrance or exit of libraries and so on. This is very popular in the United States and is beginning to spread in France. Surveys of the employees of firms are more difficult. The management is not always well disposed and when it is, the employees are often suspicious and do not reply frankly (this varies according to the country and to the intensity of class consciousness).

Group investigations can also be made of audiences of a theatre or cinema or meeting, the congregation at a religious service, etc. Some investigations of the effects of advertising films have been made by inviting an audience to a free film show after which a request is made to fill in a questionnaire. Studies in religious sociology which have been extensive in France since 1945 have used questionnaires handed out at the entrance of the church, briefly explained from the pulpit and collected at the exit.

Until now the largest group questionnaires are those contained in the *American Soldier*. Starting in 1941 the 'Research Branch of the Information and Education Division of the War Department' undertook a series of sociological studies in depth of American soldiers. This important study was a significant step forward in the social sciences. It appeared in four volumes in 1949–50 and contained 3,000 pages of reports of four years of inquiry. Questionnaires were widely used: more than 20,000 questions were asked of eight million soldiers. The questionnaires were given to groups of soldiers collected in a particular place; a soldier investigator explained the significance of the inquiry and guaranteed absolute anonymity.

B. Oral questionnaires

With this type of questionnaire the subjects are asked questions individually by a specialist investigator and the investigator writes down the replies. The actual questionnaire is never in the hands of the subject.

Training investigators presents a series of difficult problems. They have to help the subjects to 'relax', explain the questions to them and accurately record the replies: they should not exert any influence over the subjects by direct suggestion, by their appearance or by their general behaviour, etc. Despite all precautions, distortions are inevitable: the lack of secrecy in replying, the personal appearance, the opinions and views of the investigator all have effects which can be measured but which are difficult to eliminate completely.

(a) ANONYMITY

The questionnaires bear no trace of the name and address of the subject and they are to this extent anonymous. But the responses are made orally in the presence of the investigator who knows their content and at the same time knows the subject. This produces phenomena connected with prestige and with distrust.

1. *Prestige.* All men seek in social relationships to increase their own prestige in comparison with those with whom they come into contact. Subjects questioned tend to present themselves in an advantageous light *vis-à-vis* the investigator and thus distort their replies. Several examples can be given.

When subjects are asked about educational background they tend to exaggerate their educational level. If they are asked how much they give in subscriptions and gifts to charities, they tend to exaggerate the amount. In the United States an inquiry was made in 1944 on people of whom it was known had cashed their war bonds. 17 per cent replied that they had not cashed them and the proportion of lies was even greater for subjects higher in the socio-economic scale.

Another experiment made in the United States during the war is even more interesting. The same questions were asked of two identical samples in the first by investigators, in the second on confidential forms. In the replies to questions I and II (see fig. 5), it is obvious that some subjects sought to give the impression to the investigators that they did not hold opinions generally not regarded as not respectable: in the replies to question III which were put to subjects of a lower socio-economic level (and therefore unsuccessful people), many subjects sought to create the impression that misfortune and not incompetence explained their failure. Choosing investigators of the same level and social class as the subjects has been suggested as a way of reducing the effect of this phenomenon, but this does not eliminate it entirely.

Questions	Replies	Investigators	Confidential forms (in percentages)
I. Do you think that the English will try to make us do as much of their fighting as possible?	Yes	25	42
	No	57	42
	No opinion	18	16
II. Do you think that the Jews have too much power and influence in the United States?	Yes	56	66
	No	27	17
	No opinion	17	17
III. Do you think that success depends on luck, talent or influence?	Luck	14	9
	Talent	64	76
	Influence	8	7
	No opinion	14	9

Fig. 5.—Verbal replies and replies on confidential forms

2. *Distrust*. Subjects fear that the anonymity of the answers will not be respected absolutely and investigators will tell other people the opinion expressed. Consequently, subversive opinions tend to be disguised and respectable opinions emphasized even if they are not what the subject really thinks.

In post-war Germany, which had suffered successively nazi persecution and purges of the armies of occupation, distrust of opinion polls was such that the number of non-responses was very high. It has been noticed in France in the past few years that the difference between the results of opinion polls and votes actually cast in elections has often been greater for the Communist Party than for the other parties; replies in the polls tend to underestimate the size of communist opinion. The fact that it is regarded as subversive and that avowal has a certain risk (the sack, etc.) results in dissimulation.

An American investigation has shown that the correlation between the real cases of absenteeism and the answers made to investigators is only .60.

(b) PERSONAL APPEARANCE OF THE INVESTIGATOR

The phenomena relating to prestige and distrust, as has been said, can be diminished if investigators belong to the same social class as the subjects. However, generally speaking, the personal appearance of the investigator has an effect over and above these phenomena. Several examples can be quoted from American investigations which provide evidence of the effects of social appearance, colour of the skin and general racial appearance.

1. *Social appearance of the investigator.* An investigation made in 1941 in the United States on the opinions of trade unionists about the law forbidding strikes gave very different results according to whether the investigators belonged to the working class or the lower middle class.

	Lower middle class investigators	*Working class investigators*
For	59%	44%
Against	29%	39%
No opinion	12%	17%

To some extent these results illustrate the fact already mentioned that distrust is diminished if investigators are chosen from the same social milieu. But there are probably other factors: a worker confronted by another worker may tend to harden his class position. There are various kinds of prestige.

2. *Colour problems in the United States.* These produce important distorting effects. An inquiry was made in 1942 on negro sugjects in the South. The results differed according to the colour of the investigator. Differences were present whether or not the question was about a racial matter.

To the question 'Would the negroes be better or worse treated if the Japanese conquered the United States?' the following replies were made:

	Negro investigator	*White investigator*
Better	9%	2%
The same	32%	20%
Worse	25%	45%
No opinion	34%	33%

DIRECT EXTENSIVE OBSERVATION

To the question 'Do you think that it is more important to devote all our efforts to defeating the Axis or to get democratic reforms passed at home?' the following replies were made:

	Negro investigator	White investigator
Defeat the Axis	39%	62%
Democratic reforms	35%	26%
No opinion	26%	12%

The results of this test are very important in estimating the degree of real integration of the negroes into the American community. It is pointless to hope for objective replies in these cases: distortions of one kind or another will always be present according to the appearance of the investigator. Comparison between distortions provides valuable information about the basic opinions of the subjects.

3. *Problems of anti-semitism.* The influence of the appearance of the investigator was illustrated by the tests made by Robinson and Rodhe in the United States in 1941. Two questions were put to identical samples of the population: 'I. Do you think that there are too many Jews in public offices and jobs? — II. Do you think that the Jews have too much power in the United States?' The subjects were divided into four identical groups, each being questioned by different investigators: the first with Jewish appearance, the second with non-Jewish appearance, the third with Jewish appearance and a Jewish name, and the fourth with Jewish appearance but with a non-Jewish name. These were the responses:

Investigators	Question I 'Yes'	Question II 'Yes'
Jewish appearance	15.4%	15.6%
Non-Jewish appearance	21.2%	24.6%
Jewish appearance and name	11.7%	5.8%
Jewish appearance but non-Jewish name	19.5%	21.4%

(*c*) EFFECTS OF THE OPINIONS OF THE INVESTIGATOR

The role of the investigator is not purely mechanical and is not limited to reading questions and recording replies. The investigator must help the subject to understand the question, overcome his distrust and interpret his reply. In these operations the investigator can be influenced by his own opinions and can also influence the subject.

1. *Measuring the distortion.* An American inquiry of October 1940

gives valuable information on this subject. Two examples only will be quoted.

The investigators were divided into two groups, one composed of isolationists, the other of interventionists (supporters of aid to Britain at war with Hitler) and each questioned an identical sample of the population, asking the same question: 'Which attitude do you think that the United States should adopt: keep out of the conflict or help Britain?' These were the responses (after the non-responses had been eliminated):

	Isolationist investigators (in percentages)	Interventionist investigators (in percentages)
Help the British	44	60
Keep out of the conflict	56	40

The results are striking as the proportions were almost reversed. A more complex analysis was made of the replies to the same question, distinguishing between four groups of investigators, firstly according to isolationism and secondly according to their preference for Wilkie or Roosevelt in the presidential elections. The results for the subjects having a preference for Roosevelt or Wilkie were also calculated separately. These were the results:

Percentage of replies
'It is better to keep out of the conflict.'

Investigators' preference	Subjects' preference	Isolationist investigators	Interventionists investigators	Difference
Roosevelt	Roosevelt	51.1	30.9	20.2
Wilkie	Wilkie	64	43.4	20.6
Roosevelt	Wilkie	56.2	49.6	6.6
Wilkie	Roosevelt	47.8	37.7	10.1

2. *Methods of correction.* Several methods have been suggested to prevent these distortions. There have been attempts to assemble teams of investigators with different views so that the distorting effects would cancel one another out: but this has little real chance of success. Teams of investigators can also be recruited who are neutral politically—but this neutrality is often illusory. A neutral investigator on one question can have partisan views on another.

The best method is the careful training of investigators putting them on their guard against these distorting effects. The results obtained can be very good, especially when compared with other methods. Experienced investigators can achieve a very satisfactory level of objectivity.

DIRECT EXTENSIVE OBSERVATION

On opinion polls: HADLEY CANTRIL, *Gauging Public Opinion*, 3rd ed., Princeton, 1947; F. F. STEPHAN and P. J. MACARTHY, *Sampling Opinion: an analysis of survey procedure*, New York, 1958; M. H. HANSEN, W. N. HURWITZ, G. W. MADOW, *Sample, Survey Methods and Theory*, 2 vols., New York, 1953; M. B. PARTEN, *Surveys, Polls and Samples*, New York, 1950.

On the design of questionnaires: S. L. PAYNE, *The Art of Asking Questions*, Princeton, 1951; R. L. KAHN, *A Comparison of Two Methods of collecting data for Social Research*, Ann Arbor, 1952.

On the general theory of opinions: R. K. MERTON, *Social Theory and Social Structure*, Glencoe, 1958; N. POWELL, *Anatomy of Public Opinion*, New York, 1951; M. B. SMITH, J. S. BRUNER, R. WHITE, *Opinions and Personality*, New York, 1955; W. ALBIG, *Modern Public Opinion*, New York, 1956.

Section III. The results of investigations

Firstly, the technical problems have to be considered: the results have to be processed, interpreted and their validity assessed. Secondly, sociological and ethical problems have then to be taken into consideration: what will be the consequences of publication of the results? What rules should be applied to publication? The second category of problems will only be examined briefly because they tend to fall outside the scope of a methodological study.

1. PROCESSING THE RESULTS

This comprises a series of technical operations so that categories of replies can be expressed in percentages. The percentages have themselves to be interpreted. Errors are frequently committed because more is demanded of a survey than it can give.

A. Technical operations

These fall into two separate categories. The first is coding which is as delicate an operation as designing the questionnaire. The second is routine arithmetical or mechanical operations.

(a) CODING
This consists of assigning each category of responses a number which will determine the place of the perforation on the punch card.

1. *Constructing the code.* The operation presents no difficulty for closed questions when it is easy to distinguish between the replies (yes, no; complete approval, qualified approval, neither approval nor

disapproval, qualified disapproval, complete disapproval; etc.). It is also very easy for questions of fact (sex, age, residence, party, religion, etc.). On the other hand, it is very difficult for open questions with completely free replies and no 'sample' of replies: these questions are, however, most important for investigations in depth.

A code is constructed in several stages. A preliminary code is established based on possible types of replies. This is applied to a sample of interviews so that the categories of the preliminary code can be corrected experimentally. The final code is established in this way and is usually verified by a 'coding-test' (a sample of interviews are coded separately by different people to test the reliability of the code) before it is finally used.

The code is not constructed after the investigation but is usually commenced at the same time as the questionnaire. Questions are to some extent prepared with the coding in mind. In serious investigations a 'pilot-survey' is carried out on a small sample and the results of this are coded. The final questionnaire is drawn up using this coding.

2. *The coding operation.* This consists of entering each reply in one of the categories defined by the code. This is the job of specialist coders. Next to each reply the coder writes a code number.

However precise the code is, coding always contains an element of interpretation by the coder and distortions are always possible. The opinions of a coder can influence him to interpret in one way rather than another without him being aware of it. Attempts are made to eliminate these distortions by a careful technical training. These are easier to detect than the distortions in the inquiry itself because the information collected in interviews can be subjected to many tests. By having the same interviews coded by different people (after tests of reliability have been conducted by experienced coders) personal distortions can be measured.

(b) MECHANICAL AND ARITHMETICAL OPERATIONS

These are used to process the results once the coding is completed. Various mechanical means make the processing simpler and quicker.

1. *Punch cards.* The results of each interview are recorded on punched cards. Standard punched cards usually have eighty vertical columns each comprising ten figures so that a great number of replies can be recorded on each card. If each question has ten possible replies then the replies of eighty questions can be recorded. Most questions have only two or three possible answers and, therefore, two questions can

Direct Extensive Observation

be recorded on a single column (this creates some additional sorting difficulties).

Special machines which are similar to typewriters punch the cards. Reproductions can be made so that other research institutions can use the results. The process of checking the cards against the original coding is also mechanized.

2. *Sorting.* The punched cards are placed in a sorting machine which counts each category of answers or, alternatively, the categories of subjects who make the same reply to the same question.

The principle of the sorting machine is very simple. A 'reading brush' is placed before the column corresponding to a particular question and all the cards are passed in front of it. When the column is punched there is an electric contact which causes the card to fall into a receptacle and the total number of cards falling into each receptacle appears on an instrument. Further sorting within each group of cards produces figures for each reply.

3. *Calculation of percentages.* The counting instruments of the sorting machines only give totals and not percentages. These can be quickly worked out on calculating machines and slide rules. As the figures of opinion polls are never absolutely accurate it is not worth calculating decimal parts of percentages. This can even be regarded as harmful because this introduces an illusion of precision into the results.

B. Value of the results

There are two principal problems. How accurate are the results? How can they be interpreted?

(a) DEGREE OF ACCURACY

Preceding analyses have shown that imprecision in the results can be the consequence of two kinds of distortion: distortions resulting from chance which can be measured; non-random distortions which cannot be measured.

1. *Chance distortions.* These result from possible incongruity between the sample and the population from which it is drawn. Probabilist methods and random sampling make it possible to measure these distortions (or, more exactly, the probability that these distortions will not pass certain limits). It should be clearly understood what is meant when it is stated that the margin of error is not greater than 5 per cent more or less. In the first place, the 5 per cent applies to all

results. If it is stated that 20 per cent of a population are opposed to the banning of atomic tests, this means not less than 15 per cent and not more than 25 per cent are opposed. The margin of error in this case is 5 in 20 (or 25 per cent). In the second place, these are not absolute margins: they represent certain thresholds of probability. For example, with a probability threshold of 95 per cent using the previous example, one can say that there is no more than a 5 per cent chance that the opponents of atomic tests are less than 15 per cent and more than 25 per cent. It is always possible that the sample belongs to this 5 per cent and thus the whole poll is false.

2. *Distortions resulting from psycho-social phenomena.* It is impossible to eliminate all the psycho-social distortions previously described and there is always a danger of a cumulative effect: the opinions of the investigator aggravating the effects of prestige or distrust relating to the subject, the opinions of the coder superimposing themselves on the investigator and so on. Results of polls are therefore only approximate. This must never be forgotten and one should not demand of the method more than it can give.

This does not justify the suspicion held by some people of these methods of extensive observation. They alone make possible the exploration of certain areas of social reality which would otherwise be completely inaccessible: approximate information is better than none at all and surveys are worth more than the gratuitous suppositions or empirical views sometimes used to cover up ignorance. Results of opinion polls give sufficiently accurate indications of the main tendencies of opinion and their distribution. Even distortions and errors have borne fruit. American inquiries into the distortions produced by prestige, distrust, personal appearance and opinions of investigators have thrown light on certain social and political phenomena. It does not matter much that the extent of error cannot be measured and that the true opinion with no distortions cannot be exactly known; comparison of the various distortions is a worthwhile analytical tool.

(*b*) DIFFICULTIES OF INTERPRETATION

Interpretation of the results of a poll is always difficult and prediction based on these results always hazardous. The problem of non-response represents a supplementary difficulty.

1. *The problem of non-response.* If refusal to reply (or 'no opinion' replies) were distributed in the same way as the replies, it could be ignored and the percentages of replies be calculated without taking

non-response into account. In election analyses the percentages are often calculated on the basis of the votes cast, ignoring the abstentions. But the non-responses introduce an element of error into the survey method by seriously modifying the composition of the sample and falsifying the calculation of the probability of errors. Certain procedures to diminish this have already been described.

Comparative analysis of groups of 'abstainers' and respondents has shown that their composition is not the same. Usually a higher proportion of women than men and, in some countries, of old people do not reply to political questions. There are no means of testing whether the groups of men or women who do not reply have the same composition as those who do: if the two groups are heterogeneous it is possible that small differences between the replies given by men and women result from a disproportion of non-responses and not from a real difference in distribution of opinion.

2. *The problem of prediction.* The public success which opinion polls have had partly results from the predictions based on them. The first polls were made in the United States and attempted to predict the results of elections (the first, on a presidential election, was published on July 24, 1824, by the *Harrisburg Pensylvanian*; it was very simple and unscientific). Large newspapers have for sometime past ordered polls from institutes of public opinion in the weeks before general elections and published the results. There were many successful predictions before the startling failure for the American presidential election of 1948, when all the institutes of public opinion predicted victory for Dewey.

This failure made a deep impression on public opinion and it is always recalled to dispute the findings of polls. Too much importance should not be attached to it because important research was done on the polls of 1948 to uncover the sources of error, improvements in methods have resulted from this research. It was, for example, noticed that in previous polls the proportion of Republican votes had always been overestimated. This appeared to arise from the fact that the socio-economic level of the subjects questioned was higher than the national average. It was also shown that the non-responses had not been taken seriously. Above all, it was apparent that not enough notice had been taken of the trend in opinion which had been shown in previous polls and which continued between the date of the last poll and the election itself.

In any case the problem of prediction is secondary. It is of small importance that survey methods only permit tentative predictions. The successes of the method have, however, been more numerous than the failures. For the political scientist the important thing is that the results of the survey and of the elections should be sufficiently close for polls to be considered as good analytical instruments.

2. PUBLICATION OF THE RESULTS

Publication of opinion polls can have direct effects on public opinion and on those who govern. Not only do they reveal an existing situation, but to a certain extent they also tend to change it. This presents ethical and legal problems. To what extent ought the results of public opinion polls be published? What rules should govern their publication?

A. Practical effects

To a certain extent, to know oneself is to change oneself. Psychological treatment of mental illness is based on this idea—an essential stage in the curing process is to make the sufferer aware of the subconscious phenomena which are the source of the illness. There is an analogy in the social context: selfconscious public opinion is not the same as unselfconscious public opinion—it reacts to the image it has of itself.

Not enough work has been done on this aspect of opinion polls, so only a few brief remarks can be made on the possible effects on the public and the governors in democratic régimes.

(a) THE MAJORITY EFFECT

It is usually admitted that the publication of the results of an opinion poll tends to strengthen majority and weaken minority opinions. The scope of this effect, however, seems to be limited.

1. *The majority effect in practice.* The majority effect is a particular case of the 'Panurgic complex' already mentioned which in turn is part of a general tendency in human societies towards conformity.

The independently minded who wish to differentiate themselves from the mass are a small proportion of the total population. Most people aspire to be like others and submerge themselves in the group. Fear of sanctions plays an important part but it is not the only factor: the tendency to 'shout with the crowd' is very strong. It is strengthened by the search for communion, the desire to escape loneliness and be surrounded by gregarious warmth. Democratic doctrines which make majority opinion the arbiter of the truth tend to encourage this, but the diametrically opposed doctrines such as totalitarian fascism are even stronger supporters of conformism.

2. *Limits to the effect.* It only operates if there is a clear majority. If a poll reveals a narrow majority it is very likely that the minority draws strength and encouragement from this. But if the distribution is of the order 70–30 per cent the majority effect undoubtedly comes into play.

The effect probably varies according to the country. The United States is an example of a country where the tendency to conformism seems strong, France a country where it seems less strong, but the differences are smaller than is often supposed. It is also probable that there are differences between social categories.

Publication of forecasts of election results has shown that the effect does not always operate. It often happens that minority opinion steadily increases and majority opinion decreases. A Gallup Poll of 1938 provides an example. The following were the changes in opinion about two candidates for the Senate in Kentucky between April and August 1938:

Date of publication of the polls	Chandler (in percentages)	Barkley (in percentages)
April 10th	33	67
May 15th	35	65
July 8th	36	64
July 24th	39	61
August 5th	41	59
Results of election August 6th	43	57

This evolution, the opposite of the majority effect, can be explained by the effect of the election campaign or general political factors.

(*b*) EFFECTS ON GOVERNMENT

Polls have considerable significance in democratic systems because they can in the last resort result in a kind of direct democracy which can paralyse government.

1. *Direct democracy.* Polls create the possibility of a new type of direct democracy. A representative random sample can be constructed using all possible precautions and investigators can question the subjects in the sample about measures proposed by the government: if there is a majority in favour they could then have the force of law.

It is interesting to recall that the ancient democracies widely used the procedure of drawing lots to elect political assemblies. This was regarded both as the judgment of the gods and in accordance with egalitarian principle. Mathematical theory alters the ideological basis, but in practice reaches analogous conclusions.

The idea of an assembly composed by a scientific sample is a prophesy, a kind of science-fiction fantasy. No one has yet suggested attaching legal consequences to the results of a poll. However, polls influence parliaments and, significantly, parliamentarians regard the development of political opinion polls unfavourably. In the United States where they are common many protests about them have been made in the Senate and the House of Representatives. Parliaments, the organs of representative democracy, are aware that these techniques threaten their prerogatives.

2. *The risk of governmental conformism.* An inquiry conducted in the United States in 1940 by H. L. Childs showed that 70 per cent of the politicians in Washington thought that their decisions and those of their colleagues were influenced by public opinion polls. This influence is usually thought to be in the direction of conformity with public opinion. A democratic government has a natural tendency to follow public opinion and has indeed been described as government by opinion. The more important opinion polls become the greater will be the tendency for governments to align themselves with the results.

This is a danger because the duty of a government is not to follow all expressions of public opinion, however short-sighted, but to provide the means by which the public can really understand the problems and thus act in an appropriate manner to solve them. Polls reveal unbelievable ignorance of the facts, uncertainty about the main problems and bias induced by the mass circulation press. In a politico-economic system where the formation of public opinion is anarchic and where it is influenced by a press which is in private hands, following public opinion is not in accord with the basic aims of democracy which are to give men the means of emancipating themselves and thus of governing themselves. The tendency of representative authorities to follow the results of polls could end in demagogy and not democracy.

But one should not be too pessimistic. The polls provide governments with evidence of the state of opinion and something can therefore be done about the ignorance revealed. Even though the polls have defects, defective information is better than none at all. Opinion polls are not in themselves dangerous but the propaganda which can be made out of the results is.

B. Rules for publication

This problem has two different aspects. It can be asked whether or not the results should be published at all. It can also be asked whether publication should be accompanied by guarantees to prevent sub-

Direct Extensive Observation

sequent distortion. There are no legal rules at the moment so one has to suggest the principles on which desirable rules could be based.

(*a*) THE PRINCIPLE OF PUBLICATION
This is a different problem for governments, for private and for foreign organizations.

1. *Publication of governmental inquiries.* It is normal and desirable that the government should inform itself of the state of public opinion (this is one of the primary duties of a democratic government) by conducting polls.

A government seems justified in not publishing these polls. The dangers of public conformism and the government following majority opinion have just been pointed out. A government should seek to avoid these things.

A government is faced with the alternative of not publishing the results of its polls or conducting polls on minor matters only or not conducting them at all. No government wants to make sticks with which it can be beaten by publishing results of polls on grave and controversial matters. As it is preferable that the government is informed, unpublished opinion polls must be regarded as legitimate. In the interests of science the results should be placed in the archives and opened to the public after some delay.

2. *Publication by private organizations.* Many polls are conducted by private organizations such as industrial and commercial firms, newspapers and periodicals, etc. If the investigation concerns purely commercial or industrial matters or matters related to the firm or institution which conducts the poll (such as market analyses) it is usual that results remain the private property of the firm or institution which can keep them secret.

This conclusion is not valid when the investigation concerns political, intellectual, religious, etc., attitudes and opinion. To apply the rules of free competition and private property to these fields would give a monopoly in practice to the richest firms and organizations—a monopoly of particularly valuable information since it can be used to influence public opinion. According to democratic principles anybody should be free to pursue any inquiry on the condition that the results are published without delay.

3. *Publication by foreign organizations.* Some institutions occasionally make investigations in another country. For example, American institutions often conduct investigations in European countries.

The investigations can provide useful information for the purpose of influencing public opinion; foreign institutions can put the information at the disposal of their governments. This can take the form of a kind of sociological espionage: it is therefore proper to forbid investigation of this kind. It is not practical to authorize only university or scientific institutions because in some countries it is often difficult to distinguish these from government. The best solution is simply to insist on the immediate publication of the results: the espionage aspect then disappears.

(b) FORM OF PUBLICATION

The form of publication is important. The publication of badly done investigations and garbled and distorted results is dangerous.

1. *Publication of badly done investigations.* Given the influence of publication of polls on opinion, badly executed investigations which probably have inaccurate results present serious dangers. It has been suggested in the United States that a kind of label of quality or regulations against fraud should be established to guarantee the quality of the polls. These would be difficult to operate in practice.

The public should be educated. Opinion polls require a complex organization, specialist personnel and long experience; in practice only a few institutions in each country are capable of conducting valid polls and it should not be difficult to know which these are. The public should also be taught about the relativity of the results, of the difficulty of eliminating all distorting factors and so on so that the usual errors of interpretation will not be committed.

2. *Tendentious or garbled publication.* This is a difficult problem in the present state of the law. Institutes of public opinion usually attach some conditions about publication of results by the organizations which pay for them. It is usually stipulated, for example, that the result of election polls are published without explanation and in their entirety in order to avoid tendentious presentation.

An odd incident in France in November 1953 showed this precondition to be insufficient. A monthly ordered a poll from IFOP on the controversial question of the attitude of the French to the European Defence Community. When it obtained the results of the poll the periodical published only those favourable to its own position (pro EDC), arguing that it owned the results and therefore refused to allow the IFOP the opportunity of rectifying the tendentious presentation. A journalist took personal responsibility for complete publication, defying the monthly to sue him. It did not.

DIRECT EXTENSIVE OBSERVATION

Critical works: L. ROGERS, *The Pollsters: public opinion, politics and democratic leadership*, New York, 1949; W. HENNIS, *Meinungsforschung und repräsentative Demokratie*, Tubingen, 1957; J.-B. DUROSELLE, *De l'utilisation des sondages en histoire et en science politique*, Brussels, 1957.

H. CANTRIL, *Public Opinion: 1935–1946*, Princeton, 1951; G. SCHMIDT-CHEN, *Die befragte Nation*, Fribourg-en-Brisgau, 1959; the periodicals *Sondages* and *Public Opinion Quarterly*.

On the failure of the opinion polls' predictions in the 1948 American Presidential elections: the report of the Social Science Research Council, *The Pre-election Poll of 1948*, New York, 1949; D. KATZ, 'Polling Methods and the 1948 polling failure', *International Journal of Opinion and Attitude Research*, Vol. 2, No. 4, Winter 1948–49; G. GALLUP, 'The Gallup Poll and the 1950 Elections', *Public Opinion Quarterly*, 1951.

CHAPTER III

DIRECT INTENSIVE OBSERVATION

Direct extensive observation is conducted on large and populous communities through representative samples. As a general rule the size and composition of these samples allow only superficial studies. Observation is extensive but not profound. Direct intensive observation has exactly the opposite characteristics. It is carried out on small groups and even on individuals. It is therefore not as wide but it is more detailed and has greater depth.

As has already been said, the dividing line between the two types of observation is hard to draw. Small samples of large groups can be subjected to intensive analysis in depth. Some techniques can be adapted for use in both types of observation. This is true for the interview: opinion polls are only a particular variety adapted for extensive observation. Tests and attitude scales, followed by intensive observation, can also be used in simplified forms for the study of samples of large populations. But there are other techniques which are peculiar to intensive observation such as participant observation.

Section I. Interviews

As has just been remarked, the interview is a technique common to both intensive and extensive observation. A general examination of the interview will, therefore, be made before moving on to the special procedures used for observation in depth.

1. GENERAL EXAMINATION OF THE INTERVIEW

There are as yet few written works on the general theory of the interview. Special forms of it have been examined but there is no satisfactory general theory. It must be remembered that the interview is used in fields other then scientific research and is one of the main techniques of contemporary journalism. This has not raised its prestige with sociologists and the frivolity of many journalistic interviews has thrown ill-merited discredit on the method.

Direct Intensive Observation

A. Forms of interview

The forms of interview will be discussed according to their purpose here and their technical variations (interviews with or without questionnaires, free or directed, etc.) later (see p. 183). Two distinctions cut across one another—interviewing for opinions or personality characteristics and documentary interviews; interviews with prominent people and with 'ordinary' people.

(*a*) INTERVIEWS FOR OPINIONS OR PERSONAL CHARACTERISTICS AND DOCUMENTARY INTERVIEWS

This is scientifically an essential distinction. A person can be asked what he is or what he knows—more precisely, what he knows about himself or what he knows about other men, things and events. The first is an opinion interview, the second a documentary interview. Both are used in political science.

1. *Opinion or 'personal' interviews.* The purpose of these is to find out attitudes or opinions. Most polls questionnaires are opinion interviews. They are an attempt to discover the opinions of a large population—'public opinion'—through a sample. The interview is also applicable to intensive observation. Interviews in depth of a few typical people can complement and illuminate the results obtained from polls (although it must be realized that these cannot be representative). Systematic interviews of small groups—such as leaders or prominent people—can be carried out.

In social psychology the interview is extensively used to examine personality and this goes beyond the concept of the opinion interview. It is a more specialized and profound variety of 'personal' interview. But exploration of the whole personality structure and character and the construction of a psychoanalytical profile is not irrelevant to the other social sciences.

2. *Documentary interviews.* When a subject is being questioned about what he knows, he is a source of information in the same way as a book or an archive.

Documentary interviews have always played a great part in the social sciences, particularly in political science, economics, etc. *Democracy in America* is based on this type of procedure and so too are the main works of M. André Siegfried (direct human contact and conversations—which are interviews—play a greater part in them than work on books).

In political science the rarity of archives and written documents and the difficulty of gaining access to them creates the situation in which questioning the people who know, those who were the participants or observers of events is the only means of obtaining information. Even where this is not the case their testimony can fill gaps, correct errors and illuminate the significance of events. Naturally people are not always willing to talk and when they are it often happens that they have forgotten, are unconsciously mistaken or distort the truth by omission. Oral testimony, like written testimony, must be subject to critical analysis.

(*b*) INTERVIEWS WITH LEADERS AND WITH 'ORDINARY' PEOPLE
In opinion polls ordinary people are usually questioned and there is an attempt to make them as 'ordinary' as possible since they are intended to be representative. Investigators are instructed to avoid eccentric and atypical people (including important and prominent people). In contrast, direct intensive observation can include both documentary and opinion interviews of leaders and of the prominent.

1. *Interviews for the opinions of leaders.* These are often made for prestige reasons in journalism—the opinion of a prominent personality is asked because his prestige reinforces the opinion which he gives or simply because it increases the prestige of the newspaper. Commercial publicity uses the same technique: if Brigitte Bardot expresses her preference for a certain make of soap this encourages sales. Political propaganda also uses analogous methods. But prestige interviews are objects of study for the sociologists, not analytical techniques.

Investigations by interviewing leaders and social élites can be a useful means of studying social phenomena. It is important to know the differences between the opinions and attitudes of élites and the masses (in various groups and levels). The interview has in this case a secret and impersonal nature proper to studies of opinion. In the last few years studies of leaders, social élites and establishments through the interview have been greatly developed. Sampling and the techniques of extensive observation have even sometimes been used in them; this is a doubtful procedure unless the sample is large.

2. *Documentary interviews of leaders.* Élites, leaders and prominent people are approached because they alone can give information about certain things. In political science political leaders must be approached for documentary interviews since they are the holders of power.

These interviews are often disappointing in practice, because the political leaders will not talk freely and consider much of what they know as State secrets. When they talk they are more inclined through altruism or ideology, or in the interests of the party or the doctrine which they support, or through a desire to appear in a favourable light, to distort the truth than other men. It must be remembered that for politicians prestige has greater importance than for ordinary men and their public appearance is part of their job.

Documentary interviews with leaders are, however, indispensable. Contacts with them are essential for studies of parties, pressure groups, decisions, institutions, etc. Often little is gained from these contacts, but it sometimes happens that information, unobtainable by other means, is uncovered. Retired political leaders are often very interesting: interviews can replace memoirs. It is also of great interest to interview second rank leaders from the middle and lower levels of groups and parties. These people possess information of great value, have great experience and knowledge and usually talk much more freely than leaders of the front rank.

B. Interview technique

Extensive interviews by questionnaire have precise and rigid technical rules. In intensive interviews subtlety, tact and qualities of adaptation are more important than very carefully prepared questions. The technique of opinion and documentary interviews can be distinguished although the two are often the same.

(*a*) TECHNIQUE OF OPINION INTERVIEWS

This can be deduced from what has already been said about designing and administering opinion polls. The same basic problems are present although the context is very different.

1. *Gaining the confidence* of the subject has particular importance because he is asked many more things than in an opinion poll. The analysis is more profound and therefore more indiscreet. Without real confidence in the investigator the subject will not talk.

It is therefore important (although not necessary) that the investigator is known to the subject. The recommendation of a third party, the reference of a learned institution or a well-known personality can be very useful in this respect. Sympathy with the political position of a political leader is a consideration: it often happens that only people belonging to the same party or having the same views or, alternatively, people whose neutrality and impartiality are guaranteed, have a real chance of having a serious interview. It is a curious fact that in France foreigners have often obtained information about pressure groups which would have been refused to Frenchmen.

There are particularly gifted investigators who have personal aptitudes for making men talk and for putting people at their ease. Others find it more difficult. This should be remembered in collective research projects. Psychologists and social psychologists are almost alone in using the interview scientifically and their methods ought to be used in the other social sciences.

2. *Organization of the interview.* Intensive interviews can be free or take the form of a questionnaire. The free ('non-directed') interview is as carefully prepared as the questionnaire: the themes to be introduced are defined and the interviewer prepares his questions in advance. These questions are not written down and the form which they take is determined by the context of the interview; they do not follow a rigid order and replies produce further questions, etc. The free interview is more like a conversation than an interrogation. The tape recorder can be usefully employed.

The interview with a questionnaire (the 'directed interview') is derived from the procedures examined during the discussion of polls. Open questions obviously predominate and the questions are usually more complex. Hybrid procedures can be used: the questionnaire can be used as a framework on which one can elaborate. The advantage of the questionnaire is that it allows comparison and statistical assessment. The procedure is therefore more like extensive direct observation. But the freer the interview is the greater can be its depth.

(*b*) TECHNIQUE OF DOCUMENTARY INTERVIEWS

The problem of gaining the confidence of the subject and the personal qualities of the investigator are about the same as in opinion interviews, but the preparation and conduct of the interview are very different.

1. *Preparation of the interview.* This mainly consists of collecting as much documentation as possible on the problems which are to be discussed. The investigator should have a very wide background knowledge of the period in question so that he can immediately place the facts alluded to in the interview in their context, assess their importance and know when to ask for clarification. He must also have gone through all existing written documents on the questions he will raise during the interview.

The basic rule is that the interview must take place after research on the written documents. The interviews must be the last stage of research if full benefit is to be derived from them. It is then possible

Direct Intensive Observation

to prevent the interview straying on to topics for which there are other available sources of information. Above all it is possible to probe more deeply if the person interviewed is under the impression that the interviewer is well informed.

2. *Conduct of the interview.* The problems to be tackled are prepared but the actual form of the questions is left to the inspiration of the moment. New questions can be asked following the course of the conversation. The investigator should ask for clarification, point to possible contradictions with the interpretations of the facts already known and do everything possible, using the maximum tact and adroitness to get to the bottom of the problem.

It is desirable that the interview has two stages: firstly, a preliminary series of interviews to compare the results with each other and with the facts available from other sources; secondly, interview some people a second time to ask for complementary explanations and clarification and discuss disputed points. The subject interviewed has time for reflection between interviews and can think about the important points.

Interviews can also present an opportunity of gaining access to the archives of the person interviewed. The maximum of discretion has to be used to avoid compromising the outcome of the interview. Experience has shown that in so far as one can interest the interviewee in the research and convince him of the importance of his collaboration, good results can be obtained.

2. SPECIAL INTERVIEW TECHNIQUES

There are various special techniques used and others can be envisaged. Interview technique provides wide scope for the ingenuity of social scientists. It is an individual thing which does not require complicated equipment nor collective preparatory studies. However, only the procedures of repeated interviews ('panel interviews') and various methods of interviews in depth will be examined here. These are concerned primarily with 'personal' and opinion interviews rather than documentary interviews.

A. Repeated (panel) interviews

This technique was perfected by Lazarsfeld: an example of its use in a study in his depth on the presidential elections of 1940 in the district of Erie (Ohio), published as *The People's Choice*. A group of people were subject to repeated interviews at various intervals.

(a) TECHNIQUE OF THE PANEL

Essentially the panel is based on two ideas: (1) Repetition of the same questions at regular intervals; (2) the same people are interviewed throughout the inquiry.

1. *Repetition of the interviews.* Panels are designed mainly to study the evolution of attitudes and opinions over a short period of time. The group is questioned at regular intervals to obtain a series of 'snapshots' of its opinions and a comparison of these gives an accurate idea of the evolution of opinion.

The interviews can be about attitudes and opinions (for example, political attitudes and opinions as in the Erie inquiry), about those things which are likely to influence opinion (radio, books, newspapers and various other things) and about attitudes and opinions which are thought to be linked with the aim of the inquiry. A preliminary systemization of the problem is therefore necessary for the preparation of panel questionnaires. The basic hypotheses must be defined for the panel to test their accuracy.

The frequency and the total period of interviewing varies considerably, depending on the nature of the inquiry and composition of the groups interviewed. In the Erie investigation, the interviews were repeated six times with a month and a half between each. Another inquiry by Lazarsfeld at Cornell University concerning students' ideas about careers was spread out over two years. The only limitation is the difficulty of maintaining a homogeneous sample over a long period of time.

2. *Homogeneity of the sample.* The panel technique differs from repeated opinion polls in that the latter are based on new samples each time a poll is taken.

The panel technique is used in two different ways—either it is applied to a representative sample of a population established by the techniques described in the previous chapter, or it is used to observe the whole of a small group, for example, the pupils of a school or the students of a college. The panel is used more in the former case.

'Mortality' has to be taken into account in all panel groups. Some people leave for good, others are absent for a period during the inquiry, others become tired of interviews and do not co-operate, etc. This 'mortality' can be circumvented by starting with a larger sample than necessary. But those who disappear often constitute particular types and their distribution is often not representative of the sample. Distortions result and they can be serious when 'mortality' is high. Lazarsfeld consequently called the method a means of studying 'social change in the short-term'.

DIRECT INTENSIVE OBSERVATION

(*b*) LIMITATIONS OF THE METHOD

The most important difficulty raised by the method is the distorting effect of repetition.

1. *The distorting effect of repetition.* The care which is taken to construct questionnaires so that the interviewee does not guess the questions to be asked has already been mentioned. In the panel system the subjects know the questions after the first interview and they therefore prepare their replies. Repetition of the questions increases the subjects' awareness of the problems and they think more and more before replying. The apparent changes brought to light can result from a progressively deepening awareness of an opinion which has not basically changed as well as through real modifications of opinion.

To measure this distortion, other different samples can be questioned at the same time as the panel sample. These samples would not suffer the effect of repetition. But it can legitimately be asked why the panel technique is used rather than repeated polls with different samples.

2. *Study of the distorting effect.* The panel technique has all the advantages of interviewing a group or a small community as compared with a sample. Also the distorting effect is interesting in itself because it reveals many things about the nature and consistency of opinion and in the same way as the distorting effects in polls.

The works of Lazarsfeld tend to show that the important aspects of an opinion or an attitude and the factors which have a great influence on them, are hardly changed at all be repetition. But the secondary factors or the unconscious aspects of opinions and attitudes are influenced by repetition. Analysis of repeated interviews of the same group and of simultaneous interviews of different groups to some extent allows a distinction to be made between various elements in opinions and even to form hierarchies of these elements.

B. Interviews in depth

Under this general heading various interview techniques are grouped which attempt a deeper understanding of opinions, attitudes and even the whole personality of the subject. The terminology is not well established in this field and classification is not easy. Some techniques differ very little from one another but two categories can be clearly distinguished.

(a) SINGLE INTERVIEWS IN DEPTH

In principle the subject is interviewed only once although clarifications can be sought in a second interview.

1. *Focused interviews.* This technique was invented by the American sociologist R. K. Merton. It consists not so much of an interrogation as assisting people to illuminate some factor or stimulus acting on them and the results of this on their attitudes. The interview takes place following a particular situation common to all the people being interviewed—a film, the reading of a newspaper, listening to the radio, participation in a psychosocial experiment, etc. The aim is to study in depth the influence of this situation. The procedure was invented to analyse the effects of 'communications'.

Firstly, the content of the basic situation is subject to detailed analysis after which hypotheses are made about the significance and effects of the situation. These hypotheses determine the main areas of inquiry and act as a guide for the interviews (the main aim of which is to verify these hypotheses). The guide to the interview is only a framework on which the investigator can elaborate. The main object is to make the subject aware of the hypothesis which one wants to analyse and then allow him to comment on his own experience. The conversation between the investigator and the subject is recorded in full and subjected to detailed analysis.

2. *Clinical interviews.* The term is used here in a wider sense than that generally applied to it in the United States and more in keeping with the idea expressed by the word 'clinical'. An interview of this kind resembles the methods of questioning used by a doctor on a sick person in order to diagnose him.

In the American sense of the term the clinical interview was extensively used to gather material for the study of the 'authoritarian personality' published in the United States in 1950. The technique resembled the focused interview to the extent that after a preliminary analysis the interview is 'focused' and directed (in a flexible manner) by the investigator. The difference was that the focus of the interview was not a particular experience but the basic motivations of the opinions and attitudes which the investigator was trying to characterize. The interview guide comprised a series of basic questions and a list of more direct questions related to them; the investigator has a certain freedom to diverge from this guide.

In non-directed interviews the subject is allowed as much initiative as possible during the whole of the interview. The investigator limits himself to helping the subject to express himself and to guide the interview towards the relevant subject or subjects. This procedure is used in social psychology, psychotherapy, etc. In general its use in the social sciences seems to be spreading.

(b) MULTIPLE INTERVIEWS

These are used more rarely because the subject has to submit to numerous interviews over a fairly long period and therefore must show considerable patience. Multiple interviews provide knowledge in depth of personality, opinions and attitudes, and provide valuable documentation. They can be classified in several categories: 'memoir' interviews, interviews of prisoners and people in detention and psycho-analyses.

1. *Memoir interviews.* This type of interview has been little used until now but it seems to have great possibilities. The procedure is for an investigator to obtain permission from a person to see him regularly over a period of time to question him on events in which he has been involved. To a certain extent the investigator plays the role of the memoir writer. The subject is invited to give his souvenirs orally, the investigator encouraging him in the right directions. Full notes and, if it does not make the subject over-cautious, a shorthand record or a tape recording should be made.

The type of person who could be interviewed are retired politicians of the second rank, directors and secretaries of committees, parties and groups, local élites and notables, higher civil servants, etc. Out of active political life and partially isolated they usually welcome the opportunity to communicate confidences and to recover prestige in their own eyes and those of their interviewers. The interviewer must, of course, have a profound knowledge of the period studied and be sympathetic and tactful.

2. *Interviews with prisoners.* Prisoners are in an available condition in that replying to interviews is a distraction for them and they will do so willingly. But there are two serious difficulties. In the first place the prisoner must not get the impression that the interview is a new form of interrogation designed to extract from him information which could be used against him or his friends. The interviews must be made after the sentence and the investigator must provide guarantees; the prisoner must be free to accept or refuse to see the investigator, etc. A prisoner also has a natural tendency to self-justification; his replies tend to be tendentious (this is a less serious drawback than the first because the responses of all subjects tend

towards self-justification). The procedure was used for social psychology investigations on nazi war criminals after the Nuremburg trials.

3. *Psychoanalysis*. This is not the place for a full description of psychoanalytical methods of interviews. It is a long process resembling the general idea of multiple interviews. It is a therapeutic method, a technique for treating mental disorders and personality troubles and can only be used by a very experienced specialist.

Psychoanalytical methods are naturally used in social psychology but much more rarely in other branches of the social sciences. An attempt has been made to use it in political science but there is hardly any possibility of psychoanalysing political leaders. However, some examinations of nazi war criminals were conducted with more or less rigorous psychoanalytical methods.

Some American sociologists tend to explain much political behaviour in psychoanalytic terms but by indirect psychoanalysis which takes away much of the significance of the conclusions.

On the general technique of the interview: R. L. KAHN and C. F. CANNELL, *The Dynamics of Interviewing*, New York, 1957; the special number of the *American Journal of Sociology* on 'The Interview in Social Research', 1956, No. 2; H. H. HYMAN, W. J. COBB (*et al.*), *Interviewing in Social Research*, Chicago, 1951; the introduction to A. C. KINSEY (*et al.*), *The Sexual Behaviour of the Human Male*, Philadelphia, 1948.

On the panel technique: F. LAZARSFELD, B. BERELSON, H. GAUDET, *The People's Choice*, New York, 1948; B. BERELSON, F. LAZARSFELD, W. N. MACPHEE, *Voting*, Chicago, 1954; P. F. LAZARSFELD, 'The Use of Panels in Social Research', *Proceedings of the American Philosophical Society*, 1948, pp. 405–10.

On interviews in depth: H. D. LASSWELL, *Psychopathology and Politics*, Chicago, 1930; R. K. MERTON, M. FISKE, P. F. KENDALL, *The Focused Interview*, Glencoe, 1956; R. A. FEAR, *The Evaluation Interview*, New York, 1958.

On psychoanalysis and social science: W. MUNSTERBERGER and S. AXELROD, *Psychoanalysis and the Social Sciences*, New York, 1955; J. C. FLUGEL, *Man, Moral and Society*, New York, 1955; M. GINSBERG, 'Sociology and Psychoanalysis', *British Journal of Sociology*, 1951, p. 76; F. W. MASON, 'The Political Implications of Psychoanalytic Theory', *Journal of Politics*, 1954, pp. 704–25.

On 'clinical' interviews: T. ADORNO (*et al.*), *The Authoritarian Personality*, New York, 1950; *Studies in The Scope and Method of 'The Authoritarian Personality'*, Glencoe, 1954; D. M. KELLEY, *Twenty-two Cells in Nuremberg*, New York, 1947; H. V. DICKS, 'German Personality Traits and National Socialist Ideology', *Human Relations*, 1950, pp. 111–54.

Direct Intensive Observation

Section II. Tests and the measurement of attitudes

The notion of the test has already been mentioned during the discussion of questionnaires. 'Test questions' can be inserted in questionnaires. The answers to them are not in themselves interesting but they provide indications about opinions and attitudes. In the widest sense a test is a series of questions by means of which the personality of the subject is indirectly explored. Conscious analysis of his own personality is not asked of the subject. His behaviour in the test reveals the relevant information.

Opinion and attitude scales are particular instances of the test method. The most frequently used procedure is a series of standardized test propositions which form a 'scale'; a grading of all responses is based on approval of some and disapproval of others. The technique of attitude scales will be compared with two other procedures for measuring attitudes and opinions.

1. TEST METHOD

Tests are very widely used today in psychology, social psychology and in psychiatry. They are used as guides for the academic careers of school children, vocational aptitudes, management selection, selections of army officers, etc. Its use in other branches of social science is less widespread. Like many other methods it was invented and perfected by social psychologists.

A. Survey of test methods

To understand the current use of tests and their possible development it is necessary first of all to make a general survey of the method. A description will be given of the various categories of tests.

The general characteristics of a good test are almost the same as those of a good questionnaire: reliability, validity, sensitivity. These qualities—especially validity—are even more important in tests. Tests do not provide direct knowledge but give indications of behaviour, opinions and personality factors and it is therefore essential to ensure an exact correspondence between the indication and the thing itself.

(*a*) TESTS OF APTITUDE AND KNOWLEDGE
These are for measuring the level of intelligence, the extent of knowledge and the nature and degree of skills. In tests of knowledge and aptitude there is an objectively correct answer to all the questions: the answer '9' to the question 'How much is 5 plus 4?' is

objectively correct. The nature of the tests varies greatly: three types will be distinguished.

1. *Intelligence tests.* These can be based on questions designed to determine level of information. Some use immediate memory, the solving of simple arithmetical problems, common sense problems, discovering common characteristics in groups of words (aptitude for abstraction), etc. Pictorial and graphical procedures are also used: labyrinths, puzzles, cubes to be fitted together, pictures to be completed.

2. *Aptitude tests.* These are currently used in the army, air force, public services and in private firms. They are even more varied then intelligence tests because of the range measured: motor, visual, hearing aptitudes and aptitudes in the higher intellectual functions, etc. Most are composite tests designed to test several aptitudes at the same time. Many tests are constructed on a basis of factorial analysis. The use of this method in the social sciences, which was perfected for aptitude tests, will be discussed later.

3. *Tests of knowledge.* These can replace essays and examinations to measure the knowledge of individuals. They have been extensively developed in the United States and Britain. In France where the system was invented (by Binet in 1910) these tests are looked on with disfavour and there is much prejudice against them. A detailed examination of the results of examination and *concours* made twenty-five years ago showed the faults in traditional methods. The conclusion of this study seems incontrovertable: 'It is obvious that these tests cannot be introduced in every case. It is doubtful whether French composition, style, manner of expression, intellectual creation of the first order can ever be reduced to a precise test. But in other educational matters when it is a question of determining whether a candidate knows the facts, understands the laws and problems, tests are more efficient.'[1] Tests of knowledge are used in educational institutions and even more in professional recruitment.

(*b*) PERSONALITY TESTS

The following definition is given by Pichot: 'Personality tests explore all the non-intellectual (in the widest sense) aspects of the personality, in other words the conative (or volitional) and affective aspects.'

---

[1] Laugier, Piéron, Toulouse, Weinberg, *Etudes docimologiques sur le perfectionnement des examens et concours*, Conservatoire des Arts et Métiers, 1934.

Personality tests are more difficult to validate than knowledge or aptitude tests because the questions do not have objectively true replies (this is the main characteristic of these tests). There is no objectively true reply to the question: 'Do you prefer to have numerous acquaintances or two or three good friends?' Both alternative replies are valid; they show a different kind of personality.

Personality tests can be divided into two broad categories—objective tests and projective tests. The difference is not always easy to establish. The former are concerned only with certain aspects of the personality: the links between the 'indications' (the actual reply to the questions) and the basic phenomena are closer and the results can therefore be quantified and processed by statistical techniques. The latter attempt to analyse the whole personality: the links between the indications and the basic phenomena are not so close and the results cannot therefore be quantified.

1. *Objective tests.* These can take the form of questionnaires or projects to be performed or both.

(*a*) Questionnaire tests are concerned with tastes, feelings, interests and behaviour. They are designed in much the same way as opinion questionnaires but many of the questions are 'camouflaged' (making it difficult for the subject to find out the exact nature of the problem being probed). Test questions of honesty are often included: subjects are asked about behaviour in circumstances where almost all (95 per cent) normal subjects look unfavourably on a certain type of behaviour. For example: 'Have you never sworn in your life?'—A reply of 'no' is evaluted 'not as a tendency towards lying in general but of a tendency of the subject to wish to present himself in too good a light' (Pichot). The final results can be corrected according to the 'lying score' of subjects. There are questionnaires measuring personality traits, adaptation to social situation, attitudes and interests. Among the latter 'value' questionnaires are particularly noteworthy.

(*b*) Project tests do not differ from knowledge and aptitude but the 'projects' to explore personality are more difficult to perfect. An example can be given of tests of moral sense: to assess the honesty of a subject two exactly equivalent tests can be given and the subject can be allowed to correct one of them himself without any supervision. A significant difference between the results would suggest a lack of honesty. There are tests to distinguish between normal and the neurotic personality, the tendencies towards introversion and extroversion, of instability, meticulousness, aptitude for bluff, aspiration to success, etc.

2. *Projective tests.* The term 'projection' is borrowed from the terminology of psychoanalysis but it is not used in the same sense which Freud gave it. Projective tests consist of 'confronting the subject with a situation to which he answers according to the meaning this situation has for him and according to what he feels during this reply'. (L. K. Frank.) They are an attempt to analyse the whole personality and their interpretation is consequently very difficult. Precise assessment and statistical analysis are almost impossible.

There are a great number of projective tests. Some are called constructive such as the mosaic test of Löwenfeld which consists of the free grouping of 475 plastic plaques: the design made is assessed by a complex method. Another of Löwenfeld's tests is the 'world test'. The subject is given wooden toys representing houses, trees, motor cars, people and so on and he arranges these on a sand tray. The behaviour of the subject, his successive choices and the whole construct are noted. This test was first used for children but it has proved equally useful for the analysis of adult personality. Another test consists of giving the subject a miniature theatre and actors, etc.

Other tests are based on the 'completing' method. The task of the subject is to complete something which is presented to him in an unfinished state. The great Swiss psychoanalyst Jung invented a word association test: the subject has to say the first word which comes into his head when a word is spoken to him. The most famous and frequently used projective tests are the Rohrschach test, the Murray test (Thematic Apperception Test—TAT) and the Rosenzweig test ('frustration test'). The Rohrschach test dates from 1921. The bibliography of works on it amounts to over a thousand items and a special institute and numerous scientific societies are devoted exclusively to its study. This test is composed of ten reproductions of ink blots made by pressing two sheets of paper together. The subject must say what these blots represent for him (they represent nothing in particular). After Rohrschach the most frequently used test is the TAT which is composed of a series of thirty drawings of scenes containing several people, which have ambiguous meanings. The subject has to say what the drawings represents, what has happened previously to lead to the situation shown in the drawing and what the conclusion of the story is. Rosenweig test is used much less but some tests in political science are based on an analogous technique. It consists of a series of twenty-four drawings of two people in frustrating situations. The person on the left is represented as saying several words (using the technique of the comic strip) and the subject has to write the reply of the person on the right.

Direct Intensive Observation

B. Use of tests in the social sciences

As has been said already, tests are mainly used in social psychology and psychiatry. They have been developed for the selection of managers and leaders. Their use in the analysis of opinions and attitudes could obviously be extended.

(a) SELECTION OF LEADERS

The selection of leaders and establishments of all levels and in all fields falls within the field of political science. It is directly associated with problems of authority and power. If political science is limited to the study of the State only the selection of administrative, political and military cadres fall within its scope. In either case the selection of heads of firms and the lower ranks of management is the concern of economic science and in its general aspects the problem also falls within the scope of social psychology.

1. *Selection of civil servants.* Tests are widely used for the selection of the entry to the administrative class in the British civil service and to the Foreign and Colonial offices.

Tests are used for the first two of the three stages of selection of the graduate candidates for the administrative class. The first stage, which eliminates 40 per cent of the candidates includes essays on economic, social and political questions, verbal tests, choice of synonyms, etc., as well as tests of aptitude and knowledge. The second phase includes projective personality tests: Murray's TAT (adapted), tests of word associations and a biographical self-portrait.

2. *Selection of military officers.* Tests are more widely used in this field than in the selection of administrators; practical tests are mainly used.

Tests were started in the German army in 1926 and used in conjunction with other examinations for the selection of trainee officers. Intelligence and mental aptitude tests were adopted first, then a reaction test (in which the subjects were faced with sudden stimuli) and these were subsequently associated with practical tests of command, individual performance, analysis of verbal expressions, gestures and writing and a biographical examination.

Since 1941 the British army has used intelligence and projective tests in association with group tests (see p. 250) for selecting officer cadets. The methods perfected in the British army have been the basis of those used subsequently in the French and Belgian armies.

The Australian army adopted tests in 1943 and used them even more extensively: aptitude and intelligence, word association, personality and the Rohrschach tests are applied together.

In the American army also tests were used for the selection of officers during the Second World War in conjunction with practical tests and sociometric evaluations (see p. 331). Special tests were drawn up specifically for the selection of officers (Officer Classification Test and the General Survey Test).

3. *Selection in industry.* Tests are still little used in industry. In a survey done in Britain in 1951 of a sample of eighty-seven firms, sixteen had commenced to use systematic techniques in the selection of personnel and only eight of these used up-to-date methods. In the United States the proportion appears to be higher. On the continent of Europe more and more important firms are starting to use selection tests.

In Britain several medium-sized firms in the coal distribution trade commissioned the National Institute of Industrial Psychology to select candidates for management positions and the Institute used, among others, intelligence and personality tests. In Australia the collective application of the Rohrschach test has been used in conjunction with other procedures for the selection of candidates for management functions in a shoe factory, etc.

(*b*) OPINION AND ATTITUDE TESTS

It has been mentioned that opinion questionnaires generally include test questions. The test technique has, however, been used in the analysis of attitudes and opinions in a more profound and systematic fashion, mainly in the form of projective techniques. The basic difficulty lies in interpretation: the problems posed are generally more difficult than in personality tests.

1. *Examples of projective tests in social science.* These have mainly been developed in the United States. The Prohansky test (1943) transposed the principle of Murray's TAT to the analysis of social conflicts and syndicalism: it comprises a series of newspaper photographs showing scenes of strikes, unemployment, riots, squalor, etc. The Sanford test (1945) uses the same procedure to analyse anti-semitic attitudes. The Fromme test (1941) used to analyse attitudes towards the methods for solving international tensions is based on analogous principles. Others are based on the Rosenzweig frustration test for the analysis of the authoritarian or democratic temperament, racial conflicts, etc.

Direct Intensive Observation

An interesting test was made in France by the French Institute of Public Opinion during an inquiry on the Left for the review *Temps modernes* in 1953 (published August-September 1954). It comprises firstly a series of ten photographs based on the TAT technique showing scenes linked to various aspects of the Right/Left distinction: scenes of strikes and syndicalist riots, arrests of North Africans and colonialist attitudes, military parades and patriotic ceremonies, religious charities, etc. The subject had then to assess a series of nine accounts of analogous themes. This was, however, not a test but a preliminary to the administering of an opinion questionnaire. The results were used mainly to give depth and complement the answers to the questionnaires.

2. *Difficulties of projective tests in the social sciences.* Interpretation is the common difficulty of all projective tests. A test ought to be objective, in other words there should be precise bases for assessing the results. It is particularly apparent in the social sciences that projective tests, which concern the whole personality, do not lend themselves well to objective interpretation.

Tests such as the Rohrschach test and the TAT have been applied to a large number of subjects of many nationalities over many years and they have been subjected to numerous validating and control tests. Serious bases for an objective assessment exist but, despite this, assessment of them remains highly controversial.

Various other tests have only been applied to a small number of subjects. Validating tests have been done for some of them: for instance, the results of the Prohansky test have been compared with opinion questionnaires covering the same problems; tests given by different people to similar samples have been compared, etc. These have, however, been too few to constitute a real validation. Also the very nature of political events make it difficult to transpose political science tests from one country to another. Tests on the Right and the Left, for instance, are valid only for France. Many tests must be rapidly adapted to keep pace with events: some of the photographs or accounts of 1953 no longer correspond to the problems of today.

This does not mean that the tests cannot be validly used in the social sciences. It means that none of the tests actually used at the moment has the same degree of validity as the Rohrschach test or TAT (and their validity remains controversial). But it is not impossible to overcome the difficulties. Until they are overcome, projective tests which have not been seriously verified should be treated with caution: intuitive interpretation can result in serious errors.

2. MEASUREMENT OF OPINIONS AND ATTITUDES

Tests are an attempt to measure a psychological element. The results of intelligence and aptitude tests, for example, are in the form of a statistical assessment which claims to be a measure of a degree of intelligence or degree of skill: there have been various controversies about this, notably about the assessment of 'mental age' in intelligence tests.

Personality tests are less precise: in a sense they are qualitative rather than quantitative. This is not true of all of them. 'Attitude scales' have been constructed to analyse attitudes and opinion and it is claimed that these give very precise measurements of opinions and attitudes. There will be an attempt to define their place in the context of all the techniques used to measure attitudes and opinion: then they will be discussed in detail.

A. Methods of measuring opinions

The preliminary theoretical problem—is it possible to measure an attitude or opinion—will not be examined here. Is it possible to say that someone is twice as socialist as someone else? Is it not more true to say that people are socialists in different ways? Is not the apparent difference of degree between opinions a qualitative difference—a difference of nature? This is, in fact, a problem of all measurement: a man who weighs twice as much as another is a 'fat man' compared to a 'thin man'—which is a difference in nature. It nevertheless remains true that weight can be measured and the measurements can be used to analyse differences between human beings. Even if differences of opinion are basically differences of kind, from the moment that measuring instruments can be applied to them, the measurements are an element in social reality.

The real problem is not theoretical but practical. Is it possible to construct precise and objective measuring instruments for opinions? Three categories of techniques can be proposed: self-assessment, assessment by a judge and attitude scales.

(*a*) SELF-ASSESSMENT

This has already been touched on in the discussion of opinion questionnaires.

1. *The technique.* This consists of asking the subject to assess the intensity of his opinions; there are two principal procedures used. The most frequent and the least ambitious is asking the subject to choose between various qualifications of an attitude. He can be asked whether he completely approves, approves to some extent,

is neutral (neither approves nor disapproves), to some extent disapproves or disapproves completely of an opinion. The measurement is approximate and vague.

The other procedure is apparently more precise. The subject is asked to define his position in relation to an opinion by placing himself on a scale ranging from one extreme to another. One could, for example, ask a subject to assess his political position by placing a cross on the line:

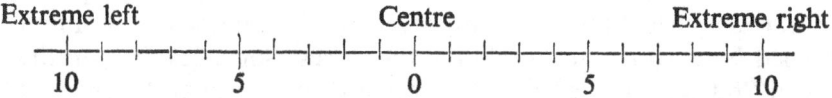

A kind of vertical thermometer graduated from 0 to 100 is often used in the United States. When a subject has given his opinion he is asked to mark on the thermometer the intensity of this opinion.

2. *Defects of self-assessment.* The main defect of self-assessment is that it is subjective. Valid measurement is based on a scale which is identical for all the objects measured. This scale does not exist in this case. Two subjects can in good faith place themselves at different places on the scale although they hold a position with equal intensity because they have not the same conception of the degrees of opinion possible.

There are other defects which are common to all questionnaires: insincerity on the part of the subject and his tendency to place himself in an advantageous position *vis-à-vis* the investigator, etc. But these are less serious than the subjective character of the measurement. Self-assessment can only be used to complement other procedures. It can complement extensive inquiries in which there is no real attempt to measure opinions: it can furnish supplementary information to that provided by questionnaires. It can also be used with other measuring procedures—comparing the results can be interesting.

(*b*) ASSESSMENT BY A JUDGE

This is analogous to the system used in assessing written and oral academic examinations. A judge assesses the intensity of opinions and attitudes after various tests. As in academic examinations, the mark depends on the personal assessment of the judge.

1. *The basic tests.* There is a great variety of possible tests on which a judge could base his assessment.

The judge could observe the behaviour of the subject in real life. This is difficult in practice: it is possible to analyse the intensity of political opinions by examining speeches in parliament or in meetings or the behaviour of voters in the voting booth, etc. Behaviour in artificial situations is easier to analyse: series of standardized tests are used in the selection of leaders.

The judge can also base his assessment on replies to questionnaires or on free and directed interviews. The assessment is made in the form of a particular kind of 'coding'. The different types of response are not classified but marks are given to the intensity of opinion revealed by all (or a group of) the responses. Some inquiries in the United States have been based on analysis of personal documents: analyses of the mail in German civilians were carried out during the war to discover the level of morale; of the biographies of 238 people to assess their attitude towards prohibition, etc. The correlation between the assessment of various judges was .96. The correlation between the assessments of the judges and self-assessments was .81.

Replies which can be assessed objectively (placed on an attitude scale) and those which cannot, should be distinguished. In the latter case judges can interpret the tests to assess the intensity of attitudes.

2. *System of assessment.* There are two main ways of assessing: either it is done relatively, the responses being classified in relation to one another and the subjects ranked (the intervals between the ranks not necessarily being equal). This is valid only for the group of subjects being examined. Or, each subject is assessed separately against a theoretical value scale. The introduction of an apparent precision which does not in fact exist should be carefully avoided. A classification according to a scale of approximate categories is usually preferred to a statistical classification.

(c) ATTITUDE OR OPINION SCALES

Attitude scales are an attempt to establish an objective system of measurement. A measuring instrument constructed in advance assesses intensities of attitudes or opinions. The general technique is to present the subject with a series of standardized propositions and to ask him which he approves and which he disapproves. The combination of responses automatically determines the intensity of the opinion.

There is a variety of tests incorporating attitude scales. An attempt has been made by means of attitude scales to make personality tests as precise as intelligence and aptitude tests. Establishing the scales has two main difficulties.

1. *Equality of intervals.* The ideal scale would have equal intervals between gradations. Thurstone's attempt at this in his scale with 'apparently equal intervals' will be discussed later. The other scales are less ambitious. Two scores on the same scale can be compared but one cannot take an average of the scores of the same subject on different scales. Measurement remains very imprecise.

In several types of scales the various positions are not put in a strictly rank order: this means that assent to a proposition of a certain intensity does not necessarily imply assent to a proposition of lesser intensity on the same scale. It will be seen that only Guttman's scale has a strict hierarchy.

2. *The zero point on the scale.* The scales are established on the principle that an attitude or an opinion is characterized by a sign. Opinions are divided into two groups—the favourable and the unfavourable. Thus on each scale there is a 'zero' point. The interpretation of this zero point has given rise to many difficulties which will not be gone into here. It can, however, be pointed out that zero may have two meanings according to the scale. It either represents a position of neutrality towards all propositions on the scale or the adoption of a position favourable to some and unfavourable to others. It depends on the scale which of these is the more probable. It is difficult to define the significance of a zero score and the zero raises difficult theoretical problems. An example from political science can be quoted: is the Centre a position of neutrality between Right and Left or the combination of some Leftist positions and some Rightist positions?

B. Attitude scales
Most methods of constructing attitude scales are difficult, long and expensive. The results obtained often do not seem to justify the effort (as in many other fields). Despite this, the method is worth fostering because introducing quantification and measurement into a science is essential to its development.

(*a*) RANKING SCALES
Each subject is invited to rank in order of decreasing preference a number of similar objects such as politicians, ideologies, nationalities, professions, etc., and a score is established. In practice, the ranking can have two aspects: direct classification or indirect classification by binary comparisons.

1. *Direct classification.* This corresponds to the definition just given.

The subject is, for example, invited to classify by order of preference the candidates at an election, various political parties, etc. The nuances of the attitudes towards each element can be seen.

This method is sometimes used for other reasons than the measurement of attitudes: for example, to find out the attitude of a subject to a single element without drawing his attention to it; to find out the opinion of a worker on the efficiency of his foreman he can be asked to rank all his colleagues.

2. *Binary comparisons.* This technique was invented by Thurstone in 1927–28 and should not be confused with the Thurstone scales which will be discussed later.

The subject is presented with a series of objects in pairs and is asked which he prefers. The final order of preference is established automatically according to the relative place given to each in the whole series. The advantage of this method is that a much greater accuracy of replies is obtained. The disadvantage is that it involves excessive work if there is a large number of objects to be compared. In Guilford's study (1931) on the comparison of fifteen national groups each subject had to make 105 successive comparisons.

The method also allows the establishment of comparisons between the relative distances between several objects. The percentage preference in binary comparisons is taken as a measurement of social distance. If the percentage of subjects who prefer Italians to Russians is the same as for Greeks to Chinese, then it can be said that the relative distance of the Italians to the Russians is the same as that of the Greeks to the Chinese. A scale of relative social distance can thus be constructed.

(*b*) THE BOGARDUS SCALE AND ITS DERIVATIVES

The Bogardus, called the 'scale of social distance', is the oldest scale used. It was invented in 1925, widely used since, and often transferred into other fields.

1. *The Bogardus scale.* Its purpose is to measure the intensity of national and racial attitudes. The subject is asked the following question: 'Do you freely admit, if you allow yourself to be guided solely by your feelings, that the members of the races and countries which are on the attached list should occupy the following positions: 1. Close relations by marriage; 2. Personal friends in your club; 3. Neighbours in your street; 4. Colleagues at work; 5. Citizens of your country; 6. Tourists in your country; 7. Forbidden to reside in your country. You ought to consider each race or nationality as a

whole without taking into consideration individuals whom you have either liked or disliked personally.' Separate replies are made for each of the races or nationalities.

The Bogardus scale is constructed in a very empirical way, and because it is simple, it is easy to handle. It has been argued that the 'social distance' is not a function of sympathy or antipathy: many American subjects have, for example, placed the French at a greater social distance than the English whilst declaring a greater sympathy for them. It is revealing that unknown nationalities (for example, the 'Brombinians', a fictional nationality which Bogardus included in his questionnaire) are placed very low on the scale.

2. *Scales derived from Bogardus.* Dodd in 1935 measured attitudes towards various groups (national, religious and social) by means of a five degree scale: '1. I would willingly marry one of them if I wanted to marry; 2. I would readily invite one to dinner; 3. I would prefer to consider them as people one knew by sight and with whom one would exchange a few words on chance meeting; 4. I would find no pleasure in meeting these people; 5. I wish all these people were done away with.'

Crespi used in 1944 a scale which he called a 'thermometer of social rejection' to analyse attitudes towards conscientious objectors. These are the six propositions on this scale: '1. I have no reason for treating a conscientious objector differently from anyone else and I would not mind if one entered my family by marriage; 2. I would accept conscientious objectors as friends; 3. I would have only passing relations with conscientious objectors; 4. I do not want anything to do with conscientious objectors; 5. I think that conscientious objectors ought to be put in prison; 6. I think that conscientious objectors ought to be shot as traitors.'

Scales of the same kind could be established quite easily to measure a great number of political opinions and attitudes.

(c) THE THURSTONE SCALE

In 1929–31 Thurstone perfected a very different attitude scale from the method of binary comparisons mentioned above.

The scale takes the form of a series of propositions which are submitted to the subject who merely indicates whether or not he agrees with them. These propositions are drawn up so that agreement with the first indicates the most favourable reaction, agreement with the last the most unfavourable and agreement with the middle one indifference or neutrality (the zero point). The intervals between the various propositions are equivalent from whence comes the name sometimes given to the Thurstone technique—'the method of the apparently equal intervals'.

1. *Constructing a Thurstone scale.* This is a delicate operation and comprises the following stages:

(*a*) The greatest possible number—at least several hundred—of propositions or assertions about the opinion or attitude to be analysed are collected. These propositions are stated as clearly as possible, in a way which calls for unequivocal agreement or disagreement.

(*b*) The propositions are then submitted to a numerous (about a hundred) group of experts and they are asked to classify the propositions in a certain number of columns—usually seven to eleven—corresponding to declining degrees of attraction to the opinion or attitude under consideration.

(*c*) Propositions which are spread over a great number of columns are rejected, those which are spread over a small number of neighbouring columns are kept and they are classified according to their average distribution.

(*d*) The propositions retained are sorted again to sift out the least clear, the most ambiguous and the least direct. Fifteen to thirty questions are finally retained and these are chosen so that there is an equal distance between them (calculated according to the median of the distribution of each question): thus a continuum going from one extreme to the other in principle in a regular manner is plotted.

(*e*) The proposition on the scale are shuffled in a random manner and presented to the subjects; each subject singles out those with which he agrees; the attitude or opinion of each subject is assessed according to the median of the values on the scale of the propositions to which he has agreed.

2. *Use of Thurstone scales.* The personal opinions of the judges have no influence on their assessment of the propositions since they classify them simply in relation to the attitude under consideration without giving their personal opinion. It was shown in 1935 in America that a scale constructed by a group of violently anti-negro students and one constructed by negro students about attitudes towards the racial question had a correlation of .97.

Thurstone scales have been widely used in the United States to analyse political opinions, notably racism and anti-negro prejudice, nationalism and the attitudes towards war, etc. As an example, these are seven of the propositions (or items) of the Drobna scale (1930) on attitudes towards war:

Scale	Propositions
1.3	A country can never attach too much importance to its national honour and war is the only way of maintaining national honour.
2.5	When war is declared one's duty is to enrol to fight.
5.2	Wars are only legitimate if their aim is to defend weak nations.
5.4	War and peace are both essential to progress.
5.6	The best one can hope for is the partial abolition of war.
8.4	The contempt for life and the rights of man implied by war results in the increase of crime.
10.6	All nations should disarm immediately.

The length and complexity of the operations necessary to establish Thurstone scales is their main disadvantage: it is a difficult and costly business to collect a hundred expert judges to place several hundred propositions in eleven categories. An attempt has been made to replace particular scales by 'universal scales' which could be applied to a whole series of opinions and attitudes. Universal scales were constructed by Remmers and Silance in 1934. In some cases they have given results identical to those obtained from scales specially established. But in many other cases their results have been unusable. The correlation between the Drobna scale on war and the results of a universal scale applied to the same subject was only .28.

(c) LICKERT SCALES

In 1932 Lickert suggested a different and simpler (because it did not require experts) method of constructing attitude scales.

1. *Constructing Lickert scales.* This comprises the following operations:

(*a*) A large number of propositions relating to the object under consideration are collected; but unlike the Thurstone method these can have either a direct or a very indirect connection with the subject being considered.

(*b*) These propositions are then submitted to a number of subjects and they indicate their reactions by marking 5, 4, 3, 2 or 1 which correspond respectively to complete approval, approval, neutrality, disapproval and complete disapproval.

(*c*) Each subject has a total mark obtained by adding all the individual marks together.

(*d*) The correlations between the marks for each proposition and the total marks are calculated; propositions with a low correlation are discarded (their disagreement with the total mark shows that they are not measuring the same thing as the other propositions).

Lickert constructed scales in this way to study attitudes towards imperialism, internationalism, the colour problem, etc. Great use of Lickert scales was made by Rundquist and Sletto in 1936 in their study of the morale of the American people during the great depression.

2. *Differences with Thurstone scales.* The validity of the two types seems almost the same. Some think that the Lickert scale makes possible a more subtle analysis because there are five possible attitudes to each question rather than the simple 'yes-no' of the Thurstone scale. There does not seem to be a great difference in reliability between the two procedures.

But the significance of the two scales is very different. The Thurstone scale is more rational: expert judges have classified the propositions in an objective order. The mark which each subject obtains is independent of the marks given to the other subjects. It has therefore an absolute character (at least in a particular culture and civilization). In contrast, the Lickert scale is relative: the results can only be interpreted by reference to the group studied since each subject can only be assessed in relation to his place in the whole group of the subjects questioned.

(*d*) HIERARCHICAL SCALES AND THE GUTTMAN SCALOGRAM

In the studies of American soldiers during the war, Louis Guttman invented a new technique of attitude scales which he called the 'scalogram'. The name scalogram applies to the propositions, the replies and the apparatus for classifying them. The scale itself is usually called a 'hierarchical' scale.

1. *The notion of a hierarchical scale and the scalogram.* Guttman's intention was to construct a strictly hierarchical scale, in other words a scale in which agreement to a proposition at a particular level implies agreement with propositions at an inferior level. Thus the following five propositions are hierarchical: (1) Are you *agrégé*? (2) Are you *licencié*? (3) Have you the *baccalaureat*? (4) Have you been to an institution of secondary education? (5) Have you been to school? The reply 'yes' to question 1 implies yes to the rest; the reply 'yes' to question 2 implies yes to 3, 4 and 5, and so on.

It is only by assembling this kind of hierarchical group of propositions that attitudes and opinions can really be measured and subjects given precise ranking and exact measurement. Some other scales attempt a similar hierarchy but they only succeed approximately. Even the scalogram cannot achieve a perfect hierarchy.

Direct Intensive Observation

It is usually allowed that a hierarchical scale is valid if its reproduction coefficient is at least 90 per cent. This coefficient represents the extent to which subjects follow the order of the scale; it also corresponds to the degree of accuracy with which one can reproduce all the replies of a subject from his ranking on the scale. The coefficient of reproduction is calculated by the formula $R = 1 - \dfrac{E}{Q \times S}$ in which E is the total number of errors, Q is the number of questions and S is the number of subjects. The errors must also have a random distribution. 'Weak' scales with a coefficient of between 80 per cent and 90 per cent are sometimes used if the errors have a random distribution.

In the Guttman scale the hierarchical series of propositions are placed on a graph in the form of a parallelogram (this was the first meaning of the word scalogram). Using the example already cited, if thirty subjects were questioned, one answered 'yes' to question 1, two to question 2, four to question 3, eight to question 4, ten to question 5, five to none of the questions. This would produce the scalogram shown in fig. 6 (the highest rank is given to the subjects which answered 'yes' to the greatest number of questions). The scalogram shows the attitudes of all subjects and their distribution over the various ranks. The attitude of different groups can be easily compared.

2. *Establishing a hierarchical scale.* Two successive series of operations are necessary to construct a strictly hierarchical scale.

Firstly, all the questions related to the attitude studied are submitted to a group of subjects and they are required to answer yes or no to them. The number of questions and subjects are limited by the dimensions of the scalogram (in the second sense of the word: apparatus for constructing a hierarchical scale). Secondly, a table of all the replies is drawn up and an attempt made by trial and error to see if it is possible to classify the questions and replies in a hierarchical order (in other words, make a parallelogram like the one in figure 6 with less than 10 per cent aberrant cases).

This classification can be made by mechanical or by graphical (paper and pencil) methods. The most frequently used method is a special apparatus—the scalogram (in the second sense of the word). There are various types. Some consist of large level surfaces of wood or metal with grooves sunk into them so that small coloured or numbered balls which represent the responses can be placed in them: the balls can be easily slid from one groove to another for successive 'trials'. Others take the form of bar lines on which the results can be marked with chalk or crayon and easily erased and put in other places. One of the most convenient forms is the cube which can be moved

INTRODUCTION TO THE SOCIAL SCIENCES

en bloc by slipping rods into grooves: the responses are marked on each cube by colours or by numbers. The main advantage is that all the responses of a subject or all the replies to a question can be moved together.

The operation is mainly one of trial and error and can take a long

Subjects		Yes					No				
		Questions					Questions				
Rank	Number	1	2	3	4	5	1	2	3	4	5
5	1	×	×	×	×	×					
4	2		×	×	×	×	×				
	3		×	×	×	×	×				
3	4			×	×	×	×	×			
	5			×	×	×	×	×			
	6			×	×	×	×	×			
	7			×	×	×	×	×			
2	8				×	×	×	×	×		
	9				×	×	×	×	×		
	10				×	×	×	×	×		
	11				×	×	×	×	×		
	12				×	×	×	×	×		
	13				×	×	×	×	×		
	14				×	×	×	×	×		
	15				×	×	×	×	×		
1	16					×	×	×	×	×	
	17					×	×	×	×	×	
	18					×	×	×	×	×	
	19					×	×	×	×	×	
	20					×	×	×	×	×	
	21					×	×	×	×	×	
	22					×	×	×	×	×	
	23					×	×	×	×	×	
	24					×	×	×	×	×	
	25					×	×	×	×	×	
9	26						×	×	×	×	×
	27						×	×	×	×	×
	28						×	×	×	×	×
	29						×	×	×	×	×
	30						×	×	×	×	×

Fig. 6.—A hypothetical scalogram

DIRECT INTENSIVE OBSERVATION

time. But there are several basic rules to be followed in the groping. A first stage is to classify the questions according to the frequency of positive responses, eliminating those with aberrant frequencies. The subjects are then classified according to the frequency of their positive

			No									Yes					Number of the subject	Rank
9	8	7	6	5	4	3	2	1	9	8	7	6	5	4	3	2		
									×	×	×	×	×	×	×	×	×	1
				×					×	×	×	×	×		×	×	×	2
								×	×	×	×	×	×	×	×	×		3
								×	×	×	×	×	×	×	×	×		4
								×	×	×	×	×	×	×	×	×		5
								×	×	×	×	×	×	×	×	×		6
×									×	×	×	×	×	×	×	×		7
	×								×	×	×	×	×	×	×	×		8
								×	×	×	×	×	×	×	×	×		9
				×					×	×	×	×	×		×	×		10
				×					×	×	×	×	×		×	×		11
					×				×	×	×	×	×	×		×		12
							×		×	×	×	×	×			×		13
								×	×	×	×	×	×	×	×			14
					×				×	×	×	×	×	×	×			15
	×							×	×	×	×	×	×	×				16
					×	×			×	×	×	×	×	×			×	17
					×	×	×		×	×	×	×	×	×	×			18
					×	×		×	×	×	×	×	×	×				19
			×		×	×		×	×	×	×	×	×					20
					×	×	×	×	×	×	×	×	×					21
	×				×	×	×	×	×	×	×	×	×					22
				×	×	×	×	×	×	×	×	×						23
				×	×	×	×	×	×	×	×	×						24
				×	×	×	×	×	×	×	×	×						25
				×	×	×	×	×	×	×	×	×						26
				×	×	×	×	×	×	×	×	×						27
				×	×	×	×	×	×	×	×	×				×		28
				×	×	×	×	×	×	×	×	×				×		29
				×	×		×	×	×	×	×	×		×				30
				×	×		×	×	×	×	×	×		×				31
	×			×	×	×	×	×	×	×	×	×						32
				×	×	×		×	×	×	×				×		×	33
				×	×	×	×	×	×	×	×			×				34
				×	×		×	×	×	×	×		×					35
				×			×	×	×	×	×		×					36
				×		×	×	×	×	×	×							37
				×	×	×	×	×	×	×	×							38
				×	×	×	×	×		×	×							39
	×	×		×	×		×	×				×		×				40
	×	×		×	×	×	×	×										41
	×	×		×	×	×	×	×										42
	×	×		×	×	×	×	×										43
	×	×		×	×	×	×	×										44
	×	×		×	×	×	×	×										45
	×	×		×	×	×	×	×										46
	×	×		×	×	×	×	×										47
	×	×		×	×	×	×	×										48
	×	×		×	×	×	×	×										49
	×	×	×	×	×	×	×	×										50

Fig. 7.—Scalogram of political militancy
(S. Moscovici, 'L'analyse hiérarchique', *L'Année psychologique*, 1954, pp. 83 ff.)

responses. Another elimination of questions then takes place—those to which subjects have made numerous aberrant replies (not conforming to the patterns which are beginning to appear). Finally, the questions are ordered so as to make as nearly as possible, with the minimum of errors, the form of a parallelogram.

Figure 7 is an example of a hierarchical scale of political militancy. Fifty subjects belonging to the same political party were asked fifty questions. By elimination a scale of nine hierarchical questions were obtained, which were, in descending order: (1) Have you posted political posters? (2) Have you had political conversations with a colleague? (3) Have you tried to convince people to join a party? (4) Have you been to political meetings? (5) Have you given money to a party? (6) Do you like to have political discussions? (7) Do you consider yourself well informed politically? (8) Did you vote in 1946? (9) Did you vote in 1951?

The order of the questions and the distribution of the subjects were different for other political parties: even the content of the questions on the scale was sometimes different.

General introduction to test methods: A. ANASTASI, *Psychological Testing*, New York, 1954.

On projective methods: S. E. BELL, *Projective Techniques*, New York, 1948; L. E. ABT and L. BELLACK, *Projective Psychology*, New York, 1950; O. K. BUROS (*et al.*), *Mental Measurements Yearbook*, 4th ed., 1953.

On the Prohansky test: H. M. PROHANSKY, 'A Projective Method for the study of attitudes', *Journal of Abnormal and Social Psychology*, 1943, pp. 393–5.

On the Fromme test: A. FROMME, 'On the Use of Certain Qualitative Methods of Attitude Research', *Journal of Social Psychology*, 1941, pp. 429–59.

On attitude scales: A. L. EDWARDS, *Techniques of Attitude Scale Construction*, New York, 1957; M. W. RILEY (*et al.*), *Sociological Studies in Scale Analysis*, Brunswick, 1954.

On binary comparisons: L. L. THURSTONE, 'The Method of paired Comparisons for social values', *Journal of Abnormal and Social Psychology*, 1927, pp. 384–400, and 'An experimental Study of Nationality Preferences', *Journal of General Psychology*, 1928, p. 405.

On the Bogardus scale: E. S. BOGARDUS, 'Measuring Social Distance', *Journal of Applied Sociology*, 1925, p. 290, and 'A Social Distance Scale', *Sociological and Social Research*, 1933, p. 267; A. I. SIEGAL and F. L. GUER, 'A Variation of the Bogardus Technique', *Journal of Social Psychology*, 1956, p. 275; L. P. CRESPI, 'Attitudes towards Conscientious Objectors', *Journal of Psychology*, 1944, p. 81.

On Thurstone scales: L. L. THURSTONE and E. J. CHAVE, *The Measurement of Attitudes*, Chicago, 1929; D. D. DROBNA, *A Scale of Measuring attitudes towards war*, Chicago, 1929; H. H. REMMERS and E. B. SILANCE, 'Generalized Attitude Scales', *Journal of Social Psychology*, 1954, p. 24.

On Lickert scales: R. LICKERT, 'A Technique for the measurement of attitudes', *Archives of Psychology*, 1930, p. 140; R. LICKERT, S. ROSTOW, G. MURPHY, 'A simple and Reliable Method of scoring the Thurstone Attitude Scales', *Journal of Social Psychology*, 1934, p. 228.

On the Guttman scalogram: L. GUTTMAN, 'The Quantification of a Class of Attitudes' in P. HORST (*et al.*), *The Prediction of Personal Adjustment*, New York, 1941, and 'A Basis for scaling qualitative data', *American Sociological Review*, 1944, p. 139.

Section III. Participant observation

All the procedures of direct observation—whether extensive or intensive—described up to now are based on individual contacts between the observer and the people observed. There is an attempt to define the behaviour or the attitudes or obtain information on the life of the group by examining some of the members of the group. Participant observation, on the other hand, consists of examining the group itself as a whole. This is global observation differing from the atomistic procedures of observation which have just been described.

It is called participant observation because the observer always involves himself to some extent in the life and activities of the group. This participation is sometimes passive and limited to the role of a spectator—but a spectator who is forced by the circumstances to be involved in the show and be amongst the actors. Moreover, the participation is often more active and can be divided into two types. Either the observer is external to the group to start with and involves himself in the group to be able to observe or he is originally a member of the group who endeavours to acquire the quality of an observer. Although the two situations can shade off into one another it is important to distinguish between 'participant-observers' and 'observer-participants'.

1. PARTICIPANT OBSERVERS

Sociologists wishing to observe collective behaviour within certain groups, become involved in the life of the group and participate in its activities. They are observers first and participants second; their participation has no other *raison d'être* than their wish to observe. The participation can vary in intimacy and duration: sometimes the observer involves himself only briefly and superficially in the life of the group but sometimes the symbiosis is long and profound. They represent two very distinct varieties of the method although there are a great number of intermediary cases.

A. Observation by individuals and small teams
The observer either observes and records without really becoming part of the group or takes part in the whole life of the group for quite a long period. The former type is derived from reporting, the latter from anthropology.

(a) REPORTING
The technique of reporting used by journalists has to be made more systematic, precise and rigorous for use in the social sciences. It is an appropriate method for the study of meetings, demonstrations, assemblies, congresses, etc., and in general for observing the discontinuous activities of groups, rather than for the study of their structure and routine existence.

1. *Study of meetings, demonstrations and assemblies.* The collaboration of professional reporters in these studies can often be very useful: journalism is moving in the direction of accuracy and seriousness and some newspapers require from their contributors qualities analogous to those of good scientific observers.

The main difference lies in the systematic character of social inquiry. The plan of research and the working hypothese must be determined in advance. For the French elections of January 2, 1956, for example, a plan for the study of public meetings was established giving very precise instructions to the investigators (these have been improved on since). Procedures drawn from content analysis (check lists of key words) were used in conjunction with others. Observation was conducted by small groups—two to three 'reporters' for each meeting.

Numerous studies of this kind could be made. There is little serious literature on party congresses and congresses of other political associations, on the atmosphere of sittings of parliament or parliamentary committees or the meetings of groups: in this field parliamentary journalists, suitably directed, could provide valuable assistance to social science research. In spite of the efforts of UNESCO, studies of international conferences are also few: they could form a contribution of the first importance to the science of international relations.

2. *The study of group structure and behaviour.* The reporting method is excellent for describing particular incidents, but it is less appropriate for the study of the everyday life, the structure and the behaviour of groups (unless the groups under consideration are parliamentary

assemblies, committees, etc., the main activities of which are meetings and sittings). In these fields the reporter can only gather a superficial impression of the whole—the behaviour of a crowd in the street, the style of and reception in party offices, etc. The value of these impressions, of these direct contacts must not be over-estimated. Nothing serious can be based on them alone but they are useful, even indispensable, in evoking general atmosphere.

Describing a political party, for example, without knowing the atmosphere of its meetings and of the party offices, the tone of discussion between militants and their behaviour, etc., would be a cold, dead and incomplete picture. Similarly the analysis of the *grand corps* of the State, the description of a trade union or a pressure group, the study of a newspaper, etc., should rest on direct personal contacts. Social science is concerned with living men: it is necessary to watch them live in order to understand them.

(*b*) ANTHROPOLOGICAL OBSERVATION
This is derived from ethnological methods and applied to communities in so-called civilized countries.

1. *The method.* The ethnologist who wishes, for example, to study a tribe of the upper Amazon will live with it for a long period (several months at least). He will attempt to gain the confidence and integrate himself into the community. He will probably never succeed completely but, helped by familiarity, the group will eventually more or less adopt him. Little by little people will come to behave naturally in his presence and will show themselves without posing as they really are. The ethnologist will watch them live, question them on the significance of their acts as they perform them and accumulate observations from which he will later establish a general picture. Usually he has preconceived ideas in the form of theories and hypotheses which guide his research.

Transposing these techniques to the study of civilized societies has been considered for several years. A sociologist can enter a social group—a small town, a working-class area, a factory, etc.—to study it. He can follow almost the same line of conduct as the ethnologist, win people's confidence and get himself adopted by them, without hiding his role as an observer—quite the reverse: he would try to make the subjects of the inquiry understand its significance whilst guaranteeing their anonymity.

Another element of the ethnological method is present—the 'other', 'different', 'foreign' character of the observer in relation to the group observed. It is often foreigners to a country who make the best studies of it (the subjectivity of the observer is less and people talk more freely to him). They can also be 'foreigners' from the social point of view; for example, a middle-class sociologist studying a working-class area or a group of gangsters.

2. *Application.* This method can be widely used and it has the great advantage of studying social phenomena as a whole. Basic relationships in their various aspects can be clearly seen. It is a method of observation in depth. But it calls for great subtlety, understanding and intuition, and it is difficult to use. Also the results do not have an appearance of rigour and most of them cannot be quantified.

Only two examples of anthropological observation which have produced important results will be quoted. Firstly, the study made by William Foote Whyte, *Street Corner Society* (1937), on a working-class area of a town in the East of the United States almost exclusively inhabited by Italian immigrants and their children. The author lived in the area for three-and-a-half years, sharing the daily life of the inhabitants, developing sympathies with them, trying to understand them and analysing the social structure of the community and its political life. He examined in depth the formation of gangs of young people, the development of 'rackets' and their significance. This work is an important contribution to the study of social structure at the working-class level.

The second example is the book by Laurence Wylie, *Village in the Vaucluse* (1957). This American author lived with his wife and two children for a year in a village perched on top of a hill about 50 kilometres from Avignon. He taught English at the school where his children were pupils. He was progressively adopted by the population. His work is probably the best on France for a long time. He describes all aspects of the village life and the analysis of political life is very important. Wylie shows that State, parties and politics in general are distrusted by the villagers: they are all a part of an external world, the universe of 'them' which is distrusted on *a priori* grounds. Except in municipal elections all the votes are protests against 'them' and the power of the outside: the degree of protest varies only according to social and economic status. Politics is a means of obtaining favours through the mediation of representatives who have no other functions. The State is a kind of enemy. Wylie intends to study other villages in France to determine to what extent these characteristics are general.

B. Team observation

The difference between individual observation and observation by small groups lies rather in the number of observers than in the manner of inquiry. In the methods which have just been described the investigators are few in number (one to three) and, above all, observer participation is practically their only method of inquiry (not counting the preliminary scrutiny of all the documents concerning the community being studied).

In collective observation, on the other hand, participant observation is associated with other techniques such as opinion polls, interviews and tests: scrutiny of documents is conducted on a very large scale, hence the necessity of a much more numerous team of research workers. This team usually has a hierarchical organization with a director, two or three senior research workers and a varying number of assistants. The assistants are often recruited amongst the members of the group being observed.

(*a*) THE TEAMS

There is not an absolute difference between team work and the technique described previously. Often, observation of an anthropological type is used as a basis and nucleus of other inquiries. This was the case with the inquiry conducted at Vienne (Isère) by Pierre Clément and Nelly Xydias in 1949–50. After living for three months in the community and using ethnographic analysis, P. Clément and N. Xydias made a poll of the population, a series of tests on school children and on small samples of adults, etc., whilst at the same time continuing their ethnographic observations.

1. *Method.* The preceding example provides a good example of the difference between team observation and individual observation.

The first difference is in the size of the team, which can vary greatly. There are always a fairly large number of assistants—investigators, interviewers, test specialists, secretarial staff, etc.—helping the specialist, or specialists, who direct the project. Some of them are recruited on the spot: members of the group studied thus collaborate in the observation. Some American investigations have employed very large teams. Lloyd Warner had thirty collaborators, without counting secretarial assistance, in the work on *Yankee City*.

The length of 'participation' in the life of the community studied varies a great deal. In Yankee City research on the spot lasted five years. The period is usually much shorter, often limited to several months. The form of participation is often different to that of anthropological studies. Work is done on the documents in the local archives, the authorities are contacted, opinion polls are made, etc. The place of direct daily observation of people and things is more restricted. But a phase of the inquiry is often given over to ethnographic inquiry or some members of the team are assigned this task.

The essential characteristic of the method is the association of various techniques of observation—'participation' is only one of these techniques. In a sense it is a comparative method since the results obtained by using different techniques are compared. In most cases the study has an interdisciplinary character and the team directing the work is composed of specialists in various branches of the social sciences—psychologists, anthropologists, political scientists, etc. We will return to this aspect of the method during the examination of comparative methods (p. 268).

2. *The results.* Only a few typical examples from the most important works of this type will be quoted. The largest work remains the one which under the direction of Lloyd Warner commenced in 1930 and continued for five years in a typical small American town, baptized 'Yankee City'. Assessing the information gathered took nearly twenty years. Publication of the report began in 1941.

The most interesting contribution of Warner's research concerned social stratification, the definition of six 'classes': upper-upper, lower-upper, upper-middle, lower-middle, upper-lower and lower-lower. These are not only a reflection of standard of living but also a feeling about social prestige: members of the community placed people according to these ranks. The theory, which can be criticized from many points of view, will not be examined here: in the United States it came as a revelation, showing that contrary to the traditional views, there was a class system.

A very interesting inquiry, conducted with small resources, was made by Robert and Helen Lynd on another small American town in 1927 and re-examined eight years later. This allowed a study in depth of the evolution of the town (baptized 'Middletown'). This inspired work in France: Ch. Bettelheim and S. Frére on Auxerre (1947–48, published in 1950) and the work already cited by P. Clément and N. Xydias on Vienne-sur-Rhône (1949–50, published in 1955).

(*b*) PARTICIPATION OF OBSERVERS

When members of the group being observed collaborate in the inquiry under the direction of the specialists who conduct it, there is an intermediary situation between the 'participant-observer' and the 'observer-participant'. It is nearer the former because the inquiry is not under the direction of members of the group observed (these have only an auxiliary role). There are various possible situations and the main ones will be examined.

Direct Intensive Observation

1. *Collaboration between the observed and the observers.* In most team inquiries part of the team is recruited on the spot. This is partly explained by reasons of convenience and economy, but more by the usefulness of participation of members of the group observed.

The main advantage is the confidence inspired in the subjects questioned. Commenting on the poll conducted in Auxerre, Bettelheim wrote: 'The success was due equally to the personalities [of the investigators] and their position in the town.' This problem has already been touched on in examining opinion polls. The only aim here is to overcome the natural distrust of people subject to the investigation. There is no connection with 'observer-participants'.

2. *Technique of mass observation.* This was invented and perfected in Britain but it has also been used in the United States. It rests on a network of informants in a country (or region or town). They record all they observe of interest to the inquiry. The inquiry itself is directed by specialists who synthesize and analyse the reports sent to them by their local informants.

An example of this technique is the wartime activities of the Domestic Branch of the Office of War Information in the United States. The Office organized a network of key people as informants—journalists, businessmen, trade unionists, farmers, clergymen, members of social organizations, etc. Each had to record how the members of his milieu reacted to important current events: The information gathered illuminated many aspects of the morale of the civilian population and the reactions of public opinion.

3. *Lewin's 'social laboratories'.* A psychologist, Kurt Lewin, has done important work in psycho-sociology; his theories which transpose Gestalt theory into sociology have had a considerable influence. One of his positions is the refusal to separate research from action. He invented 'social laboratories', a method of observing social reality and at the same time changing reality. These laboratories have two forms—seminars and 'collective auto-analysis'. The seminars are a variety of experiments on small groups which will be examined later (see p. 249). Collective auto-analysis should be mentioned here as a very special form of participant-observation.

An example of collective auto-analysis was a study done in an American town on 40,000 inhabitants which the investigators called 'Northtown'. An attempt was made both to study the attitude of the inhabitants to two minorities (Negro and Jewish) which were victims of discrimination and to make discriminatory practices cease —or at least alleviate them. An executive committee for the inquiry was established, composed of representatives of about fifteen organizations such as trade unions, ex-servicemen's organizations and social organizations. An interview plan was put into operation by volunteers from these organizations. Reports were submitted to the organizations concerned. A plan of reform was then adopted and publicized by the press, the local authorities, the organizations, etc. Some positive results were obtained.

The method has naïve aspects but it merits examination. It would be interesting to compare some collective auto-criticism procedures with educational sessions organized in some popular democracies, particularly China and Vietnam. The techniques differ greatly in detail but the basic ideas have some similarities.

2. OBSERVER PARTICIPANTS

The procedures just examined are moving from participant observation to observer participation. Mass observation and 'social laboratories' are not put in the latter category only because the directors of the observation remain outside the group observed. In the methods which will now be studied members of the group—'participants'—observe the social realities of their own group. Two main techniques should be distinguished. The observer either practises introspection and studies social reality through the medium of his own consciousness or he observes his colleagues in the group, the institutions in which he operates, etc.

A. Introspection in social science

In social science the observer is subject and object at the same time in that he observes and is an element in the thing observed. Social phenomena are to a large extent phenomena of consciousness and an observer naturally looks at their reflection in his own consciousness. Introspection was widely practised in the 'pre-history' of the social sciences: before the eighteenth century the main works are based, not only on the observation of external facts and historical comparisons, but also on the personal reactions of the observer.

Today introspection has a bad scientific reputation. Psychology has spared no effort to free itself from introspection and to establish objective research methods. The social sciences have followed a parallel route. It does not, however, seem possible to exclude self-observation completely. In practice, it is the basis of a large number of documents such as memoirs and autobiographies which are widely used in the social sciences. Since this indirect introspection is

Direct Intensive Observation

acceptable there is no reason to exclude direct observation. The limits of the procedure should, however, be clearly understood.

(*a*) USE OF INTROSPECTION

A large proportion of social phenomena are only known to us through their repercussions in individual consciousness. When an individual is questioned in an interview or opinion poll, he is asked to express what he feels; in other words he is asked to practise introspection. But this procedure differs in two ways from the usual form of introspection in that it is superficial and the results are used in an indirect manner by the investigator. From these points of view introspection is undoubtedly superior.

1. *Analysis in depth by introspection.* To apply the precept of Socrates 'know yourself' requires practice and apprenticeship. The methods of investigation already described nearly all rest on the assumption that the subjects questioned spontaneously confide their thoughts and rapidly expose their thinking. But the picture which people give of themselves can only be superficial because they are usually not accustomed to analysing themselves.

This explains the superiority of some testimonies derived from novels over direct inquiry. The writer, whose profession is introspection, sees further into real life than the subjects of a poll and gives to his characters a depth which the subjects possess but which they cannot make explicit. The sociologist can go even further in using introspection because he has a better professional training to ask the relevant questions and to decide the ways in which introspection can be extended (on condition, of course, that he practises introspection and acquires expertise in this field).

It should be remembered that a trained and experienced man is the best tool in the social sciences. No machine, however complicated, can yet produce the same result as some French parliamentarians—to predict before a vote the result of a division with a very small margin of error. This requires a considerable gift for observing others and intuition. But to observe others in any profound way, it is essential to possess a deep knowledge of oneself through introspection.

2. *Direct analysis by introspection.* Polls and interviews require the subject examining himself and the observer recording and interpreting the result of this examination. Introspection does away with the second stage. The one who is analysed himself expresses the results of the analysis. The risk of distortion is less great and the possibility

of accuracy is greater. Experience and practice are necessary not only for observing but also for expressing meaningfully the results of observation. The superiority of writers which has just been mentioned is not solely because they are better at analysing themselves but also, and often mainly, because they can express themselves better.

In this field, too, the sociologist's experience is invaluable. He alone knows the significance and the importance of the various aspects of the facts studied. He alone can give precise and rigorous expression to phenomena which he observes in himself. He is, in a manner of speaking, a 'privileged' observer—a more perfect instrument of observation than others.

(b) LIMITS OF INTROSPECTION

Social science cannot be divorced from introspection. In fact, it is often used more or less unconsciously. It is preferable that people should be aware of this. In many fields introspection provides information which could not be obtained by other means. But the limits of the method should be known. It presents three main dangers, subjectivity, distortion and apparent facilty.

1. *Subjectivity.* Phenomena present in *one* individual consciousness (the observer's) can be known through introspection. But one cannot conclude that all consciousnesses in the group observed will contain the same reactions. The results of introspection are valid only as individual testimony. There are undoubtedly many common elements in the consciousnesses of members of the same group but they cannot be separated from personal idiosyncracies by the introspective method.

This does not undermine the value of the results but means simply that the results should not be generalized. Introspection thus has significance only in conjunction with other methods already described. The general configuration of attitudes and the outlines of phenomena can be discovered by these other methods. Introspection allows the deepening of the analysis at isolated points in the form of testimonies, illustrations and examples. It is desirable that there should be as many of these as possible covering very different cases.

2. *Distortion.* It has been said introspection requires experience and patience. There is, however, a danger of over-subtlety in analysis. In order to disentangle his feelings an observer may introduce a subtlety which was not there in the first place. It is also possible that the habit of self-analysis leads to an unconscious pose. One some-

Direct Intensive Observation

times has the impression that writers experience rather artificial and forced feelings as a result of a *déformation prefessionnelle*.

This does not mean that introspection should not be used in the social sciences, but it is another reason for taking precautions. The dangers should not be exaggerated and even artificial complex and over-subtle schemes are useful in analysing more simple feelings and reactions. The main thing is to avoid giving the results of introspection a general significance and to consider them as a means of complementing results of objective methods which must always be used.

3. *Facility*. This has to be mentioned only because some French sociologists (lawyers and philosophers) tend in this direction. The advantage of introspection is that it can be practised in comfort and tranquility between the four walls of an office, seated in front of several sheets of paper. One looks at one's own soul in a moral mirror and regards oneself as exemplifying the whole community. The task is easier, less unpleasant, less lengthy than observation in the field, scrutiny of documents, long inquiries and tedious calculations. It is a solitary occupation which avoids the difficulties of co-operation with others.

B. Observation of one's own group

The attitude here is the reverse of that described concerning 'participant observers'. Instead of a specialized sociologist, originally a stranger to the group, entering it and to some extent becoming a part of the group, a member of the group turns himself into a sociologist and tries to acquire the qualities of a qualified observer in order to observe his own community.

(*a*) NOTION OF OBSERVING ONE'S OWN GROUP

A preliminary distinction can be made between observation made only by members of the group and inquiries in which outside observers collaborate. The latter have already been examined and only the former really comes within the category of observer participants. Two other categories will be examined: contemporary observation and *a posteriori* observation; observation by members and by apostates.

1. *Contemporary and* a posteriori *observation*. In contemporary observation members of a group study its activities as they take place. In this respect they are in the same situation as the participant observers described in the previous paragraph. A group of

Parliamentarians can study the work of the National Assembly, the reactions and behaviour of its members: a group of socialists can analyse the life of the Socialist party, the influence of the leaders and the militants, etc.

In *a posteriori* observation the member or members of the group analyse the past activities of their group. The memoirs of a politician or higher civil servant are a form of *a posteriori* observation. But there are many others. Members of a group generally have greater freedom of access to the archives of a group and can interview people in the group more easily.

It is necessary to distinguish between these two forms of observation because *a posteriori* observation is not really participant observation but using membership of a group to further research by other means. Contemporary observation uses other means such as polls, questionnaires, etc., but also uses direct observation.

2. *Observation by members of the group and by apostates.* Participant observation rests on the assumption that observers are members of the group observed, participate in its activities and remain faithful to it. Observation by former members of the group who have left and broken with it is rather different in kind: this can be called observation by apostates.

These latter observations have, however, some importance. Many closed and secret groups cannot be observed by outsiders nor by their own members (or, at least, their own members cannot communicate their observations). Only apostates can give accurate information on the activities of these societies. They can write the history of the groups from memory and their experience helps them to interpret current reactions and behaviour of the group to which they once belonged; they alone can assess the significance of various external manifestations which outsiders can easily misunderstand.

Observation by apostates provides information which cannot be acquired elsewhere. But it should be received with great caution. The personal deformation of the observer can be very great. An apostate often seeks to justify his apostasy both in his own and other people's eyes; he tends to blacken the reputation of the group which he has left and interpret unfavourably its activities (more so, if there is material advantage to be gained which was illustrated by the behaviour of ex-members of the communist party in the United States in the pay of the FBI). The faithful have undoubtedly a tendency to distort in the opposite direction but generally this is done with less passion; and love makes for better understanding than hatred. Also groups evolve quickly; apostates have a tendency to interpret current behaviour in the light of memories of past events.

1. *Advantages of the procedure.* There are three main ones. As has been said, in some cases members of a group can benefit from certain facilities. This is particularly true in the field of political science where distrust of motives and keeping of 'secrets' are widespread. Except in unusual cases the freedom of an external observer in political parties and pressure groups is very limited. Only members of the group can make observations in depth.

Members of the group also have the advantage of being intimately involved in the life of the collectivity being studied. Apart from documents and material facts, the communal atmosphere composed of imponderable factors can be easily understood only by members of the group. Observation of one's own group is certainly deeper and more intimate than observation of groups to which one does not belong, even if one tries to participate fully in their life for the purpose of the inquiry.

Some sympathy is necessary for any complete understanding. Sympathy can distort but it is also a source of understanding. The unmarried cannot describe married life. The unbeliever cannot describe religious experience. It must be remembered that all areas of social life are steeped in faith, passion and enthusiasm. No external observer can grasp the nature and intensity of this: only an authentic participant, and not an occasional provisional participant, can grasp it.

2. *Dangers of the procedure.* These are obvious. The observer's sympathies influence him, usually in good faith, towards favourable interpretations. Conscious distortion is relatively rare but unconscious distortion is frequent. An extensive as possible technical training in the social science to develop the objectivity of the observer can alleviate this to a certain extent.

Pressure from the group itself must also be taken into account. The more strongly integrated it is the more difficult it is for it to permit other than laudatory publications about it. There is, therefore, a natural tendency to exert pressure to conform on observers who are members of the group. But the advantages accruing from an objective study—which shows the dark places as well as emphasizing the highlights—are considerable. An evolution towards objectivity can be discerned in commercial advertising and political propaganda will probably follow suit. This evolution has, however, scarcely started. In conclusion, observation of groups by their own members should be treated with reserve and this should increase in proportion as the group is rigid and integrated. But observation of this kind is indispensable.

On sociological investigation in general: P. V. YOUNG, *Scientific Social Surveys and Research*, New York, 1956; C. A. MOSER, *Surveys Methods in Social Investigation*, London, 1958; H. HYMAN, *Surveys Design and Analysis*, Glencoe, 1955; E. SHEVKY and W. BELL, *Social Area Analysis*, Stanford, 1955; A. J. REISS, *A Review and Evaluation of Research on Community*, Nashville, 1954.

On participant observation: M. S. SCHWARTZ and C. GREEN-SCHWARTZ, 'Problems in Participant Observation', *American Journal of Sociology*, 1955, p. 343.

On anthropological methods: M. GRIAULE, *Méthodes de l'ethnographie*, 1957; C. LÉVI-STRAUSS, *Anthropologie structurale*, 1958; W. F. WHYTE, *Street Corner Society*, Chicago, 1937; L. WYLIE, *Village in the Vaucluse*, Cambridge (Mass.), 1957; A. H. BIRCH, *Small Town Politics*, Oxford, 1959; L. BERNOT and R. BLANCARD, *Nouville, un village français*, 1953; A. LEIGHTON, *The Governing of Men*, Princeton, 1945.

The main American collective studies: L. WARNER (*et al.*), *Yankee City Series*, Yale University Press (I. *The Social Life of a Modern Community*, 4th ed., 1946; II. *The Status System of a Modern Community*, 2nd ed., 1947; III. *The Social Systems of American Ethnic Groups*, 3rd ed., 1947; IV. *The Social System of the Modern Factory*, 2nd ed., 1948; V. American Symbols Systems (to be published)); R. S. and H. LYND, *Middletown: a study in Contemporary American Culture*, New York, 1929, and *Middletown in Transition: a study in Cultural Conflicts*, New York, 1937.

The main French studies: C. BETTELHEIM and S. FRÈRE, *Une Ville française moyenne: Auxerre en 1950*, 1950; P. CLÉMENT and N. XYDIAS, *Vienne sur le Rhône*.

On mass observation: C. MADGE and T. HARRISON, *Britain by Mass Observation*, 1939; S. DERI (*et al.*), 'Techniques for the Diagnosis and Measurement of Intergroup Attitudes and Behaviour', *Psychological Bulletin*, 1948, p. 251; A. BARTH, 'The Bureau of Intelligence', *Public Opinion Quarterly*, 1943, pp. 73–4.

On social laboratories: K. LEWIN, *Resolving Social Conflicts*, 1948; R. LIPPITT, *Training in Community Relations*; the special number of *The Journal of Social Issues*, December 1948.

On observation of one's own group: H. E. DALE, *The Higher Civil Service of Great Britain*, 1941; D. MCKEAN, *Pressures on the Legislature of New Jersey*, New York, 1938; B. BETTELHEIM, 'Individual and Mass Behaviour in an Extreme Situation', *Journal of Abnormal and Social Psychology*, 1943, p. 417; E. KOGON, *The Theory and Practice of Hell*.

An example of introspection: L. STEFFENS, *Autobiography*, New York, 1931.

PART TWO

SYSTEMATIC ANALYSIS

To seek facts and record observations without any systematization is not scientific. It makes no difference if the research is conducted on a large scale using modern techniques: mechanized empiricism is empiricism all the same. For this point of view American social science took a wrong turning between 1920 and 1940; there has been a reaction and theories and systems are now given pride of place. Perhaps the reaction has been too sharp but in principle it is sound. To talk today of 'Anglo-Saxon empiricism' simply shows ignorance of what has happened in the last twenty years.

On the other hand to systematize in the void, using always the same few and out-dated facts hinders progress in the social sciences. There is little chance of finding better arrangements for the pieces of the puzzle: synthesizers in an ivory tower are presumptuous. Nothing meaningful is said when it is asserted that theory should have the first place and collection of facts a subordinate place: the carburettor is not subordinate to the motor nor the motor to the carburettor. After periods of 'super-systemization' research and observation of the facts should be emphasized; in this respect the orientation of American social science between 1920 and 1940 was salutary. After a period of 'hyperfactualism' the inverse reaction is natural. In either case observation and systematization cannot be divorced.

It cannot be repeated often enough that systematic analysis does not constitute a stage separate from observation and research. One does not first of all seek facts and then compare and systematize them. Systematization is indispensable from the very first step: all research is based on it. The essential thing is to see significance and this is impossible without systemization. 'No facts without ideas, no ideas without facts': this dictum of François Simiand admirably expresses the character of all scientific research.

An outline will be given of all the various elements of systematic analysis in the social sciences, showing their similarities and their differences with systematic analysis in the physical sciences. There will then be an examination of special techniques of systematic analysis—graphs and mathematical techniques—which warrant a more detailed analysis. Basically they are an application of the comparative method.

CHAPTER ONE

ELEMENTS OF SYSTEMATIC ANALYSIS

Following the academic schema, scientific research is divided into three phases: observation of the facts, formulation of the hypotheses and experimental testing of the hypotheses to transform them into laws. In practice things are very different. All research does not end in laws: some simply concerns facts of structure, operation and evolution. Also observation is not made without preconceptions: it takes place within a conceptual framework and like the sociologist who conducts an opinion poll, the scientist who examines 'nature' has always previously defined with some precision the questions which he is going to ask. But it remains true that the experiment is the basic procedure of systematic analysis in the physical sciences.

In this lies the main differences between the physical and the social sciences. Experiment has a secondary place in the latter: it is not and it does not seem likely ever to be highly developed. The comparative method has a place of the first order in the social sciences but it is used much less in the physical sciences (all sciences to some extent need it to stimulate ideas and hypotheses). The elements of systematic analysis in the social sciences can therefore be classified into three categories: conceptual frameworks, experiment and the comparative method.

Section I. Conceptual frameworks of research

All scientific research is conducted within conceptual frameworks. This, in the first place, implies a classification of facts and a more or less precise typology. This in turn supposes an accurate idea of the phenomena studied and the relations between them—in other words hypothetical 'theories' and 'systems'. The aim of typologies and theories is not to describe reality but to explain it through the formulation of sociological laws. It is, however, necessary to distinguish between certain levels of scientific research. As this problem dominates the others it must be examined first.

Introduction to the Social Sciences

1. LEVELS OF SCIENTIFIC RESEARCH

The first aim of science is to formulate laws which describe constant relations between phenomena. These laws have an explanatory and provisional character: they define the links existing between various aspects of reality: they make possible the prediction of the phenomenon N when phenomenon A is present. But the establishment of laws is not the only aim of scientific research even in the natural sciences. In practice the discovery of laws is possible only in the most advanced sectors of research: there are still few such sectors in the social sciences.

A. Distinction of levels of research

Three levels of scientific research can be distinguished in the physical and social sciences: the levels of description, classification and explanation. Formulation of laws is present only at the last stage; explanation and prediction are not inextricably associated with one another.

(a) THE THREE LEVELS: DESCRIPTION, CLASSIFICATION, EXPLANATION
These will be dealt with briefly.

1. *Description.* Before thinking of establishing a relationship, even a hypothetical one, between two series of phenomena, most aspects of the phenomena must be described in detail. The establishment of hypotheses and the formulation of laws must be based on the scrutiny and comparison of a wide range of material.

At the moment many fields, and often central ones, in the social sciences are at the level of description. The concrete cases of French pressure groups can be taken as an example. Their influence on government is indisputable. It would be of great importance to specify exactly what this is by defining hypotheses and attempting to verify them. In practice this is almost impossible because of the absence of sufficient basic information. It can be argued that the field of pressure groups in France still remains at the level of description. In other countries—for example, the United States—research is more advanced and the level of explanation can be reached.

The charge often made that studies in the social sciences are restricted to description without attempting explanation is very often unjustified. These works are descriptive because they cannot be anything else. Documentation is still too scarce to make valid attempts at explanation. To restrict oneself to the level of description in this case is more scientific than to look for explanations which would necessarily be illusory: it should be understood that descriptive works have great importance because they alone make it possible to move on to the level of classification and then explanation. Works of this kind can advance the social sciences in very important ways.

2. *Classification.* One usually moves from description to explanation through the intermediary stage of classification. Categories have to be determined before the relations between the categories can be defined.

The second stage of any science is the establishment of a classification or the perfecting of a typology: this will be dealt with in detail in the following paragraph (only the context is dealt with here). Description and classification ought not be regarded as distinct and necessarily successive levels of research. In practice, all description assumes the character of classification: it always implies to some extent reference, whether explicit or not, to some preliminary classification. Description and classification are interwoven and so too are classification and explanation: verification of working hypotheses and the search for sociological laws leads to the refining and eventually the correction of the classification used as the basis of the research. Distinguishing the three levels is nevertheless important and the relative succession of levels is indisputable.

3. *Explanation.* The level of scientific explanation can be approached when a sufficient mass of phenomena have been described and when the basic classifications in the field have been sufficiently refined. The number of fields in the social sciences where this can be attempted is still few: this explains why there are few real sociological laws.

Most research in the social sciences takes place on two planes at the same time. Trying to verify hypotheses and transform them into laws covers one area whilst in others the task is limited to defining the problems and suggesting general lines of a typology: this increases the number of phenomena described and refines the proposed frameworks: the activity is at the level of description and classification as well as explanation. Research is, at the same time, explanatory, descriptive and classifying. There are, however, certain fields of study which are now sufficiently worked over to permit work purely at the level of explanation.

(*b*) FROM EXPLANATION TO PREDICTION
In principle the level of explanation is also that of prediction. Since scientific explanation consists of asserting the dependence of two

phenomena, A and B, one can predict that B will be present if A is present. In all sciences, however, prediction runs into a certain number of difficulties and these are serious in the social sciences.

1. *General difficulties of prediction.* These are linked to the character of scientific determinism which will be examined later. Prediction always issues from explanation in causal determinism and in most forms of functional determinism but not in 'stochastic' determinism according to which only several possibilities can be predicted.

The statistical character which scientific laws are now recognized to have only permits a global prediction for groups of factors. But, even in the social sciences, this global prediction can be very precise: in many fields (economics, demography, etc.) the percentage of elements to be found in a certain position can be predicted, and the margin of error can itself be evaluated.

2. *Special difficulties in the social sciences.* Prediction in the social sciences is more difficult than in the physical sciences for two reasons. Firstly, social phenomena are very complex, resulting from the combination of a great number of factors which are difficult to isolate and measure. In the physical universe there is also a multiplicity of factors, but it is easier to measure them and therefore to predict the result of their combinations.

Also, and most important of all, modifications of the social context are much more rapid, profound and complex than those of the physical context. It is true that physical laws are valid only when 'all other things are equal' and in 'given conditions of temperature and pressure'. It is also true that things are never quite the same and there is never identical temperature and pressure conditions. But the differences are usually very small and superficial; they are easy to measure and predict. In contrast, differences in social context are so complex and produce so many chain reactions and 'feedback' effects that they are practically impossible to define. It is, however, necessary to distinguish two categories of sociological laws. Some refer to limited and circumscribed facts and to the short-term effects which can be predicted with some precision: this is true of some economic and demographic laws. Others refer to more complex clusters and to the 'medium' or 'long-term' and only allow very approximate prediction.

B. Scope of sociological explanation

What does explanation in the social sciences mean exactly? This brings us to the definition of social determinism and the scope of laws which arise from it. Since the founders of sociology, attempting to assert the scientific character of the subject, argued that social determinism has the same nature as physical determinism, there has been a great and unresolved debate on this subject. The position of August Comte and Durkheim has been very strongly criticized, in the first instance for non-scientific reasons: the idea of social determinism appeared contrary to human liberty. It has been seen since that the contradiction is only apparent and that this is a false problem: the existence of social determinism is hardly discussed today. But its nature and scope remain very controversial: for some it is really different from physical determinism; for others they are analogous and only secondary differences separate them. The second thesis seems closer to reality: the first seems to rest on an archaic conception of physical determinism.

(a) CHARACTERISTICS OF SOCIAL DETERMINISM

The sociologist G. A. Lundberg wrote: 'The term scientific law can and ought to mean in the social sciences exactly what it means in any of the other sciences.'[1] This is an exaggeration in so far as the word 'exactly' is used, but in general it is true. There are differences between physical and sociological determinisms, but they are of degree rather than kind. The concept of determinism in the physical sciences has changed greatly and has come closer to the concept in the social sciences.

1. *The functional character*. At the end of the nineteenth century determinism in the physical sciences was conceived almost solely in the form of causal determinism: phenomenon A being considered as the generating element of phenomenon B with which it appeared to be associated. This relationship is expressed in the famous formula: 'The same causes produce the same effects.' But the notion of cause is very obscure: Comte banished it from the vocabulary of science. The concept of causal determinism has been gradually abandoned in favour of the much more precise functional determinism borrowed from mathematics. The 'constant relations' between phenomena are analogous to the relation which unites two variables in a function: to every value of x there corresponds a value y. This expresses the current notion of a law in physical and social sciences much more than causal determinism.

Sometimes, however, both categories of science use a concept of 'stochastic' determinism; instead of each value x having a corresponding value y, each value x has a corresponding cluster of values y which are scaled between a maximum and a minimum without it being

[1] G. A. Lundberg, *Foundations of Sociology*, New York, 1939.

possible to predict which of these values of y will be present in any given case (see pp. 286–93). A large number of the relationships analysed in the social sciences are of this kind. This is so in the physical sciences on the scale of the very small—although this should not be exaggerated: in 1953, Louis de Broglie qualified his famous conclusions concerning indeterminancy in quantum physics and the scope of the equation of uncertainty.

2. *The statistical character.* The concept of statistical determinism, based on calculation of probabilities and the law of large numbers is becoming more and more important in science. It was first invented as a basis for certain sociological laws, particularly in demography. In spite of the hostility of Auguste Comte (who strongly criticized their application to sociology in the works of Bernoulli) it has become dominant in the social sciences and has also been progressively adopted by physicists. Today most physicists admit that physical laws are laws of probability of a statistical character. As Abel Roy said in 1934: 'A law is only a mathematical relation: it is only a probability and a classifying principle.' Originally sociological laws were conceived on the model of physical laws: today, it is the physical laws which tend to come closer to the sociological laws.

This statistical character allows the famous conflict between scientific determinism and human liberty to be entirely eliminated. It can be recognized as a false problem. Liberty is associated with the attitude of each individual: sociological laws only express the relationship between groups of individuals. They rest on the fact that within a group the attitudes adopted by the elements composing it are as a whole statistically determined. This simply means that the proportion of people who will submit to the influence of some factors and those who will submit to others can be predicted. Individually each remains free to act as he wishes. That 10 per cent of Parisians take the train on August 1st does not compel anyone to go to the station. The problem of human liberty is no longer brought up seriously to criticize the concept of a sociological law: but for the man in the street the question is not settled. Many qualms about the social sciences are still explained by this.

(*b*) RELATIVELY OF SOCIOLOGICAL LAWS
Sociological laws have only a relative application: this is also true of physical laws but their relativity is less accentuated. In the social realm, relativity has two aspects: historical and dimensional.

1. *Historical relativity.* This has already been dealt with during the

examination of the general character of social phenomena, in refuting the 'objection of historicity' (see p. 31). It was then stated that the regularities and liaisons are relative to a given historical context and it does not seem possible to transfer them from one context to another. These contexts are both geographical and historical: they are 'cultures' and 'civilizations' localized both in time and in space. Examples are Mediaeval Christendom, nineteenth-century Europe, twentieth-century Western industrial society and so on (see p. 65). Each 'context' has its sociological laws which are not directly applicable to other contexts. It is, perhaps, possible to define systems of transposition from one context to another; this task falls within the field of general sociology.

2. *Dimensional relativity*. The distinction between 'macro' and 'micro' has become familiar to the economists and no economist any longer contests that explanations valid for small areas are not applicable (unless modified) to large aggregations. The distinction is generally valid in all the social sciences: 'macro-sociology' and 'micro-sociology' are terms now used. But thinking about the consequences of differences in scale has hardly begun. This is a major problem which all attempts at explanation and prediction run up against.

An example from political science, the field of electoral studies, shows its importance. Studies in France of electoral sociology at the national level show the presence of great currents of opinion which can partly be identified with social class, religious attitudes and so on. In the context of the département these currents are fragmentary but their presence is quite clearly seen. If one goes further and examines small communes these explanatory factors lose much of their importance and give way to factors of another kind: influence of a certain person, of a particular fact, etc. To say that these particular factors are submerged in the general factors which have just been mentioned is meaningless—there is no fusion of the two. When one passes from one scale to another the system of explanation simply seems to change.

One of the most fruitful hypotheses which can be suggested to researchers is the distinction between two categories of social phenomena—those of macro-sociology and those of micro-sociology. Its importance is shown in the research in the United States on small groups (see p. 57): the conclusions drawn from these studies seem in part false when applied to States and large groups. There is no proven sharp and absolute difference of kind between large and small groups; but the facts known lead one to think that there is a greater probability that such a difference exists than that it does not.

One can hardly help invoking at this point differences of scale in the physical universe. Physical laws too are only valid within a certain sphere. The laws of 'our world', the laws of the infinitely large and the laws of the infinitely small have to be distinguished. The laws for the world on our scale are not valid on the scale of the galaxy nor on the scale of the atom. There is an analogy to the social universe. One cannot even say that the 'large' and the 'small' are less far removed from one another in the social universe because the distinction is between the situation where there is direct human contact and where there is not. In the physical world Einstein tried to formulate a general key, a system of transposing, which would make it possible to pass from the laws of one scale to another. Research of this kind will probably be necessary one day in the social sciences.

2. CLASSIFICATIONS OR TYPOLOGIES

Establishing a classification of phenomena is a fundamental stage in all scientific research. It is impossible to observe facts as an amorphous mass without any order. Classification groups together similar phenomena and thus reduces to a number of 'types' the numberless variety of particular facts. Different categories of typologies are possible and they can moreover be used simultaneously. The fundamental problem is to discover the natural distinctions between phenomena, to express a natural classification of facts and not to rank them in artificial and arbitrary categories.

A. The different kinds of typologies

Firstly, classifications can be distinguished according to their level of generality. There exist a general typology common to all social sciences (see p. 66), typologies relating to each particular discipline and typologies relating to special categories of phenomena within each discipline (for example, the classifications in political science of types of political parties; in economics of types of firm, etc.). At each level typologies can be established on different bases: it has already been remarked that in most of the social sciences, in the absence of a generally agreed typology, everyone has to establish his own for the particular field in which he is working. This assertion has to be qualified. The anarchy is less great than it might be because there are certain 'schools' of thought. Crudely speaking, three main tendencies can be distinguished: the institutional, the relational, and the functional tendencies.

(*a*) INSTITUTIONAL TYPOLOGIES

As their name indicates, they are based on the concept of institution.

Elements of Systematic Analysis

1. *The concept of an institution.* This is not easy to define. An institution is a cluster of ideas and beliefs, usages and ways of behaviour, and material things (insignia, emblems, buildings, patrimonies, etc.) which form a co-ordinated and organized whole. Family, marriage, elections, political parties, parliaments and so on are examples of institutions. Two elements in the notion seem basic, the organic nature of institutions—the elements of an institution are not simply added one to the other but constitute a whole of indivisible and hierarchically ordered parts; the durable nature of institutions—an institution lasts longer than each of the members which compose it; it survives them and extends over several generations.

The notion of institution is directly opposed to the idea that society is made up purely of relations between individuals. In some respects institutions are modes of relations, but they are more than this. Firstly, the relations which they engender are stable and durable. Secondly, apart from relations between each of its members, there are other non-relational elements in the institution: the idea which one forms of it, the collective images which it engenders, the material elements which are part of it. A parliament is more than the interpersonal relations of parliamentarians with each other and with people outside.

It is interesting to compare this concept of an institution with the very fashionable concept of 'structure'. In fact, the latter is barely defined. 'Structuralism', in asserting that the social universe is composed of stable and coherent clusters, is opposed to 'relational' theories, but the terms 'structure' and 'institution' do not refer to the same thing. In some respects 'structuralism' seems to come close to functionalist typologies. The notion of structure is also associated with the idea of a natural typology of phenomena (see p. 235).

2. *Institutional typologies.* These are very numerous: each social science is partly based on the definition of a certain number of institutions which, originally, was often formal: juridical institutions were often used as a basis. Originally the concepts of the family, property, marriage, association, authority, etc., were to some extent borrowed from law. Juridical typology seems to have served as the first classifying 'filter' of the social sciences. A progressive emancipation has taken place, in so far as observation of the facts has uncovered the real nature (often very different from their legal definition) of the institutions.

(*b*) RELATIONAL TYPOLOGIES

These have been mainly developed in America where they reflect a traditional individualism.

1. *Notion of relational typology.* Instead of categories of organized and structured phenomena, some people discern only systems of interpersonal relations in the social universe. This evokes echoes of the quarrels which attended the birth of sociology. Reading Durkheim makes one aware of the opposition between those who considered social phenomena as relations purely between individuals and those who believed in a social reality apart from interpersonal relations. The first tendency is 'relational', the second 'institutional'.

2. *Relational typologies.* Several typologies have been built on a relational basis. The 'behaviourist' school has succeeded in isolating some categories which can be used in certain fields such as public opinion, propaganda, the effects of 'messages' and the analysis of 'decision making'. But these fields remain limited and fragmentary. The sociometric school of Moreno endeavours to define in a more general and abstract manner, models of relations which somewhat resemble types of constellations described by astronomers (the 'stars' in this case being individuals). Social psychologists have sought to classify interpersonal relations according to human 'instincts': attraction, repulsion, affection, interest, etc. But all these attempts remain partial because societies and human groups are not limited to interpersonal relations.

(*c*) FUNCTIONAL TYPOLOGIES

These have had a growing popularity in recent years: 'functionalism' is a very important tendency in contemporary social science.

1. *Notion of functional typology.* The basic idea is to classify the various categories of social relations according to the role which they play in the community. 'Function' is a composite notion containing diverse tendencies, which often remain implicit. It is, on the one hand, associated with a certain organicist conception of society (the concept of 'function' is important in biology); and on the other, whilst giving first importance to the end pursued, it reintroduces a certain idea of value into the social sciences (teleological conceptions always tend to become confused with moral values).

A fundamental difference exists between the notion of function in the social sciences and the notion of function in biology. The biologist studies the function or functions of each organ; in other words they separate function from institution; very often the study of functions helps to illuminate the analysis of the structure of the organ. In contrast, the sociologist sometimes has a tendency to forget this association: this is why social functions tend to resemble the ends which moralists give to society rather than biological functions. The 'structuralists' attempt to avoid this: their typologies are both functional and institutional.

2. *Development of functional typologies.* The concept of functional typology is not new; Locke and Montequieu, in defining the legislative, executive and judicial powers are in fact establishing a functional classification of political phenomena. The functional approach is becoming the dominant trend of Western sociology.

From some points of view this should be welcomed. In the United States it marks an advance on the relational tendencies which are declining in relative importance. Recourse to functional typologies is indispensable for the comparative study of very different societies: institutions are too unlike to provide a satisfactory basis of comparison. It is also possible that in some respects the functional approach is more fruitful for the elaboration of general theories than the institutional approach.

But it is necessary to stress the dangers of functional typologies. Most are based on an *a priori* definition of the aims of human society, with a more or less conscious moral basis of the 'furthering the common good' type. Institutional typologies can often be criticized for being derived from legal contexts and consequently remaining very formal. Functional typologies are, on the other hand, too often derived from implicit moral beliefs with no scientific character: they describe the ideal functions according to preconceived doctrines which a society ought to fulfil and not those which it actually fulfils. The notion of 'social integration' considered as a primordial function of the group, the notions of the 'normal' and the 'pathological' which are used as the basis of many theoretical and numerous practical studies, are linked with these deviations and this places them outside science.

B. Problem of natural typology
A typology should not be artificial. If it is, it is an obstacle to research and a hindrance to the progress of science. The search for a natural typology presents difficulties in any science: the errors of the first zoological and botanical classifications illustrate this very well. But the difficulties of sociologists are particularly severe and result from the particular character of social phenomena which could be called 'amorphism': this difficulty is more apparent than real because social facts are in reality highly structured.

Introduction to the Social Sciences

(*a*) APPARENT AMORPHISM OF SOCIAL PHENOMENA

This is related to two facts: first, the various elements in the social universe are difficult to differentiate from one another; second, the general lines of their internal structure is not clearly apparent.

1. *The 'continuum'*. As a general rule it is relatively easy to isolate organisms and structures which are clearly differentiated from their context in physical and chemical phenomena: an animal, plant, geological stratum have clearly defined limits; they are clearly separate from other elements and from their context. This is not the case with social phenomena. In most instances it is, at first sight, difficult to separate elements. The social universe has the appearance of a continuum, the various elements of which are not naturally isolated from one another. Classifying operations therefore have an essential role and particular dangers.

If we take as an example a political institution, the political party, which appears clearly differentiated and which has been the subject of many studies. A political party seems an example of social reality clearly isolated from others. In fact it is not. A whole series of material phenomena—an office, name, headed notepaper, a programme, leaders, deputies, electors—can be observed. But where does the party start and finish? The reply varies according to the individual and is never very precise. The party as an organization is usually ill-defined. The party is an extreme case of a clearly defined structure so the problems are much more severe for some pressure groups, social classes, 'spiritual families', etc. The only clearly delimited elements of social reality are those with a geographical or juridical basis. But this is often formal and does not correspond to the natural divisions of social reality.

2. *Difficulty of distinguishing main and secondary elements*. It is not enough that the various elements studied are easily differentiated to establish a valid typology. Each must have a general articulation clear enough to distinguish the main from the secondary elements. Every typology is based on a distinction of this kind: organisms are classified in the same category when their main elements are the same and only differ in their secondary elements. Organisms, institutions and social structures do not usually present clearly defined features. What are the main and dominant elements of a political party? Some assert its doctrine, others its socio-economic base, others its organization and others its strategy. A typology can be established on any of these bases, but it is impossible to prove that one conforms more to reality than another.

3. *Artificial character of actual classifications.* The apparent amorphism of social phenomena has two consequences. In the first place, it is rare that a typology is generally accepted by all the specialists in a field. For example, there is at the moment no commonly accepted classification for social groups: classifications of types of family, rural community, political parties, etc., remain controversial. Each researcher thus establishes his own typology with the result that it is difficult for other researchers to make direct use of his results. In the absence of a common language researchers must make translations which are always difficult and only approximate.

The second consequence is still more serious. In the absence of a well-established typology corresponding to the general pattern of natural phenomena, artificial classifications have to be constructed. To a certain extent, research in depth will show up this artificial character and make possible a closer approximation to a natural typology (there are in practice no other means of doing this). But, because of the apparent amorphism of social reality, there is a serious danger that the phenomena studied tend to take the form of the classification adopted rather like iron filings correspond to the field of a magnet held over them. In the discussion of content analysis it was remarked that many analyses have shown that the main thing is to determine pigeon-holes into which information is channelled, and one will always succeed in filling them.

(b) THE REAL STRUCTURE OF SOCIAL PHENOMENA

The 'amorphism' of social phenomena is more apparent than real. It is an optical illusion arising from the primitive state of the social sciences rather than the real nature of the phenomena. Sociologists do not yet know how to recognize certain types of social fact rather like the white man who, in his first contact with negroes, found them all alike: he only came to differentiate them later. Social reality is naturally 'structured'.

1. *Existence of natural structures.* Clearly delimited and organized structures are apparent to observers to the extent that a field has been well worked over: ethnologists in particular have uncovered numerous examples (the research for natural social structures is called 'structural anthropology'). It seems that the social universe is highly structured: facts are not isolated, they are grouped in natural constellations or 'clusters'. In this respect the social universe can be compared to the field of physical perception described in Gestalt theory. Various elements of social reality seem to us to be difficult to distinguish and the internal hierarchy of their structures is not clear to us because our

eyes are not yet sufficiently accustomed to looking at them. The social sciences will cure themselves of this children's disease as they develop.

2. *Natural structures and ideal types.* The controversies around the fashionable term 'structure' revive the old discussions about the term 'ideal type' as defined by Max Weber. According to Weber, sociological types are not realities but abstractions: all classifications based on them are therefore ideal and not natural. There can be no true natural classification since the basic types are always defined by an intellectual operation which ignores the uniqueness of particular phenomena and retains only the elements common to a group of them.

This concept illuminates the notion of natural structure. It is true that fundamental structures are always distorted to some extent by particular elements because of the complexity and uniqueness of social phenomena: 'pure' structures dissociated from concrete examples are necessarily abstractions. But the process of abstraction is identical in all sciences: the concept of the 'mammal' is also an 'ideal type'. It nevertheless corresponds to reality to the extent that the abstraction does not distort the facts but extrapolates their meaning: thus the ideal type is also a real type and classification based on it is a natural classification.

2. THEORIES AND HYPOTHESES

A theory synthesizes the results of observation, experiment and comparison and expresses in a co-ordinated and coherent manner all that is known and implied by a group of phenomena.

A theory is a statement of the results of research already made and a programme for future research. The distinction between two separate moments in the construction of a theory between *a priori* systematization and *a posteriori* systematization is rather artificial: the first attempts to define the context of research and the questions to be asked, etc.; the second extracts from the results obtained by research, a coherent description of reality in an attempt to explain and predict. In practice these two things are often merged and there is a perpetual dialogue between defining questions and systematizing the results.

More important is the distinction, already referred to, between the different levels of systematization. At the level of field research theorizing consists of the formulation of working hypotheses which, by a process of verification, can be transformed into sociological laws. At the highest level, that of the social sciences as a whole, one seeks to construct general theories, 'cosmogonies' intended to explain the whole mechanism of social life. At the intermediary level, partial theories synthesize the results produced by a branch of a discipline: they can take the form of collections of co-ordinated hypotheses which are called 'models'.

A. General theories

In the last fifty years the social sciences have made big advances in the field of specialist research. A host of new techniques of observation have been perfected and widely used. A mass of facts has been collected. The sum total of concrete knowledge has greatly increased. But there has not been the same development in theory. There has been no, or at least very little, real progress in the last fifty years. At the present time this inertia of general theory constitutes the principal obstacle to the development of the social sciences: it holds back research or makes it sterile because of the lack of a suitable organizing principle.

(a) THE NUMBER OF GENERAL THEORIES

It is hardly an exaggeration to say that each sociologist has his general theory. There are 'schools' but most of them are small sects without an audience. There are only two great categories of theories—Marxist and 'psychologist'—which have a large number of adherents. The second is a tendency rather than a theory.

1. *Marxist theory.* It has already been said that Marxism is the first general theory and remains the only 'cosmogony' of the social sciences. It has been criticized but not replaced.

The fundamental basis of the Marxist schema can be summarized as follows: technical/economic situations engender class situations: class conflict is the basis of the social dynamic. These relationships are indisputable, but it is doubtful whether they are the only important ones or whether they are always and everywhere the most important. Many social phenomena can be explained in terms of the class struggle —but not all. The main lines of Marxist explanation seem to correspond to reality from the middle of the nineteenth to the middle of the twentieth century in Europe. The industrial revolution, stimulated by technical change, produced a new economic structure: this new structure unleashed a violent struggle between the working class and the bourgeoisie (in the wide sense of the term); political, social, intellectual, moral and other changes largely reflected this class situation. Other, many other, phenomena were present which the Marxist tends to minimize, but the Marxist analysis remained accurate in outline.

It is very doubtful whether this is so for other historical periods. The Marxist schema always remains valid in the sense that the influence of techniques on economic change, repercussions of the latter on class conflicts and a transposition of these conflicts into the fields of politics, religion, art and so on can always be discerned. But this influence does not always seem to be decisive and other influences probably play a more important role. For long historical periods the 'basic producers', the workers and peasants, played no role; they were in a way outside society and class conflicts were secondary; the main conflicts were of other kinds—religious, national, racial, family, etc. And will there be no conflicts in the classless society promised to us in the 'higher stage of communism'?

It is a curious fact that Marxist theory is more fruitful in social science in non-Marxist than in Marxist countries. In the former its conclusions are used as useful hypotheses to guide research and the results of the research modify the theory. In Marxist countries, Marxist theory is raised into a dogma and tends to paralyse instead of stimulating research: 'Stalinist' sociology in effect abandoned the experimental method and took refuge in scholastic reasoning based on the principles in the sacred texts of Marx, Engels, Lenin and Stalin.

2. *Psychologist theories.* It is an exaggeration to say that there is a 'Western' theory of social science opposed to Marxist theory. Western sociology borders on anarchy and is characterized by a multitude of rival theories. It is obvious, however, that 'psychologist' tendencies are very widespread in the Western countries under the influence of the United States. It would be inaccurate to allege a reaction against Marxist theory because psychologist, 'relational' and 'behaviourist' tendencies were strongly represented in Anglo-Saxon countries, especially the United States, long before Marxism was taken seriously here.

Psychologist 'tendencies' and not 'theories' are talked of because they represent a general orientation rather than a precise system. The tendencies consider society as a collection of interpersonal relations and give psychological elements pride of place in explaining social phenomena. The weakness of this position is the absence of a generally acceptable psychological theory: the controversies between psychologists are reflected in those between sociologists. The growing influence of psychoanalysis (although there has been something of a decline in recent years) has produced a certain, although a very relative, unity.

In the main, however, psychological theories are in retreat. They are still dominant in the West and their influence remains strong

Elements of Systematic Analysis

because of the development of techniques already described which apprehend social reality through individuals (opinion polls, interviews, tests, attitudes, scales, etc.). Efforts to construct an anti-Marxist communal sociology based on Pareto and Mosca with a vertical 'mass-élites' division as opposed to a distinction between classes have virtually collapsed: this was political rather than scientific venture. Contemporary development of research on 'structures' and 'systems' seems more important, in much the same way as the development of macro-economics which marks the abandonment of psychologism in economics. The growing acceptance of 'functionalist' theories which go beyond the purely relational and interpersonal to consider the community as a whole (at least in its aims) operates in the same direction: it is a stage in the progressive abandonment of psychologist theories in the West in favour of strictly sociological theories.

(b) THE PARTIALLY NON-SCIENTIFIC CHARACTER OF GENERAL THEORIES

General theories are necessary to science: on the one hand, they synthesize the results obtained by fitting them together like pieces in a puzzle: on the other hand, they assist and stimulate new research, by separating the known and unknown, the certain from the doubtful, making possible the correct formulation of the problems, the definition of the general framework of a typology and suggesting working hypotheses. It is pointless to ask whether the theory comes before or after empirical research: it comes both before and after. Theory is perpetual movement: synthesis of results provides the basis for new research which necessitates modification of the old theory and a new synthesis which opens other avenues of research, etc. But, in this movement, theory transcends the limits of scientific knowledge.

1. *The unknown.* A general theory does not consist only of synthesizing all the known facts. It implies going beyond these facts and the formulation of comprehensive hypotheses which also cover unexplored areas: all systematization is in part a work of imagination, invention and intuition.

At the level of general theories or 'cosmogonies' complete objectivity is impossible and the most serious error is to give the appearance of objectivity to conclusions which are not objective. Social science is still in a primitive stage and too few facts are established to construct a cosmogony in which the objective predominates. At the present stage (in which the science will remain for some time) a general synthesis is based on beliefs and intuitions rather than established facts. It must integrate all the facts, but it is compelled by the force of circumstances to give a large place to doubtful facts.

2. *The presence of non-scientific beliefs.* The whole man is involved in the creative activity of constructing a general theory. In the natural sciences the thinker can be moved purely by the passion for objective truth: this is hardly conceivable in the social sciences. The practical consequences of general theories are too serious, profound and immediate for the theorist to ignore them. Science and action are associated whether one likes it or not: the beliefs of the man intervene in scientific research. Specialist work can be done without this problem presenting itself: an opinion poll, a study of electoral geography or a content analysis can be completely objective and need not be influenced by the opinions of those who make them. But there never has been and cannot be complete objectivity in the construction of a general theory. All general theories have been formulated with a view to practical action as much as (and often more) than to the disinterested pursuit of knowledge: this is admitted by some theorists whilst others tend to hide it.

The presence of these beliefs produces serious errors from the scientific point of view in the form of limited objectivity, unconscious distortion of reality, underestimation of some facts and overestimation of others. It should always be remembered that in strictly scientific research such distortions are sometimes present: academic passions are narrower but not less violent than political passions. Despite these distortions the theories still have utility in scientific research: they can be considered as working hypotheses and their conclusions should be approached with systematic scepticism.

B. Partial theories and models

In the last few years the term 'model' has been widely used in the social sciences. It is part of the fashionable vocabulary (there are scientific fashions just as there are fashions in clothes). But the meaning given to the word varies greatly. There are two main classifications: firstly, mathematical and non-mathematical models; secondly, models of prediction and models of investigation. These do not coincide although many predictive models have a mathematical basis.

(a) PREDICTIVE MODELS

In the original sense of the term, as used in economics, a model has two characteristics: firstly, it is a mathematical construction and, secondly, an instrument of prediction. One must go beyond this precise concept to understand subsequent uses of the procedure.

Elements of Systematic Analysis

1. *Economic models.* The first outline of a construct of this kind is to be found in Quesnay's famous economic tableau: this was a kind of miniature model of reality representing in a simplified manner the production, distribution and consumption of wealth. This tableau did not have a mathematical character. The reduction of reality was made by a qualitative assessment of the factors present. It was an approximate schema with great illustrative and pedagogic value but from which it is impossible to extract any precise information.

Quesnay's idea has simply to be transferred into a mathematical and statistical framework to arrive at the modern concept of the model. From the multitude of factors which coalesce in the production and distribution of goods, certain of them, considered characteristic, are isolated. A reduced model of economic reality is constructed on the basis of these variables. The inventor of this method was Professor Wassily Leontief, of Havard, who established his famous diagram in the form of a double-entry table: this forms the basis of all contemporary calculation of national accounts.

Great progress has been made in recent years in the technique invented by Leontief. Most governments use it for national accounts to assess decisions in the economic, financial and social fields. Models thus play an important role in practical political science.

2. *Predictive models in other social sciences.* Use of predictive models is much rarer in the other social sciences. The slow growth of statistics and, above all, the fact that many essential facts cannot be measured by valid instruments are obstacles in the way of the use of predictive models. An example can be given of the attempt by the American writer K. W. Deutsch to establish a model of nationalism.

Deutsch tried to define a systematic framework in which could be placed a wide variety of statistics (social, cultural, economic, political, etc.). The framework itself has a qualitative character: all the data within it is quantitative and statistical. This is an interesting essay but it must be doubted whether it can produce serious concrete results. The author believes that his model could lead to predictions about the assimilation or differentiation of populations in a given geographical area and even indications of the length of the process of assimilation. One must remain sceptical of these claims: the model ignores political organization, historical decisions, the role of dominant personalities (all of which seem crucial factors).

(*b*) INVESTIGATORY MODELS

The term 'model' tends to be used more and more in a very different sense to the one just described. This other meaning is a number of co-ordinated working hypotheses which give a simplified and schematized picture of reality. The purpose is not prediction but scientific inquiry. It should always be remembered, however, that prediction and investigation are closely linked.

Usually these descriptive models make much less use of mathematical procedures and the majority do not have a mathematical basis. Games theory presents some possibility of investigatory models with mathematical bases.

1. *Non-mathematical models.* The idea behind these is exactly the same as that of partial systemization (the intermediary level between working hypotheses and general theories). Working hypotheses are systemizations of particular elements, phenomena or groups of phenomena, of social reality. General theories attempt to give a comprehensive picture of social phenomena and their reciprocal relationships. Non-mathematical models attempt to systematize a sector of reality which forms a more or less homogeneous whole.

Such models assume as precise a typology as possible although this typology is usually largely hypothetical (given the backward state of the social sciences). The use of descriptive models is one of the most effective ways of making progress in typology. Research in depth by means of models makes possible the verification of a hypothetical typology and its modification in the direction of a true and natural typology.

Descriptive models are more than a typological framework and a scheme of classification. Relations between various phenomena are defined, some by sociological laws (if they exist), others by working hypotheses (which is usually the case). Models are used to verify the accuracy of these hypotheses. It is not, of course, possible to test several hypothese at the same time: experiments and observation are never conducted on more than one element of the model at a time. But the construction of the model makes it possible to place various elements in relation to others and, by using the observations already made, introduce order, define the extent of what is known and the gaps in each category of phenomena, etc.

There are great possibilities for development of models in the social sciences because of the lack of general theories. In the absence of general theories the best solution is to establish partial systemizations of particular sectors of social reality: parties, pressure groups, organizations, communications, public opinion, etc. An example of this is my book on *Political Parties* (1st edition, 1951: since 1951 the models have been modified on the basis of subsequent research). In general, the designing of non-mathematical models is characteristic of the present state of the social sciences.

2. *Games theory and strategic models.* It has already been remarked that operational research is partly based on mathematical games theory. Occasionally games theory is used to build predictive models and can also be used for some descriptive models (prediction and investigation can never be absolutely separated).

A great number of social rivalries and conflicts can be expressed in terms borrowed from games theory. 'Strategic models' defining a type of pure theory of decisions can be constructed. This kind of model can be used in operational research to throw light on a political choice, an advertising campaign, etc. It can also provide a basis of scientific research by providing descriptive models. Exaggerated hopes should not be entertained: games theory will not illuminate the whole of social life. Too many strategic models leave out the most important elements of a decision because they cannot be calculated mathematically, and they thus are reduced to elementary schema far removed from living reality. But excesses should not lead to blanket condemnation of a method which can be useful.

C. Working hypotheses

Observation does not bear fruit unless questions have previously been defined. As far as possible these questions ought to take the form of working hypotheses in that an answer is invented at the same time as the question; the aim of research is to find out whether this answer is correct. A working hypothesis is in effect a proposed sociological law: if it is verified it becomes a law; if not, it is abandoned and another hypothesis is formulated which in turn is tested.

(a) DEFINITION OF HYPOTHESES

There are no precise rules for drawing up hypotheses. We are again in the realm of invention, creation and intuition which is outside any rigorous methodology. General guides, however, can be given.

1. *The general schema.* The phase of elaboration of hypotheses is usually characterized by extensive research. Instead of trying to go deeply into a limited field, an attempt is made to consider the maximum possible number of facts covering a wide field. These facts will be acquired through rapid and superficial inquiries covering the widest possible range of circumstances, countries, etc., and by scrutinizing the maximum number of existing documents, etc. In general, classical comparative methods are widely used. 'Close comparisons' will be complemented by 'distant comparisons' (see below p. 265). The more facts are gathered and the more they belong

to different fields of experience, the more chance there is of a basic hypothesis occurring. An aptitude for synthesis and for seeing possible relations between apparently independent phenomena plays an essential role.

Teamwork can be useful in this field, Not that ideas are produced in collaboration—their creation is an essentially individual thing—but the association of several researchers increases the chances of one of them inventing a hypothesis: comparing experiences can stimulate one of the team. A team also makes the collection of more facts possible. The hypotheses can be refined; it is not enough to have an idea, it must also be refined and formulated in a rigorous manner. Working hypotheses must be defined with the greatest possible clarity and precision.

2. *An example.* An inquiry was conducted under the sponsorship of UNESCO on the participation of women in politics. The investigation specifically covered four countries—France, Norway, German Federal Republic and Yugoslavia. It was preceded by a preliminary investigation covering the widest possible number of countries (reports were received from seventeen). These preliminary reports were written by specialists chosen by the director of the inquiry who supplied them with a document defining the scope of the inquiry, the questions to be asked, the fields to explore and the nature of the documents to be supplied. The director synthesized the seventeen reports obtained in order to define working hypotheses. These were discussed by a large group at the International Congress of Political Science held at The Hague in 1952. The definitive working documents integrating the points made in this discussion was finally established as a basis for the second phase of research (the verification of the hypotheses).

(*b*) VERIFYING THE HYPOTHESES

This is the strictly scientific part of the work. In constructing hypotheses one is limited to collecting the already known elements of the problem. This is done in as thorough and systematic way as possible, trying to take into consideration all useful elements and to compare elements directly bearing on the subject with others not so closely associated but which might illuminate some of its aspects. In the second phase new elements are sought and virgin territory explored.

1. *Experiment.* In the natural sciences experiment is the main method of verifying hypotheses. A hypothesis has the form of a proposed law

expressing a relationship between two phenomena; the conditions under which one or the other appear are varied and the influence on the other is recorded. There is an attempt by artificial means to isolate some of the supposed factors of a phenomena in order to determine whether they have or have not an influence and eventually this influence is measured.

2. *The comparative method.* In most cases in the social sciences it is not possible to use the experimental method. It is usually impossible to vary the 'conditions of temperature and pressure' and to isolate phenomena in order to establish reciprocal relationships. One is compelled to use direct observation. One seeks to multiply observations in the widest possible variety of natural conditions as different as possible. The comparative method is used extensively and, as has already been said, it tends to play the role of a substitute for experiment in the social sciences.

On the characteristics of social determinism: G. GURVITCH, *Déterminismes sociaux et liberté humaine*, 1955; R. MACIVER, *Social causation*, 1942; G. A. LUNDBERG, *Foundations of Sociology*, 1939.

On the distinction between the 'macro' and the 'micro': J. MEYNAUD, *Bibliographie sur les problèmes du changement d'échelle dans les sciences sociales*, UNESCO, 1958.

On the notion of structure: C. LÉVI-STRAUSS, *Anthropologie structurale*, 1958; T. PARSONS, *Structure and Process in Modern Society*, Glencoe, 1960; S. F. NADEL, *The Theory of Social Structure*, Glencoe, 1957; A. R. RADCLIFFE-BROWN, *Structure and Function in Primitive Society*, 1952.

On ideal types: M. WEBER, *Essays in Sociology*, New York, 1946; *Methodology in the Social Sciences*, Glencoe, 1949; *The Theory of Social and Economic Organization*, New York, 1947.

On the behavioural tendency within American political science: H. EULAU, S. J. ELDERSVELD, M. JANOWITZ, *Political Behaviour*, Glencoe, 1956; L. FESTINGER and D. KATZ, *Research Methods in the Behavioural Sciences*, 2nd ed., 1956; D. WALDO, *Political Science in the United States of America*, 1956, especially pp. 21–31; the collective work, *Research Frontiers in Politics and Government*, Brookings Institute, 1955.

On functional typology: R. K. MERTON, *Social Theory and Social Structure*, 2nd ed., Glencoe, 1957; S. M. LIPSET, *Political Man*, New York, 1960; G. ALMOND and J. S. COLEMAN, *The Politics of Developing Areas*, Princeton, 1960.

On general theories: N. S. TIMASHEFF, *Sociological Theory*, New York, 1955.

On the relation between theory and practice in the social sciences: E. S. JOHNSON, *Theory and Practice in Social Studies*, New York, 1956; W. H. J.

Sprott, *Science and Social Action*, Glencoe, 1955; B. Moore and G. R. Leslie, *The Sociology of Social Problems*, New York, 1955.

On mathematical models: P. F. Lazarsfeld (*et al.*), *Mathematical Thinking in the Social Sciences*, Glencoe, 1954; H. A. Simon, *Models of Man*, New York, 1957; K. W. Deutsch, *Nationalism and Social Communication*, New York, 1953.

On non-mathematical models: J. Bates, 'A Model for the Science of Decision', *Philosophy of Science*, 1954, pp. 326–39; M. Duverger, *Political Parties*, 1955; J. A. Slesinger, *A Model for the Comparative Study of Public Bureaucracy*, Ann Arbour, 1957.

On games theory: J. D. Williams, *The Compleat Strategyst, being a primer on the theory of games of strategy*, New York, 1954; D. Blackwell, *Theory of Games and Statistical Decisions*, New York, 1954; R. M. Thrall, C. H. Coombs, R. L. Davis, *Decision Process*, New York, 1954; M. Shubik, *Readings in Games Theory and Political Behaviour*, New York, 1953; K. W. Deutsch, 'Game Theory and Politics', *Canadian Journal of Economic and Political Science*, 1954, pp. 76 ff.

Section II. Experiment

Experiment can be defined as provoked and directed observation. One or more artificial factors are introduced into a natural process and the results are compared with what happens when no extraneous factors are introduced (thus the effect of these factors can be measured). Experiment can take place under laboratory or natural conditions, the former being more conducive to the isolation of factors. In all cases experiments are made to verify hypotheses previously defined.

Experiment is an essential tool of research in the natural sciences and through it hypotheses are transformed into laws. In the social sciences, experiment in the proper sense of the word is rare. All the ethical problems encountered in biology with experiments on human beings are encountered in an even more acute form (in one sense) because experiments have to be conducted on whole communities and not on individuals. Unfortunately, there are no substitutes for human beings, like animals in biology.

There are several experimental procedures in sociology. These will be described briefly along with those instances where the introduction of an extraneous factor does not affect the course of the phenomena but merely allows information on the phenomena to be obtained: this is not strictly an experiment but a procedure for obtaining documentation. A distinction will be drawn (although this is often difficult) between laboratory experiments and experiments in the field.

Elements of Systematic Analysis

1. LABORATORY EXPERIMENTS

In these, experiment takes place under artificial conditions. People who submit to them know that they are subjects of an experiment; they know the artificial character of the undertaking although all aspects of it and particularly its basic aims are not always revealed to them. Laboratory experiments do not raise the same ethical objections as experiments in the field: firstly, the subjects submit to them voluntarily; secondly, they know that it is a kind of game which will not influence the course of their real life. In spite of this the game can have consequences and the participants might in some way be marked by it.

A. Artificial groups

This technique has been greatly developed in the United States for the study of interpersonal relations, group 'morale' and leadership. The method has been widely used in some countries as a means of selecting people for positions of command.

(*a*) ARTIFICIAL GROUPS AS A TECHNIQUE OF SOCIOLOGICAL EXPERIMENT

A group of people are gathered together for a certain length of time in the same place (hotel, large country house, college, etc.). They live together, sometimes performing certain tasks. Observers record carefully all the details of the life of the group.

1. *Single group experiments.* Observations are usually made on a single group. The composition of the group is carefully studied at the start. Tests, questionnaires and various examinations are given to those who take part.

The simplest form of the experiment is to leave the group entirely free in its activities and give it neither tasks nor leaders. The spontaneous appearance of leaders, the attitude of the group towards them, the conflicts between aspirant leaders, the formation of cliques and so on can be observed. Factors can subsequently be introduced into this spontaneous process to measure their influence on the behaviour of the group. The group can be given a certain task to perform. Certain obstacles can be put in its way or the group can be faced with a certain situation. Disturbing elements can be introduced into the group and it can be subjected to influences and propaganda to measure its receptivity. In short, the group is treated as an object for experiment.

The artificial conditions of the experiment obviously diminish its significance. This objection is less strong with groups of children, where an artificial group can have a real existence. On the part of adults the experiment requires considerable goodwill, seriousness and a certain amount of naïvety. Members of the group must take themselves very seriously and not play practical jokes. The results can be quite false if they do not co-operate in good faith.

2. *Comparative experiments on several groups.* The principle is the same if the experiment is conducted on several groups simultaneously each being submitted to a range of factors. There is also an attempt to make the composition of the groups as close as possible. Comparison of the reactions of the groups makes possible a better assessment of the various factors studied.

An example can be given of the experiments made in 1940 by Lewin, Lippitt and White on the consequences of three different social climates—authoritarian, democratic and anarchic. Four groups were assembled and each was submitted successively for a period of three weeks to the three climates. The experiment was made on children aged eleven. The authoritarian atmosphere was created by an adult taking all the initiatives, criticizing without explaining his criteria, etc.; the democratic climate, by the adult attempting to guide the children through mixing with them, suggesting various solutions amongst which they were free to choose, trying to stimulate teams to take responsibilities, etc.; the anarchic climate, by leaving the members of the group strictly to themselves and not guiding them.

Observers recorded the behaviour of the children minute by minute for the whole period of the experiment which was spread over six months. Very interesting results were obtained, particularly on the development of aggressive feelings during the authoritarian period. Experiments of this kind would be difficult to conduct on adults. But in spite of this the technique has made possible studies in depth on the nature of authority in small groups.

(*b*) ARTIFICIAL GROUPS AS A SELECTION TECHNIQUE
The best indication of the importance of the technique is its use in many countries as a selection procedure. Group tests can be conducted with or without a designated leader.

1. *Without a leader.* Candidates are observed as a group in situations without a leader being appointed: it is assumed that 'leadership' shown in these experimental situations would be identical to that shown in real situations.

One situation is a discussion on a subject chosen by the group itself. Members of the selection committee join informally with the group around the same table and take part in the discussion. This system is used in the selection of military leaders and in the recruitment of some civilian managers. It has been used in selecting health service officers for New York City: six to nine candidates hold a round table discussion on a medical problem, having been allowed five days in which to prepare; four examiners sat in a corner observing them and marked them according to certain criteria.

Another technique is giving the group a certain task to perform. In the British army, for example, a group of six to eight potential officers have to build a bridge with planks and ropes across a ditch. Tests of this kind are often used for personnel selection in private firms: members of the group are asked to consider themselves as a board of directors and information concerning a certain technical problem is given to them. On the basis of this information they are required to draw up a plan for the firm.

2. *Group tests with leaders*. These tests are designed to assess leadership qualities. A subject is given the leadership of a group and confronted with several concrete situations as in the previous example. This is a test of an individual—the leader. The members of the group take it in turns to fill the position. The essential part of the test is the relations between the members of the group and the leader.

Examples can be given of two techniques used in the British army for the selection of officers. In the first, the group is presented with a model containing all the tactical details of a terrain: houses, roads, fields, woods, railways, etc. The leader has a specific task to accomplish (for instance, capture a bridge with the enemy holding certain positions). He must draw up a plan and give precise orders to each member of the group. The second test takes the form of a game on a lawn. The terrain is divided into two halves and each half is assigned to a group of six or seven men with a leader. All members of the team, except the leader, are blindfolded and they can only move under the instructions of the leader who states the number of paces forward, backwards and so on. The attacking team must carry three sacks of straw into the terrain of the defending team and place it at the rear without being touched by the defending team.

B. The sociodrama

The 'sociodrama', invented by the American psychologist Moreno, has a much more limited use than artificial groups. It has not the same value either as an instrument of scientific observation or as a useful practical device. It is worth mentioning because of its originality, its success in the United States and its analogies with other, apparently very different, techniques.

(*a*) THE TECHNIQUE OF THE SOCIODRAMA

The sociodrama—or psychodrama (it will be seen that there is little difference between the two terms)—can only be understood in the context of the general theories of the very strange person who invented them.

1. *The sociology of Moreno.* Born in Bucharest in 1892, Moreno studied medicine and psychiatry in Vienna. He was influenced by Freud, Marx and the German philosophers. After settling in the United States in 1925 he developed sociological theories which he called 'sociometry'. Some other aspects of his work, notably sociograms (p. 331), will be mentioned later.

Moreno's sociology is based on his own very personal religious ideas. He said himself that very little was needed for him to have become founder of a sect and not a science. He believes fundamentally in a higher plane of existence characterized by a spontaneous creativity; through this, man tends to identify himself with God (considered as the absolute spontaneous creativity). This spontaneous creativity is at the moment in an embryonic state in man but it can be liberated by men and has immense possibilities of development. Moreno compared this liberation to atomic fission.

Moreno's techniques, notably the sociodrama and the psychodrama, are aimed at assisting men to achieve the plane of spontaneous creativity. From this point of view they can be compared with the techniques suggested by the surrealists—psychic automatism, automatic writing, day-dreaming, etc.—for the liberation of man. According to Moreno, liberation through spontaneous creativity comes from collective action from which all psycho-social elements, forming a barrier to it, are removed. This follows a sort of social catharsis which merges the deepest part of the human personality, the true nature of relations between men and attainment of man's full creative capacity.

2. *The psychodrama and the sociodrama.* The two terms are almost synonymous. It can be alleged that the psychodrama is concerned with throwing light on the individual personality whereas the sociodrama with relations between individuals, but for Moreno the individual personality cannot be separated from inter-personal

relations. The techniques are identical although the psychodrama extends over a longer period.

The technique of the sociodrama is rather like that of the *Commedia dell'Arte* or of Pirandello in *Six Characters in Search of an Author*. It consists of a play leader (and assistants to the leader whom Moreno called 'auxiliary egos').

An example of a sociodrama is one led by Moreno himself in a University in the West of the United States, concerning the race problem. A negro couple were invited from the audience and by careful questioning came to present their case and react as in a real life situation. A white woman was then introduced as an 'auxiliary ego' who provoked changes in attitude and illuminated the attitude of the two protagonists. The 'auxiliary ego' withdrew and the leader asked the 'actors' to imagine what they would be like in ten years. A discussion, with the audience participating, about what had happened took place. The reactions of the audience were an important element in the sociodrama. The experiment ended by indicating to those concerned how the situation could be improved.

(*b*) USE OF THE SOCIODRAMA

For Moreno the sociodrama is something quite different from a laboratory experiment. Its practical utility is much greater than its scientific results. It is not only intended to improve social relationships but allow men to liberate themselves from the shackles which prevent them from attaining the level of creative spontaneity. To the extent that the sociodrama attains its objectives, opinion and attitudes and their deeper significance can be better known: it is thus a means of sociological investigation.

1. *Use of sociodramas and psychodramas in the United States.* These techniques have been used to a certain extent. The Mansfield Theater, the first psychodrama theatre, was founded in 1940 and had considerable success. The techniques have been developed in practice in two directions.

One direction is in the field of therapeutic psychiatry. Dr W. A. White, director of the St. Elizabeth hospital in Washington, started in 1931 to treat his patients with the technique. During the Second World War it was widely used because the shortage of specialists often made individual therapy impossible. Hundreds of soldiers and sailors seem to have been cured of 'shell shock' by it. The same methods were applied to ex-servicemen. The technique was somewhat modified—the leader tended to play a less active role and the patients collaborated together.

The second field is that of human relations in firms. The reflection of a fundamental ideological position is seen here—a refusal to admit structural antagonisms of the class struggle type and the belief that tensions and conflicts between social groups are abnormal and can be resolved by social therapy. An example can be given of the Harwood Manufacturing Company which used the sociodrama as a means of finding out the best means of stopping gossiping on the night shift which was having a serious effect on production: it could apparently be established 'that the employees had not understood that the management wanted to increase production for everyone's benefit and that continual gossip prevented this'.

2. *Collective self-criticism in popular democracies.* Although the theoretical bases and the practical conduct are different, collective self-criticism which takes place in some popular democracies can in some respects be compared to sociodrama. Officially there is no play-acting: the participants are well aware that they are not on the stage and the practical consequences of self-criticism can be serious. But the difference is more formal than real: the employees of the Harwood Company also knew that the 'game' was not a real game and that there would be practical consequences; the mental patients who take part in psychodramas know this too. Also, all real trials have a theatrical aspect (the best dramas are trials) and the sessions of collective self-criticism are no exception.

The idea of catharsis by liberating deep feelings is also present: the presence and participation of the whole group aids catharsis which in turn assists the achievement of a higher level of purity. The theatrical element might be more highly developed in these sessions than in psychodramas because the actor often lies to save his skin and the spectators, knowing that he is lying, enter into the game. The purpose of the mechanism of overlapping lies is to create an artificial truth, a theatrical truth and make it become progressively the real truth, to make actors and spectators adopt in real life their allotted roles. But it is naïve to suppose that there is no lying in psychodrama.

2. EXPERIMENTS IN THE FIELD

It is often difficult to distinguish these from laboratory experiments. Sessions of collective self-criticism are not laboratory experiments because the participants risk life and liberty. Some groups in experiments are in almost entirely natural conditions such as school classes, students in colleges, etc.

Elements of Systematic Analysis

But it is easy enough to differentiate experiments conducted in the field which tend to alter the structure or behaviour of real groups. These methods are rarely used for both ethical and practical reasons.

A. Passive experiments

An experiment is passive if there are no consequences on the group which submits to it: this avoids the ethical objection of treating men as objects—there is no 'manipulation' by the experimentor. In a strict sense it is not a real experiment and is sometimes called a pseudo-experiment. There are two kinds: induced observation and *ex post facto* experiments.

(*a*) INDUCED OBSERVATION

This consists of introducing an artificial element into a natural social process, not in order to interfere with its progress but to make it possible to collect information which would otherwise be inaccessible. The purpose of the outside 'stimulus' is strictly documentary. A good example is the idea of recorded votes.

1. *Recorded votes:* With a secret ballot there are no means of finding out by direct methods the distribution of votes in an election between the different parties according to age, sex, religion, etc. The method normally used is the opinion poll and because of non-responses this is an inefficient procedure.

To circumvent this difficulty it has been suggested that, without interfering with the secrecy of the ballot, a system of recording votes could be established which would differentiate between sex, age group, etc. This procedure was used several times before 1939 in the United States and in certain towns in Germany to analyse the results of female suffrage. Separate ballot boxes for the sexes were generally used. Similar experiments were made after 1945 in France at Vienne (Isère), Belfort and Grenoble.

During the UNESCO inquiry into the participation of women in politics in 1952–53, a proposal was made to extend the procedure further. This proposal no doubt has something to do with the German electoral law of 1953 which allows the Minister of the Interior to authorize the use in some constituencies of ballot forms with indications on the back of sex, age and religion. Valuable information has been collected by this means.

2. *Assessment of the procedure.* It has been sharply criticized by women's organizations which consider it discriminatory, by politicians who think it interferes with the secrecy of the ballot and by

lawyers who regard it as contrary to the principle of national sovereignty (which is indivisible).

None of these arguments bears examination. They camouflage hidden motives. The women's organizations feared proof that women did not vote in exactly the same way as men which would destroy the myth of identity between the sexes; politicians have fears of the same kind—to prove that a particular party attracts women's votes and another does not, would hinder the propaganda of both; lawyers are either hiding analogous preoccupations behind legal principles or they are impenitent theorists fearing that their theories would not withstand the first breath of reality.

The use of the technique has not in practice given rise to any difficulty or incident. No one has asserted that it has altered the result nor that it has constituted an inadmissible manipulation of a human group. As the scientific results obtained are very interesting it is desirable that the method should be extended (and in different fields).

(*b*) 'EX POST FACTO' EXPERIMENTS

The sociologist Greenwood has made a special study of this method. It consists of looking back on the chain of factors which gave rise to a particular situation. Certain phenomena are isolated and the process of evolution is studied through them: this gives it an experimental aspect. The technique of isolation resembles the introduction of an external factor, but, in fact, nothing is introduced. One merely isolates a variable. There are two forms of the method—tracing the causes from the effects or taking certain factors and following their consequences.

1. *Consequences of particular factors.* Certain historical factors are isolated and the influence which they have on the contemporary situation is examined. The best example is the work of H. F. Christiansen in 1935 on the relations between education and social success: the hypothesis was that a better education assured greater success. All the people who had left the same school nine years previously (1926) were looked for and 1,194 out of 2,127 were traced. These were divided into two groups—those who had completed their schooling and those who had left school prematurely. Each group was then reduced in order to balance (at least in theory) the social origins, the condition of the parents, intellectual standard, national origin, etc., so that the only variable was educational level.

It was found that 88.7 per cent of the members of the group who completed their education and 83.4 per cent of those who did not survived the economic depression with an unchanged situation. The difference is too small (given that each group had only 145 members) to be really significant. The great difficulty of the method is eliminating all the variables but one and one can never be sure of having done it.

2. *The factors in certain situations.* The opposite procedure to the one just described can be followed. An attempt can be made to work backwards from a given situation to try to discover the causes which could have produced it. For example, one can try to discover the causes of antisemitism by analysing the past of the members of a group of antisemites.

This technique has been used in Minnesota in comparing a group of fifty delinquents with fifty non-delinquents. The hundred had gone through the same educational institution, had the same level of intelligence, the same home background, etc. The factors leading to delinquency were isolated.

B. Active experiments

Active experiments raise a fundamental moral problem. Men cannot be treated as objects for experiments and one cannot push a community in directions which might be harmful simply to collect scientific observations. This point of view can be disputed—and it is certainly even less permissible from a moral point of view to 'manipulate' a community through propaganda either for racist or nationalist ends or to defend certain classes and groups.

This type of experiment also encounters numerous practical difficulties. It is possible, however, to use it in limited fields and study of aberrant cases is a very fruitful kind of active indirect experiment.

(a) DIRECT ACTIVE EXPERIMENTS

The definition has already been given—the introduction of an artificial element into a natural social process—and, as has been said, this is very rare. They can either take place 'in the field' or under conditions which, without being artificial, are rather special.

1. *Experiments on groups of a special character.* This covers experiments made on students in Colleges and Universities, soldiers, prisoners and deportees. These are not artificial groups in the sense that has been given to the term. They are natural groups in which individuals live real lives but they are rather marginal groups and are easily available for experiments.

Examples of their use are the experiments made on American soldiers to measure the influence of film propaganda. Two groups are balanced by test questionnaires: one group sees the film, the other does not. Both groups are interviewed before and after or only after the showing of the film. The effect can then be measured. The experiment can be further extended by submitting one of the groups to intensive propaganda for a long period of time and the result compared with the group which was not subject to it. Members of both groups are kept in ignorance of the exact nature of the experiment.

In some American Universities experiments of the following kind have been made. M. Smith in 1939 in the University of Kansas arranged courses and lectures for a group of students in ethnography designed to destroy racial prejudice and a control group of similar composition was formed and kept out of these sessions. Remmers has made similar experiments on antisemitism. F. T. Smith in 1943 sent a group of fifteen students into Harlem to make personal contacts with negroes and a control group was kept away from contacts. Other experiments have been made on the influence of newspapers, periodicals, pamphlets, etc.

2. *Experiments on ordinary groups.* These are more difficult. The most interesting is undoubtedly the one made by Hartmann in the elections for an administrative post in Allentown, Pennsylvania. Hartmann himself was the socialist candidate. He drew up two manifestos, one based on rational arguments, the other on strongly emotional arguments. In some polling stations the voters were given the former, in others the latter and in others none at all. Comparison of the results of the three is an interesting measure of the influence of these categories of arguments.

Lewin conducted experiments of the type previously described, removed from the context of university and army. To examine the best ways of persuading people to change their food habits, he arranged for one group of women a series of lectures and for another group a series of discussions opened by a short introduction. The attempt was made to impose new principles on the first group and the second group was led to adopt them through a collective decision. Lewin found the 3 per cent of the subjects of the first group changed their habits against 32 per cent of the second. This experiment inspired him to invent the technique of 'social laboratories' which has already been described.

Another type of experiment was conducted by Lapiere to verify the correlation between actual behaviour and answers to opinion questionnaires. He went into a large number of hotels and restaurants in the United States accompanied by a coloured person and observed the behaviour of the management towards him, having previously given an opinion questionnaire to the management. He found that their actions were ninety times less coloured by racial prejudice than their responses to questionnaires (this may simply prove a lack of courage or duplicity on their part).

Experiments on the spread of rumours in a community are possible. Having established the main points in a small town where stories and gossip are exchanged, some rumours could be started (in various places) by way of experiment: the speed and channels of circulation could then be established.

(b) INDIRECT ACTIVE EXPERIMENTS

This is the study of a new factor in a social process which has not been introduced by the sociologist. The factor is introduced for their own purposes by people who participate in the social or political life of the group.

1. *Technique of 'aberrant cases'.* The study of the effects of a political or social reform is, to a certain extent, an experimental study. Basically it does not matter who has introduced the extraneous factor into the normal social process or for what motives: it creates an experimental situation which can be treated as such.

Although the study of all political reforms can be regarded as experimental, it must be remembered that they are largely the product of the situation they are intended to change. It is therefore often difficult to isolate, in what subsequently occurs, the results of the reform and the consequences of normal evolution. There are no 'control' groups which alone can give precision to the experimental method.

In certain special situations—aberrant cases—a measure is applied locally and the rest of the country remains under the old dispensation. The changes in the 'aberrant' locality can be compared with the changes elsewhere. This can be called indirect experiment.

2. *Use of the technique.* A few concrete examples can be quoted from the electoral field (the technique can, of course, be used in many other fields).

A study of the propaganda of the German Social Democratic Party was made by Tchakhotine in the Hesse by-elections of 1932. Tchakhotine, who was head of propaganda for an anti-nazi organization of the Social Democratic Party, introduced new factors, giving to these elections the character of 'aberrant cases'. Since, almost everywhere, the Social Democratic Party opposed the Nazis with the old classical campaign techniques, Tchakhotine obtained permission to use techniques borrowed from the Nazis: obsessional slogans, sensational posters, extensive use of chalked slogans and symbols (the three arrows), ceremonies, monster processions and mass meetings. The Social Democratic Party, which had previously been losing votes everywhere, increased its votes in Hesse.

The use of modern advertising procedures in France in the local elections of 1953 and in the general election of 1956 in Oise could be studied in depth in the same way. Other constituencies where the traditional methods were used provided control group comparisons. The way in which a particular Senator literally 'bought' his seat was analysed in this way. The method of indirect experiment using aberrant cases can be widely used.

On experiment: F. S. CHAPIN, *Experimental Designs in Sociological Research*, New York, 1947; E. GREENWOOD, *Experimental Sociology*, New York, 1945; J. C. TOWNSEND, *Introduction to Experimental Method for Psychology and Social Science*, London, 1953.

On experiments with artificial groups: E. A. SHILS, 'The Study of the Elementary Group' (and bibliography) in H. D. LASSWELL and D. LERNER, *The Policy Sciences*, New York, 1951; R. LIPPITT, 'An Experimental Study of the Effect of Democratic and Authoritarian Group Atmospheres', *University of Iowa Studies in Child Welfare*, 1940, pp. 43–198; R. LIPPITT, *Training in Community Relations*, New York, 1949; L. CARTER, W. HAYTHORN, M. HOWELL, 'A Further Investigation of the Criteria of Leadership', *Journal of Abnormal and Social Psychology*, 1951, pp. 589 ff.; M. W. BARNARD, 'A New Method of Selecting Health Officers in Training', *American Journal of Public Health*, 1947, p. 715; J. M. FRASER, 'An Experiment with Group Methods', *Occupational Psychology*, 1946, p. 63; A. W. GOULDNER, *Studies in Leadership* (especially pp. 626–8), New York, 1950.

On the sociodrama: J. L. MORENO, *Who Shall Survive?* Washington, 1934; *Sociometry and the Science of Man*, New York, 1956; *Psychodrama*, New York, 1946.

On *ex post facto* experiment: M. F. CHRISTIANSEN, *The Relations of School Progress to Subsequent Economic Adjustment of Students attending four St Paul High Schools*, Minnesota, 1938; F. S. CHAPIN, 'Social Participation and Social Intelligence', *American Sociological Review*, 1939, pp. 157 ff.

On experiments with groups of soldiers: C. I. HOVLAND, A. A. LUMSDAINE, F. D. SHEFFIELD, *Studies in Social Psychology in World War II*, Vol. III, Princeton, 1949.

Active experiments: M. SMITH, 'A Study of Change of Attitudes towards the Negro', *Journal of Negro Education*, 1939, p. 64; H. H. REMMERS, 'Further Studies in Attitude', Series II and III, *Studies in Higher Education* and

Purdue University Bulletin, 1936 and 1938; F. T. SMITH, *An Experiment of Modifying Attitudes towards the Negro*, New York, 1943.

On recorded votes: *Statistisches Jahrbuch für die Bundesrepublik Deutschland*, 1958, pp. 108–9; G. BREMME, *Die politsche rolle der frau in Deutschland*, Göttingen, 1956; F. GOGUEL (*et al.*), *Nouvelles études de sociologie électorale*, 1954.

G. W. HARTMANN, 'A Field Experiment on the comparative effectiveness of "emotional" and "rational" political leaflets in determining election results', *Journal of Abnormal and Social Psychology*, 1936, pp. 99–114; M. F. GOSNELL, *Getting out the Vote*, Chicago, 1927; S. TCHAKHOTINE, *Le Viol des foules par la propaganda politique*, 2nd ed., 1952.

Section III. The comparative method

Auguste Comte and Durkheim considered comparison the fundamental method of the social sciences, having the role which experiment held in the physical and biological sciences. In *The Rules of Sociological Method* the study of 'concommittant variants' is described as 'the primary instrument of sociological research': Durkheim regarded analysis of the similarities and differences between societies and institutions as the best means of discovering sociological laws—a view shared by the majority of sociologists. Comparisons are indispensable in the social sciences but certain precautions are necessary in using them. The old adage 'comparison is not reason' must always be remembered. According to Littré, to compare is 'to examine simultaneously similarities and differences'. The definition shows that comparison assumes similarities and differences—one does not compare things which are exactly the same, nor completely different. Comparison requires a certain analogy between the things compared. The difficulty is determining the degree of this analogy. The danger of the comparative method is the making of artificial comparisons based on distortions of the objects compared.

There are two broad categories of classical comparative methods. One is to compare analogous phenomena, studied according to the same technique of analysis—this is the strict current notion of comparison. One can also compare different views of the same phenomena obtained by using different analytical techniques. This is somewhat removed from the traditional concept of comparison but it forms part of the comparative method.

1. COMPARING ANALOGOUS PHENOMENA

Phenomena of the same kind which are spatially separated can be compared; for example, contemporary parliamentary institutions in France, Britain, Germany and Scandinavia; or phenomena of the same kind which are separated by time: the French parliament under Louis-Philippe, between 1875 and 1914, between the two wars, in the Fourth and Fifth Republics; or the same kind of phenomena in a different context: the administration of nationalized industries, private firms, large cities, etc. Many other combinations are possible.

In all cases the fundamental problem is the same—how to avoid artificial comparisons. The further removed from one another in space, time and context the things compared are, the greater are the chances of artificiality. The danger is equally great when large and complex phenomena are compared. But it is not easy to go beyond these brief statements and define precisely rules for the use of the comparative method.

A. General technique of comparison

There are two main types of problems, both concerning the degree of analogy of the things compared: those of structure and those of general context.

(a) PROBLEMS OF STRUCTURE AND TYPOLOGY

A previously established typology is necessary to use the comparative method: comparison is valid only between two facts of the same type and between facts with analogous structures.

1. *Necessity of structural analogy.* The term structure is used broadly. Structural analogy means two things: the facts compared must have close general characteristics and their degree of complexity must not be too different.

The French National Assembly, the British House of Commons, the German Bundestag and the Italian Chamber of Deputies can be compared. These institutions have identical general characteristics. But a comparison between these assemblies and the Estates General of the *ancien régime*, the general assembly of the French clergy, the Diet of the old Polish Kingdom would have little validity: the structures of these institutions have very different characteristics. This is not to say that comparisons are impossible or entirely useless but they are inevitably superficial.

It is possible to compare the office of Prime Minister in all the great countries of the contemporary world. But it is hardly possible to compare the governments of real States to the organization of the executive in Andorra, Monaco and the tribes of the Amazon because of the difference in structural complexity. Similarly, comparing the

Elements of Systematic Analysis

contemporary communist and socialist parties to the eighteenth-century Whigs and Tories would not be very fruitful.

2. *Institutional and functional comparisons.* All the preceding examples are institutional comparisons. These are most common because the structural analogy is easy to determine. It is, however, necessary to be wary of nominalism and not to be taken in by appearances. Professor Gunnar Heckscher asked: 'Is the Saudi Arabian monarch really comparable to the Danish? Is an election the same thing in India and America?' Obviously not. The notions of structural analogy and of context must come into play.

Functional comparisons are much more difficult. The notion of function is less easy to use than the notion of an institution. One can compare the mechanism of decision-making in various institutions (Chamber of Deputies, party, trade union, large firm, etc.); the way in which order is maintained in a class, a congress, public meeting, sporting occasion, etc. Such research is interesting, particularly for 'distant comparisons' (see p. 266), in which the institutions are too different to provide an adequate framework for comparison. The difficulties and consequently the precautions necessary cannot be overemphasized. It is easy enough to establish a typology for institutions but there are very few clear functional typologies, except in limited fields (for example, functions of the State), and establishing them is a delicate operation.

(*b*) PROBLEMS OF CONTEXT

Social facts are not isolated and cannot be isolated: they are elements of a whole from which they cannot be separated without losing all meaning. Comparing two institutions or two functions without taking into consideration the total reality of which each is a part cannot produce any valid result. Context has to be taken into account. Except in 'distant comparisons' (p. 266), phenomena whose contexts are too different ought not to be compared.

1. *The spatial context.* Legalism has caused this to be forgotten although it was strongly emphasized by Rousseau and the eighteenth-century authors. Problems of small states are not the same as those of large ones. Observation has general significance in the social sciences, so differences of scale have great importance (they are really differences of kind). A gathering of 1,000 people is not a group 100 times larger than a gathering of ten people: it is a different phenomenon. This is the distinction, the importance of which has already been stressed, between the 'macro' and the 'micro'.

Only phenomena of analogous dimensions or belonging to aggregations of analogous dimensions can be compared. A party with a million members and one with 5,000, the budgetary procedures of Andorra and the United States, cannot be validly compared. This rule must, of course, be applied with some flexibility; there are no criteria for defining precisely a scale of dimensions. Naturally, it often happens that institutions belonging to unequal aggregations are compared (for example, the parliamentary régime in Norway and France); even so the dimensional factor should never be forgotten.

The concept of dimension is difficult to define. Size of population is not an accurate measurement of the power of states: other factors count such as the political consciousness of the inhabitants, the socio-economic level and so on. China has three or four times more inhabitants than the United States but is not three or four times 'greater'. The dimensional concept here impinges on the concept of the 'cultural context'. It is within the terms of fairly close cultural levels that the dimensional factor is significant.

2. *The cultural context.* In the absence of a better term, 'cultural' is here used in a broad sense. It is associated with the idea that social phenomena are relative to types of 'civilizations', 'epochs' and 'cultures'. A particular example will illustrate this. An American ethnologist, Murdock, has studied the balance of powers in the Berber tribes of southern Morocco and this led him to compare their organization with modern states where various procedures try to maintain equilibrium. Basically this is a functional comparison. The analysis is interesting, but the conclusions should be treated with caution because the cultural contexts (and the dimensional contexts) of the tribes and modern states are very different.

Murdock also compared the Anglo-Saxon two-party system to the dualist organization existing in some Indian villages in the south-east of the United States, where lineage is divided into two and division of powers and functions is made in a complex fashion between the two halves. Here, too, the cultural context is too different for the comparison really to have any meaning. This is not to say that it is entirely useless—the possible role of these 'distant comparisons' will be discussed later—but research in depth cannot be made on such bases.

The rule of cultural analogy leads not only to caution in comparisons between institutions from what are now called 'different civilizations' but also to care in historical comparisons within the same civilization and even the same country. If the periods are close then the comparison is valid, if they are not so close comparison is hazardous. Serious distortion is produced by the common tendency to project on the past present ways of thinking, feeling and living. Here again one must be wary of nominalism: in spite of the similarity of words, the democracy of Athens cannot be validly compared with Western democracy.

3. *Significance*. The problem of significance can be linked with the problem of context. The dualist division in the tribes studies by Murdock does not seem to be associated with the same intentions, needs and basic beliefs as Anglo-Saxon two-party systems: the significance of the phenomena is different. Examples can be found of analogous institutions having different significance although they belong to very close, even identical, cultural and dimensional contexts. One of the difficulties of comparative study of political parties is that the significance which a party has for its followers often differs greatly according to country and also according to party in the same country: being a communist in France has not the same significance as being a radical or a moderate. The same remark holds for pressure groups, trade unions, associations, etc.

If one makes the requirements of analogy too strict comparative studies become impossible. One should be cautious without making comparison impossible. False, hasty and superficial comparisons do great harm to the social sciences. On the other hand, excessive rigour tends to paralyse them. Also, as we will now show, superficial and hasty comparisons can be useful in a clearly defined field and with a precise object.

B. The two categories of comparisons

All scientific invention consists of relating two apparently far removed things: it involves using the comparative method outside the limits just prescribed. There are two uses and techniques of comparison corresponding to two phases of research. The two techniques can be called 'close comparisons' and 'distant comparisons'.

(a) CLOSE COMPARISONS

These have just been described. They are the type most frequently used by research workers and correspond to the level of research of students, assistants, technical collaborators, etc.

1. *The notion of close comparison.* It is enough to summarize what has already been said in order to define close comparison. Close comparison is made between analogous types of structures, is generally an institutional comparison and more rarely functional. The contexts

of the objects compared are as similar as possible in dimension, cultural background and significance.

Close comparison aims above all at precision. It is as thorough and detailed as possible. Its principal objective is the search for differences since, by definition, the similarities are as numerous as possible. When the differences have been isolated and their significance discovered, one attempts to explain them by possible differences of context and structure. Only then is an appeal made to other types of explanation, avoiding verbal explanations such as 'national character', 'racial temperament' and so on which are the equivalent in social science of the soporific effects of opium.

2. *Use of close comparisons.* Close comparison is essentially a substitute for the experimental method. Being unable to isolate a variable and submit it to various conditions of temperature and pressure, a great number of natural conditions of temperature and pressure are observed at the same time. This assumes the prior formulation of hypotheses which one seeks to verify by observation. The phenomena are not brought together merely 'to look at them': it is known in advance precisely what one wants to observe and define. The use of the comparative method cannot be separated from previous systemization, not only in the definition of a typology to decide which are comparable structures, but also in the construction of a theory, a hypothetical model whose correspondence with reality one seeks to verify.

The distinction between close and distant comparisons is not, of course, rigid. Each has an area of its own to which it is particularly appropriate. But both can be used outside their own areas. More rapid and superficial close comparisons can be used to formulate hypotheses and to construct a typology. It is perhaps possible to distinguish between limited and wide comparisons: the first corresponding to the verification of hypotheses, the second to the formulation of hypotheses and the establishment of a typology. My book on *Political Parties* attempted to construct a basic typology and was mainly based on large-scale use of close comparisons.

(c) DISTANT COMPARISONS

These relate mainly to the level of scientific invention: their use is therefore much more rare.

1. *The notion of distant comparison.* This is contrary to the general rules of the scientific method which have just been described. Different types of structure or institutions from different cultural contexts or of different dimensions or of different significance, are compared. They

are either historical comparisons covering widely separated periods or ethnographical comparisons.

One is mainly looking for resemblances. The things compared are far removed from one another, so it is natural that they are different. The extent to which they are the same and the significance of these resemblances are the main points of interest. The technique of comparison is not rigorous. There is really no comparative method in this field. Some people have an aptitude for seeing hidden analogies, for synthesis which produces distant comparisons. These comparisons are different to what Murdock has been accused of doing (see p. 264): he applied the detailed and careful method of close comparison to widely separated phenomena.

2. *The use of distant comparison.* It is a means of looking for hypotheses, general ideas, theories, elements of typologies and systems. General culture (in the widest sense) is here indispensable to the social scientist, or at least to one who is capable of invention. This is the mysterious realm, already referred to, of scientific invention which is in many respects close to creation in the arts, poetry, etc. A wide culture and an ever-present curiosity nourishes the creative aptitude.

The distance between phenomena should not, of course, be too great: if there is no analogy at all between phenomena comparison is impossible. Comparisons are first looked for within the specialist social sciences. The specialist then tries to follow developments in other social sciences (even if only as an 'amateur') in order to advance his own discipline by discovering analogies which could form the basis of hypotheses for new research.

It must be emphasized that distant comparisons are not the only means of arriving at new typologies and systems. It is only one means amongst others of provoking the shock which produces discovery. Intuition feeds on everything. Distant comparisons are more an attitude of mind consisting of keeping eyes open for relationships, analogies and resemblances when faced with any phenomena, rather than a rigorous method.

2. DIFFERENT VIEWS OF THE SAME PHENOMENA

This extension of the comparative method is becoming more and more widely developed in the social sciences. A single phenomena is examined by different approaches and techniques and the results are compared. This method makes possible studies in depth and is well suited to team work and interdisciplinary researches.

A. General description of the method

A single phenomenon or a single group of phenomena are the objects of study: an institution, decision, community (village, party, trade union, association, district, etc.), country, geographical region, etc. It is analysed by various methods each giving a particular 'view' of the phenomenon. These are then compared (this is the comparative character of the analysis). Two varieties of the method can be distinguished (although distinguishing them in practice is often difficult).

(*a*) WITHIN A SINGLE DISCIPLINE

It has been said that the frontiers between the various social disciplines are artificial but university organization is giving them a practical reality. Most research is carried on within the context of university departments.

1. *The different 'views'* are obtained from the simultaneous use of various techniques of analysis belonging more or less to the same discipline. For example, in the study of a political party one would make a legal and political analysis of the structure, statutes and their application, real organization, leaders, etc. A questionnaire would be given to the office holders and a poll taken of its members and electors. Doctrine and programme would be analysed through its publications, strategy by a study of the votes of its deputies, by a content analysis of their declarations in Parliament, by studies of the party press, etc.

2. *Character of teamwork.* It is practically impossible for one person to make detailed analyses using all these techniques, so it is usual that a team is formed of specialists in the different techniques. But all will be political scientists. All the disciplines useful to political science are employed but one does not go outside political science. This is the difference in principle with the other variety of the method: it will be seen in practice this difference is often blurred. The best example of research of this kind is the co-operation of numerous political scientists with considerable resources in the study of selection of candidates for the presidency of the United States in 1952.

(*b*) INTERDISCIPLINARY RESEARCH

Various specialists, for example, geographers, demographers, social psychologists, historians, anthropologists, sociologists, political scientists and so on are associated in the study of the same phenomena using the techniques of their own discipline.

Elements of Systematic Analysis

1. *Interest of this research.* Since many disciplines borrow techniques from neighbouring disciplines there is not always a clear difference between interdisciplinary researches and research with different techniques within the same discipline. The absurdity of university partitions has already been sufficiently emphasized and will not be dwelt on here. But the orientation towards a widening of the horizons of research embodied in the second variety is very important. The development of interdisciplinary research in recent years assists the progress of the social sciences. They ought to be extended and each discipline would gain from it.

2. *Difficulties of interdisciplinary research.* Unfortunately there are two obstacles in the way of the extension of this research. In the first place there is academic conservatism and attachment to sects, to partitions, etc.; fortunately the younger generation of researchers seem to be emancipating themselves from this unfortunate state of mind. The second and more serious obstacle is financial. This kind of research requires large resources. In the United States private foundations can provide sufficient financial backing. In France, the *Centre national de la Recherche scientifique* is much poorer and its structure, which parallels the traditional university divisions, is an obstacle to the financing of interdisciplinary studies.

B. Main uses of the method

The method is becoming more widely developed. In some fields it is well adapted to the research framework—for example, area studies, electoral sociology, collective monographs (community studies), decision making, etc. The bringing together of these various research techniques can cause surprise at first sight; but it is, in fact, the adaptation of the same general procedure of comparative analysis to different frameworks.

(*a*) AREA STUDIES

Since the Second World War 'area studies' have been developed mainly in the United States. Some regard this as the consequence of the expansion of the American role in international affairs necessitating the development of geopolitical knowledge. 'Perhaps also, in a country where geographical studies are so underdeveloped—several great American universities have no chair of geography—but where the teaching of international relations reaches a very high level, area studies are a spontaneous means of associating spatial considerations with examination of general political data.' (J.-B. Duroselle.) Area studies have, however, become more numerous outside the United

States in recent years. In France the *Fondation nationale des sciences politiques* has encouraged them.

1. *Notion of area studies.* Area studies are mainly a method of analysing international relations. A region with a certain social and political unity is examined and an attempt made to explain its place and role in international society. All the disciplines which might throw light on the problem can be associated with this study.

Duroselle assigns a well-defined place to area studies in the field of international relations, in which he distinguishes three stages. The first is the collecting of documentation through various disciplines. The second is to confront the studies of phenomena concerning a territory or a group of territories in a way in which contingencies can be separated from the basic permanent elements. The third stage is the establishing of a comprehensive theory of international relations; in other words, defining the fundamental elements which explain relationships independently of geographical areas. The second stage exactly corresponds to area studies.

This framework can be criticized in that it presents the three stages as successive. As in all other branches of the social sciences the third stage is necessary at the beginning of the research in the formulation of theories and hypotheses. Similarly the accumulation of documentation and area studies are not always two distinct phases; area studies are a framework within which materials are accumulated.

Area studies can also be useful for considering government, political life, public opinion in a group of countries. One could examine, for example, the political parties in the Far East or the Middle East, the press of Scandinavia or of North Africa, without paying much attention to international relations. The 'geographical area' would have to be a homogeneous context in the sense which has already been given to this term. Until now area studies have been mainly in the field of international relations, but there is no reason why they should be limited to it.

2. *The technique of area studies.* The method presents two main technical problems: the choice of the area and the choice of disciplines to be associated in the work.

The smallest geographical area which can be the basis of an area study in international relations is the State (or dependent territory): only States or dependent territories have an international personality. This rule applies to other area studies, except in the case of large States in which regions can have a definite political character: examination of the Muslim regions of the Soviet Union can be regarded as an area study. Groupings of states present delicate problems. Several great constellations are apparent—Scandinavia, the Middle East, South East Asia, Latin America—but their boundaries are not easy to define (in Latin America, for example, the Portuguese and Hispanic have to be distinguished and there are several sub-divisions within the latter).

The choice of discipline is also difficult. Duroselle—who is concerned purely with international relations—considers that there must be at least three: history, geography and sociology. This list seems very short unless 'sociology' covers a whole group of social sciences and research techniques. If fields other than international relations are considered an even greater range of disciplines must be used. No *a priori* list can be established. The main point is that the interdisciplinary character is basic to the method. The analysis of an area by a single discipline is not an area study.

(*b*) ELECTORAL SOCIOLOGY

Electoral studies are carried on in a large number of countries but electoral sociology is a French research technique which is being imitated abroad (Belgium, Italy, etc.). It was founded in 1913 by M. Andre Siegfried in his famous *Tableau politique de la France de l'Ouest sous la IIIe République*. It was neglected between the two wars but interest revived after 1945 under the influence of Francois Goguel and his study group, at the *Fondation nationale des sciences politiques*.

1. *Techniques of electoral sociology*. Electoral sociology is a comparative method of research mainly based on geography. It consists firstly of drawing up a series of maps using the smallest possible administrative areas of the results of elections. Various other maps of soil, products, methods of exploitation, distribution of wealth, types of activity, social class, religious practice, communications, etc., are established. These are compared with the electoral maps in order to find resemblances and, eventually, correlations.

The method is not, of course, limited to the comparing of maps. The area under consideration must be studied as comprehensively as possible—its history, mentality, daily life, etc. Many of these things cannot be recorded on maps. Comparison of maps is only one, and often the most superficial, element of electoral sociology. As soon as one tries to define the correlations and explain one has to use other methods.

2. *Problems of electoral sociology*. Two categories of problems are found in almost all branches of the social sciences: they are particu-

larly acute in electoral sociology because the research technique is becoming very refined.

The first problem is that of explanation. The coincidence between the electoral map and some other map suggests a correlation. It is easy enough to find out whether this is a coincidence or a true correlation but it is much more difficult to say on what this correlation is based. A famous example, taken from Siegfried, illustrates the problem. Siegfried noticed a coincidence in the west of France in 1913 between the nature of the soil and voting behaviour: inhabitants of granite regions voted Right, limestone regions Left. Siegfried explained this by saying that in granite regions the soil is not porous, water can be found everywhere and habitations are dispersed; the isolation of the farms encourages a turning in on oneself and reliance on tradition. In limestone regions where the soil is porous, water is rare and the inhabitants are grouped around wells: contacts encourage the exchange of ideas and therefore change. This seems probable but it remains a hypothesis.

The other problem is the dimensions of the research (similar to the delimitation of the area in area studies). Except for the general maps published by Francois Goguel to summarize the different elections at a national level, studies of electoral sociology have been conducted within the framework of the département. Raymond Aron has denounced this narrowness. Others have adopted the opposite view. M. Arambourou has argued for 'micro-sociology' in the form of electoral geography based on detailed study of the results for each commune. This is an important question because there seem to be different modes of explanation according to scale. This has already been examined in the discussion of the scope of sociological laws.

(*c*) DECISION MAKING.
This is the study of the way in which decisions are made.

1. *The development of the study.* Like many social science techniques it originated in the United States. Its development seems to have resulted firstly from a desire to study the mechanisms of social life dynamically: the traditional approach centred on institutions, situations and structures is essentially static. This attitude is particularly useful in political science because it facilitates a more complete emancipation from legal frameworks. Secondly, studies in decision-making are probably a derivation of the behaviourist attitude which tends to replace institutional frameworks by relational frameworks (see p. 233): the making of a decision is *par excellence* the occasion

of the development of a series of relations between individuals, groups, institutions, etc.

The technique has been particularly developed in international relations. In this field institutions are comparatively few and play a secondary role; decisions (treaties, alliances, declarations, etc.) are, in contrast, important and numerous. But there are also numerous studies of decision-making in domestic politics, economics, etc. The situation is very different from that of area studies which are still almost exclusively confined to international relations.

2. *The technique of studying decisions.* Only a brief outline will be given. The framework of the study can be, but is not always, provided by a series of associated methods as in area studies or electoral sociology. Research can be organized according to the factors which influence the decision or according to the people who take part in the decision (which comes almost to the same thing); or according to each stage of the decision; etc. All these elements can be examined from different points of view. It is therefore necessary to make a short preliminary study to establish a framework of research and the working hypotheses.

The unity of the decision studied is also important. All important decisions are, in fact, made up of a group of lesser decisions and are themselves part of a group of larger decisions. It is difficult to lay down general rules about the level at which the study should be made or which category of decisions should be covered. In the international relations field, J.-B. Duroselle has suggested a distinction of four levels: elementary decision (nomination of an ambassador, deletion of an article on a list of prohibitions, etc.); an 'evolved' decision, which assumes a series of steps and preliminary decisions (the French decision to sign the ECSC treaty in April 1951 which terminated a process which started in 1950); the foreign policy 'complex' and the 'play' of opposed or divergent policies around a problem (Agadir affair, Suez affair, etc.); the whole area of foreign policy which is a 'complex of complexes' (the Eastern question, decolonization, the awakening of the Middle East, etc.). Decision-making research should take place mainly at level of illuminating the process of transforming groups of elementary decisions into 'evolved' decisions. This scheme could be used in other fields, notably in domestic politics.

Studies of decision-making ought to place decisions in their institutional context, in other words in the framework of the organization or organizations in which they are taken. It is important here to distinguish between the official actors who seem to decide—

and who in practice often, but not always decide—and the unofficial actors who operate publicly or behind the scenes. Decision-making seems an excellent technique of studying the latter type of actor; it is, for example, an excellent means of approach to pressure groups in domestic politics. Their structure, sociological basis and so on must still be analysed but many of the obstacles which hinder these direct analyses disappear or diminish in importance in the context of the study of a decision. The very concept of a pressure group tends towards this kind of research: rather than exerting constant pressure on institutions they exert pressure on particular decisions.

(*d*) COLLECTIVE MONOGRAPHS
Under this title are grouped studies, associating different disciplines or techniques, on small groups (communes, associations, political parties, firms, institutions, etc.) or even on individuals (case studies).

1. *Community studies* are the commonest form of collective monographs. One technique (participant observation) has already been described. The American inquiries on Yankee City and Middletown, and the French studies (see p. 222) on Auxerre and Vienne-sur-Rhône can be cited again.

It is interesting to relate these great and profound studies to the depth to the method designed in France by Lebret and the collaborators in 'Economie et humanisme' to establish a preliminary 'diagnosis'. The procedures differ according to whether the inquiry is urban or rural. The presentation of the results is even more original than the technique of research; a system of graphs gives a very clear synthetic picture and makes possible numerous comparisons using classical comparative methods. These techniques have been developed to a certain extent in France and elsewhere—notably in Brazil.

2. *Studies of organizations.* Until now collective monographs have been mainly limited to studies of local communities but they can be used in other fields. They ought to be extended to the study of political or para-political, groups: parties, trade unions, pressure groups, etc., and in general to all organizations whether political or not (see p. 68). Individual monographs based more or less on a single method have mainly been used until now for these kinds of study. Collective monographs by organized teams using similar methods to community studies would be quite feasible and very fruitful.

3. *Case studies of individuals.* The term 'case study' means in practice

two different things: firstly, analysis in depth of individual behaviour either by means of personal documents or through biographical interviews.—this is the original sense of the term; secondly, a wider meaning including all monographs on an event, decision, particular 'case' (a secondary distinction should be made between studies of real cases which are a method of scientific research and studies of hypothetical cases which are only a pedagogical procedure): American lawyers have used this method for the study of law and it has subsequently been used by sociologists. The term is here used in the first sense; the second cuts across several research techniques, for instance, that of decison-making.

A large number of case studies can be compared to discover the outlines of the characteristics of a group: this was the method used in the famous sociological work in 1918–20 on the Polish peasant in Europe and America (see p. 95); this was a comparison of the classical type resting on the confrontation of analogous phenomena. An individual can also be analysed through personal documents (correspondence, various writings, etc.) and by numerous interviews in depth; this constitutes different simultaneous 'views' of the same fact.

On the comparative method in political science: R. MACRIDIS and R. COX, 'SSRC Interuniversity Seminar on Comparative Politics', *The American Political Science Review*, 1953, p. 641; R. MACRIDIS, *The Study of Comparative Government*, New York, 1955; S. BEER and ULAM, *Patterns of Government*, 2nd ed., 1962; S. NEUMANN, 'Comparative Politics: a half-century appraisal'. *Journal of Politics*, 1957, p. 369.

On the comparative method in historical studies: H. PIRENNE, 'De la méthode comparative en histoire', *Congrès des sciences historiques de Bruxelles*, 1923; H. SÉE, *Science et philosophie de l'histoire*, 2nd ed., 1933; A. MEILLET, *La Méthode comparative en linguistique historique*, Oslo and Paris, 1925.

On the comparative method in ethnology: L. SHAPERA, 'Comparative Method in Social Anthropology', *American Anthropological Review*, 1953, p. 350; W. L. THOMAS (*et al.*), *Current Anthropology*, Chicago, 1956.

Collective investigations: P. T. DAVID, M. MOOS, R. M. GOLDMAN, *Presidential Nominating Politics in 1952*, 4 vols., Baltimore, 1954; *Studies in Social Psychology during World War II*, 4 vols., Princeton, 1949–50 (usually called *The American Soldier*); G. MYRDAL, *An American Dilemma: the Negro Problem and Democracy*, New York, 1944.

On area studies: special number of the *International Bulletin of the Social Sciences*, UNESCO, 1952, Vol. IV; C. W. BENNETT, *Area Studies in American Universities*, Social Science Research Council, 1951; J. H. STEWARD, *Area Research*, SSRC, 1950; US DEPARTMENT OF STATE, *Area Study Programmes in American Universities*, Washington, 1956.

Introduction to the Social Sciences

On decision making: R. C. SNYDER, H. W. BRUCK, B. SAPIN, *Decision-making as an Approach to the Study of International Politics*, Princeton, 1954; H. A. SIMON, *Administrative Behaviour*, 2nd ed., New York, 1957; D. DAVIDSON and P. SUPPES, *Decision Making*, Stanford, 1957; S. BAILEY, *Congress makes a Law*, New York, 1950; P. WASSERMAN and F. S. SILANDER, *Decision Making: An Annotated Bibliography*, Ithaca, 1958.

On electoral sociology: A. SIEGFRIED, *Tableau politique de la France de l'Ouest sous la IIIe République*, 1913; F. GOGUEL and G. DUPEUX, *Sociologie électorale*, 1951; G. DUPEUX, *Current Sociology*, 4, 1954–55; the articles of R. ARON and R. ARAMBOUROU in *Revue française de science politique*, pp. 5 ff., 1955, and pp. 521 ff., 1952.

On community studies: L.-J. LEBRET, *Guide pratique de l'enquête sociale*, 3 vols., 1952–55.

On organisations: J. G. MARCH and H. A. SIMON, *Organizations*, New York, 1958; R. K. MERTON, *A Reader in Bureaucracy*, Glencoe, 1959.

On case studies: J. S. SCHLESINGER, *How to become Governor*, East Lansing, 1957; the monographs in the series *Case Studies in Practical Politics*, Eagleton Foundation, 1958.

CHAPTER TWO

MATHEMATICAL AND GRAPH TECHNIQUES

Mathematical techniques are improved versions of the comparative method. The expression of phenomena by figures and symbols allows a large number to be compared simultaneously, their respective characteristics can be set against one another with great accuracy, and their analysis taken much further. In striving to introduce 'quantification' and mathematics into their disciplines as far as possible, specialists in the social sciences, contrary to what many laymen think, are not merely deferring to a fashion, but are recognizing that mathematics provides analytical tools incomparably more effective than classical comparative methods. The results obtained by methods described in previous chapters are as different from those which mathematics can achieve as walking is from travel by jet aircraft.

This much said, the opposite extreme should be considered. An American political scientist, in criticizing colleagues almost exclusively devoted to fields in which mathematical techniques are possible, likens them to the drunk who persists in looking under the lamppost for the watch which he has lost in a dark alley—it being the only well-lit spot. It may be that the most interesting areas of the social sciences will elude quantification and mathematical analysis for a long time to come. This is not a reason for ignoring these areas. Nor is the fact that at present the fields in which mathematics can be used are comparatively few a reason for not knowing what these are.

Mathematical techniques are here considered together with graph techniques, which are also advanced applications of comparative method and make it possible to survey a very large number of facts simultaneously, isolating both their similarities and differences. Some graphs are simply visual translations of mathematical functions or enumerations—others, such as those based on maps, have no mathematical aspect.

Section I. Mathematical Techniques

Our description of the various uses of mathematical techniques in the social sciences will be only a summary account designed to be comprehensible to readers without advanced mathematical training (which includes most social science students). No attempt will be made to give even an outline of analytical techniques which are complex and can be used only by specialists. When the techniques require only fairly simple calculations, the formulae and instructions for using them will be given, with no attempt at (theoretical) justification; to drive a car properly no acquaintance is needed with the theory of combustion engines.

1. EXPRESSING PHENOMENA MATHEMATICALLY

Mathematical analysis assumes that the material studied has been expressed in figures. These figures express those common characteristics of phenomena which serve as a basis for comparing them. Two stages are involved (i) the transposition into numerical form, called *quantification*; (ii) the isolation, from tables of figures thus obtained, of values which express them synthetically—*averages and indices*. The first stage brings us clearly up against the difficulties of applying mathematical methods to the social sciences. As for the second, no more than a few elementary concepts will be dealt with here.

A. Quantification in Social Science

Mathematical analysis can be applied only to phenomena which can be counted or measured, i.e. expressed in figures. Such figures must be exact, or analysis based on them will be fundamentally unsound. Here lies the crucial obstacle to the development of the methods of mathematics in the social sciences; only a few areas can really be quantified and even in these the exactness of the figures obtained must be regarded with caution.

However, recent developments in mathematics present new possibilities. The terms 'human mathematics' and 'qualitative mathematics' have been coined; these, it is asserted, would reflect faithfully the nature of social facts. At the moment such prospects remain fairly limited.

(a) SCOPE OF QUANTIFICATION

Two kinds of quantification can be distinguished in social studies. Some phenomena are measurable physically and thus lend themselves to quantification which is, at least apparently, rigorous. Others can be measured by more approximate methods, and the figures obtained are fairly imprecise.

1. *Physically measurable phenomena.* Despite the difficulties these are quite numerous. Demographic facts, most economic phenomena, many aspects of geography, etc., can easily be measured. In politics, elections are the perfect example of a physically measurable event, and there are others—newspaper circulations, party support, membership of groups and social classes, and so on. Admittedly, statistics about these things are not always exact. But they may be—the only obstacles to overcome are material ones (excluding the desire to keep information secret, which many observers have encountered).

There are those who criticize the scope of these figures. A series of calculations and mathematical analyses can be carried out on the basis of electoral statistics, to correlate, for example, the Communist vote in France and standard of living, or the Communist vote and the position of the wage earner. But, the critics assert, it is forgotten that voting communist does not mean the same thing for the workman in the Paris region and the peasant in Lot-et-Garonne. The Communist Party means entirely different things for these two voters, and their political attitudes are fundamentally different. Simply to add the two is contrary to the very foundation of mathematics which requires that units are identical.

This is not a valid argument. Every quantification is an abstraction consisting of isolating some elements in a totality and disregarding others. In a forest of 10,000 trees there are no two identical ones; all are different in some way or another. But the total is correct because all share the character of 'tree' which is defined *a priori*. Similarly among the four million Communist voters there is a common element—every one of them has put in the ballot-box a voting slip supporting a Communist candidate. If—but only if, we remain within the terms of this definition quantification is valid.

And yet a part of the objection remains. Imagine a vague concept 'trunk', applied both to tree-trunks and to human bodies. A forest of 10,000 'trunks' will include both trees and bodies. Mathematically, calculations based on this figure will be valid, within the terms of the definition 'trunk'; but in forestry or in physiology they will be meaningless, for the complex trees/bodies is not a significant category The same thing may occur in social studies—for example in local elections, where parties count for little, some do not constitute a valid category (e.g. in France, 'Radical' votes in the cantonal and municipal elections). The fault lies not in the quantification but in the typology. This problem has already been studied.

2. *Approximately measurable phenomena.* With some other material quantification is much less rigorous. The most typical case is the measurement of attitudes or opinions. We have already shown how the intensity of an attitude or an opinion can be assessed (p. 196) and the approximate nature of the results obtained was emphasized. Despite efforts to establish objective and accurate scales, we are left with a high coefficient of subjectivity. This is not to say that the figures are meaningless, but that they only give orders of magnitude or indications.

This observation applies also to the majority of replies to opinion questionnaires. In matters of fact, only material errors or lies which are few, impair the exactness of the results. In opinion polls, the respondent's interpretation of his own opinion, the interviewer's interpretation of the reply, the coder's interpretation of the results, all introduce elements of distortion, not to mention sampling errors and so on. It must be reiterated that these faults do not invalidate opinion polls. However approximate the results may be, they nonetheless mark an immense advance compared to a total lack of information. But the figures into which such results are cast must be considered as orders of magnitude, a fact which is openly recognized by the specialists.

But it is impossible to use such figures as the basis of complex mathematical operations. The uncertainty of the data would be magnified by the processes of calculation, so that the results obtained would lose all meaning and would be misleading. This does not mean that all mathematical analysis based on such figures is impossible, but it must be limited to rough calculations and not extended to refined techniques. We shall see, for example, that in the social sciences graphs are often preferable to calculation of the coefficient of correlation, the basic figures being too inexact to produce a valid result (see below, p. 290).

(*b*) POSSIBLE APPLICATIONS OF QUALITATIVE MATHEMATICS

The use of mathematics is envisaged by some outside the fields in which quantification is possible. There are two main possibilities of advance in this field (i) contemporary evolution of mathematical theory; (ii) computers.

1. *Evolution of mathematical theory.* Contemporary theory in the field of discontinuous values suggests striking points of comparison

with the problems studied in the social sciences. Set theory, group theory, topology, all set out to establish exact relationships between classes of terms separated by discontinuous values. Discontinuity is an essential trait of the relationships between qualitative groups, e.g. those studied in the human sciences. From this comes the term 'qualitative mathematics'; but the term is wrongly used because it is impossible completely to equate discontinuity with qualitative characteristics.

Claude Lévi-Strauss has given memorable expression to the still remote possibilities which may be opened up for the social sciences: 'Human mathematics for which neither mathematicians nor sociologists yet know quite where to look and which to a great extent have yet to be created, will undoubtedly be quite different from those with which social science now tries to give rigorous form to its observations. Human mathematics attempt to escape from the plight of "large numbers"—that raft on which, lost in an ocean of figures, the social sciences have been floundering. Their ultimate object is not to express in simple curves progressive and continuous evolution. Their field is not that of the infinitesimal variations revealed by analysis of vast agglomerizations of data. The prospect offered to us is rather that of *small* numbers and of *great* changes caused by the movement from one number to another. If I may use a metaphor, we shall devote less attention to the theoretical consequences of a 10 per cent population increase in a country of fifty-million inhabitants and more attention to the structural transformations which result when the simple marriage relationship becomes the eternal triangle. Examining the potentialities and limitations of membership of very small groups (which in this sense remain "very small" even if the participants are numbered in millions) a link with a very old tradition is established, the earliest Greek philosophers, sages of China and India, and thinkers in the heart of pre-colonial Africa and pre-Colomban America were all concerned with the meaning and the inherent virtues of numbers. The Indo-European civilization, for example, has a predilection for the figure 3, whilst Africans and Americans preferred to think in 4's; quite distinct logical and mathematical properties are involved in such choices.'

2. *Electronic calculators*. The most recent electronic computers raise the possibility of handing over to them the analysis of problems whose terms have not been properly quantified.

Electronic computers are based mainly on a binary system, i.e. the information fed into them must be broken down into a series of elements based on a scale of 2—the same basic method as that of the old botanists' handbook determining the names of plants with pairs of opposed characteristics ranged in series of different lengths. This form imposes a particular programming method on the operations which the machine performs, but at the same time it enables the machine to handle other material than figures. 'Binary language' means that the machine tends naturally to work with questions of the 'yes-no' type, which are not mathematical questions, but the sort of questions which the social sciences have to resolve. One observer writes: 'The computer plays the game of "guessing identities" at the speed of light; we conceive the possibility of reconstituting *any* thought process through the series of yes/no answers found in this game.' (M. Sauvage.) But this potentiality has not yet been realized.

B. Synthetic Expression of Quantities[1]

Most of the quantities to be analysed in the social sciences are in the form of statistical series expressing the features of a large population or of an evolution in time. From these series are derived 'characteristics' which give a synthetic and reasonably close account of them. These characteristics can also be compared with one another through indices or percentages.

(*a*) AVERAGES

The most important of these are the arithmetical mean, the geometrical mean and the median.

1. *The arithmetical mean.* This is defined as the sum of the terms of a series divided by the number of the terms. Its algebraical symbol is:

$$\bar{a} = \frac{a_1 + a_2 + a_3 \text{--------} a_n}{n}$$

The arithmetical mean is the best known and the most widely used of the characteristics of magnitude. It has the advantages of depending upon the value of all the terms in a series, of being comparatively immune to fluctuations in sampling, and of lending itself easily to algebraic comparisons and calculations. But the largest terms in a series have much more weight than the others in the arithmetical mean, and it is therefore not used in certain cases.

2. *The geometrical mean.* The geometrical mean is the nth root of the product of the n terms of a series:

[1] This section merely describes the few elementary mathematical concepts indispensable for every student of the social sciences.

$$Mg = \sqrt[n]{a_1 a_2 a_3 \ldots a_n}$$

It is usually calculated by the use of logarithmic tables. The logarithm of the geometrical mean is equal to the arithmetic mean of the logarithms of the terms of the series. The arithmetic mean of the logarithms of each term of the series is the logarithm of the geometrical mean.

The geometrical mean is always less than the arithmetic mean. Its main advantage is to minimize the effect of the largest terms in the series upon the mean.

3. *The median.* This is the middle term of a series arranged in order of magnitude. In the series, 55, 58, 62, 63, 65, 69, 71, 77, 83, the median is 65. If the series has an even number of terms the median is the arithmetical mean of the two middle terms: in the series, 55, 58, 62, 63, 65, 69, 77, 83, the median is $\frac{63+65}{2}$ i.e. 64.

The median has two main advantages. Firstly, it is very simple to work out; secondly, it eliminates the influence of aberrant terms which greatly affect the calculation of means. On the other hand, it is less readily amenable to algebraic operations and is more sensitive to the effects of sampling errors.

(*b*) DISTRIBUTION

Averages give us only an incomplete idea of a series, which we must supplement by discovering how the terms of the series are distributed. The characteristics of distribution, e.g. quartiles, mean deviation, variance or standard deviation, and coefficient of variation, give an overall view of distribution.

1. *Interquartiles.* The median divides a series into two half-series with an equal number of terms. Taking the median of each half-series, we get the first and the third quartile (the median is, of course, the second quartile):

	Q_1		Median Q_2		Q_3	
25% of series		25% of series		25% of series		25% of series

The difference between the first and the third quartiles is the central range, containing 50 per cent of the terms; it gives the characteristic of distribution known as the interquartile, $Q_3 - Q_1$. We can use, too, the demi-interquartile, called the 'quartile deviation', i.e. $\dfrac{Q_3 - Q_1}{2}$.

To compare the distribution of two series whose elements are measured in different units, or whose orders of magnitude are different, the 'relative interquartile' is used; this is the ratio of the interquartile to the median, $\dfrac{Q_3 - Q_1}{\text{Median}}$.

2. *Mean deviation.* Mean deviation, also called arithmetical deviation, is the arithmetical mean of the differences between the individual terms as positive values whether they are positive or negative. The (arithmetical) mean of a range of hourly wage-rates (in francs) of 55, 58, 62, 63, 65, 69, 71, 77, 83, is 67. The differences between each term and this mean are as follows:

55	58	62	63	65	69	71	77	83
−67	−67	−67	−67	−67	−67	−67	−67	−67
−12	−9	−5	−4	−2	+2	+4	+10	+16

The algebraic sum of these deviations is obviously 0. Disregarding the signs, we can simply add the values of the differences: $12+9+5+4+2+2+4+10+16=64$; This is then divided by the number in terms in the series: $\dfrac{64}{9} = 7.11$, to give the mean deviation.

Mean deviation gives a fairly accurate picture of distribution: but it is only occasionally used, since absolute quantities are almost incompatible with algebraic operations. Because of this, variance and standard deviation are used instead.

3. *Variance and standard deviation.* Variance is the mean of the squares of the deviation from the arithmetical mean of a series. Taking the squares of the deviations and not the deviations themselves, we automatically eliminate the negative sign, which permits algebraic operations. In the previous example, variance is:

$$12^2 + 9^2 + 5^2 + 4^2 + 2^2 + 2^2 + 4^2 + 10^2 + 16^2 = \dfrac{646}{9} = 71.8.$$

The defect of this procedure is that our result is itself a square; still using the previous example, the figure 71.8 represents 'francs squared', which is not a readily understandable concept.

We therefore arrive at another characteristic of distribution, the

MATHEMATICAL AND GRAPH TECHNIQUES

standard deviation or 'mean quadratic deviation', which is simply the square root of the variance. Standard deviation is usually expressed by the symbol σ. In our example $\sigma = \sqrt{71.8} = 8.45$.

To compare the distribution of two series whose elements are of widely differing magnitudes, we use the coefficient of variation which is the ratio $\frac{\text{standard deviation}}{\text{(arithmetic) mean}}$. This coefficient may be expressed as a percentage. In the example, the coefficient of variation (v) is: $\frac{8.45}{67} = 0.126$, or 12.6 per cent.

Frequently, as the terms of a group vary, the mean varies in roughly the same proportion. The coefficient of variation remains relatively constant.

(c) INDICES AND PERCENTAGES

'Characteristics' enable us to extract from a series some fundamental features: they are established independently for each series studied. The purpose of indices and percentages is to provide a scale of measurement common to several elements (or several series of elements or several characteristics).

1. *Indices*. Particular and synthetic indices must be distinguished; the latter are sub-divided into simple and weighted indices.

To calculate an index one figure is taken as the base and the ratio between it and each figure in the series is worked out. The ratios obtained are usually multiplied by 100, and in this case the base figure is 100. To illustrate this let us assume that in one departement in the elections of 1946, the Radical Party obtained 25,000 votes, 30,000 in 1951 and 40,000 in 1956. Taking 1946 as base:

$$1946: \ldots\ldots\ldots\ldots\ldots 100$$
$$1951: \frac{30{,}000}{25{,}000} = 1.2 \times 100 = 120$$
$$1956: \frac{40{,}000}{25{,}000} = 1.6 \times 100 = 160$$

Price indexes offer the best example: they illustrate the distinction between simple and weighted indices. A simple index is one in which all the particular elements are assessed at face value. In general the simple index is the arithmetical mean of the particular indices composing it. For example the index of wholesale prices of the forty-five commodities covered by the French National Statistics is arrived at by means of the formula:

$$Ig = \frac{i_1 + i_2 + i_3 \cdots + i_{45}}{45}$$

An index is weighted when the particular indices for each of the items composing it are assessed at less or more than par. In other words, each particular index is weighted with a coefficient corresponding to its importance in the context. In the cost-of-living index, for example, the price of bread is given a higher coefficient than the price of braces (and so on).

2. *Percentages.* Though the use of percentages is familiar, attention must be drawn to a few glaring errors to be avoided in their interpretation.

Firstly: if percentages are used to compare the terms of a single series with one another and to express for each one the increase or decrease in relation to the previous figure, it must be remembered that these percentages cannot be added to one another. In a previous example the Radical party increased its votes by 20 per cent between 1946 and 1951, and by 33⅓ per cent from 1945 to 1961, but the total increase in 1956 on the 1946 figures is not 53⅓ per cent but 60 per cent. Secondly, percentages are not reversible; if a party's vote increases by 100 per cent between 1946 and 1951, a 100 per cent reduction in the 1956 election does not bring us back to the 1946 figure.

It is different when percentages are used to compare the division of similar totals into various classes. Here the basis of the comparison is the total of terms of each aggregate. For example, the number of Radical votes cast in the elections of 1946, 1951 and 1956 can be expressed as a percentage of the total number of votes cast at each election. We can in this case subtract these percentages from one another to measure the increase or decrease. If the relevant figures for the Radicals are, for instance, 25 per cent for 1946, 28 per cent for 1951, and 35 per cent for 1956, we can say that the party increased in absolute strength by 3 per cent in 1951 and by 7 per cent in 1956. This calculation is in fact open to criticism; it involves subtractions of fractions of different aggregates—the electorate of 1956 is not the same as that of 1951 or that of 1946. In practice, however, it is useful, giving an indication of the relative increase or decline.

2. MATHEMATICAL ANALYSIS

Two kinds of methods are used. One consists of comparatively simple techniques requiring no advanced mathematical training and using such elementary equipment as slide rules and ordinary adding machines. The other uses complex techniques which can be understood and applied only by highly trained mathematicians and normally require the use of computers. For the first category the basic formulae and instructions for their application, omitting all discussion of mathematical validity and significance, will be given; for the second, the general import of the techniques will be briefly treated without mathematical details, and some practical uses will be indicated.

A. Analysis of association and correlations

The concepts of dependence and correlation are linked to the concept of stochastic association as opposed to the idea of functional association. In a functional association for every value of variable x there is a corresponding value of variable y, and these are grouped in an aggregate with a specific form.

Association must be distinguished from correlation. Correlation is concerned with the comparing of two or more series of measurements. Association deals with the comparison of two or more series of features which are not measurable—social categories, political opinions, colours, etc. In practice the contrast between quantitative and qualitative features is not absolute. If we compare the political and the religious affiliation of a series of individuals we are seeking to associate qualitative features. If we compare the same things in different groups (constituencies, towns, etc.), the features are measurable within each group; the number of individuals displaying a feature can be counted and thus a quantitative comparison is possible.

(*a*) ESTABLISHING ASSOCIATIONS

If we ascertain the proportion of persons voting for parties of the Right and the Left and the proportion of Christians and atheists in a given group we can attempt to discover an association between religious and political factors, i.e. whether the fact of being a Christian is associated with voting for a party of the Right, or conversely.

1. *Presentation by graphs: contingency tables.* Analysis of the association (or lack of it) between the features in a given population group may take the form of double-entry tables, called 'contingency tables' and make possible an overall view of the distribution of the features in question. For example, it was found through an opinion poll that the respective distribution of atheists and believers and of

voters for Left and Right; of 6,800 people polled 5,943 are believers and 857 atheists; 2,945 vote for the Right and 3,855 for the Left. The results are shown in the table below (fig. 8).

Religion	Vote		Total
	Right	Left	
Believers	2,814	3,129	5,943
Atheists	131	726	857
Totals	2,945	3,855	6,800

Fig. 8.—Contingency table for contrasting pairs

A contingency table can also be established for more than two characteristics to establish association or independence. See, for example, figure 9.

Religion	Vote				Total
	Conservatives	Liberals	Socialists	Communists	
Catholics	1,768	807	189	47	2,811
Protestants	946	1,387	746	53	3,132
Atheists	115	438	288	16	857
Totals	2,829	2,632	1,223	116	6,800

Fig. 9.—Contingency tables for multiple characteristics

2. *Determining association and independence.* There is independence between two characteristics a and a', when the proportion of people in one of the states of a is the same as in various categories of a': for example, if the proportion of religious believers is the same in those who vote for the Left as those who vote for the Right. If the proportion is different there is an association of characteristics. Association does not mean that one of the characteristics is a factor of the other but simply that they have a tendency to be found together.

The most frequently used mathematical method to determine whether or not there is an association of characteristics is the χ^2 test. This test, in effect, is a comparison between two distributions: the actual distribution and the theoretical independent distribution. The theoretical distribution is the distribution into classes of a category of the population defined by a particular characteristic, in the same proportions as in the whole population. In the example already cited (fig. 8), the proportion of Rightest voters amongst believers would be, by definition, the same as in the whole sample: $\frac{2,945}{6,800}$; there would thus be:

$$5{,}943 \times \frac{2{,}945}{6{,}800} = 2{,}574 \text{ Rightest believing voters}$$

and $857 \times \dfrac{2{,}945}{6{,}800} = 371$ Rightest unbelieving voters.

Similarly the proportion of Leftist voters would be the same amongst believers as amongst atheists: $\dfrac{3{,}855}{6{,}800}$; in other words there would be:

$$5{,}945 \times \frac{3{,}855}{6{,}800} = 3{,}369 \text{ Leftist believing voters}$$

and

$$857 \times \frac{3{,}855}{6{,}800} = 486 \text{ Leftist atheist voters.}$$

There are, therefore, the two following distributions:

	Observed distribution	Theoretical distribution (independence)
Rightest voters (believers)	2,814	2,574
Leftist voters (believers)	3,129	3,369
Rightest voters (atheists)	131	371
Leftist voters (atheists)	726	486

The divergence between the two distributions is:

$$\chi^2 = \frac{(2{,}814 - 2{,}574)^2}{2{,}574} + \frac{(3{,}129 - 3{,}369)^2}{3{,}369} + \frac{(131 - 371)^2}{371}$$

$$+ \frac{(726 - 486)^2}{486} \# \boxed{313}$$

The number of the degrees of freedom is one, since given the frequency of one of the classes the others can be deduced from it (the totals of each column and each line being fixed). Under these conditions the value of χ^2 is 3.84 for a coefficient of reliability of 95 per cent and 6.64 for a coefficient of 99 per cent. The χ^2 is very high which demonstrates that the difference between the two distributions does not come from an error in the sample: there is therefore an association between the characteristics.

(b) CORRELATIONS

If for the same population there are two series of associated quantified characteristics, one can try to establish a correlation between them: as has been said, if each term in the series is a group of individuals, the qualitative characteristics of each (political and religious persuasion, etc.) can be measured by their proportion in the group, and correlations can be sought.

Correlations are established by lengthy calculations to determine a coefficient of correlation. A much less rigorous but a rapid and simple method is making a graph of the characteristics. In many cases in the social sciences this latter method is sufficiently accurate because the basic statistics are not precise enough to warrant rigorous calculations.

1. *Distribution graphs.* The simplest method of finding a correlation is to plot pairs of phenomena on a graph. For instance, one can study the correlation between the proportion of workers in the active population and the proportion of votes obtained by the Communist Party in an election. This is possible if one has two quite long parallel series of groups of elements: for example, if the distribution of the active population for a large number of polling areas and the corresponding distribution of votes is available.

If we suppose that the percentage of working class and of communist votes are the following:

Polling areas	Percentage of working class	Percentage of communist votes
1	60	40
2	50	25
3	70	55
4	30	20
5	25	15
6	40	30
Etc.		

x being the proportion of working class and y being the proportion of communist votes the following graph can be plotted:

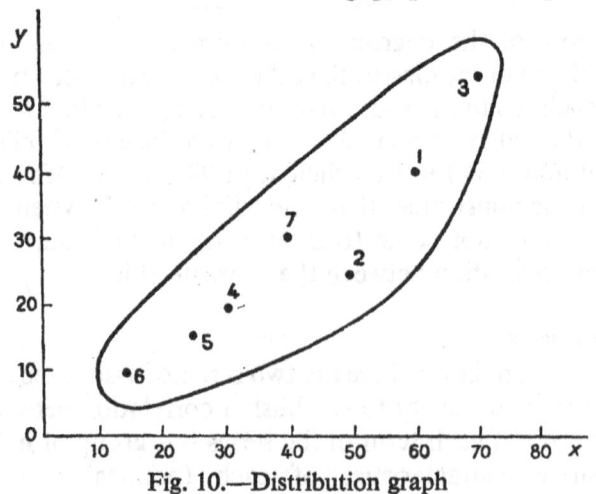

Fig. 10.—Distribution graph

Mathematical and Graph Techniques

When this is done for a large number of cases (and this is essential), a scatter of points is obtained. A correlation exists if this scatter is in the form of a more or less elliptical band which slopes in relation to the co-ordinates.

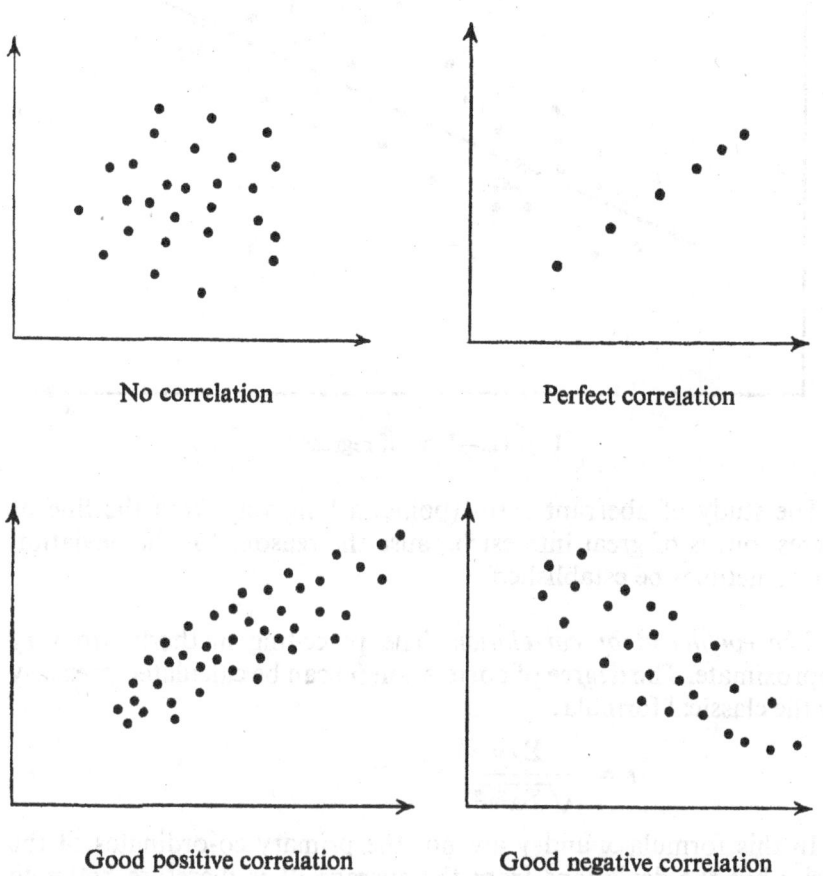

Fig. 11.—Correlations in distribution graphs

The flatter the ellipse the stronger is the correlation: in a perfect correlation ($r = \pm 1$) the points are in a straight line. The correlation is positive when the phenomena tend in the same direction and negative when in opposite directions.

The 'line of regress' can be traced on the distribution graph to represent the supposed relationship between the two phenomena studied. The line is more accurate if one divides the points on the graph into two groups and establish the median points, M^1 and M^2, and draw the line through these points.

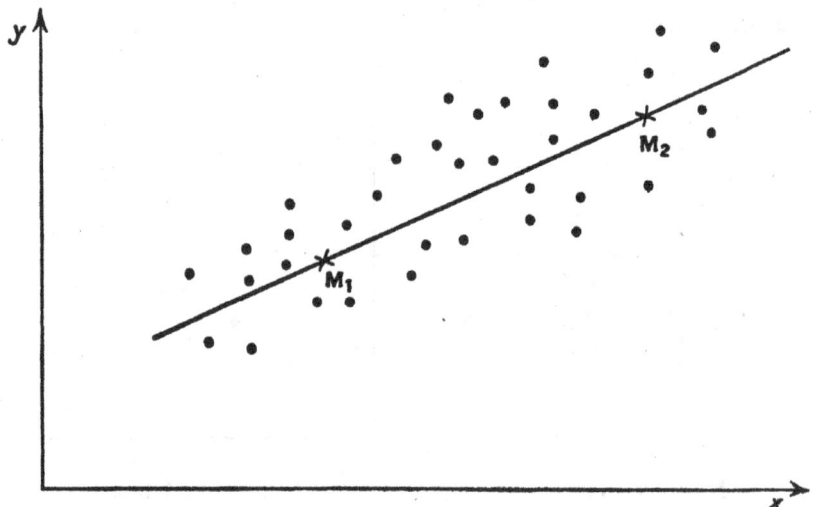

Fig. 12.—Line of regress

The study of aberrant cases (points a long way from the line of regression) is of great interest because the reasons for the deviation can sometimes be established.

2. *The coefficient of correlation.* The preceding methods are very approximate. The degree of correlation (r) can be calculated precisely by the classical formula:

$$r = \frac{\Sigma xy}{\sqrt{\Sigma x^2 y^2}}$$

In this formula x and y are not the primary co-ordinates of the series but the deviations from the average. It is therefore better to write:

$$r = \frac{\Sigma (x-x)(y-\bar{y})}{\sqrt{\Sigma (x-\bar{x})^2 \Sigma (y-\bar{y})^2}}$$

The calculations can also be made by a simpler formula in which N = the number of observations, and sx and sy the divergent types:

$$r = \frac{\Sigma (x-\bar{x})(y-\bar{y})}{N.sx\ sy}$$

Elementary works on statistics should be consulted on these points. The equation of the 'line of regression' (which is a stage on the way to the calculation of the coefficient of correlation) can be calculated so that it can be drawn accurately. More precisely the equations of two 'lines of regression'—regress of x in relation to y and y in relation to x—are calculated. The greater the correlation the smaller is the angle between these two lines.

A correlation is expressed by a number between 0 and 1. It should be remembered that a high index of correlation is not absolute proof that there is a dependence between the two phenomena—a correlation of .99 has no value in itself. Yule's famous example of a .95 correlation between death rate in Britain and marriages solemnized by the Church of England is a classic example of this. The coefficient of correlation only gives an indication.

When the coefficient is calculated on the basis of samples, errors in the sample introduce an additional area of uncertainty. This area can be accurately measured. Curves make it possible to assess it quickly (see fig. 13).

B. Factorial analysis

Factorial analysis is based on correlations. If we take the ranking of school children in different tests: literature, history, mathematics, geography, natural science, physics, etc.: correlations between pairs of rankings can be calculated.

If the ranking is identical between, for example, literature and history the coefficient of correlation is $+.1$. If the ranking is absolutely the opposite in two tests, the first one being the last in the other and so on, the correlation would be $-.1$. In practice the coefficients found lie between these two extremes.

The coefficients will not be identical for all tests. It is possible that the correlation will be high between literature and history and low between history and mathematics, etc. Factorial analysis makes possible analysis of the differences between correlations and isolation and measurement of the variables.

(a) FIELDS OF FACTORIAL ANALYSIS

Factorial analysis is mainly used in social psychology to study aptitudes: many experiments have been conducted in this field in the last fifty years. It has been applied to other fields but since its use is more recent and more limited the results obtained are less reliable.

1. *Factorial analysis of questionnaire (or test) correlations.* If a large number of people are subjected to questionnaires or tests the correlations between the results of each can be examined. This

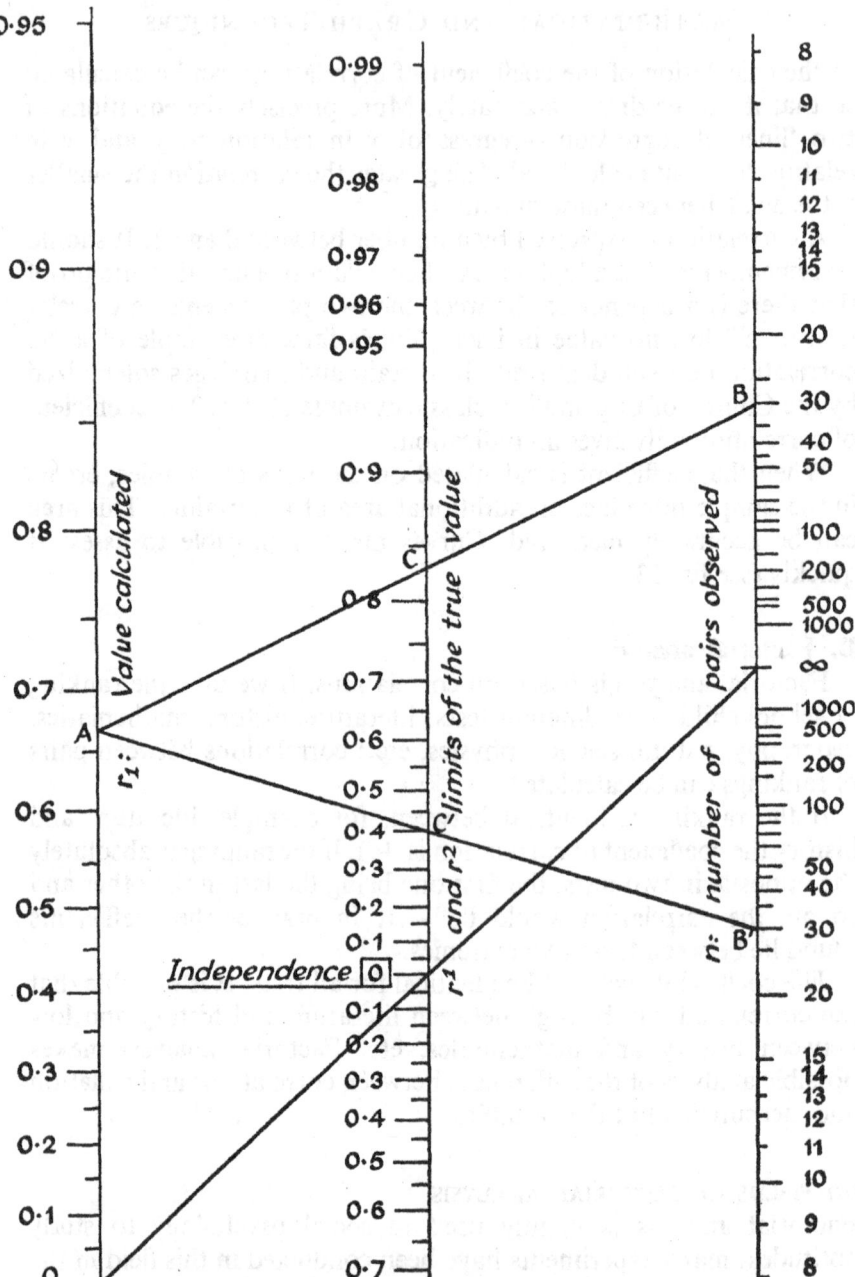

Fig. 13.—Degree of uncertainty of the coefficient of correlation

The scale on the left (r_1) is the value of the coefficient calculated on a sample of n pairs: for example, the value A.

The scale on the right (n) gives the value of the sample in two symmetrical points, for example B and B'.

AB and AB' are joined: the intersections on the centre scale (C and C') give the limits between which the true value of the coefficient of correlation is found (with a given coefficient of reliability—in this case 95 per cent).

method is widely used in social psychology. Attempts have been made to determine human aptitudes using factorial analysis: the 'factors' isolated by the analysis (which are themselves only mathematical symbols) can be assimilated with intellectual aptitudes. This assimilation creates difficulties and no conclusive results have yet been obtained despite numerous analyses and a great amount of work.

In the other social sciences, factorial analysis has been less used. There seem to be possibilities of developing it. One could, for example, administer questionnaires or attitude scales to the same group of people on religion, democracy, liberty, racism, militarism, etc., and establish correlations between the results and make factorial analyses. It would be possible in this way to isolate different factors making up political attitudes (with a reservation, which will be discussed later, on the reality of 'factors').

A variety of factorial analysis can be used to establish correlations between the replies to different questions in the same test or questionnaire. Eysenck has analysed political attitudes on the basis of a forty question questionnaire. Duncan Macrae examined the political preferences of French people through the ranking given to ten politicians by the subjects questioned in January 1955: correlations were established between the politicians according to the rank given them.

2. *Factorial analysis of correlations between individuals.* A questionnaire or test is given to a group of people and the replies of each person to each question recorded. Correlations are then established between individuals—not between the questionnaires or the questions. In practice this can be done in various ways.

The first corresponds exactly to the description just given, using either questions or ranking tests. The method has been used in social psychology especially in the analysis of aesthetic aptitudes. For example, Peel made a group classify thirty-one drawings or pictures by order of preference and correlated the classification of each individual. Eysenck did the same thing with poems. This method can be used in political science, for example, by the ranking of politicians and analysing the replies to questionnaires.

Another method could be very useful for the political scientist. Instead of establishing correlations between individuals they could be established between groups of individuals. For example, a table of replies could be established separately for those who voted for the communist, socialist, radical and other parties and the correlations calculated between pairs of parties.

3. *Factorial analysis of correlations in time.* This is much more rarely used than the preceding procedures. It consists of asking the same individual (or group of individuals) the same questions at different times and establishing correlations between the replies. The evolution of attitudes can thus be measured.

This procedure runs into serious difficulties. Repetition of questions introduces a distorting factor (this has been discussed in the section on the 'panel technique'). It is not easy to follow individuals over a long period of time but it can be done for relatively short periods. The method can be used to analyse the results of a panel and the variations in the attitudes of voters of the same party in their replies to opinion polls (but the changes in the group questioned introduces another element of distortion here).

(*b*) METHODS OF FACTORIAL ANALYSIS

The technical aspects of factorial analysis will not be described here because they cannot be understood without advanced mathematical training. But it is worth knowing the basic principles of the various methods. Broadly speaking there are two systems: Spearman's bifactorial method and Thurstone's multifactorial method, each having a variety of forms. The first is mainly used in Britain, the second in the United States.

1. *Spearman's bifactorial method.* Charles Spearman, an English psychologist, invented this method and it has been modified by Holzinger. It is based on the distinction between two categories of factors: a general factor (g) common to all tests and questionnaires (in direct factorial analysis) and group factors, common to a range of tests or questionnaires. When these two categories of factors have been extracted there remains a residue in each test or questionnaire of a third category of factors—specific factors (but these are uninteresting because they are specific).

The part played by a factor in the result of a test, in other words the proportion of this factor in the test, is called 'saturation'. It is measured by the correlation between the test and the factor. The sum of the squares of saturation of factor g and of the factors of groups for a given test is called the 'community' (h^2). The sum of the squares of all factors being 1, the specific factor is equal to $1-h^2$: this is the part which escapes factorial analysis.

The notion of the general factor which is central to the method has been much criticized. The hierarchy of the general factor and the group factors is associated with 'a strong tradition of English psychology which antedates factorial analysis' (P. Pichot). The difficulties arising from the attempt to identify this general factor will be discussed later.

2. *Thurstone's multifactorial method.* The basic idea is to explain correlations by group factors without taking into account the general factor (g). Some have seen in the conflict between the English 'bifactorists' and the American 'multifactorists' a reflection of two social structures, the first hierarchical with the crown at the apex (image of the g factor), the second egalitarian. Without going as far as this, it is possible to discern an egalitarian attitude in American psychology in the tendency to discount dominant elements in the structure of attitudes and behaviour. It should, however, be remarked that the rivalry between the two schools has decreased in recent years.

The Thurstone method has two main variants; in one of them traces of the general factor can be found under a different form. This is called the 'orthogonal axes method' because the group factors are represented geometrically by two axes which are oblique to one another. By this means the correlation between the factors can be established and one can also go further and examine the correlation of factors by the presence in each of them of a certain common element called a second order general factor (the general factor thus reappears but at the second stage of the analysis).

(*c*) SCOPE OF FACTORIAL ANALYSIS

Factors are mathematical expressions. Some consider that they are no more than this and that factorial analysis is 'a branch of statistical theory whose object is to resolve a series of descriptive variables to a small number of categories or factors...; the main aim... is economy in description'. (Burt cited by Holzinger and Hartman, 1941.) The majority of social psychologists and sociologists who use factorial analysis would not agree with this: they seek a reality behind the mathematical factors which express it. It is very difficult to find out how far they do express reality so the scope of factorial analysis is limited.

1. *General limits of factorial analysis.* Factorial analysis measures accurately the saturation of each element by a certain mathematical factor. But giving a concrete element equivalent status to this mathematical concept is a hazardous business. The precision of factor analysis must be seen only as a symbolic and synthetic expression of reality. If one considers the factors as 'hypothetical causal influences, underlying and determining the relations observed

between a series of variables' (Eysenck's definition), the precision disappears; for making a mathematical factor equivalent to an 'hypothetical causal influence' must remain a largely hypothetical operation.

The methods of finding this equivalence are numerous and they will not be dwelt on here. The most commonly used is the 'rotation' of factors. The tables of correlation used in factorial analyses can be represented by points localized in space in relation to systems of axes on which the co-ordinates of these points are measured. But there is more than one system: any system of perpendicular axes can be rotated around the base point to discover correspondences between the real variables and the mathematical factors.

It can never be certain that the correspondence is either real or accurate. Approximation which mathematical analysis attempts to eliminate, reappears at this stage. Eysenck has sought to define correspondence between mathematical factors and real variables by what he calls 'criterial' analysis based on 'the maximum agreement between the final factorial structure with a criterion chosen according to a certain theory'. This presupposed 'reference groups which to a certain extent incarnate the theory in question'. Normal and neurotic groups serve to control groups for a hypothetical factor in neuroses; groups of communists, socialists and conservatives serve as control groups for a presumed factor in conservatism, etc. But the identification of factors remains hypothetical.

2. *Factorial analysis in political science.* The limits of factorial analysis seem narrower in political science. For more than thirty years numerous factorial analyses have been conducted in the field of social psychology; a solid basis for the identification of factors has thus been provided. On the factor g, for example, the works published would fill a library. There is no agreement yet but the available material for reaching agreement is vast.

In political science the number of factorial analyses is very small. Political attitudes are more compartmentalized and analyses are valid only for a particular country and a particular time, whilst the human personality has a certain identity of structure and the results of analyses in social psychology can be more easily generalized. The identification of factors in politics is more difficult and hazardous: the analysis of the political preferences of Frenchmen made by Duncan Macrae, for example, has provoked much criticism.

Factorial analysis has, however, already obtained important results in political science mainly due to the work of the British psychologist Eysenck. He has demonstrated two 'dimensions' of political behaviour; the radical/conservative and the tough/tender. The two do not coincide: there are tough conservatives and tough radicals and there are tender conservatives and tender radicals. Fascism is a tough conservatism and communism is a tough radicalism; the classical Right is a tender conservatism and socialism is a tender radicalism. This conception can be criticized in detail but it seems to explain some phenomena.

C. Operational research

Operational research was invented during the Second World War for the study of strategic decisions. It has been developed since for the analysis of commercial and industrial problems, economic planning, financial policy, etc.

(a) NOTION OF OPERATIONAL RESEARCH

Operational research is the 'science of decisions' in complex human organizations where very many diverse elements have to be taken into account.

1. *The object.* Every decision implies a choice: the object of operational research is to define the exact limits of this choice and the exact consequences of possible choices. It does not substitute a mechanical decision for a voluntary decision, but gives information on which a voluntary decision can be based.

The idea of a science of decision originated in the revival of mathematical games theory in the works of Emile Borel (1921) and Johan von Neumann (1927). The publication of the fundamental work of von Neumann and Morgenstern in 1944 aroused great scientific interest in this field. Strategic models giving probabilities of certain results following certain decisions can be based on games theory. In operational research a great number of variables are introduced into the models.

In operational research it is necessary, firstly, that the objectives are clearly defined (the consequences of the decision can be evaluated in terms of these objectives); secondly, that the various eventualities can be clearly expressed and probabilities of realization can be determined. This presents various problems of evaluation which do not, however, differ from the general problems of evaluating social and human phenomena.

2. *The context: complex organizations.* There is an obvious difference of scale between an artisan's workshop and a modern factory. Ford cannot take decisions in the same way as the village wheelwright: the

latter can easily assess the situation in an empirical and intuitive manner and make a choice on this basis; the former cannot. This is also true of political decisions: in the Greek polis the government could take decisions by analogous methods to the village wheelwright; governments of modern states cannot.

The idea and also the method of operational research originates in the problems of scale. Instead of isolating and analysing each element separately and then reconstituting the whole, operational research considers all the relevant factors at the same time. The problem is not sub-divided as in the cartesian method: it is treated as a whole and approached from as many different angles as possible. A variety of specialists (mathematicians, physicists, social psychologists, sociologists, political scientists, etc.) usually collaborate in operational research. 'Models' of reality, integrating as many variables as possible, are used as the basis of the research.

(b) OPERATIONAL RESEARCH AND THE SOCIAL SCIENCES

Operational research is carried on in the commercial, industrial, technical, economic, financial and military fields. It is directly related to the object of political science.

1. *Practical applications.* These are very important in two fields: the military and the financial and economic policy fields.

It was first developed during the Second World War to solve problems of military strategy and tactics. In Britain and the United States it was mainly used for naval and air problems: the problems presented by aerial location and attacking of enemy submarines, by methods of bombing, by the laying of mines, etc., were submitted to operational research. Precise measurements of the efficacy of the research were possible: the proportion of ships hit by bombs in convoys which followed the advice of the Operational Research Group was 29 per cent, whilst in others it was 47 per cent. Research of this kind has widened its scope since the end of the war.

Operational research in financial and economic policy is backward in America because of the liberal economic system. It has been more widely used in Britain during and after the war. At the moment work in this field is probably most advanced in France: the statistical and financial study service of the ministry of Finance under the direction of MM. Gruson and Nora is a notable example of operational research.

2. *Science of decision and science of power.* In the field of political decisions operational research is little developed: in the United States, however, some political problems have been analysed by

operational research methods to provide information about decisions The difficulty of evaluating the variables constitutes the main obstacle. But the aim of operational research is very close to that of the science of power—political science. The exercise of power consists of taking decisions: all decisions are manifestations of power and authority. Operational research is a comparative method of studying the various manifestations of power: it applies the same techniques to different categories of decisions (military, industrial, commercial, financial, etc.).

On the general problems of applying mathematical methods in the social sciences: special number edited by C. LÉVI-STRAUSS of the *International Bulletin of the Social Sciences*, 1954, No. 4; J. C. KEMENY, J. L. SNELL, G. L. THOMSON, *Finite Mathematical Structures*, New York, 1959; P. F. LAZARSFELD (*et al.*), *Mathematical Thinking in the Social Sciences*, Glencoe, 1954; M. J. MORGENTHAU, 'Reflections on the State of Political Science', *Review of Politics*, October, 1955; M. ZELDITCH, *A Basic Course in Sociological Statistics*, New York, 1959; D. HUFF, *How to lie with Statistics*, 1954; K. J. ARROW, S. KARLIN, P. SUPPES, *Mathematical Methods in the Social Sciences*, Stanford, 1960; L. COHEN, *Statistical Methods for Social Scientists*, New York, 1954; R. A. FISHER, *Statistical Methods for Research Workers*, 2nd ed., Edinburgh, 1954; R. G. D. ALLEN, *Statistics for Economics*, 1954; W. Z. HIRSCH, *Introduction to Modern Statistics with Applications to Business and Economics*, New York, 1957.

On factorial analysis: P. E. VERNON, *Personality Tests and Assessments*, 1957; D. MACRAE, *Dimensions of Congressional Voting*, California, 1958; W. F. OGBURN and N. S. TALBOT, 'A Measurement of the factors in the Presidential Elections of 1928', *Social Forces*, December, 1929; M. F. GOSNEL, *Machine Politics: Chicago Model*, Chicago, 1937; N. N. CAGE and B. SHIMBERG, 'Measuring Senatorial Progressivism'. *Journal of Abnormal and Social Psychology*, 1949, pp. 112-17; M. J. EYSENCK, *The Psychology of Politics*, 2nd ed., 1957.

On operational research: J. F. MCCLOSKEY and F. N. TREFETHEN, *Introduction to Operational Research*, New York, 1956; C. W. CHURCHMAN, R. L. ACKROFF, E. L. ARNOFF, *Introduction to Operations Research*, New York, 1957.

On the mathematical analysis of elections: D. BLACK, *The Theory of Committees and Elections*, Cambridge, 1958.

Section II. Graphs

Graphs represent phenomena in diagrammatic form and are easily compared with one another by juxtaposition or superimposition. Comparison of the various methods of graphs is the only way of assessing the qualities and limitations of each and the potentialities of all of them taken together.

Graphs should have two main qualities: simplicity and accuracy. If a diagram is complex and difficult to read, comparison between several diagrams becomes difficult: the current tendency to make diagrams more complicated should be avoided. The impression of complexity, however, often comes from ignorance: training is necessary to construct and interpret some graphs. Two broad categories of graphs can be distinguished: mathematical graphs which are based entirely on numerical data, and non-mathematical graphs in which numerical data is partly or not at all involved. The second category is obviously much more suspect than the first.

1. MATHEMATICAL GRAPHS

In these all elements used are mathematical: all can be measured. This type of graph should not be confused with curves representing mathematical functions. The latter are a method of representing functions whereas graphs represent visually a group of measurements without there necessarily being an established mathematical relation between them.

The graphs also should not be confused with tables based on squared paper, giving a visual representation of a series of figures without really translating them into diagrammatic form. The uses of tables in the analysis of associations have been given (p. 288). They can be regarded as a stage on the way towards graphs.

A. Various types of graphs

Graph methods vary greatly and it is difficult to classify them in a logical manner. A few of the main types will be described here.

(*a*) DIAGRAMS BASED ON A SYSTEM OF CO-ORDINATES

Most are based on cartesian co-ordinates, i.e. on a system of axes (usually set at right angles) against which measurements are made. Cartesian co-ordinates can be either arithmetical or logarithmic. Polar co-ordinates are another possible system.

1. *Arithmetical co-ordinates.* The two axes of the graph are divided into equal gradations. Squared paper is generally used for this kind of graph. Some are made on paper with very thin lines which do not show on a photograph so that the final printed reproduction appears on plain paper.

If there are no negative measurements the axes start in the bottom left hand corner of the diagram (fig. 14); if there are two series of negative measurements, the point of origin is the middle of the diagram (fig. 15); if there is only one series of negative measurements, the point of origin is either in the middle of the left hand side, or the middle of the lower side of the diagram (fig. 16).

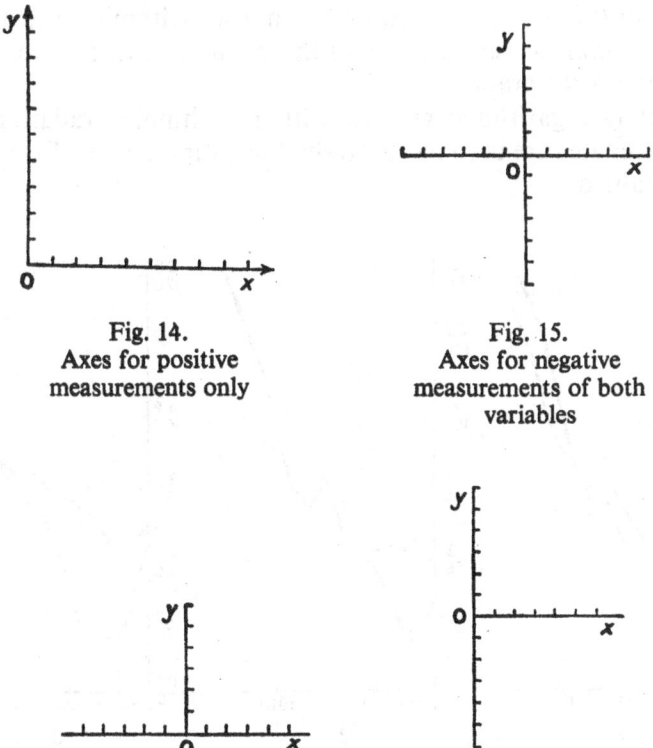

Fig. 14.
Axes for positive measurements only

Fig. 15.
Axes for negative measurements of both variables

Fig. 16.—Axes for negative measurements of one of the variables

The main problem of these graphs is to choose appropriate units of measurement for each axis. The general rule is that the relation between the two scales must show all variations considered significant. It should be remembered that there is a very different slope according to the choice of scale, as illustrated in figure 17.

2. *Logarithmic co-ordinates.* In arithmetic graphs the gradations on both co-ordinates are equidistant. In logarithmic graphs the scales are graduated in logarithms—the lengths measured are proportionate to the logarithms of the observations.

In practice semi-logarithmic graphs are usually used; only the vertical is graduated in logarithms. Paper can be obtained to make graphs of this kind. This procedure has two advantages over arithmetical representation. The logarithmic scale enlarges the small values and diminishes the large ones so that the latter can be contained in the graph without sacrificing the former. The logarithmic scale represents rates of variation and shows the relative value of the observed variations and not their absolute value. Secondly, the logarithm of 0 is $-\infty$, the zero point on a logarithmic vertical; the curve can commence anywhere and the whole of the available area can be used for the graph.

Completely logarithmic graphs, with logarithmic gradations on both co-ordinates are used more rarely, but graph paper of this kind can be obtained.

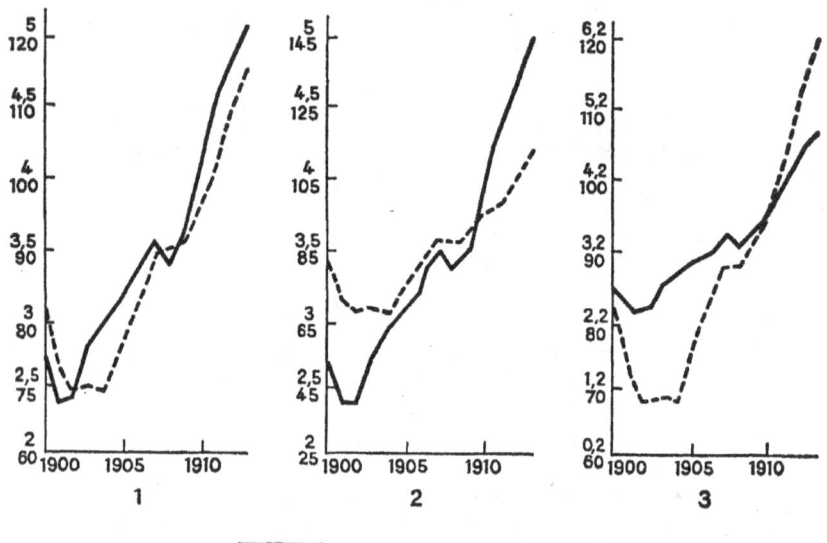

Fig. 17.—Changes of scale on the co-ordinates

——— Production of cast-iron in millions of tons
(the first figure of each gradation).

- - - - - Numbers of foundry workers in thousands
(the second figure of each gradation).

3. *Polar co-ordinates.* A single point P can be related on a graph to a single axis *ox* through the angle between the point and the origin of the axis.

It is sufficient to know the angle θ (or the polar angle) and the length of the vector OP to establish the position of point P. This procedure is very useful for representing chronological series by making successive equal periods correspond to successive equal angles: for example, by dividing a circle into twelve equal sectors

MATHEMATICAL AND GRAPH TECHNIQUES

each representing a month. The size of the phenomenon is represented by the length of the corresponding radius (fig. 18).

Representing several successive years on the same graph is difficult because this would result in a tangle unless the phenomena showing a steady increasing or diminishing tendency over the period

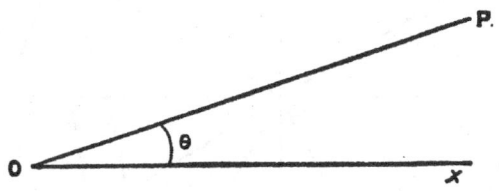

Fig. 18.—Polar co-ordinates

considered, in which case the method would give a very clear picture of the trend (fig. 19).

(*b*) GRAPHS USING BARS, AREAS, SECTIONS, AND BANDS

There is a great variety of diagrams of this kind and only a few

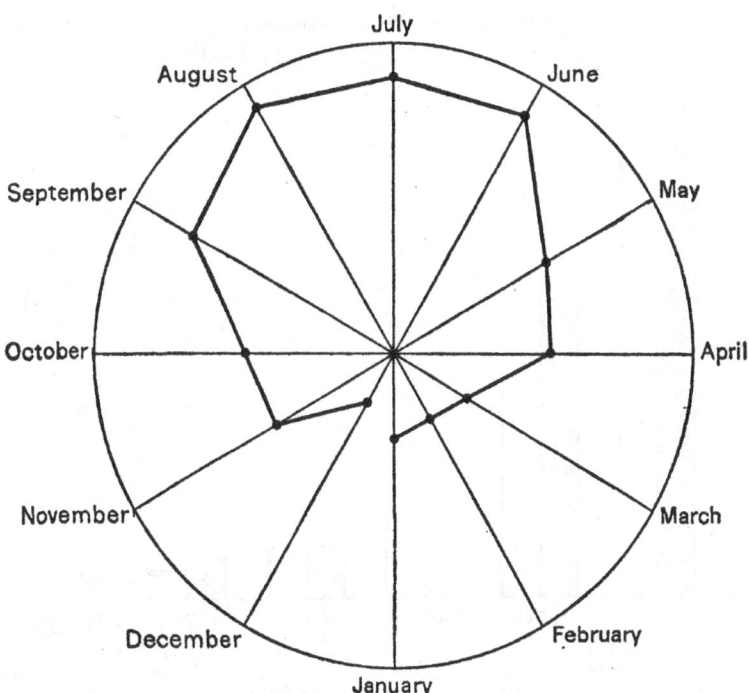

Fig. 19.—Graph with polar co-ordinates
(Mean monthly temperatures in Paris, 1939.)

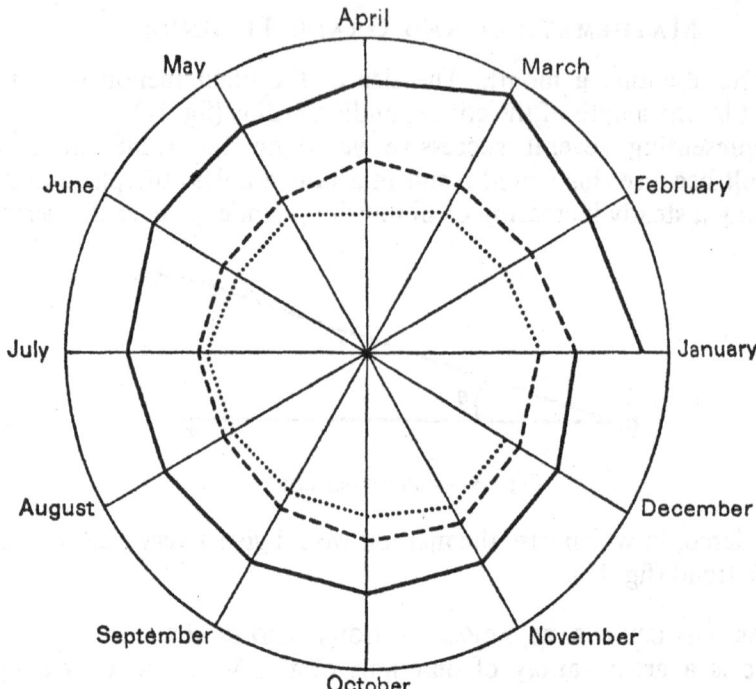

Fig. 20.—Polar co-ordinates
(Contraction of world trade, 1931–33.)

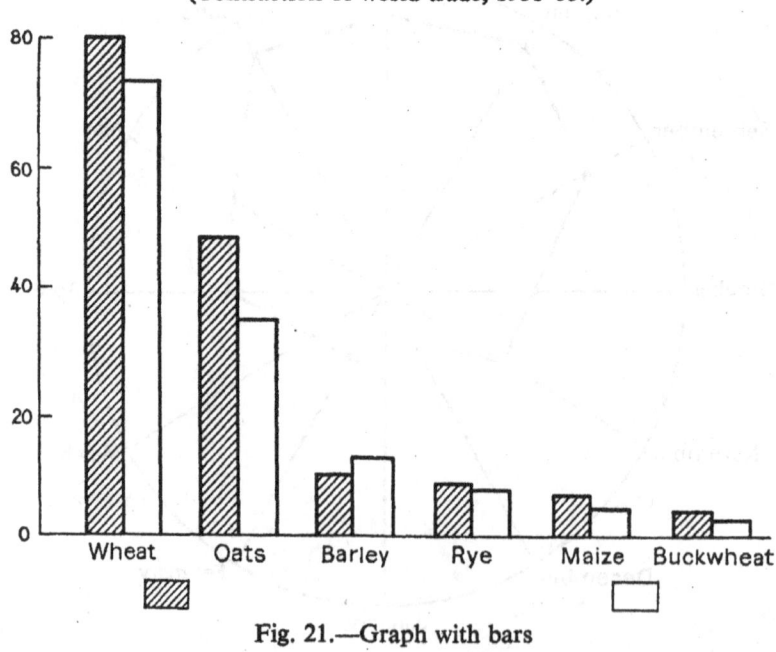

Fig. 21.—Graph with bars
(Grain production in 1948.)

Average 1930–39   1948 Production
(In millions of quintals)

Mathematical and Graph Techniques

general indications will be given. With a little imagination new ones can be invented.

1. *Graphs using bars.* Numerical size is represented by a long rectangle. Several rectangles of different colours or shadings can be juxtaposed (fig. 21). The same rectangle can be divided into sections

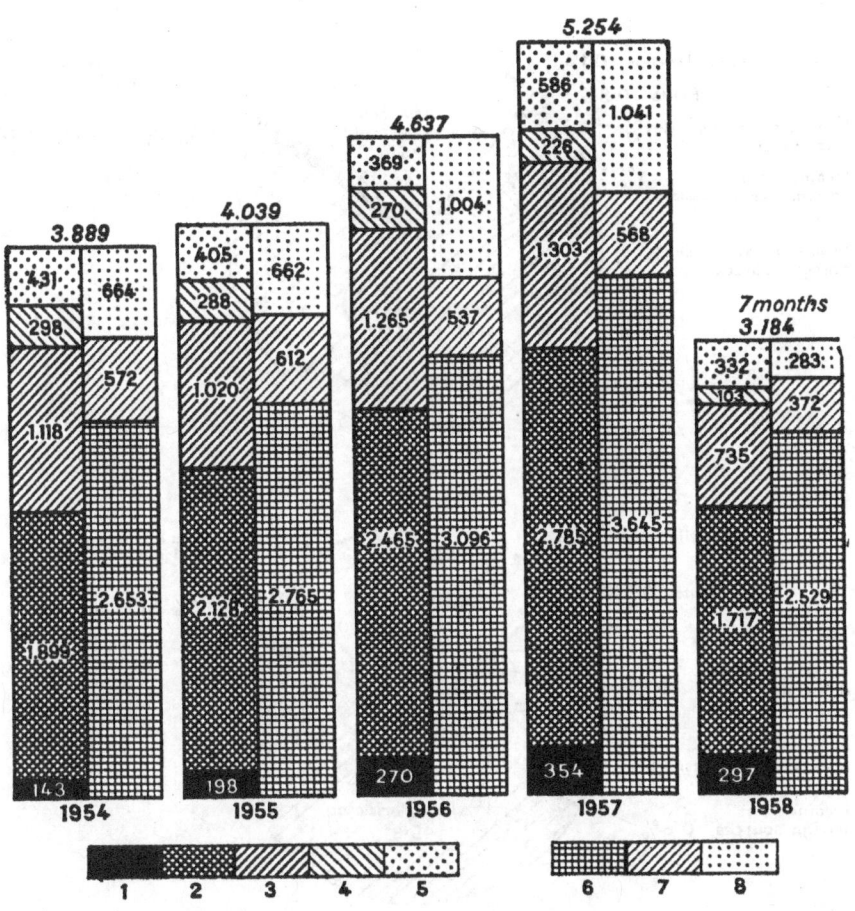

Fig. 22.—Diagram using bars with sub-divisions
(Treasury transactions in milliards of francs)

Payments
1. Preceding and following financial periods; 2. Civil budget; 3. Defence; 4. War damage; 5. Treasury charges.

Receipts
6. Taxes; 7. Other receipts (including American aid); 8. Loans.

INTRODUCTION TO THE SOCIAL SCIENCES

of different colours or shadings to represent different elements within the same total and this technique can be combined with the preceding one (fig. 22). As a general rule the bars are vertical except in age pyramids, but there is no hard and fast rule.

2. *Graphs using areas.* In the previous technique only the length of the rectangles is taken into account. The width and area are not

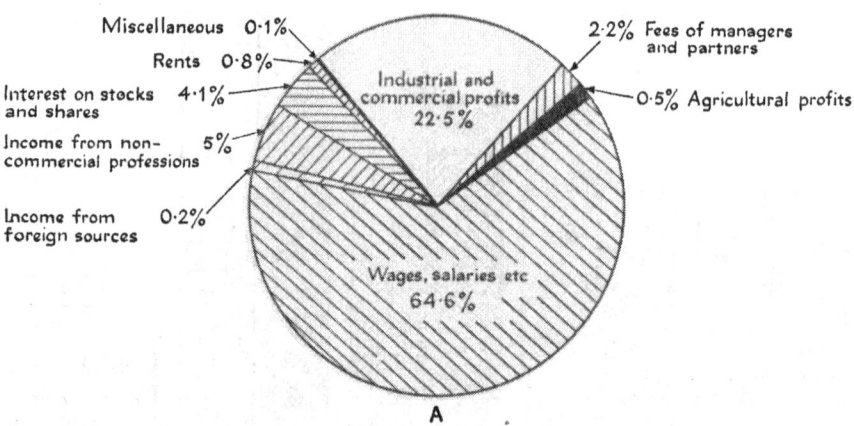

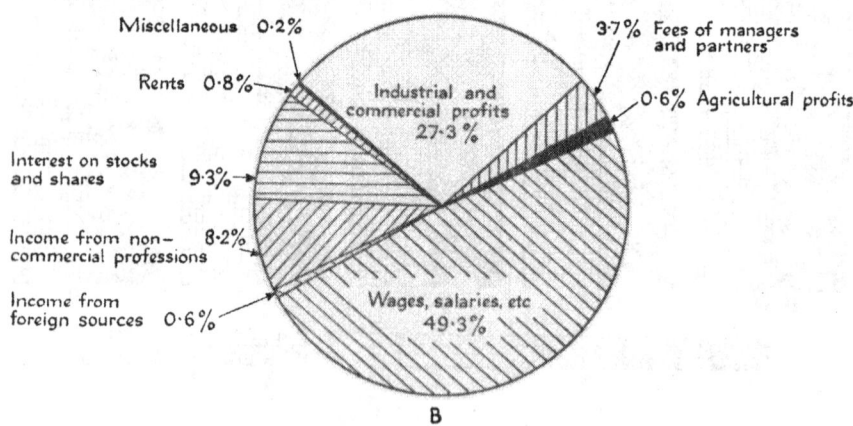

Fig. 23.—Diagram using a circle
(*Distribution of progressive surtax in 1956*)

(a) Incomes in each category as a percentage of all incomes declared or assessed for progressive surtax.
(b) Percentage of the progressive surtax from each category of incomes (approximate).

Source: *Statistiques et études financières*, No. 106, October 1957.

considered. Areas are used in 'histograms' to represent frequency series (see p. 314). They are used in the examples given in this section as illustrations rather than as accurate representations of statistics. Sector diagrams are a common form of area diagrams;

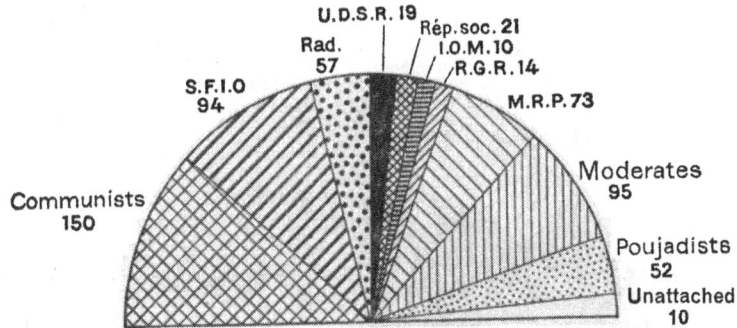

Fig. 24.—Semicircle diagram
The National Assembly elected on January 2, 1956
(Metropolitan seats)

different elements of a total are represented by proportionate sections (fig. 23). In some cases a semicircle is used (one of its current uses is to illustrate electoral results because of its similarity to the *hémicycle* of the Assembly—see fig. 24). Two juxtaposed semicircles with slightly different diameters can be used for comparisons (fig. 25).

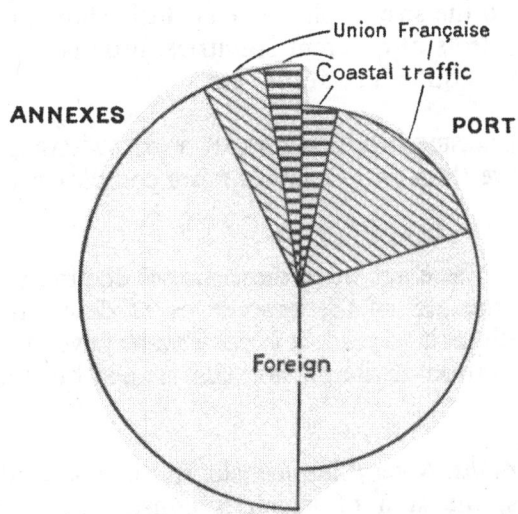

Fig. 25.—Diagram with two semicircles
(Activity of the port of Marseilles and associated wharves (dockings))

The sections can be divided into concentric bands. The preceding example of the semicircle representing the National Assembly can be used for analyses of divisions: the proportion of 'ayes', 'nays', abstentions and absences in each party can be shown by concentric bands (fig. 26).

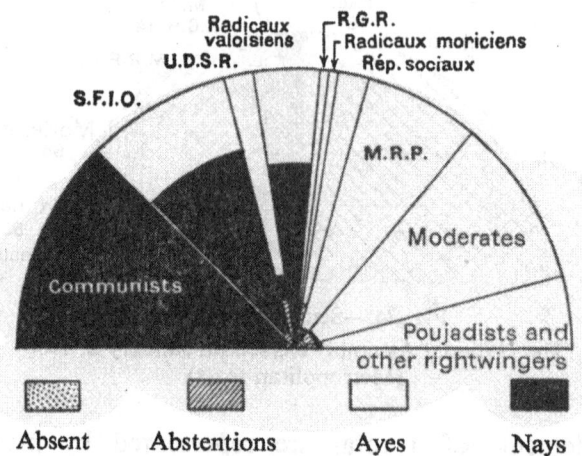

Fig. 26.—Semicircle with bands
(Investiture of General de Gaulle, June 1, 1958.)

There is a variety of other kinds of diagrams in which area is proportionate to the size of phenomena: little ships to represent the tonnage of the fleets of different countries, little people to represent the populations of different nations, etc.

(c) FIGURES REPRESENTING MORE THAN TWO VARIABLES
If there are more than two variables more complex procedures have to be used.

1. *Stereograms.* These are three dimensional diagrams. They can be designed with the aid of the procedures of descriptive geometry. They are very difficult to read. It is possible to have mock ups giving spatial representation of the phenomena studied but this is not very convenient.

2. *Triangular graphs.* A very simple technique can be used to represent three variables, the sum of which is constant: for example, the division of a percentage into three parts. One of the properties of an equilateral triangle is that the sum of the distances to the three sides

Mathematical and Graph Techniques

from a point inside the triangle is constant and equal to the height of the triangle. The intersection of the three variables is represented by such a point (fig. 27).

3. *Squared graphs.* In these there can be a simultaneous representation of an aggregate divided into two parts, the totals of which are identical:

$$a_1 + b_1 = a_2 + b_2 = K$$

The system is used in the presentation of balance sheets (fig. 28) in which the following divisions can, for example, be used:

Liabilities { Capital expenditure
Operating costs

Assets { Capital
Third party liabilities

The point of intersection represents the structure of the balance sheet. This point can be compared with others over a number of years.

B. Representation of Frequency Series

Series (whether chronological or classes of phenomena) can be represented by one or another of the procedures just described. However, there are some special rules to ensure rigorous comparison between several series or between terms of the same series.

(*a*) CHRONOLOGICAL SERIES

The rules of representation and comparisons are simple: The

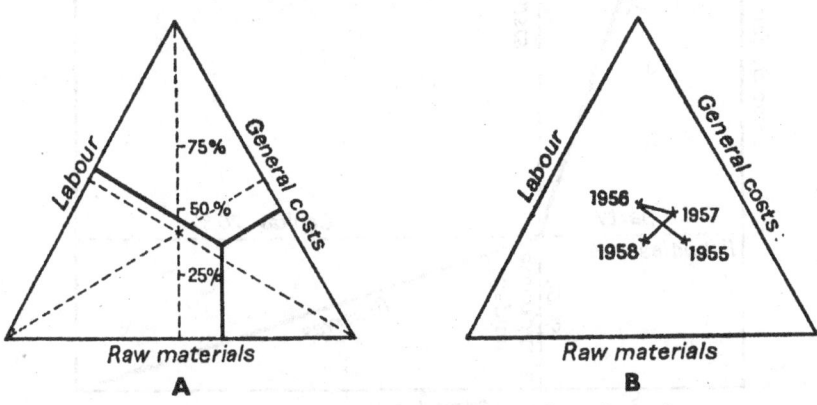

Fig. 27.—Triangular graphs (Distribution of costs)
(*a*) 1955   (*b*) Over several years

interpretation of variations can be assisted by distinguishing several types of arrangement.

1. *Rules of representation and comparison.* Elementary principles to avoid confusion are often neglected. The first amongst them is that there should be a discontinuity in the graph every time the rhythm of representation changes: if, for example, there is a change from an annual to a monthly series (fig. 29). The same rule applies if there is an interruption in the chronological series (due to absence of information, perhaps as a result of war).

In comparing chronological graphs the cautions about scales should be remembered (p. 303); when the dimensions to be compared are of different kinds there is no 'correct' relation between the units chosen. The choice of units is necessarily arbitrary; but it greatly influences the appearance of the diagram and the appearance of the relations within it.

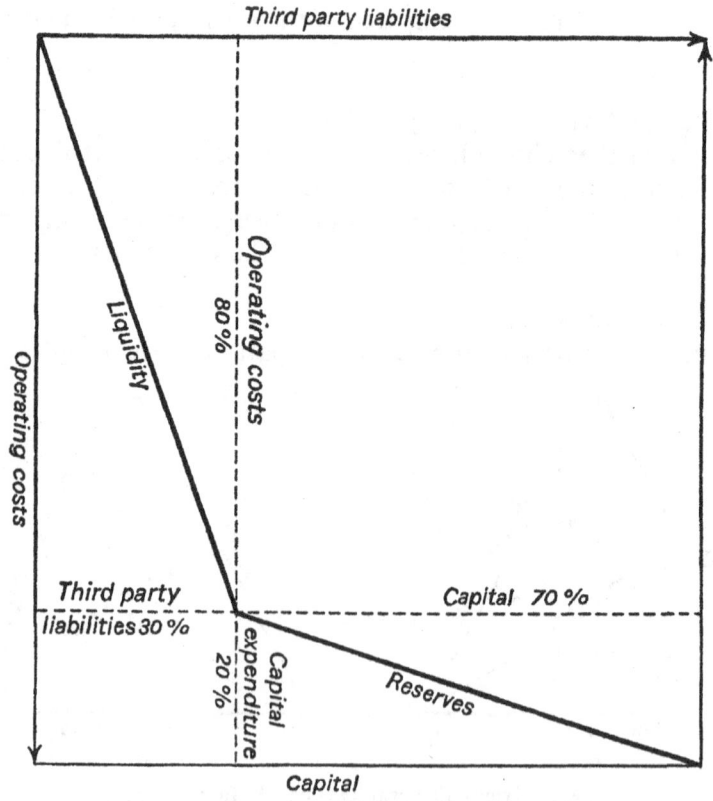

Fig. 28.—Squared graph

Mathematical and Graph Techniques

In examining variations of several phenomena it is preferable to trace the graphs on tracing paper and superimpose them according to need, rather than trace several curves on the same paper which

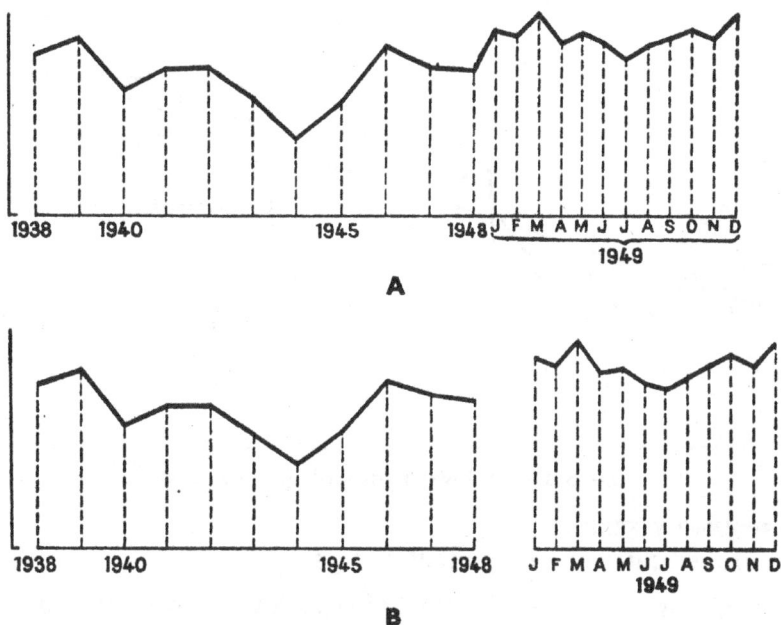

Fig. 29.—Chronological series: discontinuity when the units change
(a) Incorrect; (b) Correct.

can cause confusion. The axis y of semi-logarithmic graphs can be compared at any point but to compare arithmetical graphs the origin of the co-ordinates must coincide unless one simply wants to compare the direction of the variations.

2. *Components of chronological series*. In economics four basic temporal categories are generally distinguished: 1. A general tendency (or trend), in other words, variations over a long period of time; 2. A cyclical movement—the successive periods of prosperity and depression of economic cycles; 3. A seasonal movement, fluctuations caused by seasonal influences; 4. 'Residual' variations due to more or less accidental events (war, strikes, change of institutions, etc.).

It is interesting to transfer this schema (remembering that it is not rigid) into other social sciences. The existence of economic cycles has been called into question in the last few years. But it remains essential to distinguish between long, medium and short term movements (fig. 30).

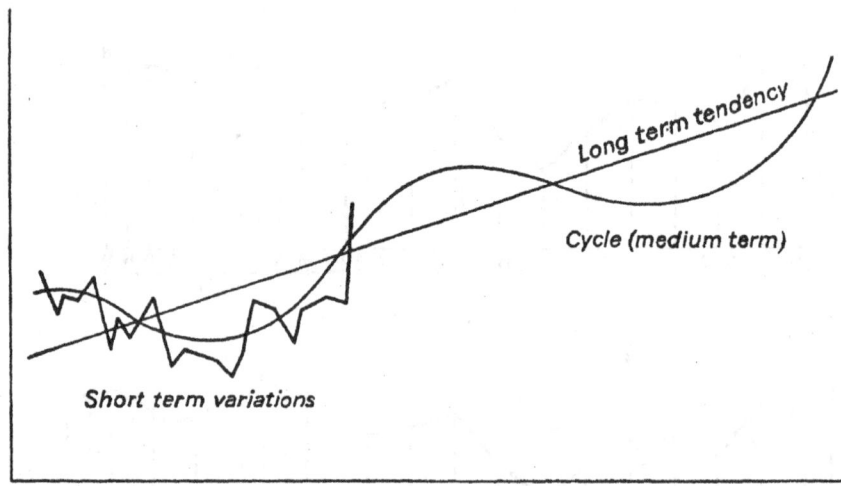

Fig. 30.—Breaking down a chronological evolution

(*b*) FREQUENCY SERIES

There are several ways of representing these.

1. *Histograms.* Each classification of a series is represented by a rectangle, the base showing the size and the height the frequency of the class. The classes must be of equal sizes to avoid producing a distorting effect (fig. 31).

2. *Frequency polygons and curves.* A frequency polygon is made by joining the centres of each classification in a histogram (fig. 32).

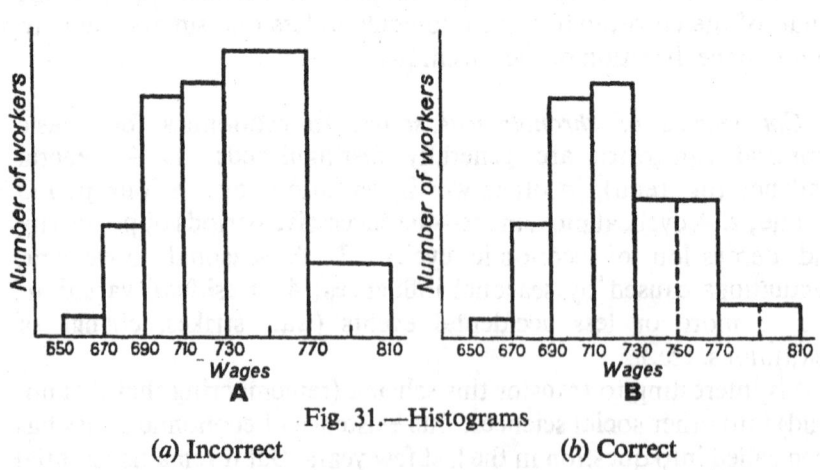

Fig. 31.—Histograms

(*a*) Incorrect   (*b*) Correct

Mathematical and Graph Techniques

If instead of joining the points (which are the middle of the histogram classifications) one draws a perpendicular line from each of them to the axis x a stick graph is produced (fig. 33). The polygon of frequency tends to become a curve as the interval between classifications becomes smaller. The curve can be traced by visual adjustment on the graph (fig. 34) or calculated on the basis of an appropriate mathematical curve.

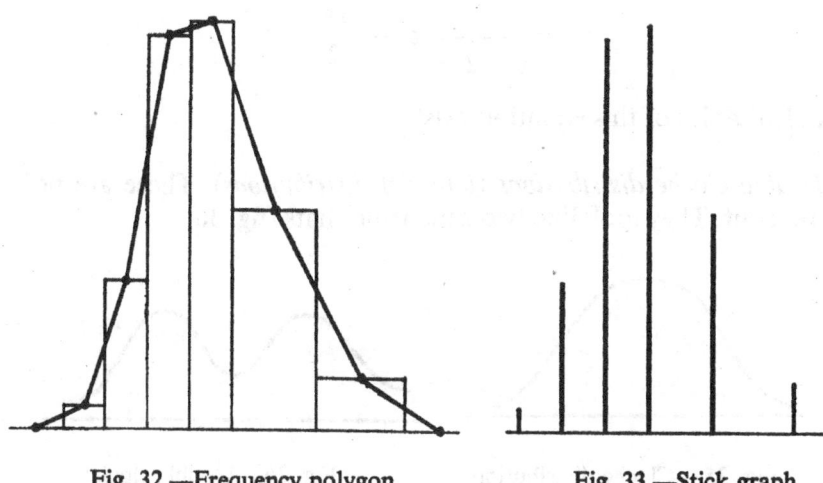

Fig. 32.—Frequency polygon   Fig. 33.—Stick graph

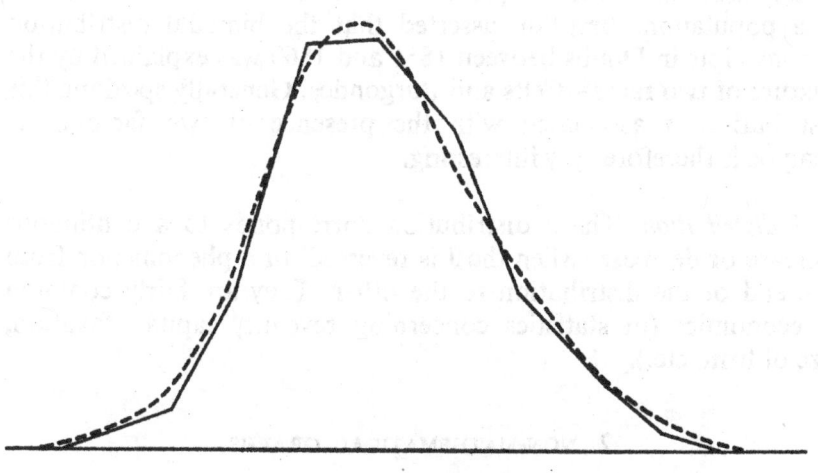

Fig. 34.—Frequency polygon and curve
- - - - - - - - Curve   ————— Polygon

(c) VARIOUS FORMS OF FREQUENCY GRAPH

It is interesting to note the similarities between these and geometric curves.

1. *Cloche distributions.* These symmetrically decreasing frequencies towards zero from a central maximum (fig. 35) are very common. They are the same as the Laplace-Gauss curve expressing random distribution, the equation of which is:

$$y = \frac{1}{\sqrt{2\pi}} e - \frac{x^2}{2}$$

Detailed tables of this equation exist.

2. *Double cloche distributions (bimodal distributions).* These are not so frequent. They look like two gendarmes hats (fig. 36).

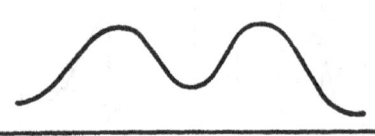

Fig. 35.—Cloche distribution (Laplace-Gauss curve)

Fig. 36.—Double cloche distribution

This is a common distribution of frequencies in biology: it is usually associated with the presence of two races or two generations in a population. Bertillon asserted that the bimodal distribution of conscripts in Doubs between 1851 and 1860 was explained by the mixture of two races—Celts and Burgondes. Generally speaking this distribution is associated with the presence of two factors. Its analysis is therefore very interesting.

3. *J distribution.* The J distribution corresponds to a continuous increase or decrease (when the J is reversed) of a phenomenon from one end of the distribution to the other. They are fairly common in economics (in statistics concerning revenue, capital, taxation, size of firm, etc.).

2. NON-MATHEMATICAL GRAPHS

Some of the elements used in non-mathematical graphs are not mathematical and are not based on measurements. They are conse-

Mathematical and Graph Techniques

quently less exact and more subjective. Some of the elements can be mathematical and the degree of vagueness, therefore, varies. From the point of view of precision two large categories of non-mathematical graphs can be distinguished: geographical diagrams and charts.

A. Geographical diagrams

These are, in principle, the most accurate of the non-mathematical graphs. Usually only their basis—one could say the system of co-ordinates—is not mathematical: it is an accurately constructed representation not of abstract space but of the real world.

One should, however, retain a healthy distrust of cartography. It often camouflages serious distortions: maps are the source of delusions. The sociologist must handle them with caution. The distortions which can result from the system of representation are well enough known, but those arising from the basic nature of the map, although equally important, are less well known.

(a) PROBLEMS OF REPRESENTATION

Several procedures are used to represent on the map the phenomena to be analysed and compared. These can be divided into two categories—continuous and discontinuous representation.

1. *Discontinuous representation* is the best known in the social sciences: every one has seen electoral maps with the percentages of votes obtained by each party in each département. Discontinuous representation utilizes either shading or colours. Shading is more common because it is cheaper (the printing can be done in a single colour). A range of shadings in the form of dots or parallel lines varying in intensity from white to black is established. The area of each section of the map is covered with the shade corresponding to the value of the phenomena studied. If colours are used cartographers have found that it is less effective to follow the order of the spectrum than to commence with the brightest (yellow) and take the next colour from one of the extremes and so on. The most frequently used combinations are: white, yellow, orange, red, violet, black; yellow, green, blue, violet, black.

These techniques produce very legible and memorable charts. But they distort the phenomena studied which have to be divided into a number of sections corresponding to the number of shades. Within each section the value of the phenomenon might vary but the representation of it is the same: if one section, in a single colour represents 15 per cent to 25 per cent of the votes in a département, a

INTRODUCTION TO THE SOCIAL SCIENCES

party might get 16 per cent in one departement and 24 per cent in another but they would be shown in the same way. This method also creates artificial disparities between close phenomena: using the example just cited a département in which a party had 15 per cent of the poll would be shown differently to a département in which it had 16 per cent.

DISTRIBUTION OF POPULATION IN 1954

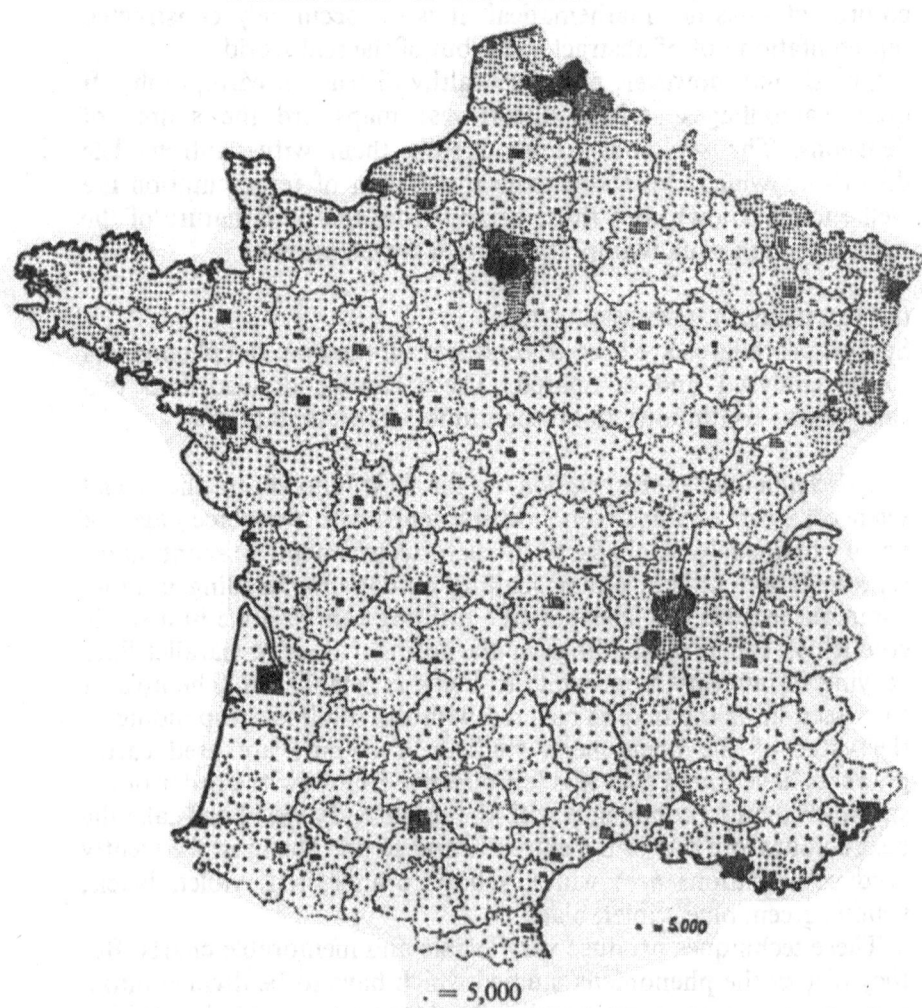

. = 5,000

Fig. 37.—Representation by dots
(Distribution of population in France in 1954, from J.-M. Jeanneney, *Forces et faiblesse de l'économie française*, A. Colin, 1956.)

Mathematical and Graph Techniques

It is difficult to avoid these disadvantages. The distortion which results from the sharp division between one level and the next cannot be eliminated but it is possible to select the least arbitrary divisions. The most reliable method of selection is by means of a frequency curve. The average value of the phenomenon is placed in the central shaded (or coloured) section and the remaining spaces are divided on both sides of it. Another method consists of inserting each value on the map in its correct location—starting from the largest each division is shaded and the successive geographical forms of the phenomenon are noted; dividing lines are drawn to illustrate characteristic forms. This is a more intuitive and dangerous method; there is a tendency to make the divisions conform to the patterns which the researcher desires. But the method can be useful for stimulating working hypotheses. It is possible by clever cartography which appears objective to falsify representation of a phenomenon: newspapers have done this in representing electoral results.

2. *Continuous representation* is more accurate but visually less striking.

Representation by dots consists of inscribing on the map one dot for each unit or multiple of a unit (for example, for every 5,000 voters). All the dots can be placed in their exact position inside each subdivision of the map either in a quincunx or an approximate geographical distribution. In the later case the system is close to that of the coloured or shaded areas but it is continuous and avoids the disadvantages of rigid categories. The great difficulty lies in deciding the value of each dot: black areas where the dots touch one another should be kept to a minimum.

Another method is using strokes corresponding in length to the number represented; the strokes always have an equal thickness (fig. 38). The stroke is usually vertical when it corresponds to a particular geographical location, horizontal when applying to a geographical area. Several strokes can be used at the same time (fig. 39). The procedure is rapid and simple but it is often difficult to read. Also, if the difference in the magnitudes to be represented is great it cannot be used.

Representation by areas avoids this last difficulty: on each section of the map, an area (square, circle) proportionate to the size represented, is drawn. A series of widely differing magnitudes can be represented when the radius of the circle or the side of the square are made proportionate to the square root of the actual numbers (fig. 40). As with strokes, the squares or circles are either centred on a parti-

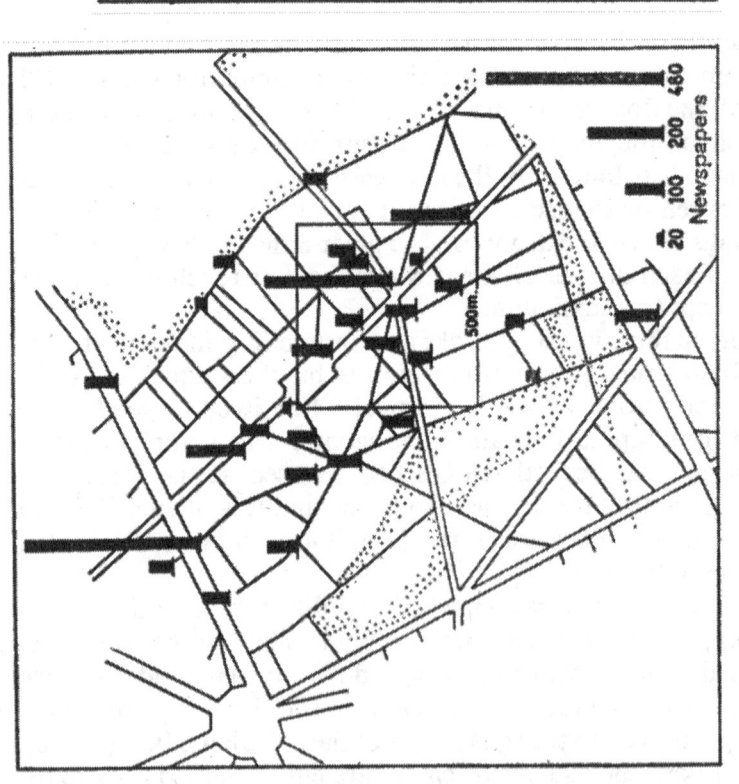
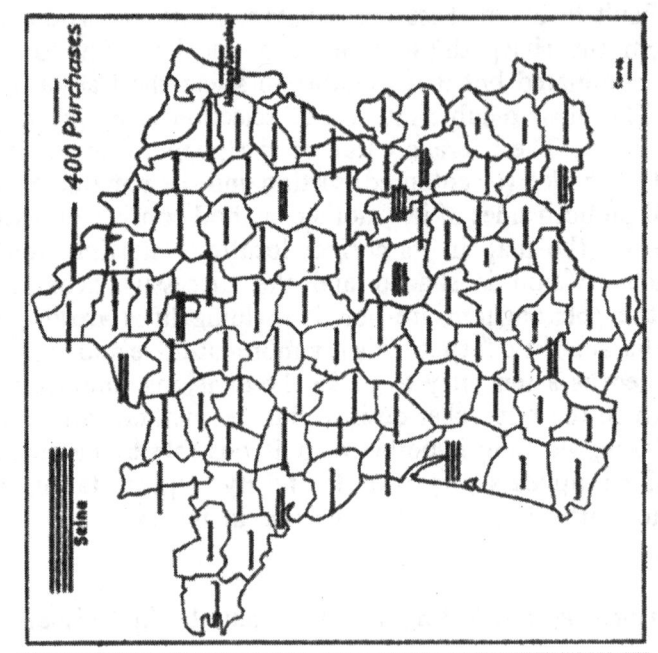

Fig. 38.—Representation by strokes

(a) *Vertical strokes*: Sale of evening papers in the district around the station, 13th arrondissement of Paris, October 1949.
(b) *Horizontal strokes*: Number of postal orders by département, December 31, 1919.

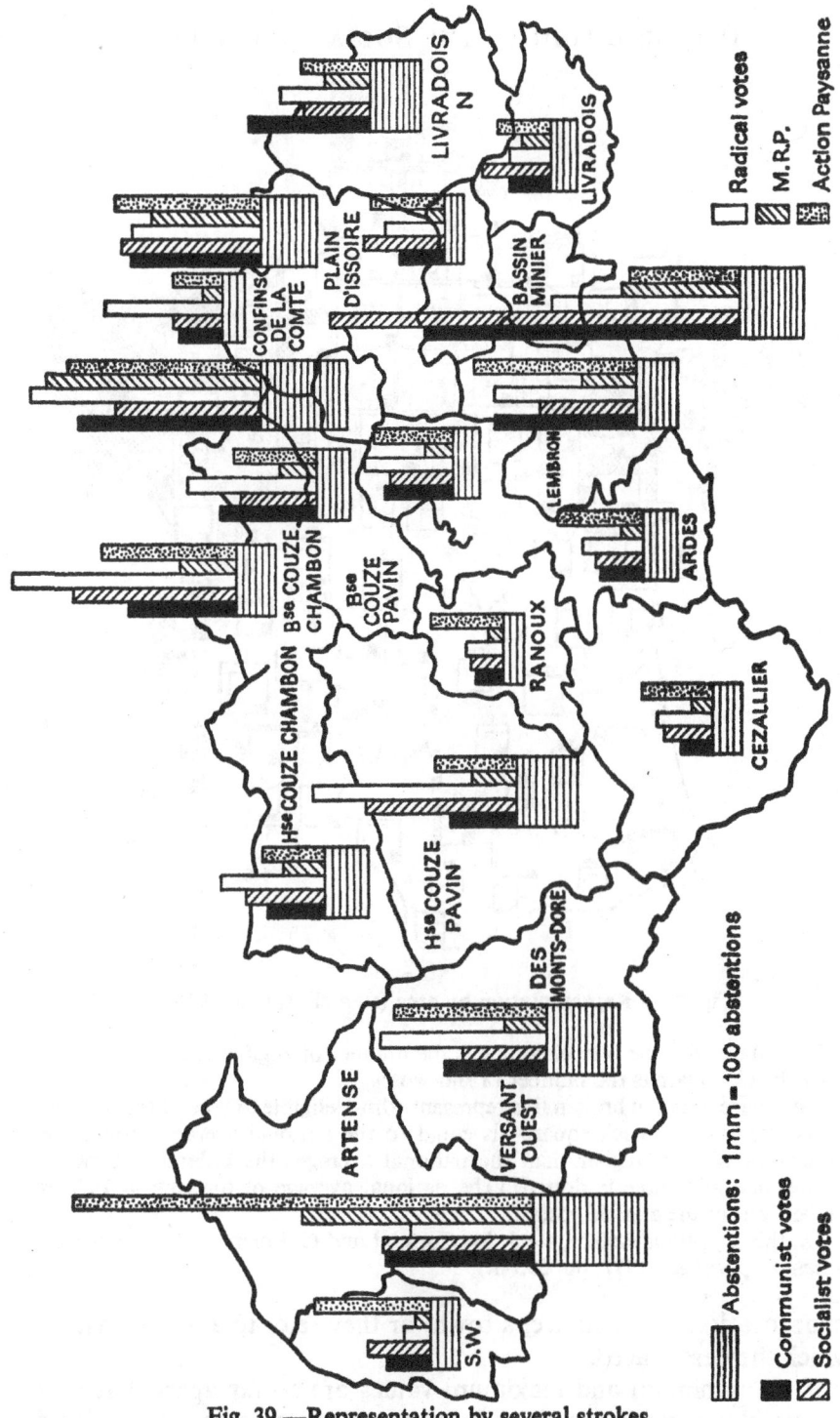

Fig. 39.—Representation by several strokes

(Legislative elections of November 1946 in the arrondissement of Issoire, from F. Goguel (*et al.*), *Nouvelles études de sociologie électorale*, 1954.)

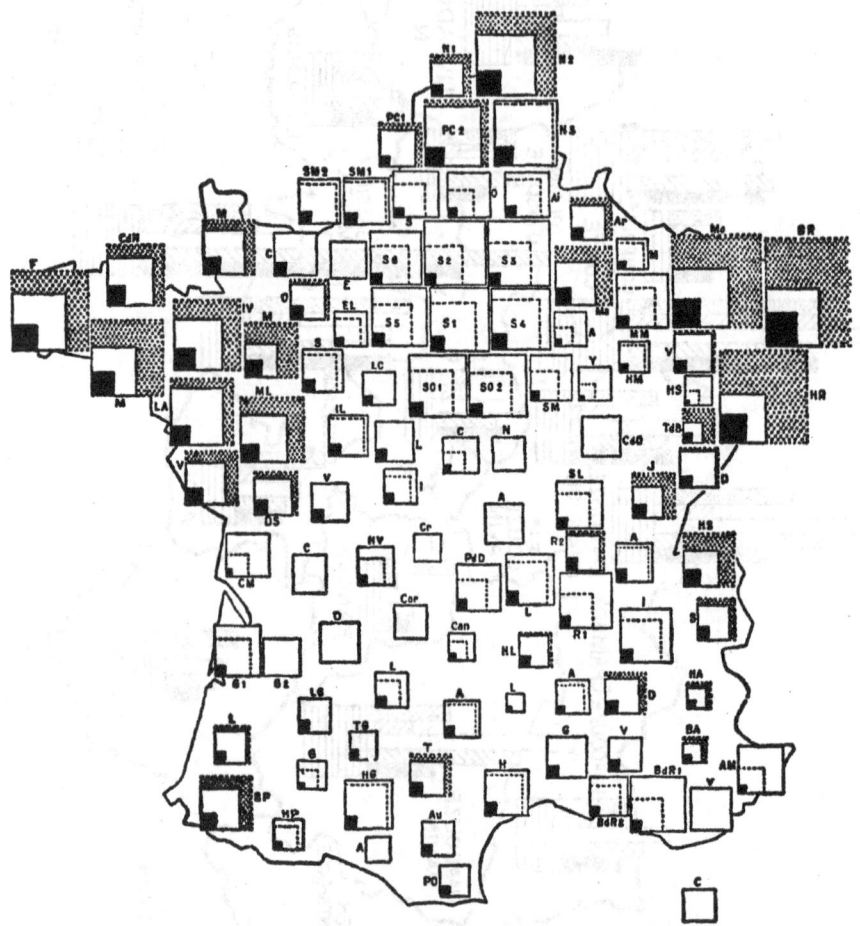

Fig. 40.—Representation by area (MRP electors in 1956)

The square with the unbroken line is the number of eligible voters.
The black square is the number of MRP votes.
The square with the broken line represents those eligible to vote, if the number of MRP votes—the black square—is equal to the national average. When the number of votes is higher than the national average, the difference between squares one and three is dotted. (The national average of the MRP in 1956 is 8.8 per cent of the eligible voters.)

(On this ingenious system, see J. M. Cotteret and C. Émeri in *Revue française de science politique*, 1957, pp. 595 ff.)

cular location (for instance, a town) or they refer to a wider area on which they are placed.

If the minimum and maximum values are so far apart that it is impossible to represent them by proportionate areas, drawings of cubes and spheres can be used to illustrate the proportions.

Mathematical and Graph Techniques

(b) PROBLEM OF THE BASIS OF THE MAP

The cartographic method consists of transcribing a political phenomenon on to a map. The use of a map introduces in principle an element of precision into the procedure. If the elements on which the map is based are accurately measured and transcribed, the map is as precise as a mathematical graph. But, in practice, cartographic methods encounter three difficulties which do not arise from the technique of representation but from the maps themselves.

1. *Distortion through the system of projection.* As the earth is spherical, representing an area on a flat surface is only possible through a distorting process called 'projection'. The choice of a system of projection is in appearance a pure convention but it has an influence on the image of reality which is derived from the map.

It would, for example, be interesting to study how the average European's image of the world diplomacy is influenced by maps centred on the equator which show Europe between the United States and the Soviet Union; these suggest that European neutralism is absurd and the Atlantic alliance, which brings together states facing one another across a large oceanic lake, is a natural growth. Polar projections, which are becoming common, stimulate quite another image: only the ice-cap separates the two great powers and Europe, in a semi-marginal position, can conceive conflicts between the USA and the USSR which do not concern her. 'Mercator, the auxiliary of NATO': what a marvellous propaganda theme! This is only intended as an example: there are, of course, a host of other phenomena not shown on maps which oppose these simplified views.

The polar projection is not more or less true than the Mercator projection. Both give equally valid images of reality. However, according to the period, the range of social data can lead to a certain projection being more valid than another. When the pole was an impenetrable barrier, the polar projection falsified reality. Since it has become very easy to cross, this representation corresponds more to reality. Public opinion has not yet become aware how easy it is to cross and in addition, the Atlantic is the focus of a more highly developed communication system than the pole: polar projections are therefore less 'true' in defining the relation between North America, Europe and the USSR than equator projections. But strategically they are becoming more true to the extent that classical methods of war decline in importance.

The distortion resulting from the system of projection is limited. It affects only large maps—in practice, only those used in the study of

INTRODUCTION TO THE SOCIAL SCIENCES

international relations. Its effects are greater on the public mind than on researchers who are aware of the conventional character of the projection. One should not, however, be too sanguine about this: some scholars are, without knowing it, influenced by the system of projection chosen. Many 'geopolitical' theories are based—consciously or unconsciously—on the various techniques of projection.

2. *Distortion through the geographical nature of maps.* Maps represent the areas of various divisions of a given territory. A distorting factor is introduced each time that a phenomena not dependent on the area of the soil is represented. Many social phenomena are in this category. In the electoral field, for example, a very great visual importance is

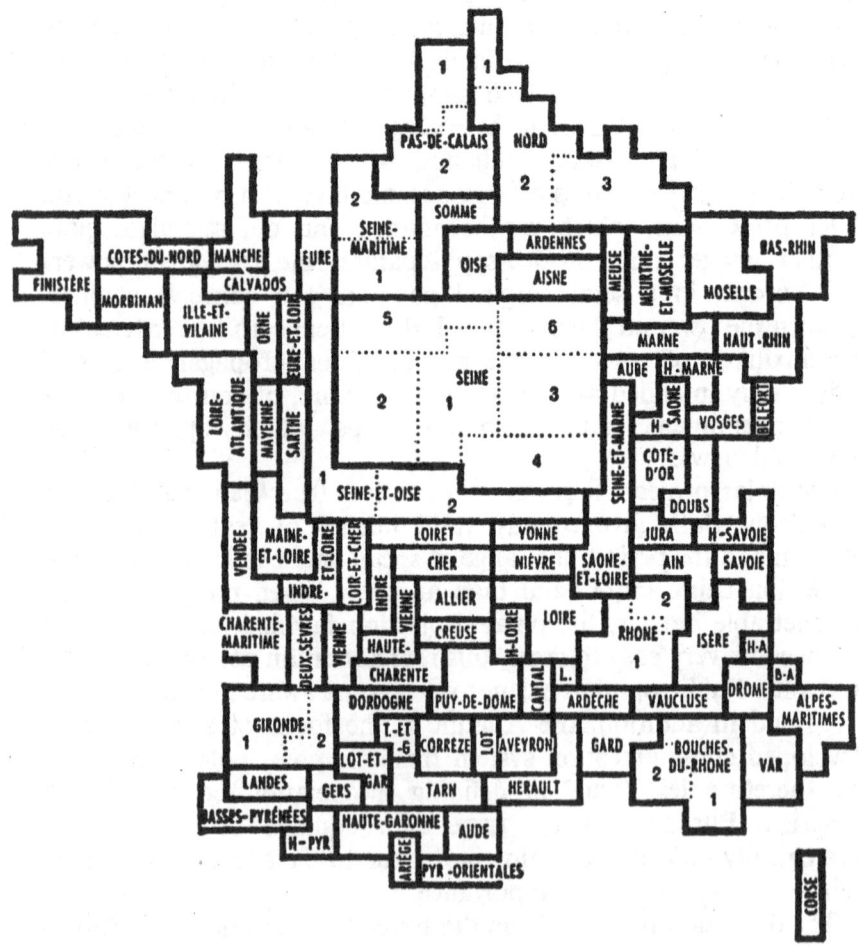

Fig. 41.—Outline demographic map

given to under-populated départements, and populous regions are reduced almost to nothing. Basses Alpes becomes much more important than Paris. All traditional maps of election results give a very false picture of reality.

This distortion can be avoided in two ways. Firstly, continuous representation by strokes, areas or volumes can be used; the size of these symbols, as has been seen, is independent of the area of the constituencies. But these symbols are not very legible. In electoral sociology colours or shading is often preferable. In this case an outline demographic map can be used in which constituencies are represented not in proportion to their area but to their population, their shape and position being respected as far as possible.

An interesting attempt has been made under my direction by MM. J.-M. Cotteret and C. Emeri to transpose the method used in international maps showing states with areas proportionate to their population (fig. 41). Comparison of maps established by this technique and conventional maps illustrates the extent of the distortion resulting from the latter (fig. 42).

3. *Accuracy of Maps.* It has been assumed that the purpose of cartographic methods is to represent measurable and measured geographical facts. But maps are often used as a basis of illustrating purely qualitative phenomena which cannot be measured exactly.

One can draw up, for example, a map of the world in which each state is coloured or shaded according to its political system; a map of France in which each département is coloured or shaded according to whether the president of the *Conseil général* is a man of the Right, Left or Centre, etc. This use of maps does not raise any objection in principle. Geographers employ the technique in maps of climate, soil, vegetation, etc. But in order to be valid two conditions must be fulfilled: 1. the classification of the qualitative elements should be rigorous; 2. the line between geographical distributions of these elements should be precise. In political maps these two conditions are not always satisfied. An example can be given of the map drawn by Charles Morazé entitled 'The Political World and its French heartland' (fig. 43): this is interesting and provocative, but it introduces an arbitrary precision which is inappropriate.

B. Charts

Under this heading come all diagrams with neither a mathematical nor geographical basis. There is practically an unlimited variety of them; anybody can invent new ones suited to the subject being studied. Only those diagrams which assist scientific research by

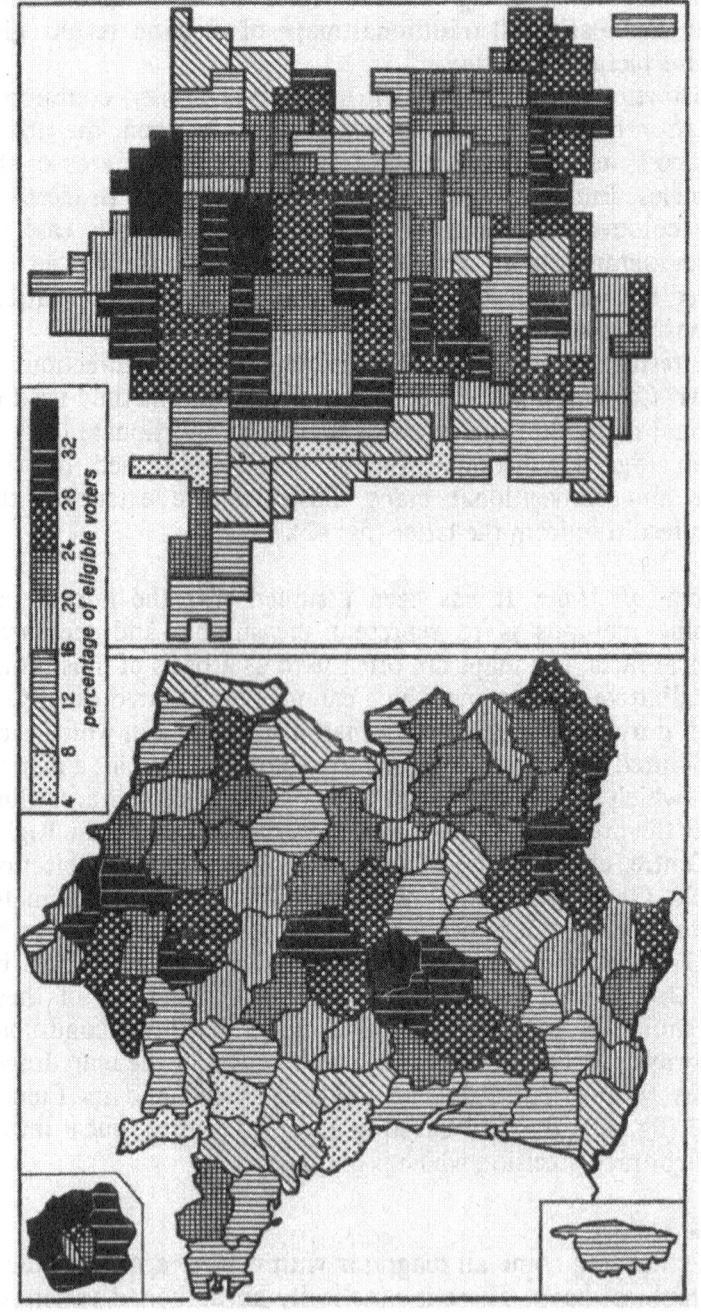

Fig. 42.—Comparison of geographical and demographical maps (Communist votes in 1956)

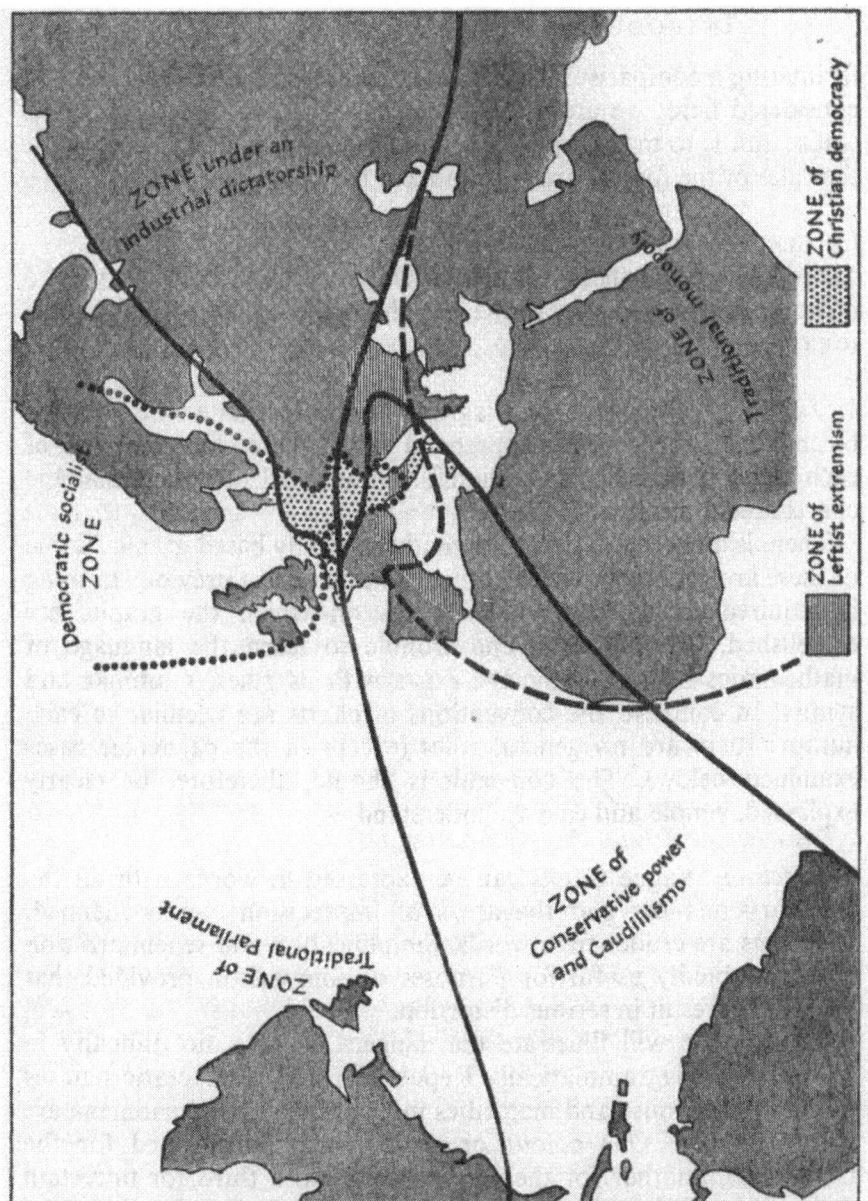

Fig. 43.—'The political world and its French heartland'
(From Charles Morazé, *Les Français et la République*.)

(1956. The author, very conscious of the artificiality of this map, remarks: 'I apologize for the excessive crudeness of these categories which are intended only to suggest and not to define a division of the world. The zone of industrial dictatorship covers those authoritarian régimes with very different characteristics which have accompanied rapid industrial development. Leftist extremism has been marked only in the typically Western Mediterranean zone. Christian democracy is also a typically Italian (perhaps Spanish?) phenomenon, and has developed particularly in Latin America.—It remains true that, taking into account nuances, France is very much the crossroads of all these régimes.')

facilitating a comparison between a large number of elements will be considered here: we are not concerned with pedagogical diagrams, whose aim is to make a problem more comprehensible. But some of the rules of the former are applicable to the latter.

(*a*) GENERAL PRINCIPLES OF CHARTS

There is as yet no theory of charts. Only two common rules will be mentioned. The necessity of these is obvious but they are not always respected.

1. *Legibility*. The aim of diagrams is to facilitate comparisons by making it possible to apprehend visually the characteristics of each element studied. It is, therefore, above all necessary that the charts used are easy to read.

There is a difference here with mathematically based graphs. Some of these are not easy to read at first sight because a previous training is required to understand the bases on which the graphs are established. It takes time and trouble to learn the language of mathematics but this language exists with its rules, grammar and syntax. In contrast, the conventions of charts are peculiar to each author: there are no general rules (except in the particular cases examined below). The conventions should, therefore, be clearly explained, simple and easy to understand.

2. *Precision*. Vague things can be expressed in words with all the necessary nuances and the areas of imprecision can be defined. Diagrams are cruder than words. Simplification and schematization are undoubtedly useful for purposes of comparison provided that they do not result in serious distortion.

An example will illustrate the danger. There is no difficulty in representing diagrammatically Republican and Democratic tenures of the White House and majorities in Congress. The phenomena are clearly defined. One colour or shading can be adopted for the Democrats, another for the Republicans and a third for uncertain majorities (where a small third party holds the balance): see fig. 44. But almost insurmountable difficulties are encountered in representing majorities of Right and Left under the IIIrd and IVth French Republics because the terms 'Right' and 'Left' are ill-defined and they vary during the period under consideration; etc. Adopting one colour for the Right and another for the Left introduces an artificial precision which distorts reality.

This does not mean that such graphs should not be used. If, for example, one wishes to make a comparative study of movements of

MATHEMATICAL AND GRAPH TECHNIQUES

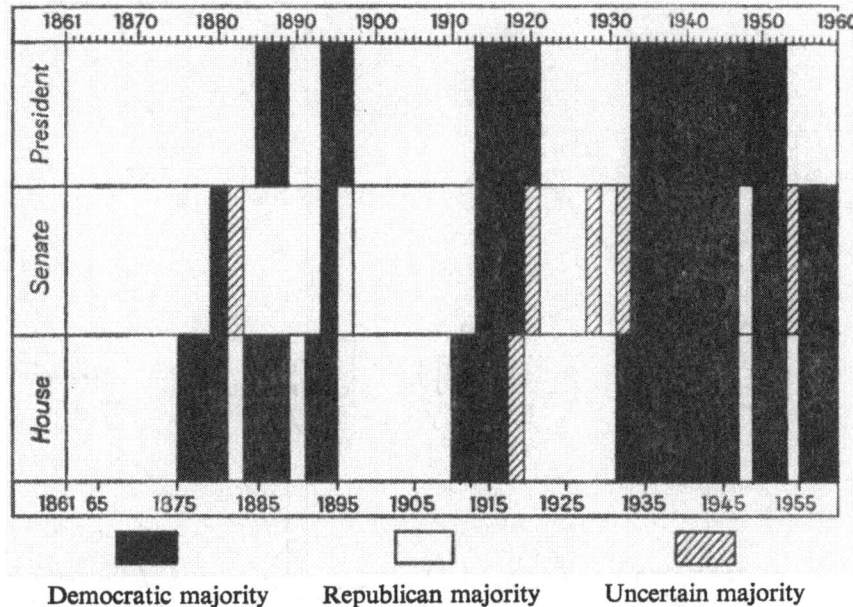

Fig. 44.—Majorities in the United States (1861–1960)
(From M. Duverger, *Les Partis politiques*, 3rd ed., 1958.)

opinion in various European countries in the last fifty years, a series of charts of elections based on a Right/Left classification would give a preliminary overall view of the problem. The method is valid to the extent that one is aware of the distortion, and the relative nature of the conclusions which can be derived from it.

(*b*) PARTICULAR TYPES OF CHARTS

If specialists in particular fields got together it would be very easy for them to agree on standard ways of representing some of the phenomena in their fields. This would greatly help comparative studies. Unfortunately congresses in the social sciences usually prefer to debate vague general questions rather than deal with these humble technical problems. Some types of charts in various fields of research are tending to become standardized without, however, their basic conventions being clearly defined. Organization charts and sociograms can be cited as examples.

1. *Organization charts.* These are charts of complex organizations (firms, groups, etc.) showing their components and the relations between them. There are several simple conventions. Hierarchies of

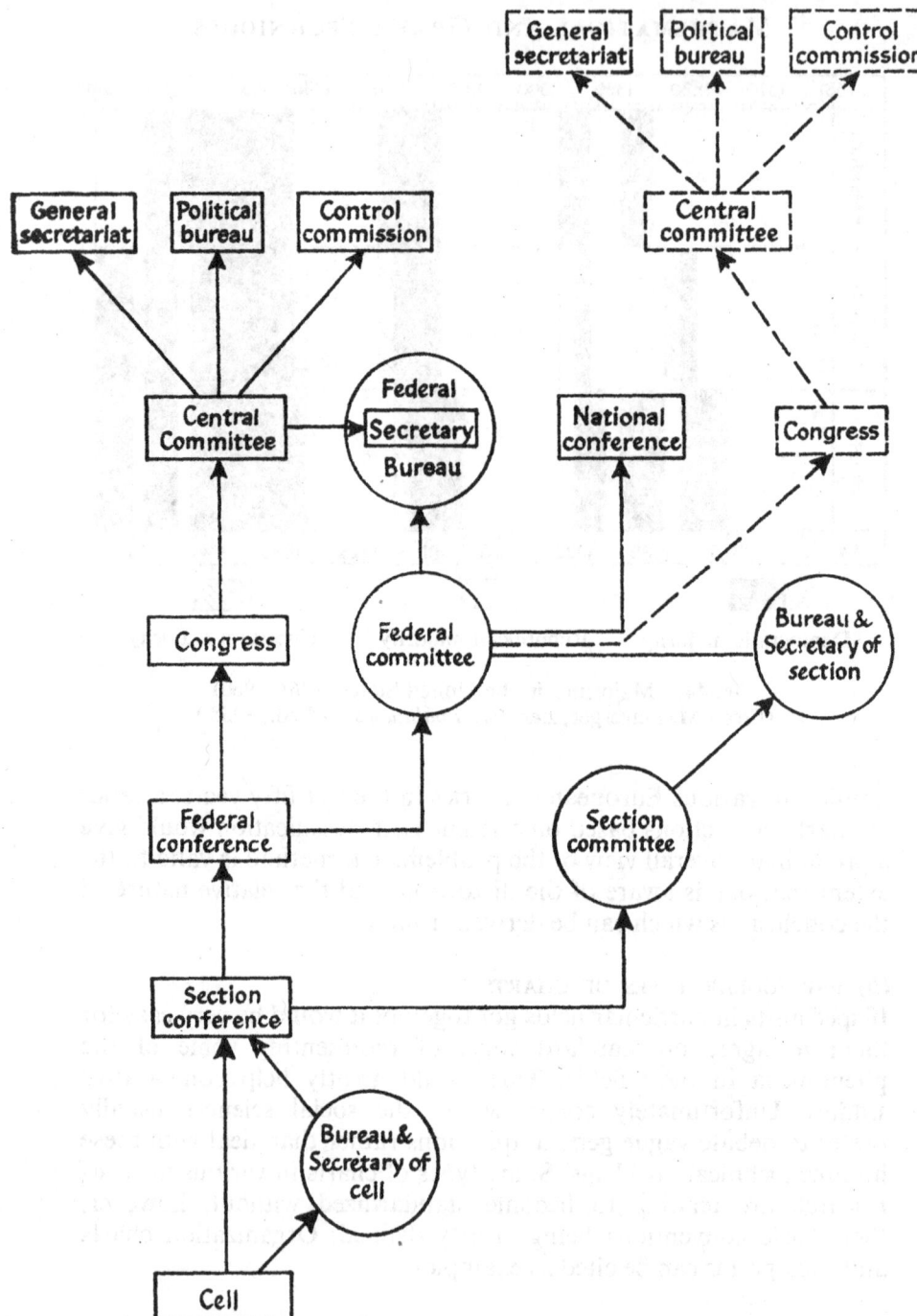

Fig. 45.—Example of an organization chart

(The French Communist Party: the dotted line represents the special organization set out in Article 26 of the Statutes.)

MATHEMATICAL AND GRAPH TECHNIQUES

elements are represented vertically, the higher elements above and the lower ones below and the equal ones on the same level. Associations between the elements are represented by an arrow: the direction of the arrow indicates which element nominates the other (fig. 45). Unfortunately these rules although brief are not always observed; organization charts are not always very legible. A general system of rules would be difficult to formulate but in particular fields (political parties, pressure groups, etc.) relatively precise conventions could be established.

2. *Sociograms.* The technique of the sociogram is associated with the sociometric method of Moreno. Its purpose is to characterize relations between individuals in a group. Each member of the group is asked confidentially which of his colleagues he finds sympathetic and wishes to have as companions at the table, at work, to share a common life, etc., and which of them he finds antipathetic and wishes to avoid. Each member of the group is represented by a dot or a small circle, arrows represent lines of attraction and an arrow with broken lines, declared antipathy.

This diagram is called a sociogram. The place of the various members of the group is determined by criteria of legibility. Moreno has invented various types of sociometric relationships: chain, star, network, etc. (fig. 46).

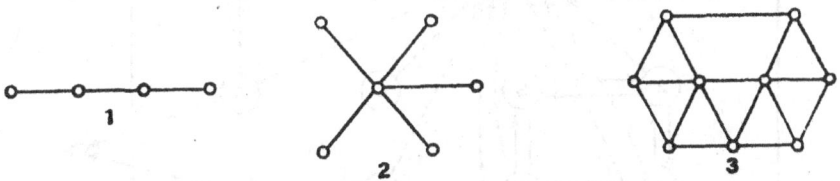

Fig. 46.—Types of sociometric relationships
1. Chain   2. Star   3. Network

The method illuminates the real psychological structure of a group. It can be compared to its formal and official structure (provided that one obtains honest answers to the questions asked). Indirect methods (tests, participant observation) can replace the direct questions about sympathy and antipathy.

An inquiry made by Jenkins on relations inside two American air force squadrons during the Pacific war provides an example of the sociometric method. The purpose of the inquiry was to find out why morale in one squadron was good and bad in the other. Jenkins asked each airman to tell him in confidence those he would

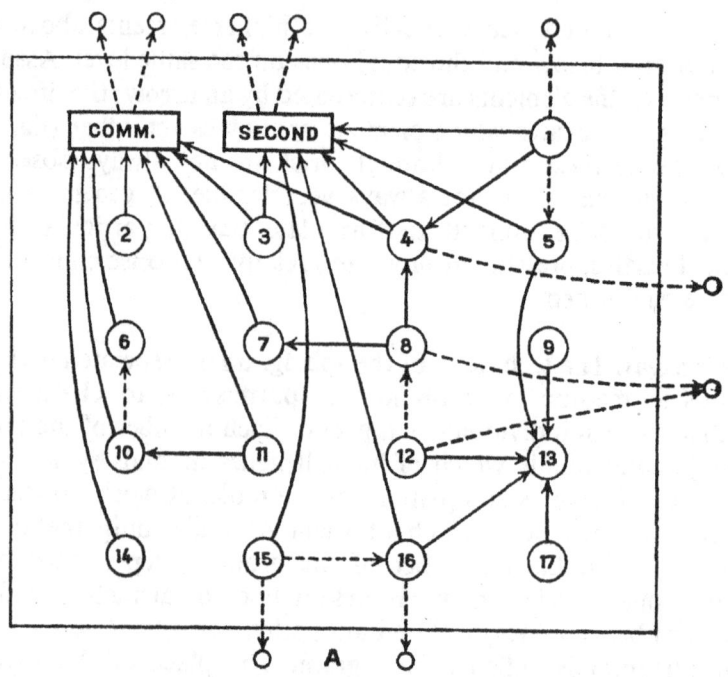

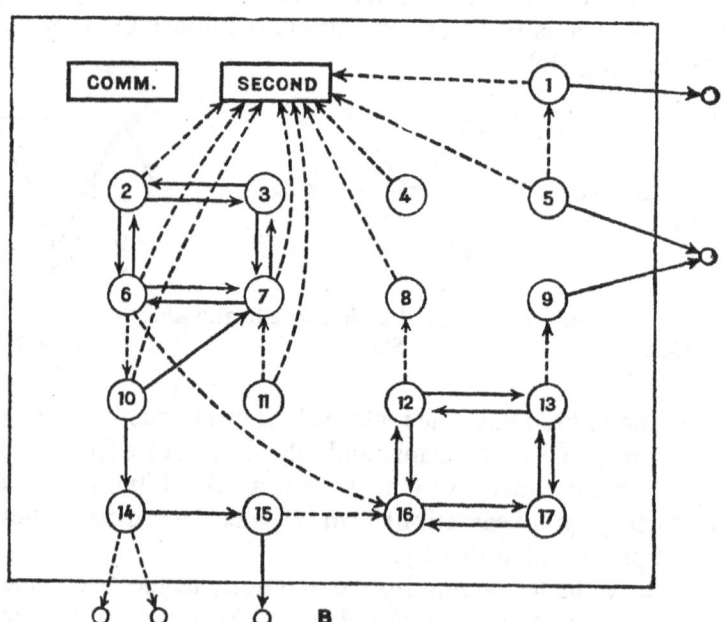

Fig. 47.—Jenkin's sociograms

(*a*) Squadron with good morale; (*b*) Squadron with poor morale.

Mathematical and Graph Techniques

like as flight colleagues and those he would not. On this basis the following sociograms were made (fig. 47).

It can be clearly seen in squadron A the official leaders (commander and second in command) were accepted as leaders by their men; in squadron B one is ignored (the commander) and the other is rejected (the second in command). It can also be seen that squadron A forms a more united group (no one outside the squadron is desired as a companion) and more homogeneous (in squadron B, there are two cliques). Similar studies, making possible comparisons on a large scale, throw light on the problem of leadership.

On mathematical graphs: P. Pèpe, *Présentation des statistiques*, 1959.

On maps and charts: A. S. Hall, *Construction of graphs and charts*, 1958; P. W. Chombart de Lauwe (*et al.*), *Paris et l'agglomeration parisienne*, 1952, Especially Vol. II, pp. 12 ff.; J. M. Cotteret and C. Emeri, 'Essai de représentation des forces politiques'. *Revue française de science politique*, 1957, pp. 596 ff.

On organization charts: R. Alusson, *Les Organigrammes*, 1958.

On sociograms: J. L. Moreno, 'La Méthode sociometrique en sociologie.' *Cahiers internationaux de sociologie*, 2, 1946; J. G. Jenkins, *The Nominating Technique*, Report to the Eastern Psychological Association, Atlantic City, 1947, and *Leadership Isolation*, 1945; P. J. Lebret, *Guide pratique de l'enquête sociale*, 3 vols., 1951–58.

INDEX

Aberrant cases, 259
Abt, 208
Ackerman, 67
Ackroff, 301
Adler, 37
Administrative Publications, 77
Adorno, 188
Aggregations, 59; supra-national, 62
Albertini, 149
Albig, 113, 114, 124, 167
Allen, R. G. D., 301
Allen, J. W., 23
Allport, 95, 101, 108, 117
Almond, 247
Althusius, 15
Alusson, 333
Amorphism (of social phenomena), 235
Anastasi, 208
Anderson, B. M., 37
Angel, 95
Anthropology (see Ethnology)
Antisemitism, 165
Apostates, 220
Aragon, 84
Arambourou, 272, 276
Archives, private, 80; of organizations, 80; of individuals, 81, 95; public, 76, 95
Area studies, 269, 275
Areola samples, 128
Aristotle, 11, 13, 39
Arnoff, 301
Aron, 37, 47, 67, 272, 276
Arquillière, 23
Arrow, 301
Art, sociology of, 52, 54
Associations, 58; sociology of, 67 (see organizations); mathematical, 287
Atkinson, 24
Attitude scales, 198, 208
Augustin, St., 14, 19
Authoritarian personality, 186
Axelrod, 188

Bailey, 276
Bales, 67
Ballot boxes (separate), 255

Balzac, 84, 103
Barber, 67
Barnard, 260,
Barnes, 23
Barodet, 104
Barre, 44, 53
Barth, 222
Batteries of questions, 151
Bazard, 21
Becker, 23
Beegle, 53
Beer, 275
Behaviourism, 30, 240, 247
Bell, S. E., 208
Bell, W., 222
Bellack, 208
Bendix, 53
Benedict, 36
Bennett, 275
Benoist, 23
Béraud, 149
Berelson, 112, 113, 114, 115, 116, 117, 118, 119, 120, 121, 123, 188
Bergel, 53
Bergson, 103
Bernot, 222
Bernoulli, 116
Bertillon, 316
Bettelheim, B., 222
Bettelheim, C., 214, 222
Bifactoral method, 296
Bigo, 24
Bimodal distribution, 316
Binary comparisons, 200
Binet, 190
Birch, A. H., 222
Black, 301
Blackburn, 36
Blackwell, 248
Blancard, 222
Bloch, 108
Blumenstock, 124
Bodin, 14, 15, 23, 46
Bogardus, 23, 200, 208
Bone, 114
Bonnard, 109
Borel, 299
Borgata, 67

334

Index

Bouglé, 37
Bourricaud, 48, 53
Bowley, 140
Braudel, 31, 33, 37,
Bremme, 261
Bridrey, 23
de Broglie, 230
Broom, 68
Brown, 95
Bruck, 276
Bruner, 167
Buchanan, 67
Bulmer, 95
Bund, 58
Burdin, 17
Buros, 208
Burt, 297
Busa, 104

Cabanis, 17
Cannell, 188
Cantril, 67, 152, 167, 177
Carbonnier, 109
Carpenter, 114
Carpentier, 123
Carro Martinez, 53
Carter, 260
Cartography, 317
Cartwright, 67
Case studies, 95, 274, 276
Cavaillès, 41
Cavan, 124
Censuses, 85
Chack, 149
Chamson, 84
Chapin, 260
Chartier, 143
Charts, 325
Chave, 208
Chauvire, 23
Chevalier, 53
Chombert de Lauwe, 333
Christiansen, 256, 260
Churchill, 112
Churchman, 301
Civilizations, 32, 64, 65; sociology of, 67, 264
Classifications, 227 (*see* Typologies)
Clément, 213, 214, 222
Clinical Interview, 186
Clusters (in samples), 129
Cochran, 143

Coders, 170
Coding, 168
Coefficient of correlation, 293
Cohen, 301
Coleman, 247
Collective character, 24, 36; consciousness, 27; images, 29, 36
Community, 58; studies of, 222, 274, 276; local, 59
Communications, 106
Comparisons, 261; distant, 266; close, 265; ethnographical, 267
Comparative Method, 261, 275 (*see* Comparisons)
Computers, 281, 287
Comte, 15–23, 33, 36, 51, 229, 230
Condorcet, 16, 19
Conformism, 172, 174 (*see* majority effect)
Conservatism, 152
Content analysis, 103; categories, 109, 114; units of analysis, 112
Context, 263
Continuous registration, 86
'Continuum' (and social reality), 236
Constraint, social, 37
Cook, 71
Coombs, 248
Co-ordinates, 302
Correlation, 287, 290; and factorial analysis, 295
Cotteret, 325, 333
Cottrell, 68
Cox, 275
Crawford, 53
Crespi, 201, 208
Crick, 37
Criminology, 50
Crozier, 69, 70
Crutchfield, 71
Cuber, 68
Cultures (*see* Civilizations)
Cuvillier, 23, 39

Daladier, 153
Dale, E., 114, 124
Dale, H. E., 222
David, 275
Davidson, 276
Davis, 247
Davy, 61
Déat, 149

335

Decision (and operational research), 299
Decision making, 272, 276
Dedieu, 24
Deffontaines, 41
Demangeon, 40
Demeunier, 16
Deming, 143
Demography, 20, 41, 53
Deparcieux, 16, 42
Deri, 222
Description, 226
Destutt De Tracy, 17
Determinism, 228; functional, 229; geographical, 40; social, 229; 247, statistical, 230; stochastic, 229
Deutsch, K. W., 67, 243, 248
Deutsch, M., 71
Dewey, 171
Dicks, 188
Diderot, 15
Dilthey, 31, 32, 37
Directories, 83
Disraeli, 87
Distribution graphs, 290
Docimology, 190 (n)
Documentation, indirect, 82
Documents, analysis of, 96; personal, 108 (see Archives, private)
Dodd, 201
Domination, 47
Drieu de la Rochelle, 84
Drobna, 202, 203, 208
Dufrenne, 28, 36
Duguit, 47, 48, 109
Dupeux, 95, 276
Dupont de Nemours, 16, 17
Duprat, 37
Durkheim, 18, 19, 26–9, 36, 37, 39, 49, 51, 52, 56, 229
Duroselle, 177, 270, 273
Duverger, 47, 53, 67, 95, 248
Dynamics, social, 17

Easton, 53
Economic science (see Political economy)
Edwards, 208
Einstein, 232
Eldersveld, 71, 247
Electoral Sociology, 271, 276
Emeri, 325, 333

Encyclopaedists, 15
Engels, 24, 240
Epochs, 63 (see Historical contexts)
Escarpit, 54, 95
Ethnology, 55, 60, 67, 211, 222
Eulau, 71, 247
Evential, 31, 62
Experiment, 246, 248, 260; active, 257; ex-post facto, 256, 260; passive, 255
Explanation, sociological, 227
Eysenck, 293, 298, 301

Factorial analysis, 293, 301
Family, sociology of, 55, 67
Favier, 95
Fear, 188
Febure, 37
Ferster, 120
Festinger, 71, 247
Figgis, 23
Finkelstein, 54
Fisher, F. M., 139
Fisher, R. A., 301
Fiske, 188
Flesch, 123
Flugel, 54, 188
Focused interview, 186
Foeden, 117
Folklore, 52
Ford, 209
Francastel, 54
Frank, 192
Fraser, 260
Frequency curves, 315; series, 311; polygons of, 315
Frère, 214, 222
Freud, 192
Fromme, 194, 208
Function, 234
Functional comparison, 263; determinism, 229; school, 247; typology, 234
Funnel (of questions), 149
Fustel de Coulanges, 55

Gage, 301
Galdston, 67
Gallup, 173, 177
Games Theory, 245, 248
Gaudet, 188
de Gaulle, 152
Geddes, 54

INDEX

Gemeinschaft, 59
General character, 31, 37
Gentilis, 15
Geography, human, 39, 53
Geopolitics, 40
Georges, 124
Geselschaft, 59
Gide, 53
Gillin, 67
Ginsberg, 54, 188
Girard, 42
Goguel, 95, 261, 271, 272, 276
Goldman, 275
Golsen, 117
Goode, 71
Goodman, 143
Gorer, 63
Gosnell, 261, 301
Gottschalk, 54, 95
Gouldner, 67, 260
Governors, 47
Governed, 47
Graphs, 301, 333
Graunt, 16, 20
Grazia, 112, 119
Greef, 25
Green-Schwartz, 222
Greenwood, 256, 260
Griaule, 95, 222
Grotius, 15
Groups, artificial, 249, 260; elementary, 55, 57, 67; intermediary, 55, 58; natural, 257; pressure, 78; small, 57; structure, 210
Gruson, 300
Guer, 208
Guerin, 69, 70
Guilford, 200
Guillard, 20, 41
Guiraud, 109
Guitton, 95
Gurvitch, 33, 37, 53, 54, 65, 66, 68, 247
Guttman, 199, 204-5, 209

Halbwachs, 39, 53
Halkin, 108
Hall, 333
Halle, 95
Halle, 95
Halley, 16, 20, 42
Hallowell, 37

Hamilton, 112
Handel, 67
Hansen, 143
Hansen, 143, 167
Hardy, 41
Harris, 117, 123
Harrison, 222
Hart, 113
Hartmann, 261, 297
Hatt, 71
Hauser, 124
Hayek, 37
Haythorn, 260
Hazard, 24
Hebb, 53
Heckscher, 263
Hegel, 25
Henmon, 103, 109
Hennis, 177
Heraclitus, 19
Herdan, 109
Herzog, 116, 124
Hess, 67
Hevner, 113, 124
Hierarchical analysis, 204 (*see* Scalogram)
Hill, 67
Hirsch, 301
Histograms, 314
Historical analysis, 99, 108; contexts, 32, 264; relativity, 230 (*see* Civilizations, Epochs)
History, 36, 62, 67; philosophy of, 64
Historicity, 31
Hitler, 92, 124, 156, 166
Hobbes, 15, 17, 23, 25
Hodges, 37
Holbach, 15
Holmes, 54
Holzinger, 296, 297
Horst, 209
Horton, 124
House, 23
Hoyland, 260
Howe, 95
Howell, 260
Hubert, 24
Huff, 301
Hume, 123
Huntingdon, 40
Hurwitz, 143, 167
Hyman, 101, 143, 188, 222

Hyperfactualism, 49, 73, 223
Hypotheses, working, 245, 247

Ibn Khaldoun, 20, 65
Iconography, 91
Ideal types, 238, 247
Independence, mathematical, 288
Indeterminacy, 230
Indices, 285
Industrial sociology, 45
Inherited wealth, 86
Institutional, 31; comparisons, 268; typologies, 232
Institutions, 233
Interdisciplinary research, 268, 275
Internal understanding, 30
Interviews, 178; clinical, 186; documentary, 179; focused, 186; of 'ordinary' people, 180; of leaders, 180; multiple, 187; for opinion, 179; of prominent people, 179; of prisoners, 187; in depth, 185; repeated, 183
Interquartiles, 283
Introspection, 217, 218, 222
Investigators, 165; reliability of, 158

Jacobs, 116
Jacobson, 95, 112
Jaeger, 23
Jahoda, 71
James, 53
Janet, 46
Janowitz, 71, 95, 247
Jaspers, 28
Jellinek, 46
Jenkins, 331, 332, 333
Johnson, 247
Journaux Officiels, 77
Jouvenel, 37, 53
Juridical Analysis, 100, 109

Kahn, 167, 188
Kaplan, 53, 117
Kappel, 123
Karlin, 301
Katz, 71, 177, 247
Kayser, 95
Kelley, D. M. G., 188
Kelley, H. H., 68
Kemeny, 301
Kendall, 188

Keynes, 44, 53
Kinsey, 52, 54, 188
Kish, 143
Kjellen, 40
Klein, 67
Klineberg, 68
Kluckhorn, 95
Knowledge, sociology of, 64, 67
Kogon, 222
Komidar, 123
Krech, 71
Kris, 118, 124
Kroeber, 67

Laboratories, social, 215, 222
Laboratory experiments, 247
Lacombe, 31, 32
Lacroix, 24
Lafitau, 16
Laicization, 51
Lange, 53
Lapiere, 258
Laplace, 316
Larsen, 68
Lascaux, 52
Lasswell, 53, 71, 109, 110, 111, 112, 115, 123, 124, 188, 260
Laugier, 190
Law, 35 (*see* Juridical Analysis); of the three stages, 17
Lazarsfeld, 71, 100, 113, 117, 124, 183, 184, 185, 188, 248, 361
Lazarus, 25
Leaders, 193, 249 (*see* Selection)
Léauté, 53
Le Bras, 52, 54
Lebret, 274, 276, 333
Lee, 124
Lefébvre, 24
Leighton, 222
Leites, 109, 118, 123, 124
Lenin, 240
Leontief, 243
Le Play, 40, 56
Le Roy, 78
Lerner, 71, 123, 160, 260
Leroi-Gourhan, 95
Leslie, 248
Levels of research, 226
Lévi-Strauss, 56, 60, 67, 93, 95, 222, 247, 281, 301
Lévy-Bruhl, H., 53

INDEX

Lévy-Bruhl, L., 24
Lewin, 215, 222, 250
Lewis, 117
Lhomme, 53
Lickert, 203, 204, 208
Lilienfield, 25
Lindbergh, 156
Lindesmith, 68
Lindzey, 68
Linguistics, 93, 95
Lippitt, 222, 250, 260
Lipset, 53, 247
Literature, 95; in the social sciences, 83
Littré, 46, 261
Lively, 124
'Living space', 40
Locke, 15
Logarithmic co-ordinates, 303
Loomis, 53
Lowenfeld, 192
Lumsdaine, 260
Lundberg, 68, 229, 247
Lynd, R. and H., 214, 222

Mably, 15
Macarthy, 143, 167
McCloskey, 301
Macdiarmid, 110, 124
Macdougall, 26
Macgranaham, 113, 124
Machiavelli, 14, 15, 23, 46
MacIver, 68, 247
McKean, 222
Maclung Lee, 124
Macphee, 188
Macrae, 295, 298
Macridis, 275
'Macro-micro', 44, 57, 231, 247, 263
Madge, 222
Madow, 167
Majority effect, 172
Malebranche, 16, 39
Malraux, 82
Malthus, 41, 43
Mannheim, 67
Mannheimer, 143
Maps, 317
March, 276
Marchal, A., 63
Marchal, J., 24
Marginalism, 44

Martin, 110
Marx, 15, 18–22, 27, 36, 44, 46, 64, 240
Marxism, 24, 26, 43, 239 (see Marx)
Mason, 188
Mass Observation, 215
Mathematical analysis, 277; characteristics, 282; techniques, 278; methods, 301
Mathematics, human, 278; qualitative, 278, 281
Mauss, 61
Mean deviation, 284
Meetings, study of, 210
Meillet, 275
Mendès-France, 110, 116, 119
Mendras, 53
Mercier de la Rivière, 16
Merriam, 53
Merton, 64, 68, 112, 124, 167, 186, 188, 247
Mesnard, 23
Measurement of attitudes, 189 (see Attitude scales)
Measurement of opinions, 194, 196
Meynaud, 67, 247
Michelet, 104
Miles, 117
Miroglio, 67
Models, 242; 248, economic, 243; investigatory, 243; non-mathematical, 244; of prediction, 242; strategic, 245
Moheau, 16
Monographs, 274; collective, 275
Montchrétien, 14, 15, 43
Montesquieu, 15, 16, 19, 24, 46, 72
Moore, B., 248
Moore, W. E., 68
Moos, 275
Morals, 35; sociology of, 52, 54
Morand, 104
Morazé, 325, 327
Moreau-Reibel, 23
Moreno, 234, 251–3, 331, 333
Moret, 61
Morgenstern, 299
Morgenthau, 301
Morre, 67
Mosca, 241
Moscovici, 207
Moser, 222
Mounin, 23

Mean, arithmetical, 282; geometrical, 282
Mueller, 124
Mukerjee, 54
Mutlifactoral method, 297
Mumford, 95
Munsterberger, 188
Murdock, 264, 265, 267
Murphy, 209
Murray, 192, 193, 194
Musset, 103
Myrdal, 37, 70, 275

Nadel, 247
Nations, 61
Neumann, 275
Nezard, 23
Nora, 300
Novack, 114

Political economy, 20
Political Science, 46, 53, 112
Political implications of the social sciences, 69
Polls, 86, 87, 125, 128, 167, 177; assessment of results of, 169; probability methods, 128; publication of, 172; of 1948, 177
Pool, 109
Positive character, 17, 33
Possibilism, geographical, 40
Powell, 167
Power, 53, 66, 300; biological aspects of, 53
Prediction, 227; through polls, 171
Prélot, 46, 53
Press, 77, 95
Prestige, 155, 162
Probability samples, 128, 143
Prohansky, 194, 208
Projection (maps), 323
Projective methods, 192, 195, 208
Proust, 103
Psychoanalysis, 30, 188
Psychodrama, 252, 253
Psychological analysis, 25
'Psychologist theories', 240 (see Social psychology),
Public Opinion, 78
Pufendorf, 15

Quantification (in social science), 278
Quantitative methods, 102 (see Mathematical analysis); semantics, 103, 109
Quartiles, 283
Questionnaires, 143, 293 (see Questions)
Questions, contamination of, 148; closed, 144; evaluative, 145; of fact, 146; open, 144; of opinion, 147; oral, 162; series of, 145; tests, 148; with written replies, 159
Quetelet, 17
Quotas, 125, 143

Racism, 164
Radcliffe-Brown, 67, 68, 247
Random selection, 125, 128
Ratzel, 40
Recorded votes, 255
Recordings, 94
Regress, line of, 292
Reiss, 222
Relational typology, 233, 240
'Relationist' school, 26 (see Relational)
Relativity, 32, 45; of sociological laws, 228
Reliability, 122, 158
Religious sociology, 51, 53
Remmers, 203, 209, 258, 260
Renan, 62, 67
Renaudet, 23
Reporting, 210
Representativity of samples, 133
Reynaud, 153
Riley, M. W., 208
Rist, 53
Robbins, 44, 55
Robin, 23
Robinson, 165
Robson, 55
Rodhe, 165
Rogers, L., 177
Rogers, W. C., 123
Rohrschach, 192, 194, 195
Roosevelt, 117, 152, 154, 155, 166
Rose, A. M., 37, 68, 71
Rose, R., 68
Rosenberg, 71
Rosenzweig, 192, 194
Rostow, 209
Roucek, 37, 68

INDEX

Rousseau, 15
Rubel, 24
Rundquist, 204
Runion, 117
Rural Sociology, 41, 53

Saint-Simon, 17, 21
Saintyves, 95
Salter, 113, 114, 121, 123
Samples, balanced, 140; compensated, 141, 143; controlled, 140; master, 132
Sampling, 125, 143, 184
Sanford, 194
Sansovino, 14
Sapin, 276
Sauvage, 282
Sauvy, 41
Say, 44
Scale, 231 (see 'Macro-micro')
Scalogram, 204, 209
Schlesinger, 276
Schmalenbach, 58
Schmidtchen, 177
Schrag, 68
Schuman, 112, 124
Schutz, 123
Schwartz, 122
Sée, 23, 275
Segerstedt, 37
Selection, personnel, 113, 250, 160
Self criticism, 254
Selltiz, 71
Systematic analysis, 225
Shapera, 275
Shaw, 95
Sheffield, 260
Shevky, 222
Shils, 260
Shimberg, 301
Shubik, 240
Shuman, 124
Siegel, 208
Siegfried, 179, 271, 272, 276
Significance, 265; tests of, 137
Silance, 203, 209
Silander, 276
Simiand, 32, 323
Simon, 248, 276
Sire, 53
Slesinger, 248
Sletto, 204

Small, 23
Smelser, 53
Smith,, A., 16, 20, 21, 26, 44
Smith, F. T., 258, 261
Smith, K., 112
Smith, M., 258, 260
Smith, M. B., 167
Smythe, 124
Snell, 301
Snyder, 276
Social economics, 45; laws, 16; morphology, 39; philosophy, 12; physics, 17; psychology, 26, 68
Sociodrama, 252, 260
Sociograms, 331, 333
'Sociologism', 24
Sociology, 17, 20, 39, 43, 67, 68; general, 22, 63, 66; of art, 52, 54; electoral, 271, 276; of the family, 55, 67; industrial, 45; of intermediary groups, 58; of knowledge, 64, 67; of morals, 52, 54; religious, 51, 53; rural, 41; of small groups, 57; urban, 41, 53; of work, 45
Sociometry, 251, 331, 333
Socrates, 217
Sola Pool, 123, 124
Sorokin, 67, 71, 113, 124
Sorre, 53
Spann, 25, 36
Spearman, 296
Specialization, 21
Speier, 124
Spencer, 25, 36
Spengler, 25, 36, 65, 67
Spieseke, 71
Sprott, 248
Stalin, 240
Stanton, 113, 124
Standard deviation, 284
Stark, 67
Starobinski, 24
Strata (of samples), 130
Statistical determinism, 230
Statistics, 42, 84, 95, 101, 301; gathering, 85; value of, 87
Staveley, 95
Steffens, 222
Steinhal, 25
Stendhal, 98
Stephan, 143, 167
Stereograms, 310

Stereotypes, 154
Steward, 274
Stewart, 116
Stochastic association, 287
Stouffer, 101, 124
Strauss, A. L., 68
Strauss, L., 23
Structuralism, 94, 235
Structures, 247, 262; natural, 238
Suppes, 276, 301
Süssmilch, 16
Symbols, 110
Symbolic analysis, 90
Sympathy, 156

Taueber, 120
Taine, 40
Talbot, 301
Tarde, 26, 27
Tchakhotine, 259, 261
Technology, 89, 95
Tests, 137, 148, 189, 208; aptitude, 190; frustration, 192; intelligence, 190; knowledge, 190; objective, 191; personality, 190; projective, 192, 194, 208; of validity, 158
Thematic apperception test, 192–5
Themes, 111
Theories, 66; general, 22, 239, 247; partial, 242
Thibaut, 68
Thomas, 36, 95, 275
Thomas Aquinas, St., 14, 105
Thomson, G. L., 301
Thomson, W. R., 53
Thrall, 248
Thurstone, 166, 199, 201–3, 204, 208, 296, 297
Timasheff, 247
Tito, 111
Tocqueville, 46
Tonnies, 23, 67
Touchard, 58, 95
Toulouse, 190
Townsend, 260
Toynbee, 65, 67
Trefethen, 301
Troubetzkoy, 95
Types, ideal, 238, 247
Typologies, 66, 68, 227, 232–3, 247, 262; natural, 235

Ulam, 275
University departmentalization, 22
Urban sociology, 41, 53

Validity, 122, 158
Value, 33, 117
Van Den Haag, 68
Van der Beke, 103, 109
Variance, 284
Vedel, 47
Vernon, 301
Vidal de la Biache, 40
Voegelin, 37
Voltaire, 15
Von Neumann, 299
Vouin, 53

Waldo, 53, 107, 247
Waller, 67
Walworth, 123
Waples, 115, 119, 120, 121
Warner, 213, 214, 222
Wasserman, 276
Wayne, 113, 124
Weber, M., 64, 65, 238
Weinberg, 190
White, R., 167
White, R. K., 115, 118, 121, 124, 250
White, W. A., 253
Who's Who, 83
Whyte, W. F., 212
Wilkie, 166
Wilks, 136, 137
Willey, 114
Williams, 248
Winch, 53
Wolfenstein, 124
Work, sociology of, 45
Worms, 36
Wright Mills, 71
Wyant, 116, 124
Wylie, 212, 222

Xydias, 213, 214, 222

Yacobson, 124
Yates, 140, 141, 143
Yinger, 54
Young, P. V., 222
Yule, 109, 293

Zander, 67
Zelditch, 301
Znaniecki, 23, 95